The vividness with which we recall unexpected and emotional events has long been the subject of theoretical speculation; William James said that they "leave a scar upon the cerebral tissues." For many Americans, the stunning news that the Space Shuttle *Challenger* had exploded gave rise to just such memories. In this fourth volume in the Emory Symposia in Cognition series, researchers who have systematically studied recollections of *Challenger* present their findings.

Although *Affect and Accuracy in Recall* begins with the space shuttle explosion, it also addresses broader issues. Are "flashbulb" memories fundamentally different from other forms of recall? Do emotion and arousal strengthen memory in general, or only in certain circumstances? If so, by what physiological mechanisms? What functions might such memories serve? Why do traumatic events sometimes produce heightened recall and sometimes lead instead to repression? The sophisticated discussions of these issues, presented by distinguished experimental psychologists, are evidence of rapid recent progress in the study of autobiographical memory. William Brewer concludes the volume with a detailed analysis of research on flashbulb memories, from the original definition of these recollections by Brown and Kulik in 1977 to the present.

Emory Symposia in Cognition 4

Affect and accuracy in recall

# Affect and accuracy in recall

**Studies of "flashbulb" memories**

*Edited by*

EUGENE WINOGRAD

*and*

ULRIC NEISSER

CAMBRIDGE
UNIVERSITY PRESS

*T.S,*

Published by the Press Syndicate of the University of Cambridge
The Pitt Building, Trumpington Street, Cambridge CB2 1RP
40 West 20th Street, New York, NY 10011–4211, USA
10 Stamford Road, Oakleigh, Victoria 3166, Australia

First published 1992

Printed in the United States of America

*Library of Congress Cataloging-in-Publication Data*

Affect and accuracy in recall : studies of "flashbulb" memories /
edited by Eugene Winograd and Ulric Neisser.

p.      cm. – (Emory symposia in cognition ; 4)

Includes index.

ISBN 0–521–40188–7

1. Flashbulb memory.      I. Winograd, Eugene.    II. Neisser, Ulric.
III. Series.
BF378.F55A36      1992
153.1'23 – dc20

92–980
CIP

A catalog record for this book is available from the British Library.

ISBN 0–521–40188–7 hardback

# Contents

# Preface

This is the fourth volume in the *Emory Symposia in Cognition* series. Like two of its predecessors, *Remembering Reconsidered* (edited by Ulric Neisser and Eugene Winograd, 1988) and *Knowing and Remembering in Young Children* (edited by Robyn Fivush and Judith A. Hudson, 1990), it deals with memory. But whereas those earlier volumes were overviews of broad fields, this book is devoted to a single problem and – in large part – a single research paradigm. That problem is the relation between affect and memory; it is studied here by examining recollections of unexpected and emotional events. Although such recollections have only been called "flashbulb memories" since 1977 (the phrase was coined by Roger Brown and James Kulik in a seminal paper), they have long been the subject of theoretical speculation. Recently they have also been the subject of empirical research, much of it focused on memories of one particular event: the explosion of the Space Shuttle *Challenger* on January 28, 1986. It is those studies that form the core of this book.

The Emory Cognition Project conference on flashbulb memories was held on February 2–3, 1990. Our primary goal was to bring together everyone who had done research on memories of the *Challenger* episode and to review each others' data and learn from each others' methods. We hoped that the conferees would reach at least a sense of the meeting on the status of such memories: How do they compare with other kinds of recollections? Are they unusually accurate, or especially long-lived? Do they reflect the activity of a "special mechanism," as has been suggested? If so, what could that mechanism be? If not, why do they often seem so vivid and certain? That hope was fulfilled: Although we did not settle any issue conclusively, we did reach some rather generally shared conclusions. Those conclusions appear informally throughout the volume, but one of them is worth mentioning here. Whatever the relation between affect and memory, there is probably no special mechanism of storage that comes into play only at moments of peak emotion. On this point at least, the state of the art has moved beyond Brown and Kulik's original claims.

The conference was not concerned only with flashbulb memories; more general issues of affect and accuracy could not be ignored. These issues are difficult, and the psychology of memory has not yet been able to resolve them. Do emotion and arousal strengthen memory? If so, under what conditions? For what kinds of materials? By what physiological mechanisms? With what eventual effect on the accuracy of what is remembered? All these issues are addressed in the following pages, but none is conclusively resolved. On one point, however, we did come close to a consensus. The classical examples of flashbulb memory, in which people recall "reception events" (i.e., hearing some piece of important public news), may very well be *less* reliable than other kinds of emotional memories. This point, made in several different chapters (Neisser & Harsch, Larsen, Brewer), is perhaps our most interesting conclusion.

Of the chapters that follow, all but the first and last are based on papers delivered at the 1990 conference. The first is an introduction; the last was written by William Brewer at our invitation. Brewer, who attended the meeting and participated actively in the discussions, is a long-time contributor to the study of autobiographical memory. He provides a detailed analysis of the flashbulb concept from its initial definition by Brown and Kulik to its present status in the light of these chapters. It is also worth noting that David Pillemer has broken up his conference presentation into two separate chapters, one empirical and one primarily theoretical.

We are grateful to the contributors of these chapters for their diligence and patience. We also appreciate the contributions of friends who traveled long distances to attend the conference and enriched it with their comments and questions – William Brewer, Darryl Bruce, Henry Ellis, John Fitzgerald, Makiko Naka, John Robinson – as well as our Emory colleagues. David Jopling and Ira Hyman did yeoman service in the organization of the meeting. We are especially pleased to acknowledge the support of the Air Force Office of Scientific Research and the Office of Naval Research, ably represented by Albert Fregly and Susan Chipman respectively; it was their sponsorship that made the conference possible. Finally, we are happy to record – for the fourth time! – that it is a pleasure to work with the editorial staff of Cambridge University Press. The Emory Cognition Project looks forward to the continuation of this special relationship.

Eugene Winograd
Ulric Neisser

# Contributors

John Neil Bohannon III is Professor and Head of Psychology at Butler University.

William F. Brewer is Professor of Psychology at the University of Illinois at Urbana-Champaign.

Sven-Åke Christianson is Associate Professor of Psychology at the University of Stockholm.

Paul E. Gold is Professor of Psychology and Director, Neuroscience Graduate Program, at the University of Virginia.

Nicole Harsch is a graduate student in psychology at Emory University.

Friderike Heuer is Assistant Professor of Psychology at Lewis and Clark College.

Leah Kaufman is a graduate student in psychology at the University of Washington.

Steen F. Larsen is Senior Associate Professor, Institute of Psychology, University of Aarhus, Denmark.

Elizabeth F. Loftus is Professor of Psychology at the University of Washington.

Michael McCloskey is Professor of Cognitive Science at the Johns Hopkins University.

Ulric Neisser is Robert W. Woodruff Professor of Psychology at Emory University.

David B. Pillemer is Professor of Psychology at Wellesley College.

Daniel Reisberg is Associate Professor of Psychology at Reed College.

David C. Rubin is Professor of Psychology at Duke University.

Jeffery N. Swartwood is a graduate student in psychology at the University of Tennessee, Knoxville.

Victoria Louise Symons is a graduate student in psychology at the University of Manchester, England.

Amye Richelle Warren is Associate Professor of Psychology at the University of Tennessee, Chattanooga.

Eugene Winograd is Professor of Psychology at Emory University.

# 1

# Introduction

EUGENE WINOGRAD

Dates are important in the study of "flashbulb memories." President John F. Kennedy was assassinated on November 22, 1963 and Brown and Kulik asked people about their memories for that event in 1975 before publishing their famous article in 1977. The 12-year retention interval lent credibility to the claim of remarkable memory; it seemed unusual then, as it does now, for people to recall events with such vividness after so long a time. The flashbulb metaphor has remained controversial since Brown and Kulik coined it, and the explosion of the *Challenger* shuttle on January 28, 1986 provided an opportunity to examine it more closely. Several enterprising memory researchers independently set out to ask subjects to describe how they had heard the news of the shuttle disaster. Unlike earlier studies about the Kennedy assassination, these studies were undertaken within a short time after the event. Some researchers then waited months or years before questioning the same informants again.

This new wave of research on flashbulb memories has been designed to approach many of the questions raised by Brown and Kulik (1977) and by their critics. Because a number of investigators had been working independently on the same problem, a conference at which they could compare findings and discuss their implications for the relationship between affect and memory seemed appropriate. That conference was held at Emory University on February 2–3, 1990. We invited specialists whose research directly assessed memory for *Challenger* and other scientists whose research interests were relevant to the problem of flashbulb memories.

The following issues were the focus of the conference:

1. Is it necessary to postulate a special mechanism to explain the persistence of flashbulb memories? Brown and Kulik had proposed the "Now Print!" mechanism of Livingston (1967), a neurophysiological hypothesis, as an explanation of the enduring memories associated with dramatic events.

2. Are flashbulb memories as accurate as the photographic metaphor suggests? The follow-up testing employed in studying memory for the shuttle disaster allows a critical examination of this basic question. If people are inconsistent in reporting the same memory on two occasions, it is difficult to argue for accuracy.

1

3. What are the implications of flashbulb memories for an understanding of the relationship between emotion and memory?

4. Are the determinants of such enduring memories to be sought at the time of encoding, or do they work over a longer period subsequent to the original event (Neisser, 1982)?

Most of our contributors have something to say about each of these issues, although in varying degrees. We have organized the book into four overlapping sections. The first two sections report new data about memories of hearing the news of a major event. In chapter 2, Ulric Neisser and Nicole Harsch report the results of a longitudinal study of memory for *Challenger*. The morning after the explosion, Neisser collected questionnaires from a large class of psychology students about how they had heard the news. After a lapse of nearly 3 years, the same informants were asked the same questions again. The most noteworthy outcome of this study is that over 40% of the informants were clearly inconsistent across the two occasions. These results bring the accuracy of flashbulb memories into question.

In chapter 3, Steen Larsen's diary study of his own memory also undermines the notion that flashbulb memories are necessarily accurate. Each night for 6 months, Larsen recorded information about two major events of the day, a news event and a personal event. It so happened that this time period included *Challenger*, the Chernobyl nuclear disaster, and the assassination of Olof Palme, the prime minister of Sweden. When testing his memory months later, Larsen made major errors in recalling how he had heard the news of these events. Nevertheless, he argues that the most significant news events can be distinguished from other news events because they are forgotten at a lower rate. Even though flashbulb memories may be neither permanent nor fully accurate, the category may have some viability.

In chapter 4, Neil Bohannon and Victoria Symons summarize the previously published research of Bohannon and his colleagues on memories of the shuttle explosion. They also present new data, including longitudinal testing of the same subjects 36 months apart. Two of their findings seem especially salient. About one-third of the informants were inconsistent in recalling where they had first heard the news about *Challenger*, casting further doubt on the photographic metaphor. But those informants who were consistent about location were also those who reported the highest initial emotional response to the news. Bohannon and Symons argue that perfect recall is an unreasonable criterion for considering a memory as having flashbulb properties. In their view, the finding that better recall is associated with high affect is enough to validate the concept.

The second section of the book includes two chapters about the memory of children for significant events. In part because there was an ordinary schoolteacher aboard the *Challenger*, schoolchildren all over the country watched the event. Many educators and psychologists became concerned about possible effects of *Challenger's* tragic outcome on the children. Amye Warren and Jeffery Swartwood (chapter 5) assessed the memories of children who were in school at the time of the event. The children ranged from kindergarten to eighth grade and the design incorporated longitudinal testing at intervals as long as 2 years. Their chapter reports extensive analysis of this unique database.

David Pillemer (chapter 6) studied memory for a local event among nursery schoolchildren. An unexpected fire alarm was a major event within the life of the school. Younger children remembered the event less accurately than older children. Pillemer relates his findings to the children's comprehension of the event, their schemas for school routines (what some have called the "disruption" hypothesis), and their understanding of causality.

Given the apparent importance of emotion in flashbulb memories, our third section is devoted to the relationship between affect and memory. In chapter 7, Paul Gold reviews recent work on the neurobiological regulation of memory storage. In the 25 years since Livingston's (1967) "Now Print!" hypothesis, a great deal has been learned about the chemical regulation of memory. Some of this work tends to bear out the early speculations. Gold reviews research with both animals and humans, including recent work from his own laboratory, on the role of glucose in strengthening memory. Although he is cautious about claiming that the same mechanisms explain people's recall of the assassination of President Kennedy or the *Challenger* explosion, Gold believes that flashbulb memories are just examples of normal neurobiological processes in memory storage.

Daniel Reisberg and Friderike Heuer (chapter 8) discuss the problem of emotion and memory in the light of their own research. They do not use naturally occurring events like *Challenger*. Instead, they present slides and films, contrived by experts to induce strong affect, to subjects in a laboratory setting. Reisberg and Heuer find that emotion slows forgetting as well as producing selectivity in encoding and postevent elaboration.

Sven-Åke Christianson (chapter 9) presents a broad review of the literature on emotion and memory. Although he concludes that emotional events are remembered differently than ordinary events, he does not think that flashbulb memories are different from other memories of emotional experiences. Christianson presents a framework that distinguishes between "core" and "peripheral" information about an event. The reader of Christianson's chapter and that of Reisberg and Heuer will gain an appreciation of the problems involved in distinguishing between the aspects of an event that have core status and those with peripheral status.

In the final chapter on emotion and memory, Elizabeth Loftus and Leah Kaufman raise fundamental questions about the nature of traumatic memories. Why do they sometimes persist as flashbulb memories but at other times lead to the opposite outcome, repression? The question is so straightforward and important that one wonders why it has been so long overlooked.

The last section contains four theoretical papers. Michael McCloskey (chapter 11) rejects the special-mechanism hypothesis and argues that ordinary mechanisms of memory suffice to explain flashbulb memories. He is critical of both the flashbulb memory concept and the methods used to justify it. Chapter 12 is a second contribution by David Pillemer, who discusses the functions of autobiographical remembering in general. Although it is important, for some purposes, to remember events accurately, this may not be as important for other functions of memory. Pillemer distinguishes among the directive, psychodynamic, and communicative functions of memory. For example, recall may have a psychodynamic function in allowing affect to be expressed or a directive function in providing prescriptions for behavior.

David Rubin (chapter 13) provides an overview of the 1990 conference. He reviews the different criteria of flashbulb memories that have been offered, including vividness, confidence, accuracy, consistency, and function. He also emphasizes a major theme that emerged from the conference: that baseline memories are needed for comparison with the flashbulb memories being studied. Rubin identifies the following typical characteristics of flashbulb memories: good narrative structure, good fit to cultural norms, rich imagery, emotionality, and rehearsal. He observes that these factors operate over time. It takes real time (Rubin estimates at least a week) to develop one's narrative of "how I heard the news" into a coherent story satisfying these constraints.

The last word belongs to William Brewer who, in chapter 14, honors Brown and Kulik by offering an intensive, detailed evaluation of their seminal paper. What did they claim, what was their evidence, and how do their claims look today? Respectfully critical of Brown and Kulik, Brewer argues that their theory was not entirely consistent and their data not appropriate to test it. Why, then, has their paper been so influential? He answers his own question by saying that it was one of the first modern investigations of personal (autobiographical) memory, contrasting sharply with the prevailing laboratory studies. Brewer then summarizes the current evidence about flashbulb memories with respect to accuracy, imagery, confidence, and rehearsal. On the question of whether flashbulb memories are "special," he argues that they are a form of personal memory tied to the structure of news reception events. The high level of recall associated with flashbulb memories does not demand a special explanatory mechanism, but can be understood as the joint product of such factors as emotion, rehearsal, and distinctiveness.

Overall, the weight of the conference came down against the need for postulating a special mechanism for flashbulb memories. We were impressed by the high degree of inaccuracy of those memories, and saw the relationship between emotion and memory as a significant research problem for the future. On the whole, most enduring memories seem to result from the interaction of encoding, rehearsal, and retrieval factors.

**REFERENCES**

Brown, R., & Kulik, J. (1977). Flashbulb memories. *Cognition, 5*, 73–99.

Neisser, U. (1982). Snapshots or benchmarks? In U. Neisser (Ed.), *Memory observed* (pp. 43–48). San Francisco: W. H. Freeman.

Livingston, R. B. (1967). Brain circuitry relating to complex behavior. In G. C. Quarton, T. Melnechuck, & F. O. Schmitt (Eds.), *The neurosciences: A study program* (pp. 499–514). New York: Rockefeller University Press.

*Part I*

# Empirical studies

# 2

# Phantom flashbulbs:
# False recollections of hearing the
# news about *Challenger*

ULRIC NEISSER AND NICOLE HARSCH

When I first heard about the explosion I was sitting in my freshman dorm room with my roommate and we were watching TV. It came on a news flash and we were both totally shocked. I was really upset and I went upstairs to talk to a friend of mine and then I called my parents.

I was in my religion class and some people walked in and started talking about [it]. I didn't know any details except that it had exploded and the schoolteacher's students had all been watching which I thought was so sad. Then after class I went to my room and watched the TV program talking about it and I got all the details from that.

The two memories above are actual written responses to the question "How did you first hear the news of the *Challenger* disaster?" The first account was given in the fall of 1988, long after the event, by an Emory senior whom we will call "RT." It was a vivid recollection, which met or exceeded all the standard tests of a "flashbulb memory." Asked for 5-point confidence ratings of various aspects of the memory, RT hit the top of the scale: 5 on *How did you hear it?* (television), *Where were you?* (her room), *What were you doing?* (watching television), *Who was with you?* (roommate), and *How did you feel?* (shocked and upset). She was slightly less confident (rating 4) about *What time of day was it?*, answering "2:00 or 3:00 p.m." (In fact, the shuttle exploded shortly after 11:00 in the morning on January 28, 1986.) But despite her confidence, RT was mistaken. Two and a half years earlier, she had answered the same question 24 hours after the explosion. The report she gave then is the second response transcribed above. It tells us that RT had originally heard about the disaster in one of her classes. She did *not* first learn about it from television, as she later came to believe.

RT is one of 44 subjects whose 1988/1989 recollections of hearing about *Challenger* are examined in this chapter. These recollections are especially interesting because in each case we also have a report written by the same subject on the morning after the event. Comparison with these original reports shows that none of the enduring memories was entirely correct, and that many were at least as wide of the mark as RT's.

This finding poses a serious challenge to current theories of flashbulb memories. It also raises a number of new questions – at least, questions that

9

are new in this context. In such cases, has the incorrect "memory" completely obliterated all traces of the original event, or could the earlier memory be
retrieved by more adequate cueing? Where do the incorrect recalls come
from? Why are the subjects so confident of them? Such questions have rarely
been asked about flashbulb memories, because we have taken their accuracy
more or less for granted. Brown and Kulik (1977), of course, postulated a
special mechanism to explain that putative accuracy. Other theorists argued
that the special mechanism hypothesis was unnecessary (Neisser, 1982;
McCloskey, Wible, & Cohen, 1988). According to them, ordinary principles
of memory – rehearsal, uniqueness, the schemata provided by narrative
conventions – were enough to explain such memories. But in making these
arguments, even the critics took the recollections themselves more or less at
face value: It was their accuracy that the "ordinary principles" were supposed to explain.

Why did we make this assumption so readily? As memory psychologists,
we were certainly aware of the fallibility of episodic recall in other contexts.
All of us know that story recall is richly constructive, that eyewitness testimony is often confabulated, and that there is at best a low correlation
between confidence and accuracy on the witness stand. A host of studies with
Loftus's (1979) misinformation paradigm has shown how easy it is to produce substantial memory errors, even in recognition. Nevertheless, we rarely
applied these lessons to the case of flashbulb memories. There are probably
two reasons for this, one practical and the other more theoretical. The
practical reason is obvious enough: In the absence of independent records, it
is hard to resist the confidence of the subjects. They are so sure of themselves
that it seems downright discourteous to dispute their claims, and (except for
a few isolated cases) we have had little basis on which to do so.

That difficulty will be at least partly remedied by the data presented in this
chapter. But there may be another reason for everyone's readiness to accept
such memories as valid, one that is related to a rarely mentioned theoretical
dilemma. In general, psychologists have found it difficult to reconcile the
fallibility of some memories with the dependability of others. After all,
whatever research may show, we know that memory is more often right than
wrong. The mundane transactions of daily life depend heavily on shared
beliefs about past events, and they usually work out. Everybody remembers
thousands of things that really did happen: one's happy weekend with X,
one's terrible dispute with Y, one's success in achieving Z. Such recollections
are repeatedly confirmed, not only by nostalgic conversations (perhaps with
X) but by one's present unpleasant relations with Y, by a life situation that
reflects accomplishment of Z.

In the face of such evidence, we cannot help believing that "memory" is
generally reliable. It seems but a short step to conclude that most individual
*memories* are reliable too. If so, the errors that appear in experiments (and

sometimes in our own experience) must be isolated exceptions. And if memories are generally reliable, what is more natural than to suppose that the most vivid and confident memories are especially so? But despite its plausibility, the easy step from "memory" to "memories" in this argument is a non sequitur. The reliability of memory in general need not depend on the accuracy of individual recollections. It may emerge, instead, from the combined effect of many memories that are not particularly accurate in themselves. The data reported in this chapter seem to suggest just such a conclusion.

The discussion to this point has skirted a crucial issue: the role of *affect* in these recollections. The events that give rise to classical flashbulb memories include not only "reception events" like hearing the news of a disaster but also passionate kisses, startling discoveries, family tragedies. These are emotional events, and they often give rise to lasting memories. There is clearly some connection between emotion and memory, but is it a direct one? Many theorists have thought so: William James believed that "an impression may be so exciting emotionally as almost to leave a *scar* upon the cerebral tissues" (1890, p. 670; italics in original). We will call this the "emotional strengthening hypothesis." Brown and Kulik's (1977) "Now Print!" mechanism is one version of that hypothesis; the arguments made in this volume by Gold, by Bohannon and Symons, and by Reisberg and Heuer are other formulations of the same basic idea.

Although the emotional strengthening hypothesis is attractively simple, it faces several difficulties. For one thing, other factors – uniqueness, rehearsal, narrative conventions, etc. – may very well explain the accuracy of such memories without any appeal to their emotionality per se (Neisser, 1982; McCloskey et al., 1988). A second critical point was made by Rubin and Kozin (1984), who asked 58 subjects to characterize their most vivid memories on a number of dimensions. Many of the remembered events were *not* described as unusually emotional. (Their most frequent characteristic was "personal importance," which is a very different matter.) A final difficulty arises from the fact, emphasized in this chapter and occasionally reported elsewhere, that many vivid memories are simply wrong. If emotion acts to strengthen memory traces, how could it produce false recollections?

To examine the accuracy of any class of memories, one needs some record of the original events themselves. One way to obtain such records is to guess in advance that a given event may give rise to vivid recollections, and act accordingly. Like several other contributors to this volume, we recognized the space shuttle disaster as a potential flashbulb event. With this in mind, a questionnaire on which individuals could record how they had first heard the news about *Challenger* was prepared early on the morning following the explosion. The questionnaire was given to 106 Emory students in Psychology 101 ("Personality Development") near the end of the 10:00–11:00 a.m. class hour, that is, less than 24 hours after the event itself. The students filled it out on the spot and returned it as they left the classroom.[1]

The completed questionnaires were left untouched until the fall of 1988. Then, 2½ years after the event, we were ready to study the accuracy of flashbulb memories. That fall, a new questionnaire was administered to all the subjects we could still find at Emory, a total of 44. When it became clear that many now had substantially incorrect memories, we decided to examine them further. Forty of the original subjects were interviewed at length in the spring of 1989, using a structured format that was designed to provide numerous recall cues. At the end of the interview we showed them the questionnaires they had filled out 3 years earlier, and recorded their reactions to the discrepancies that thus became apparent.

In many ways our design was like that of McCloskey, Wible, & Cohen (1988), who also tested and retested people about their *Challenger* memories. But the present study has two advantages over that of McCloskey et al.: The initial records were obtained earlier (less than 24 hours after the event) and the recall interval was substantially longer (2½ to 3 years). The earlier start means that we can be more sure of the accuracy of the original accounts given by our subjects, and the longer delay provided more time for the processes of reconstruction to do their work.

### Specific aims

The most important aim of our study, of course, was to assess the overall accuracy of flashbulb memories. This aim was largely achieved by the recall questionnaires administered in the fall of 1988. As already noted (and as we have briefly reported elsewhere: Harsch & Neisser, 1989), those questionnaires revealed a high incidence of substantial errors. These data will be presented in some detail below. In addition, however, the follow-up interview enabled us to explore a number of other issues.

1. It seemed important to determine whether such memories are stable over time. Would a subject who had told an inaccurate story in October tell it again in March? The results were clear on this point: The stories we obtained were remarkably consistent.

2. Flashbulb memories are often said to be unusually vivid (Rubin & Kozin, 1984); as Brown and Kulik put it, they have ". . . a primary 'live' quality that is almost perceptual" (1977, p. 74). Is this vividness any guarantee of their accuracy? Some support for that possibility comes from a recent study by William Brewer (1988), whose subjects carried random "beepers" and noted what they were doing and thinking whenever the beep sounded. A later memory test included various vividness ratings, and accuracy of recall was indeed associated with high visual vividness. This seemed to be a hypothesis worth exploring: In the follow-up interview, our subjects made

vividness ratings too. As will be seen, the results on this point are somewhat ambiguous.

3. The third aim of the follow-up seemed potentially the most interesting: We tried to help our subjects recover the memories they had lost. Some of the methods we used were derived from the "cognitive interview," devised by R. E. Geiselman and his associates (Geiselman, Fisher, MacKinnon, & Holland, 1985) as a means of facilitating eyewitness recall; others were our own invention. Subjects were asked to recall the event from a different perspective, to think of additional ways in which they *might* have heard the news, and so on. In a final effort to jog their memories, we showed them their own original questionnaires. As it turned out, none of these procedures had any effect at all.

Finally, we carried out a number of analyses addressed to specific issues. We examined the correlations between measures of phenomenal vividness and accuracy, the effects of initial exposure and rehearsal times, and – within limits set by the information available to us – the relation between initial affect and later recall. We were also concerned with the sources of the subjects' inaccurate recollections. Is there a "schema" for hearing disaster news, to which memories are gradually assimilated? Is it possible that the events described in "false" accounts really did take place, even though they were not the actual occasions on which the subjects first heard the news? (Following Brewer, 1988, we call this the "wrong time slice" hypothesis.) These analyses do not provide any definitive answers, but they suggest some interesting hypotheses.

## Procedure

The original questionnaire was filled out by 106 students on the morning after the explosion. They began by writing a free description of how they had heard the news, then turned over the page and answered a set of questions based on the "canonical categories" of Brown and Kulik (1977): What time was it, how did you hear about it, where were you, what were you doing, who told you, who else was there, how did you feel about it, how did the person who told you seem to feel about it, what did you do afterward? A final item asked for an estimate of how much time the subject had spent, on the previous day, in talking about the event or following radio/television coverage of it. (It was hoped – perhaps too optimistically – that responses to this item might provide a rough estimate of what the literature on flashbulb memories calls "rehearsal.")

By the fall of 1988, the freshmen of January 1986 had become seniors. The Emory student directory was searched for the names of students who had been in the original sample.[2] Each of them was offered $3 to participate in a brief experiment. (The nature of the experiment was not described. If they asked why they had been selected, the experimenter replied that their names had come from a list of students enrolled in an introductory psychology class several years ago.) Almost all agreed to participate; the sample included 30 women and 14 men. When they came to the lab (either individually or in small groups), the subjects were told for the first time that the study concerned memory for the *Challenger* explosion. They filled out a new questionnaire and left. The study was ostensibly complete at that point; they were not warned that they might be contacted again later.

The 1988 questionnaire closely resembled the one on which the same subjects had recorded the original event, 32–34 months earlier. They first wrote an account of how they had heard the news, then turned the page and answered canonical questions. This time each question was accompanied by a 5-point confidence scale: 1 was defined as "just guessing," 5 as "absolutely certain." As before, they were also asked how much time they had spent (on the day of the explosion) in discussing or following radio/television coverage of the event.

A final item asked whether they had ever filled out a questionnaire on this subject before. Surprisingly, only 11 subjects (25%) answered "yes" to this question; the other 33 were sure that they had not. Compared to other similar studies, this represents rather poor recall of the first questionnaire. The long delay interval (over 2 1/2 years) must be partly responsible for this. In addition, the manner in which the original questionnaire was presented probably minimized its status as a distinct event. It was an easy and undemanding task; all the questions concerned a readily memorable event of the previous day. The participants did not have to sign up or go anywhere; it was just something that filled the last few minutes of an ordinary class, and not worth any subsequent rehearsal or comment.

Some months later, when a preliminary analysis had shown that many of the memories were far off the mark, we decided to interview the subjects more thoroughly. This time they were offered $5 for their help with an experiment. Again, in calling them, NH did not say what the experiment was about. Forty of the original 44 agreed to return; NH interviewed each of them individually (in March/April 1989) for about three-quarters of an hour. During the interviews, she was "blind" with respect to the accuracy of the individual memories. She knew that some subjects' questionnaire responses had been essentially correct and others far off the mark, but with two exceptions she did not know whether any given individual had been accurate or not. The interviews were tape-recorded, and subsequently transcribed.

The subjects began by recounting, again, how they had heard the news of the shuttle disaster. They then rated the overall quality of the memory as well as its vividness on seven separate dimensions: visual, auditory, tactile, smell, taste, emotion, and thought. The question format for the vividness ratings was "When you think about the time that you heard the news about the *Challenger* explosion, to what extent do you reexperience the original visual scene (or the original sounds, touches, smells, etc.)?" These 7-point scales were modeled as closely as possible on those of Brewer (1988).

The ratings of visual and auditory vividness posed a special problem: We thought that some subjects might call to mind the familiar television image of the shuttle explosion rather than the situation in which they first heard the news. To check on this possibility, subjects were asked just what scene they had been reexperiencing in connection with these two ratings. Six subjects who reported that they had been imagining the television display were asked to make another visual rating, this time focused on their actual surroundings when they first heard the news. This latter value was then used in all analyses of visual vividness.

In the next phase of the interview, the subjects were presented with eight instructions designed to help them retrieve additional (or alternative) memories of the event. Four of these were based on the technique that Geiselman et al. (1985) termed the "Cognitive Interview." A number of studies have shown that this procedure can elicit additional information from eyewitnesses, at least after short delays. Accordingly, our subjects were asked:

1. to reinstate mentally the original context (e.g., the room);
2. to reinstate mentally the *emotional* context;
3. to recall the event in backward order;
4. to recall the event from a different perspective.

One possible problem with these cues is that they all begin with the situation as the subject presently remembers it. If that memory is basically wrong – that is, if the situation in which the subject actually heard the news was quite different – they may be of little use. For this reason we also asked each subject to try four "lateral thinking" techniques, designed to broaden the focus of attention:

1. to recall the events of the entire day in question, both before and after they found out about the explosion;
2. to describe another way they *might* have heard the news;
3. to describe how a friend of theirs might have heard it;
4. to recall whatever they could from anytime in January 1986.

Half the subjects were given the cognitive interview cues before the lateral thinking cues; the others got the lateral thinking cues first. After their response to each cue, they were asked whether they now remembered more about their own shuttle-explosion experience. They were encouraged to report everything that came to mind, no matter how trivial.

Later in the interview, NH used even more drastic cueing methods. First, the subjects were shown the questionnaires that they had filled out the previous fall, a few months before. Any discrepancies between the account just given and the earlier one were pointed out (these were usually slight), and the subject was encouraged to suggest reasons for the difference.

NH then presented a prepared *retrieval cue*. Subjects whose 1988 recall had been far off the mark were given a cue based on their original records; for example, RT was asked, "Is it possible that you already knew about the explosion before seeing it on TV?" (Subjects with relatively accurate memories were given similar cues, *not* based on their original records.) UN had prepared these cues in advance. Finally, at the end of the interview, the subjects were shown their own original 1986 reports in their own handwriting. This often produced considerable surprise, not only for the subject but also for NH, who had not seen the individual questionnaires before. Any discrepancies between the subjects' present recollections and their original records were then discussed: "Why do you suppose you said this here and something different a couple of years ago?" Finally they were asked which version of the event they liked better and believed more. After some concluding discussion of their attitudes toward NASA and the space program, they were dismissed.

## Coding

Accuracy is not all-or-none: Many subjects had memories that were partly right and partly wrong. Consider HC, whose overall statement on the 1988 memory questionaire was:

"I was returning to my room in Dobbs Hall after a morning class. . . . I heard commotion while I was walking down my hall, and I think somebody must have told me what happened because when I got to my room I turned the television on to see what I knew would be reruns of the explosion." On the backside of the same page, he recalled the *time* as 11:30, the *place* as his dorm, and the *activity* as returning to his room. In response to *who told you* he gave a specific name, X, presumably the "somebody" in the hall; in response to *others present* he said "no one."

Compare this recall which HC's morning-after account of the same event in 1986:

"At about 1 p.m. I was returning from class with a friend of mine who was visiting. Passing through the basement of my dorm, an acquaintance of mine named Y from Switzerland said 'Go turn on the TV.' When I asked why, what happened, he said 'Just go turn it on; it's all over the TV.' I ran up the stairs thinking of presidential assassinations, with my friend muttering something about war in the Middle East. When I entered my room I noticed my TV was already plugged in, telling me that the event happened earlier that morning and my roommate had watched it for a while. Then I turned the TV on." On the backside of *that* page, in 1986, he had listed *time* as 1:10, *activity* as "Worrying about how I was going to get my car started," and *others present* as "my friend Z" (yet another name).

These two accounts agree on the basic situation: HC was walking through the dorm when he encountered an acquaintance, who told him something that made him turn on his television as soon as he got to his room. But they differ in many details: What time it was, who the acquaintance was, what he said, where the encounter took place, and who else was present. Using the initial account as a standard, the accuracy of the remembered version is somewhere between zero and 100%. But where?

One way to score such responses is just to have judges make global ratings of the similarity between the two accounts. We experimented with several rating scales of this kind, but none had satisfactory reliability. The scheme we eventually selected does not require an overall similarity judgment. Instead, the rater considers five well-defined attributes one at a time. These are, of course, *location, activity, informant, time,* and *others present*. (We did not count *affect*; a separate analysis of affect appears below.) Each of these five attributes can be reliably rated on a 3-point scale. A score of 2 means an essentially correct response (within sight distance of the same location for *place*, the same individual for *informant*, etc.). A zero means that it is obviously wrong (in the dorm rather than in class for *place*, seeing the news on television rather than hearing it from a friend for *informant*). Scores of 1 were given for intermediate cases, like HC's "walking into the dorm hall" for "going through the dorm basement."

These attributes are not all equally important. We defined *location, activity,* and *informant* as "major" attributes because they seem essential to the identify of the event itself. If you misremember where you were or what you were doing or who actually told you about the explosion, you are seriously mistaken. *Time of day* and *others present*, in contrast, are "minor" attributes: You could be wrong on both and still essentially right about what happened. Using this distinction, we defined a *Weighted Attribute Score* (WAS) with a range from 0 to 7. The WAS is the sum of the scores on the three major attributes, plus a bonus point awarded if the subject scores 3 or more (of 4 possible) on the minors. HC has a WAS of four: 2 for *activity* (walking to his room), 1 for the approximately correct *location*, and 1 for an approximately correct *informant*. (He got the wrong person, but at least he remembered that it was a person and not a television set.) This coding system is quite reliable. The two coders who first used it achieved a reliability of .79; after resolving disputed cases, their combined ratings correlated .89 with those of a naive third coder.[3]

Accuracy scores for the fall 1988 recall questionnaires are called "WAS-2/1" because they compare the second reports with the first. Analogous accuracy scores for the spring interviews (again compared with the initial 1986 reports) are called "WAS-3/1"; they had a reliability of .96. We also used this method to measure consistency across the two recall sessions; these scores, called "WAS-3/2," had a reliability of .94.

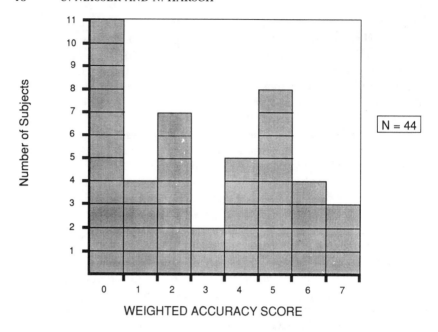

Figure 2.1. Frequency distribution of accuracy scores on the recall questionnaire, fall 1988 (WAS–2/1).

## Results

### Accuracy and confidence

The distribution of accuracies on the fall 1988 questionnaire (WAS-2/1) is shown in Figure 2.1. The mean was 2.95, out of a possible 7. Eleven subjects (25%) were wrong about everything and scored 0. Twenty-two of them (50%) scored 2 or less; this means that if they were right on one major attribute, they were wrong on both of the others. Only three subjects (7%) achieved the maximum possible score of 7; even in these cases there were minor discrepancies (e.g., about the time of the event) between the recall and the original report.

What makes these low scores interesting is the high degree of confidence that accompanied many of them. To quantify this, it was necessary to collapse the several confidence ratings on the fall questionnaire into a single value. We decided to average the ratings for the three major attributes – *place*, *activity*, and *informant*. This produced a continuous variable (confidence-T2) ranging between 1 to 5, with a mean of 4.17. Its distribution appears in Figure 2.2. To clarify the relation between confidence and accuracy, the

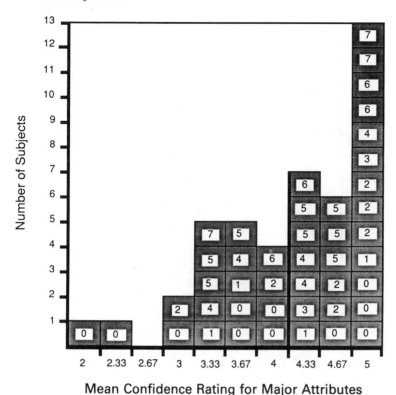

Figure 2.2. Frequency distribution of confidence ratings on the recall questionnaire, fall 1988. The number inside each cell is the subject's accuracy score, WAS–2/1.

figure also shows the WAS-2/1 score of each individual subject in the distribution.

The two subjects at the left end of Figure 2.2 exhibit an entirely appropriate relation between confidence and accuracy – they had none of either. These two subjects frankly admitted that they no longer remembered how they had heard the news. In the rest of the group there seems to be no relation between confidence and accuracy at all. (The overall correlation, based on all 44 subjects, was a nonsignificant 0.29.) The 13 subjects at the right side of the figure are particularly interesting: Their mean rating of 5.00 implies that they were maximally confident about all three major attributes. Nevertheless, they were not unusually accurate. The distribution of WAS scores in these 13 was essentially identical to that in the sample as a whole: Again, about 25% were at zero and the median was at 2.

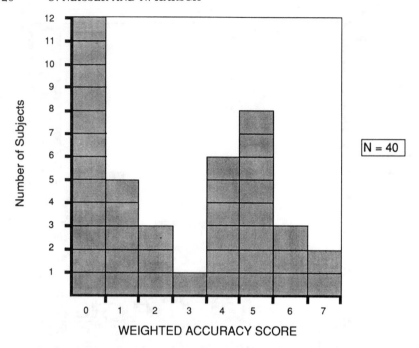

Figure 2.3. Frequency distribution of accuracy scores on the follow-up interview, spring 1989.

For the most part, our subjects told the same stories in the spring as in the fall: The average consistency (WAS-2/3) was 5.20. This result implies, of course, that the additional cues presented in the spring interviews had little effect on accuracy. Indeed, this was the case. The distribution of accuracy scores (WAS-3/1) for the interviews are shown in Figure 2.3. It is just like the distribution of questionnaire accuracies given in Figure 2.1, or perhaps a bit lower: 12 subjects are at zero rather than 11, and the mean has slipped from 2.95 to 2.75.

Instead of a series of confidence ratings for the various attributes, the interview subjects estimated the "overall quality" of their memories on a 7-point scale. These estimates (which we call "confidence-T3") were still high (mean = 5.28), and still unrelated to accuracy ($r = .30$, ns). They were positively correlated (.565, $p < .001$) with confidence-T2 (average confidence on the fall questionnaires). The most consistent subjects were also the most confident: WAS-2/3 correlated .633 with confidence-T2 and .544 with confidence-T3, both highly significant.

### Effects of additional retrieval cues

The accuracy scores in Figure 2.3 are based on the entire interview, up to the time when the subjects were shown their 1986 reports. We had originally intended to develop two such scores, one for the account given at the beginning and another after the presentation of the eight standard recall cues. This proved entirely unnecessary. Our attempts to enhance retrieval – asking subjects to reinstate the context, having them imagine how a friend might have heard the news, and the like – made no difference at all. No subjects changed their minds on any specific point after any of the eight cognitively designed retrieval cues. No one said, "Oh, now I remember how it really was!" Two subjects' WAS scores went up by a point in the interview (compared to the fall questionnaire) but six scores went down by 1 to 3 points; 32 scores were unchanged. The techniques of the "cognitive interview" (Geiselman et al., 1985) may be effective shortly after a to-be-remembered event, but they are apparently useless after a lapse of several years.

Perhaps the most interesting outcome of the interviews is what happened – and what did *not* happen – at the end. Many subjects exhibited great surprise when confronted with their own original reports. They found it hard to believe that their memories could be so wrong: "Whoa! That's totally different from how I remember it." We had expected these exclamations of surprise. But we had also expected something else: that seeing the original records would at least partially revive the original memories. If anything can recall a forgotten event to mind, it should be one's own first-hand report! In initially designing the interviews, we had anticipated a methodological problem that never materialized. How would we distinguish between (a) genuine remindings and (b) false impressions of being reminded that subjects might try to present? We need not have worried. No one who had given an incorrect account in the interview even pretended that they now recalled what was stated on the original record. On the contrary, they kept saying, "I mean, like I told you, I have no recollection of it at all" or "I still think of it as the other way around." As far as we can tell, the original memories are just gone.

### Vividness and accuracy

Our subjects had no difficulty in rating the extent to which their memories were like a "reexperience" of various aspects of the event. Table 2.1 shows that these ratings were quite high for *visual* vividness: The mean was 5.35 of a possible 7. (Six subjects reported that their first rating had been based on the television image rather than on their remembered surroundings, and were asked to make new ratings focused on the latter. With these revised ratings, which were used in all subsequent analyses, the overall visual vividness mean

Table 2.1. *Means and correlations for vividness measures*

| Experience: | Visual | Audit | Touch | Smell | Taste | Emot | Thought |
|---|---|---|---|---|---|---|---|
| Mean Rating: | 5.35 | 2.80 | 2.10 | 1.53 | 1.49 | 4.50 | 4.60 |
| *Correlations* | | | | | | | |
| Accuracy 2/1 | .286 | **.518** | −.047 | .103 | .026 | .205 | .158 |
| Accuracy 3/1 | .235 | **.510** | −.027 | .080 | −.046 | .170 | .138 |
| Agreement 3/2 | **.509** | .290 | *.337* | .271 | .075 | .109 | .259 |
| Confidence T2 | **.464** | .260 | .244 | .119 | −.057 | .093 | .290 |
| Confidence T3 | **.523** | *.353* | .242 | .159 | .042 | .250 | .147 |
| Visual | — | .196 | *.353* | .246 | *.369* | .246 | .304 |
| Auditory | — | — | .205 | .234 | .143 | .214 | .132 |
| Touch | — | — | — | .135 | *.404* | **.448** | *.325* |
| Smell | — | — | — | — | **.440** | .175 | .065 |
| Taste | — | —˙ | — | — | — | *.351* | .238 |
| Emotion | — | — | — | — | — | — | **.682** |

*Note*: *Italicized* values are significantly different from zero at the .05 level; **boldfaced** values at the .01 level.

fell to 4.92.) As in Brewer's (1988) study, visual vividness was correlated ($r =$ .523) with the rated "overall quality" of the memories (which we call confidence-T3). This means that when subjects had vivid visual images, they were very sure of their recalls. Visual vividness also correlated ($r = .509$) with WAS-3/2, the subjects' consistency across the two recall sessions. Perhaps it is worth noting the high vividness ratings for reexperienced *emotions* (4.50) and *thoughts* (4.60); these two ratings were highly correlated with each other ($r = .682$).

Unlike Brewer (1988), we found no evidence of a strong relation between visual vividness and accuracy. The correlations of visual vividness with WAS-2/1 (.286) and WAS-3/1 (.235) were positive, but did not reach statistical significance. Perhaps this is not surprising. Brewer had found high visual vividness ratings not only for correct recalls but also for those he termed wrong time slices, in which subjects seemed to be remembering (perhaps accurately) an inappropriate part of the overall event. In our scoring system, such reports would count as errors; hence their vividness would attenuate any correlation between visual vividness and accuracy. We will return to this possibility below.

Although accuracy was not strongly related to our subjects' ratings of *visual* vividness, significant correlations with *auditory* vividness appeared instead (.518 with WAS-2/1, .510 with WAS-3/1). This result was unexpected (Brewer did not report the relation between auditory vividness and accuracy in his data), and it is difficult to interpret. The sounds that some subjects said they were vividly "reexperiencing" often had little to do with the substance of the event being remembered. Subject PM, who recalled hearing the news first from a friend whose father worked in the space program, said, "My friend was . . . crying when she came to my room, so I can hear that," and gave an auditory vividness rating of "5 or 6." But PM had not heard the news from this friend; her original report shows that she heard it alone, in her dorm room, on the radio. Every aspect of her recall was right except "informant" (WAS-1/2 = 5). How could the general accuracy of her recall have been mediated by the vividness of an incorrect auditory memory?

It may be a mistake to put too much stress on the difference between the auditory and the visual vividness data. Although the auditory ratings were significantly correlated with accuracy and the visual ones were not, these two correlations (.518 and .286 respectively) are not significantly different *from each other*. Both could easily be sampling fluctuations from the same population value of $r$, perhaps around .400. The most we can say at present is that some aspects of vividness seem to be somehow related to accuracy, with the relation between them still poorly understood.

### Effects of initial "rehearsal"

The last item on the initial questionnaire asked how many hours had been spent, the day before, in discussing the disaster or watching television coverage of it. As it turned out, this variable did not correlate with either accuracy or confidence in later recall (−.132 with WAS-2/1, .234 with Confidence-T2). In hindsight, this result is not surprising. Even though we had originally included this item with the "rehearsal" hypothesis in mind, it is really irrelevant to that hypothesis. Although memory for *how one first heard the news* may benefit from repeated telling of that personal story, the hypothesis does not predict any such gain from more exposure to news about the event itself. Additional television exposure could even interfere with recall of the initial encounter, increasing the probability that subjects would remember the television-watching event in its place.

We do not know how accurate these estimates of the first day's time commitment really were. In any case, they did not hold up over time. There was no significant correlation ($r = .191$) between the amounts of "rehearsal" first reported in 1986 and the amounts estimated retrospectively in 1988. Moreover, the mean estimated time in the original reports was only 1.88 hours, whereas the 1988 estimates averaged 30 minutes longer.

### Effects of initial emotion

If affect strengthens memory, we might expect the subjects' 1986 emotions to predict the accuracy of their 1988 recalls. But what were those original emotions? The first questionnaire did not ask subjects to rate their feelings on a quantitative scale; they were simply asked, "How did you feel about it?"

Although the responses to this question are richer than a numerical estimate would have been, they are also harder to interpret. We have tried several different ways of coding them, but none has produced a significant result. Here we describe only the simplest of these schemes, which we call SH (for "Shocked & Horrified"). SH scores are defined as follows:

1.   Subjects who used at least two strong and negatively toned terms in describing their own reactions got scores of 3. *Shocked, stunned, sickened, horrified, upset, crying,* and *sad* all counted here; *surprise* and *disbelief* did not, nor did mere *sympathy* (e.g., for the astronauts and their families).
2.   Subjects who used only one such term got 2. *Sympathy* counted at this level, but *disbelief* still did not.
3.   Subjects who said only, "I didn't believe it," who reported no negative reaction, or who qualified their reactions with phrases like, "However, it's a risk people take," were given scores of 1.

As it turned out, these emotion ratings had no predictive value for later recall. The correlation between SH and WAS-2/1 was $-.171$, that is, essentially zero. Other ways of coding the reactions, including some based on the complexity of emotions reported rather than their strength, fared no better. There is no evidence for any positive relation between affect and accuracy.

We also explored the possibility that high emotion might produce later confidence (even if it did not lead to accuracy). Many people *believe* that emotions strengthen memory; they say things like, "I'll never forget this." It seemed possible that this conviction might increase subjects' confidence in their own recall of relatively more emotional events. There was indeed a trend in this direction: The correlation between SH and confidence-T2 was .254. (It was .295 with confidence-T3.) The same trend can equally well be described in terms of group means: The six subjects who were unmoved by the event (SH = 1) had a mean confidence-T2 of only 3.78, those with a moderate reaction (SH = 2) averaged 4.14, and those who had reacted strongly (SH = 3) were at 4.40. However, the null hypothesis cannot be rejected: None of these effects reached the .05 level of significance.

Perhaps it is worth reporting that the women in our sample had – or at least reported – stronger emotional responses than the men. The mean for women was 2.28; for men, 1.73. This difference is significant at the .02 level. However, there was no difference between the sexes in later confidence or accuracy.

Do subjects *remember* their emotions, 2 or 3 years later? Not as far as we can tell. Although the mean SH score of the emotions recalled in 1988 (2.21) was almost identical to the average original SH (2.19), there was no significant correlation between them ($r = .219$, ns). Moreover, these recalled emotions were not correlated with either the accuracy ($r = -.114$) or the confidence ($r = .093$) of the first recall. Whatever the source of our subjects' unwarranted confidence, it was neither their original nor their remembered feelings.

Table 2.2. *TV priority: Numbers of subjects reporting that they first heard the news via TV or otherwise, in 1986 and 1988*

| 1988 Recalls | Original 1986 Reports | | Totals |
| --- | --- | --- | --- |
| | Yes | No | |
| Yes | 7 | 12 | 19 (45%) |
| No | 2 | 21 | 23 (55%) |
| Totals | 9 (21%) | 33 (79%) | N = 42 |

### TV priority

Finally, let us look briefly at the errors themselves. When subjects' stories were wrong, what kind of mistakes did they make? A quick skim through the protocols suggests that television often played a larger role than that to which it was rightfully entitled. Recall subject RT's flashbulb account: "We were watching TV and we saw it." Like many other subjects, RT forgot the more personal way in which she had actually heard the news (some people had walked into her religion class and talked about it) and came to believe that she saw it first on television. To quantify this effect, we coded both the original records and the recalls for a binary variable called "TV Priority." Accounts in which the subjects' *first contact* with the news is via television were coded 1. (This includes cases where they were already watching television when the event occurred as well as those where they saw other people watching TV and stopped to look.) All other accounts were coded zero, even if the subject reported watching television later on. As Table 2.2 shows, our subjects' recalls exhibited significantly more TV priority than was justified by their original experiences.

The bottom line of Table 2.2 shows that only 9 of 42 codable subjects (21%) had actually learned about the disaster from television. The right margin shows that by 1988, 45% *believed* they had first heard of it in this manner. Whereas 12 subjects shifted from 0 to 1 (i.e., added TV priority), only two shifted from 1 to 0. The MacNemar Test (essentially a binomial test on the 14 subjects who changed) shows that this is significant at $p < .01$.

## Discussion

What are we to make of all this? Two and half years after the original event, many of the flashbulb memories we obtained were quite mistaken. Some subjects were both confident and right, but others – who were just as confident – were dead wrong. When errors did occur, they seemed to be permanent: The subjects pretty much stuck to their stories over the half-year between recalls. Nothing we could think of to do – up to and including showing them their own 1986 questionnaires – brought back the original memories. Where did all the errors come from? Why were the subjects so confident of them? Can these results be reconciled with the emotional strengthening hypothesis?

### The role of vividness

One reason for our subjects' confidence may have been the vividness of their recollections. High vividness is a frequently mentioned characteristic of flashbulb memories (Rubin & Kozin, 1984). The significant correlation between visual vividness and confidence fits this interpretation, and the auditory ratings are even more suggestive. Although not as strongly related to confidence as its visual counterpart, auditory vividness was substantially correlated with accuracy itself. This pattern of results can be explained in at least two ways. The first of these, which we will call Model I, takes the findings more or less at face value. It might work like this:

1. Some factor X, characteristic of flashbulb events, leads to unusually effective memory storage. (X may be a high level of affect, but the model works just as well if uniqueness or repeated rehearsal are the critical factors.)
2. High levels of X lead to rich and accurate storage of information about concrete aspects of the event.
3. This rich storage manifests itself in unusually vivid memories; hence vividness is correlated with accuracy.
4. The subjects themselves believe 1–3 above, and therefore are especially confident of their more vivid memories.

In Model I, effective storage produces both accuracy and vividness; vividness then produces confidence by a kind of metamemory judgment. The model is plausible, but it also predicts a correlation between accuracy and confidence that did not appear in our data. (It also typically fails to appear in studies of eyewitness testimony; cf. Wells & Murray, 1984.) This is not necessarily a fatal flaw: Supporters of emotional strengthening can still appeal to the wrong time slice hypothesis discussed below.

A second possibility also deserves consideration. Consider Model II:

1. Some factor Y, characteristic of flashbulb events, increases the subjects' *confidence* that they will remember the event in question. Y does not affect accuracy. (Y may be affect, if the subjects themselves believe in emotional strengthening; it could also be "personal importance," "historic importance," etc.)
2. This high confidence makes their memories unusually vivid (see Sheehan & Neisser, 1969, for evidence that vividness ratings can be influenced by demand characteristics).
3. Neither confidence nor vividness is related to accuracy.

In Model II the absence of a correlation between accuracy and confidence is easily understood, but the significant correlation between accuracy and auditory vividness poses a problem.

The available evidence does not distinguish between these models. We ourselves are inclined to think that both have some merit. Some variables, perhaps including arousal level, *do* strengthen memory and thus produce accuracy, vividness, and confidence in some subjects. In other cases, the subjects' conviction that the event was unforgettable is enough to increase the vividness of their recollections, independent of accuracy.

### Wrong time slices

One possible source of these errors is particularly intriguing: They may represent events that actually happened at another point in time. As in Brewer's (1988) beeper experiment, some recalls may have been based on wrong time slices. The subject remembers a real event, but that event was not the occasion on which he or she first heard about the explosion. RT, with whom this chapter began, is a case in point. She first heard the news when some people walked into her religion class and began talking about the shuttle. Two years later she had forgotten this entirely, but still remembered watching the news on television in her room. Because watching television in her room was the only shuttle explosion event she remembered, RT came to believe that it was the occasion on which she first heard the news. Because her memory of it was so vivid, she gave it a high confidence rating. But because she had really heard the news elsewhere, her accuracy score was zero.

Such "mislocations" are common in autobiographical memory. In his Watergate testimony, for example, John Dean frequently mislocated President Nixon's remarks: Things that had actually been said at Time A were falsely attributed to a different conversation at Time B (Neisser, 1981). Another example: In *A Collection of Moments*, Esther Salaman (1970) documents a clear case of a vivid childhood recollection assigned to the wrong setting. Memories do not carry intrinsic time tags or cross-references. However confidently we may assign them to particular points in our own lives, that assignment must be based on inference from plausible scripted sequences or contextual cues. As details fade with the passage of time, mislocations become increasingly likely.

Reception episodes like hearing the news of a public disaster may be especially vulnerable to internal mislocation. Although they produce strong feelings, those feelings are not intrinsically linked to the personally experienced sequence of events that began on hearing the news. Moreover, that sequence itself may not follow any familiar script. When some fragment of the event later comes to mind, how can the subject tell if it was the beginning of the sequence or occurred only later? This kind of uncertainty is rare with respect to directly experienced events, which usually have a clearer structure. If one narrowly escapes some danger, for example, the sequence "before it happened . . . while it was happening . . . what I did afterwards" is available to guide one's reconstruction and recall. Each phase of the sequence must have included appropriate actions and been accompanied by appropriate emotions. No such script – at least, none that necessarily fits the facts – is available for reception events.

### The bias toward television

For our error-prone subjects, the remembered event often involved television although first hearing the news had not. This shift toward "TV priority" is one of the clearest trends in the data. It probably results from the combined effect of several factors. First, most of the subjects did in fact watch a lot of television that night. For them, television coverage of the disaster was an extended, repeated, and easily remembered event. Second, most television channels showed repeated replays of the dramatic explosion itself. Those replays established a vivid and persistent visual image: Many subjects could "still see it" 2 years later. In contrast, the actual occasions of first hearing the news events usually lacked these advantages. They were brief, not visually salient, and perhaps not very interesting. Although a few subjects succeed in making personally significant narratives out of such moments (as suggested elsewhere: Neisser, 1982), many do not. What happens instead is that the original event is simply forgotten, and the more memorable one takes its place.

Another factor may also have played a role in the shift to TV priority. Although we noted above that there is no *necessary* script for hearing disaster news, there does seem to be a culturally familiar one: namely, one sees them on television. In an informal study, we asked a number of younger subjects (who had not been on campus in 1986) to imagine how Emory students *might have first heard* about the space shuttle explosion. Many of them listed "watching television" as the most plausible scenario. If such a schema does exist, subjects who no longer remembered how they actually heard the news may have relied on it in giving their responses.

### Delay of affect

We are inclined to believe that all three of these mechanisms – the fact that the subjects watched a lot of television afterward, the availability of the vivid visual image of the explosion, and the standard cultural narrative of seeing disaster news on television – played a role in the shift toward TV priority. But there is also a fourth possibility, one that is particularly relevant to the emotional strengthening hypothesis (e.g., Gold, this volume). In some individuals, affective response to the shuttle explosion may have developed only slowly. The popular concept of an instantaneous shock reaction, in which people are "stunned" by their first exposure to the news, may not be appropriate for everyone. The full import of such a disaster may not sink in for some time – time during which the subject talks to other people, watches television, and ruminates on the human consequences and social implications of the tragedy. According to the emotional strengthening hypothesis, it would be these later experiences (rather than the moment of first hearing the news) that should be most clearly remembered. This would easily explain the mislocations in our data.

We must note that this last hypothesis does not fit easily with the subjects' own reports of their feelings. Most of them used words like "shocked" and "stunned," which imply a strong immediate reaction rather than a gradual growth of affect. But for all we know, the real link between affect and memory may be some biochemical mechanism – a high level of glucose, for example, and/or a rush of adrenaline – that is not directly reflected in introspection (cf. Schachter & Singer, 1962). Such a mechanism – high arousal levels that strengthen memory and yet are not directly reflected in consciousness – could easily explain the TV-priority errors made by our subjects. (It might even explain the apparently unemotional and yet vivid memories described by Rubin and Kozin, 1984). Although we ourselves are skeptical of this explanation, it remains a possibility.

### Other types of error

Several of our subjects had false recollections that do not easily fit the wrong time slice paradigm. GA, who had actually heard the news in the cafeteria (it made her so sick that she couldn't finish her lunch) later recalled that "I was in my dorm room when some girl came running down the hall screaming, 'The space shuttle just blew up.'" GA went on to say that she "wanted to run after the screaming girl and question her," but instead turned on the television to get more information. This memory probably isn't a wrong time slice: We have no reason to believe that the screaming-girl episode ever took place. It seems more like a fantasy, based on some stereotyped conception of how people react to shocking news. We do not know when GA first had this fantasy; it may even have been very shortly after hearing the news at lunch. (Perhaps she initially imagined *herself* as the girl in question: "I feel like screaming through the dorm . . .") Later, she forgot the original event and remembered only the dramatic fantasy itself.

If this interpretation of GA's report is correct, it was based less on a wrong time slice than on a failure of "reality monitoring" (Johnson & Raye, 1981). Such failures may be rather common. Once the supporting context has been forgotten, it may be genuinely difficult to distinguish memories of events that happened from memories of those we only imagined. (John Dean did not always succeed in making this distinction either.) Another possible example: Subject MS, who had learned about the disaster at Emory like all of our subjects, later recalled being at home with her parents when she first heard the news! Did MS originally *imagine* what it would have been like to share the experience with her parents, and later mistake that imagined scenario for what had really happened? One can only speculate, and we may already have speculated quite enough.

### Conclusions

Once again it appears that establishing facts is one thing; interpreting them is quite another. Our data leave no doubt that vivid and confident flashbulb recollections can be mistaken. When this happens, the original memories seem to have disappeared entirely; none of our retrieval cues enabled the subjects to recover them. This finding rules out the simplest form of the emotional strengthening hypothesis, but it does not eliminate more sophisticated versions. Perhaps the strongest feelings took some time to develop, and thus strengthened the memory of later events rather than of the subjects' first contacts with the news. Other theories of flashbulb memories are also still in the running: The hours of later television watching may have been more strongly rehearsed, more unique, more compatible with a social script than the actual occasions of first contact. Any of these hypotheses might explain the shift to TV priority in our data.

It is not yet clear how far these findings can be generalized to other cases of vivid memory. Reception experiences – hearing the news of some tragic public event – are rather unusual in that they are not constrained by any necessary script or sequence. The emotions produced are not attached to the events that the subject actually experiences; rather, they are directed to the reported disaster itself. Thus the fragments that remain in memory some years later cannot be easily assigned to a coherent narrative – at least, not to the sequence as it actually occurred. We come, at the end, to a rather paradoxical conclusion. Flashbulb memories of reception events, like those originally described and defined by Brown and Kulik (1977), may be appreciably less reliable than other cases of vivid and confident recall.

### NOTES

1 We are grateful to Professor Alfred Heilbrun for allowing us to distribute the questionnaires in his class.
2 We appreciate the help of Jeffrey Gutkin, an Emory senior whose honors project

was based on the fall 1989 follow-up. Gutkin made about half the phone calls and administered about half the questionnaires in this phase of the study. The other subjects were called and tested by the second author, NH.
3 We are grateful to David Jopling and Julie Dunsmore for their help in coding these data.

## REFERENCES

Brewer, W. F. (1988). Memory for randomly sampled autobiographical events. In U. Neisser & E. Winograd (Eds.), *Remembering reconsidered: Ecological and traditional approaches to the study of memory*. New York: Cambridge University Press.
Brown, R., & Kulik, J. (1977). Flashbulb memories. *Cognition, 5*, 73–99.
Geiselman, R. E., Fisher, R. P., MacKinnon, D. P., & Holland, H. L. (1985). Eyewitness memory enhancement in the police interview: Cognitive retrieval mnemonics versus hypnosis. *Journal of Applied Psychology, 70*, 401–412.
Harsch, N., & Neisser, U. (1988). Substantial and irreversible errors in flashbulb memories of the *Challenger* explosion. Poster presented at the Psychonomic Society, Atlanta GA.
James, W. (1890/1950). *Principles of psychology*. New York: Dover.
Johnson, M. K., & Raye, C. L. (1981). Reality monitoring. *Psychological Review, 88*, 67–85.
Loftus, E. F. (1979). *Eyewitness testimony*. Cambridge, MA: Harvard University Press.
McCloskey, M., Wible, C. G., & Cohen, N. J. (1988). Is there a special flashbulb memory mechanism? *Journal of Experimental Psychology: General, 117*, 171–181.
Neisser, U. (1981). John Dean's memory: A case study. *Cognition, 9*, 1–22.
Neisser, U. (1982). Snapshots or benchmarks? In U. Neisser (Ed.), *Memory observed: Remembering in natural contexts*. New York: Freeman.
Rubin, D. C., & Kozin, M. (1984). Vivid memories. *Cognition, 16*, 81–95.
Salaman, E. (1970). *A collection of moments: A study of involuntary memories*. London: Longman.
Schachter, S., & Singer, J. E. (1962). Cognitive, social, and physiological determinants of emotional state. *Psychological Review, 69*, 379–399.
Sheehan, P. W., & Neisser, U. (1969). Some variables affecting the vividness of imagery in recall. *British Journal of Psychology, 60*, 71–80.
Wells, G. L., & Murray, D. M. (1984). Eyewitness confidence. In G. L. Wells & E. F. Loftus (Eds.), *Eyewitness testimony: Psychological perspectives*. New York: Cambridge University Press.

# 3

# Potential flashbulbs:
# Memories of ordinary news
# as the baseline

STEEN F. LARSEN

## Some more or less ordinary memories

On the evening of March 1, 1986, I was sitting at my portable computer just before going to bed. I was entering the following brief description into a database, adhering to a daily routine I had started on January 1 of that year:

(1)      When: 01.03.1986
         What: Prime Minister murdered
         Who: Olof Palme
         Where: Stockholm
         DetailQ: How many shots hit him?
         DetailA: Two
         —
         Source: Radio news, later "Politiken" (newspaper), TV, other papers
         ContextQ: What effects did it have for me?
         ContextA: I skipped breakfast and was 15 min late to pick up Pia.

I was in the middle of the peaceful but tedious task of performing an experiment on my own memory. This terse record of a violent and quite upsetting event was part of the material that I would be probed about some months later by the computer and try to remember. Notice particularly that I included information on both the news itself and my personal circumstances, or context, when I first heard the news.

There were other, equally upsetting, events in the database that I recorded during the 6 months of this diary keeping. Just 2 months later, this was entered:

(2)      When: 28.04.1986
         What: Big nuclear accident, indicated by extremely radioactive cloud
         Who: Soviet power plant
         Where: Close to Kiev
         DetailQ: Where was the cloud first registered?
         DetailA: Sweden, 100 km north of Stockholm
         —
         Source: Radio news, later TV evening news
         ContextQ: Where and when did I hear it first?
         ContextA: At Pia's place just after work; she was home, ill.

These two examples certainly seem to be the kind of news of which "flashbulb memories" are made – vivid memories of the circumstances of hearing shocking news, with great confidence in the accuracy (Brown & Kulik, 1977). Indeed, Christianson (1989) reported flashbulb memories of the Palme assassination in a sample of Swedish citizens, and Olof Palme enjoyed almost the same reputation in my country, Denmark, as he did in his home country, of being the most acclaimed statesman in Scandinavia. The news of the nuclear accident was particularly alarming because it mentioned the risk that part of the radioactive cloud might pass over Danish territory. The rating scales that I also filled in showed that I did in fact perceive both news items as extremely unusual and creating great personal involvement.

How accurate was my memory for this news, in particular for the circumstances in which I heard it? After 157 days had passed, the Palme item was selected by the computer for memory testing. I recalled hearing of the assassination on the radio and was pretty confident that "I heard it with Pia Sunday morning, went to buy newspaper." (For background, Pia is my wife, and at the time we were living in separate homes.) The source and the time were correct but I was obviously wrong on several other points: the place, others present, and aftermath. I did not even recognize the true circumstances as they were described in the diary.

Similarly for the Chernobyl nuclear disaster, recalled after 219 days: The source "radio" was given correctly but I remembered it to be "alone in the morning at home" – wrong on time, place, others present, and ongoing activity. Again, I did not recognize my own diary notes (and I can still "see" the erroneously recalled scene in my kitchen).

If I had not kept the diary, I would probably believe today that my memories of hearing these two news items were accurate flashbulb memories. Now, they add two well-controlled episodes to the body of examples of inaccuracies in flashbulbs (Harsch & Neisser, 1989; McCloskey, Wible, & Cohen, 1988; Neisser, 1982; Neisser & Harsch, this volume). Such examples have been used to argue that special memory mechanisms of the kind proposed by Brown and Kulik (1977) to explain flashbulb memories are unfounded because the putative flashbulbs are inaccurate and vulnerable to forgetting, just like ordinary memories.

But just how inaccurate and fragile are ordinary memories? That depends first of all upon what counts as "ordinary memories." The news stories above probably seem far from ordinary. Happily, most entries in the diary database – which ended up holding 320 events, half of them news, half of them my everyday personal experiences – were far more mundane (to me, that is). For instance, the following two:

(3)     When: 29.01.1986
        What: Space shuttle exploded
        Who: "Challenger"

Where: Jacksonville, Florida
DetailQ: What was special about the crew?
DetailA: There was a woman teacher among them

—

Source: TV evening news
ContextQ: What had kept me from noticing in the morning newspaper?
ContextA: Jesper was an overnight guest, we talked over breakfast

After 188 days had passed, I remembered none of the circumstances of watching the *Challenger* explosion news accurately, except that I was correct that the source was television news. Because I did not originally attach much significance to the event, this meager memory may be understandable. But here is a different kind of example:

(4)      When: 01.04.1986
         What: Former VS (Left Socialist) politician appointed Social Democrat press secretary
         Who: Ralf Pittelkow
         Where: Copenhagen
         DetailQ: Who is said to support him in the party top?
         DetailA: Sven Auken and Birthe Weiss (Social Democrat chairman and vice-chairman)

         —

         Source: "Information" (newspaper)
         ContextQ: What was I reminded of by hearing this?
         ContextA: Talking politics with him on train north of Copenhagen

The circumstances of this news item, on the other hand, were recalled vividly with great confidence after 243 days, and I was entirely accurate. Even though my personal involvement had only been slight, a more vivid and accurate memory had resulted than my memories of the two putative flashbulbs in Case 1 and Case 2 above. Altogether, five instances with a similar strong confidence in memory of the personal context of news (High Context Confidence memories) were present in the data; in all cases, memory of the context was quite accurate. Should these be considered genuine flashbulbs? And if the memory of hearing any piece of news is a potential flashbulb, what is ordinarily the fate of such memories?

The present chapter discusses results of the study of memory of news (from which the above examples are taken). I shall argue that memories of the personal context of ordinary, everyday news provide the most appropriate baseline against which to evaluate whether flashbulb memories are continuous in their characteristics with memories produced by ordinary memory mechanisms. The results will elucidate:

1.   memory and forgetting of the personal context of ordinary news ("potential flashbulbs");
2.   memory and forgetting of the news events themselves (considered to be the "central events" of news memories);

3. memory of High Context Confidence (HCC) news, attempting to suggest conditions and mechanisms that may turn ordinary news memories into flashbulbs.

Besides the problem of flashbulb memories, memory of news is of obvious importance to current human ecology. If autobiographical memories can be said to be "some of the things of which selves are made" (Barclay & DeCooke, 1988), news memories are "some of the things of which histories are made" (cf. Brown, 1990; Larsen, 1988a). This is what motivated the study in the first place.

## The status and structure of flashbulb memories: Two implicit assumptions

Brown and Kulik (1977) coined the term flashbulb memory to designate "a vivid recall of the circumstances in which one first learned of some important event" (p. 78). The classical example that prompted Brown and Kulik's investigation is the quite common claim of people in the United States (and many other countries) that they remember "with an almost perceptual clarity" (p. 73) the occasion in 1963 when they received the news of President John F. Kennedy's assassination. The scene appears to be preserved as in a photograph when the flashbulb is fired. Brown and Kulik emphasized that "it is not the memory of the tragic news that invites inquiry, but the memory of one's own circumstances on first hearing the news. There is no obvious utility in such memories" (p. 74). They regarded it as "a mystery" that memory of the situation where some news is heard could apparently be vivid, rich, and enduring even though this situation is utterly unimportant to the newsworthy event. Therefore, they hypothesized that flashbulbs are produced by a special, neurophysiological mechanism, the "Now Print!" mechanism, which has evolved to preserve rather indiscriminately the details, important as well as unimportant, of "biologically significant" events.

Two assumptions are implicit in Brown and Kulik's (1977) account. First, they seen to assume that the personal circumstances of hearing news will normally escape memory completely. Pillemer (1984) stated this point very clearly when he asked "why these mundane, private experiences are remembered at all . . ." (p. 77). The assumption of zero memory may be the reason why these researchers accepted memories as being flashbulbs even when subjects only claimed to recall one of the six "canonical" features of flashbulbs (cf. Brewer, this volume). Second, Brown and Kulik (1977) apparently take it for granted that the shocking news information itself would be well remembered, perhaps even without the operation of the "Now Print!" mechanism. It is somewhat peculiar that there has been no serious study of this assumption, considering that recall of the news itself is much easier to verify than the personal circumstances of hearing the news, and much more similar across individuals. The present study provides data relevant to both of these assumptions, which will be further discussed below.

## The continuity issue

The central question in recent research has been if the accuracy and permanence of flashbulb memories is really so exceptional as to motivate the postulation of a separate memory category defined by the elicitation of a special neural mechanism. Neisser (1982) pointed out that the presumed accuracy of flashbulbs was supported empirically by nothing but unverified retrospective accounts, often of events from the distant past, and scattered anecdotes. He then cited anecdotes of gross errors in such memories and concluded that "apparently flashbulbs can be just as wrong as other kinds of memories" (p. 45). McCloskey et al. (1988) systematically evaluated one version of the special-mechanism hypothesis. This strong version claims that the flashbulb memory mechanism produces perceptually vivid, complete, accurate, and permanently accessible memories. The results of McCloskey et al. (1988), concerning U.S. residents' memory of hearing about the explosion of the Space Shuttle *Challenger*, clearly showed substantial – though by no means complete – inaccuracy and forgetting across a 9-month interval, compared to the accounts given by subjects 3 days after the event.

Several subsequent studies of consistency between initial and later accounts have found similar evidence of forgetting, using delays to the initial reports as short as 1 day (Harsch & Neisser, 1989; Neisser & Harsch, this volume), retention intervals up to 3 years (Bohannon, 1988, this volume; Harsch & Neisser, 1989; Neisser & Harsch, this volume), and different news events (the *Challenger* explosion in the studies just cited; the assassination of Swedish prime minister Olof Palme in Christianson, 1989; the assassination attempt on Ronald Reagan in Pillemer, 1984). Thus, there is ample support for the conclusion of McCloskey et al. (1988) that the strong version of the special-mechanism hypothesis is untenable. Critics (Pillemer, 1990; Schmidt & Bohannon, 1988) of McCloskey et al. (1988) have argued that the strong flashbulb memory hypothesis was not intended by Brown and Kulik (1977), despite their photographic metaphor and neurological phrasing of the hypothesis, such as "permanent registration . . . of all recent brain events" (p. 76). But can a weaker version of the flashbulb hypothesis be defended?

Operationally, a weaker version might hold that even though recall of flashbulbs is less than perfect, it is still so much better than (or so different from) recall produced by ordinary memory mechanisms that a special mechanism is needed to explain it. McCloskey et al. (1988) contended that current knowledge of autobiographical memory does not necessarily predict that memory of the personal experience of learning about a surprising and consequential public event will be very poor, as assumed by Brown and Kulik (1977), Pillemer (1984, 1990), and others. On the contrary, such experiences may well be personally significant, distinctive, and frequently rehearsed, all commonly assumed to increase the vividness, richness, and durability of autobiographical memories. As long as continuity with ordinary memories has not been disproven, McCloskey et al. (1988) therefore found no grounds for postulating even a weak flashbulb memory mechanism. They concluded, "Memories for experiences of learning about surprising, consequential events are continuous in their characteristics with other autobiographical memories, and conform to the same principles" (p. 181).

## The problem of control events

These theoretical arguments notwithstanding, research into flashbulb memories has, without exception, been limited to extraordinary and shocking events, thus preventing evaluation of the issue of continuity or discontinuity between flashbulb memories and ordinary memories. Moreover, there is some confusion about what would be the appropriate kind of ordinary memories to use as a control condition or baseline for flashbulbs. It might appear logical to compare flashbulbs with autobiographical memories in general because memory of the circumstances in which some news was learned is evidently an autobiographical, or episodic, memory: The event of receiving the news occurred at a particular place and time, and this event has an "autobiographical reference" (Tulving, 1972) – "I was the one who heard it." This has been a basic premise in flashbulb memory research, but only Christianson (1989) has attempted to include ordinary autobiographical memories as a control. Christianson's subjects were asked to tell about an important personal event from the previous Saturday. However, at recall time they were not given any cues for retrieving the event, unlike the potent cue for the flashbulb, namely the assassination of Olof Palme. This invalidates the comparison, as Christianson acknowledged.

In contrast, Bohannon (1988) regarded information about the news event itself (in his studies of the *Challenger* explosion) to be "non-flashbulb information," particularly suitable as a control of the flashbulb because it is learned at roughly the same time. However, the news event is not personally experienced like the flashbulb situation. It is therefore not episodic in Tulving's (1972) sense but might rather be considered semantic or generic information, as Bohannon states himself. If this is granted, the comparison confounds the two memory categories and is therefore irrelevant to the continuity issue (cf. also Brewer, this volume).

I do not consider this argument against Bohannon very compelling because it rests on a questionable application of the episodic–semantic distinction. For example, is my memory of the *Challenger* explosion, as I saw it unfolding on the television screen, any more semantic or generic than my memory of the person watching it with me whom I saw when turning my head? Rather, Bohannon's comparison misses the continuity issue because the news information itself must also be subject to the special flashbulb mechanism – if it exists – as I shall show shortly.

## The reception context of ordinary news as control

The present study takes a more straightforward approach to the control problem. It assumes that the proper baseline for memories of hearing extraordinary news is memories of hearing ordinary news. This is in line with the phrasing used in a single place by McCloskey et al. (1988): "there is no qualitative distinction to be drawn between memories for learning about shocking, important events, and memories for learning about expected, trivial events" (p. 181). The study provides evidence to evaluate this claim. However, it also questions the assumption maintained by McCloskey et al. (1988) that experiences of learning about events are comparable, without qualifications, to direct experiences of events – that is, that flashbulb memories are conceptually continuous with ordinary autobiographical memories. Rather, the view expounded here is similar to Pillemer's (1990) by insisting that memory of learning about an event is an instance of memory of personal circumstances. In the case of news events, a more detailed analysis is given in Larsen (1988a). Only a few points need to be elaborated.

First, the circumstances in which a piece of news is learned function as the context of the news event. N. Brown (1990; Brown, Rips, & Shevell, 1985) called it the personal context of the news, but I shall use the terms news context or reception context instead of personal context to avoid confusion with the context of personally experienced events. Flashbulb memories may therefore only be comparable to the contextual part of autobiographical memories – not to the "central event" but rather to the "peripheral details" (cf. Christianson & Loftus, 1987; Reisberg & Heuer, this volume). Furthermore, the context of receiving news is usually completely arbitrary with respect to the news event. Virtually the same information might be given by radio, television, newspaper, or by another person, and the context is causally irrelevant to the news itself. Essentially, news reception is an independent context in Baddeley's (1982) sense, whereas the context and the central event in autobiographical memories tend to be interactive (which makes them hard to delimit precisely in natural situations; cf. Thomson, 1988). For this reason, it is even questionable to compare flashbulb memories with memory of the context, or peripheral details, of autobiographical events. Finally, because news reception tends to be stereotypical and repetitive (one time in front of the television set being largely similar to many other times, for instance), the distinctiveness of this kind of context is presumably very low. These arguments all imply that the appropriate and fair baseline for flashbulb memories is the context of hearing mundane news, rather than any aspect of autobiographical memories.

Second, consider the distinction between news event and reception context in relation to the special-mechanism hypothesis. Any hypothesis of relatively indiscriminate registration, whether strong or weak and irrespective of which factors are presumed to be causal, must predict that information about the two components will be equally well remembered. We may say that the memory profile of the compound news-event-plus-news-context episode is expected to be level. Thus, Bohannon's (1988) assumption that facts about the *Challenger* explosion itself should be immune to the hypothesized flashbulb mechanism because they were "not in consciousness" at the time is entirely ad hoc. Bohannon's results actually do suggest a biased profile because less was recalled from the *Challenger* news than from its reception context; however, the difficulty of his two sets of recall probes may have been unequal, which prohibited statistical testing. On the other hand, research on memory of central and peripheral events details (Christianson & Loftus, 1987; Reisberg & Heuer, this volume) suggests an opposite bias, namely, that the reception context will be less well remembered than the central, newsworthy event, particularly if the situation involves strong emotional arousal, as flashbulbs presumably do. On this background, it is interesting and important to include memory of the news itself in research on flashbulb memories, contrary to the view of Brown and Kulik (1977) and the practice of most studies.

Third, it is a standard feature of flashbulb studies that a short phrase describing the news event is used as the cue for subjects' recall of the circumstances of hearing it. The apparently high efficiency of this cue is rather surprising. The independence of the reception context suggests a very weak association with the news itself to be the normal thing. Studies of the mutual cueing efficiency of news events and their reception contexts in flashbulbs and ordinary news memories may thus shed further light on the continuity issue, as well as being relevant to theories of the structure of autobiographical and historical knowledge (Brown, 1990).

## My memory of ordinary news

The present experiment employed a method based on long-term diary studies of autobiographical memory (Linton, 1978; Wagenaar, 1986; White, 1982) to investigate my own memory of the circumstances of learning everyday news, of these news events themselves, and the association between the two. In parallel, my memory of everyday autobiographical events was assessed. Recording of events and memory testing was done entirely by computer in order to avoid the inevitable omission of personally sensitive information that would result from having another person handle the selection and presentation of events and recall cues.

A major advantage of diary methodology is that the accuracy of memory can be assessed in terms of consistency between records made shortly after the event (the same day) and later free or probed recalls. Because studies of flashbulb memories have concerned surprising, unpredicted events, researchers had difficulty collecting initial records soon after the event. Among the handful of studies in which consistency was evaluated, only one has come similarly close to the original event (Harsch & Neisser, 1989; Neisser & Harsch, this volume).

However, although it is easy to get reasonably accurate records of ordinary events by a diary method, it is hard to get records concerning events that give rise to flashbulb memories. One has to wait for them, and they occur very seldom – probably less than once a year. This problem is tackled in two ways. First, results from the present study of ordinary events are compared to previous flashbulb studies. Considering the problems of between-experiments comparisons, detailed quantitative assessment cannot be aimed for. But because the the discontinuity claim is basically qualitative, reliable conclusions may still be derived. Second, a small group of "big news" and High Context Confidence (HCC) memories are singled out for special analysis.

The body of research on flashbulbs had dealt with a very narrow range of events. The Kennedy assassination and the *Challenger* explosion have been studied extensively, with occasional studies of a few other political assassinations, the moon landing, and the Pearl Harbor attack. The strategy has been "one event, many subjects." The present approach is "one subject, many events." More subjects would be preferable, of course, but with naturalistic events that cannot be controlled by the experimenter, data that permit generalizations across events are particularly necessary. (A parallel, but more limited, multisubject investigation is reported in Larsen, 1988b).

## Method

### Subject

Male, 42 years old, Danish citizen and resident.

### Diary recording

As far as possible, one public news event and one personally experienced event were recorded every day from January–June 1986. Events were selected to be among the most remarkable of that day and to appear uniquely distinctive at the time. Recording took place in the evening as the last activity before going to sleep or, if that was impracticable, the first activity in the morning. Otherwise, the day was skipped. Out of 181 days, records were made on 161 days; on 2 days, the news event was omitted because I recalled no news from the day. Thus, records of 320 events were collected.

Records were written in English on a portable microcomputer and entered directly into a database system (programmed in dBase III) with software locks that prevented accidental inspection of past records. The diary format was similar to that of Wagenaar (1986), modified to accommodate news reception. The information recorded about each event included, first, four event elements described in response to the questions What, Who, Where, and When; the first three were allowed a maximum of 65 characters each, the last was entered as the calendar date. Second, an event detail was entered that was judged to identify uniquely the event at the time; it was written in the format of a question and an associated answer, each in a maximum of 65 characters. Third, four ratings of the event were given on 5-point scales: Frequency of occurrence of the event type (every day, every week, every month, every year, less than every year); duration of prior, related events (none, less than 1 week in advance, less than 1 month in advance, less than 1 year in advance, more than 1 year in advance); personal involvement in the event (none, slight, moderate, fair, strong); evaluation of the event (very bad to very good).

For news events, three additional pieces of information concerning the reception context were recorded. First, the source from which the news was first received; second, the number of different sources from which I had heard about it (coverage – single, double, or multiple); and, third, a context detail that was felt to be unique to the situation in which I first received the news, written in the same question-plus-answer format as the event detail. These context details usually consisted of one or more of the "canonical" features described by Brown and Kulik (1977), that is, time, location, others present, affects shown by myself or others, ongoing activity, subsequent activity, but other features (e.g., concurrent thoughts) were also used to obtain uniqueness.

### Memory testing

Memory was tested in two sessions, each one lasting about 16 hours (2 consecutive days). For the first session, a random sample of half of the news records and half of the autobiographical records was selected and scheduled for recall in random order; the remaining records were tested in the second session, also randomly ordered. The first session took place 5 weeks after recording had finished, the second session 4 months later. Thus, the period of retention varied from 1 to 11 months. The two sessions overlapped at a retention interval of 5 to 6 months, which allowed checking the stability of my selection and phrasing of material across the 6 months of diary writing and changes in recall strategies between the two sessions.

The test procedure, including scheduling of records, presentation of material, and recording of responses, was controlled by a dBase III program. Memory of each event was assessed by cued recall in two ways. First, three of the recorded event elements (What, Who, Where, When) were given as cues for recall of the fourth, omitted element; which element to omit was randomly determined on each trial. Second, the event detail answer was cued by the corresponding question in the record. For news, moreover, recall of the source and the context detail answer were cued in a similar way. A 65-character slot was provided for each item to be recalled. For the When element, however, an exact date plus an interval of uncertainly was asked for. Because these datings do not allow comparison of news event and news context (and are available for just the 80 events in which the When element was tested) they will not be reported here.

For each answer, confidence was rated on a 3-point scale (guess, uncertain, certain) combined with a three-category indication of response mode (guess, inference, memory) into one 5-point scale ("memory-certain," "memory uncertain," "guess," "inference uncertain," "inference-certain"). Then the correct answer from the original record was revealed and finally recognition of the recorded detail was judged on a 3-point scale (from "no memory" to "clear memory"). For news records, recognition of both the news event detail and the context detail were assessed. Finally, a rating of rehearsal of the event by thinking or talking about it in the period since its recording was collected.

A further manipulation was introduced in the tests of news records to study the cueing efficiency of the reception context. For a random half of the news, recall proceeded in the order described above, that is, the reception context was recalled after the news event itself had been recalled and the correct answers shown for recognition (context last condition). For the remaining half, recall of the two reception context items (source and context detail) was required before recall of the news event itself was attempted (context first condition).

## Results

### Events in the diary

The first half of 1986 turned out to be a quiet period in my personal life: My family life was stable, I did not move, nor travel abroad; I had neither great successes, nor great disappointments. The news was dramatic, however. The Swedish prime minister Olof Palme was assassinated in Stockholm and the *Challenger* space shuttle exploded, two events that have been studied in

Table 3.1. *Mean ratings of diary events*

| Event Rating | Event type | | Significance[a] |
| | News | Autobiog. | |
|---|---|---|---|
| Frequency[b] | 4.18 | 3.97 | * |
| Prior events[c] | 2.10 | 2.11 | — |
| Involvement[d] | 1.81 | 2.45 | *** |
| Evaluation[e] | 2.84 | 3.42 | *** |

*Note*: * $p < .05$; ** $p < .01$; *** $p < .001$.
[a] $X^2$ – tests performed on frequency distributions.
[b] 1 = Every day; 5 = Less than every year.
[c] 1 = No prior events; 5 = More than a year before.
[d] 1 = No involvement; 5 = Strong involvement.
[e] 1 = Very bad; 5 = Very good.

several flashbulb memory experiments; moreover, the nuclear disaster in Chernobyl took place; the United States bombed Libya; Kurt Waldheim's Nazi past was revealed and he was elected president of Austria; President Marcos of the Philippines was overthrown; and Denmark played in the soccer World Cup finals in Mexico. With such news in the "ordinary" sample, the issue of continuity with flashbulb memories would seem to get a rather conservative test.

All the news stories were first heard through the mass media, 40% from newspaper, 38% from television, and 18% from radio. News events were rated differently from autobiographical events in several respects as shown in Table 3.1. The news events were judged to occur a little less frequently $(X^2(4) = 12.85)$, though the most common rating in both cases was "once a year" (score 4). Personal involvement was clearly lower in news $(X^2(4) = 45.52)$, where the most common rating was "no involvement" (score 1) as opposed to "slight involvement" (score 2) for autobiographical events; the rating "strong involvement" was applied to none of the news and only to three autobiographical events. News was generally evaluated "neutral" (score 3) and much less positively than autobiographical events $(X^2(4) = 46.46)$, which were most commonly rated "good." Finally, the two event types did not differ in the extent to which they were seen as related to prior events; in most cases, events were perceived either as independent or as related only to events within the past week.

It is hardly surprising that the two sets of events differ as shown above, apart from their different content. However, it is not clear how this will affect memory. Memory of news should be improved because the events are relatively infrequent and therefore distinctive; but will this effect the news reception context, as it seems to happen in flashbulbs? On the other hand, greater personal involvement and more positive evaluation might improve memory of autobiographical events relative to news.

### Memory measures: General considerations

The accuracy of recall was scored by myself after finishing the second test session. The procedure was controlled by a dBase III program and the scores entered directly into the database. All information, except the ratings, from each original record was displayed with my answers to the recall questions. For each item in turn, the equivalence of recording and recall was scored on a 5-point scale (from 0 = "Totally different, no features in common" to 4 = "No difference, except wording and added information"). To assess reliability of these scores, an independent judge scored 80% of the responses (256 records, 135 of which were news) that I felt were free from embarrassing material. Correlations ranged from .92 to .97 with insignificant constant errors, which was considered satisfactory.

Instability of recording and recall practices across time were checked by comparing events from the two test sessions in the 5–6-month retention interval that overlapped between them. No significant effect of test session was found on any of the recall and recognition variables for these 108 events (examined by $t$ tests). This indicates that the difficulty of items did not change across the diary period and that recall was unaffected by practice. Data from the two test sessions were pooled in further analyses.

Memory of news events was tested with the reception context recalled either first or last, that is, before or after recall of the news event itself. Because the correct information was provided after each answer, the mutual cueing value of context and event could be studied by comparing memory in the two conditions. None of the memory variables proved significant in these comparisons, however (see details later). In consequence, data from the two conditions were pooled.

The mean results are shown in Table 3.2. Note that the three memory measures have different properties:

1.  *Recall of elements.* The three event elements (What, Who, Where) are not directly comparable in terms of the cues given, nor the information to be recalled. Thus, the Where and Who elements were inferred or guessed almost as successfully as they were remembered, according to my assessment of the response mode employed. Only the What element and the news Source achieved distinctively higher scores for remembering than for guesses and inferences (interaction between response mode and the three event elements, $F$ (4, 222) = 5.20, $p < .001$; effect of response mode on source recall, $F(2, 156) = 8.08$, $p < .001$). Such inferences inflate the element recall score and make it less useful. (Moreover, datings – "recall" of the When element – were collected for one-fourth of the events but they will not be considered here.)

Table 3.2. *Mean recall scores and recognition percentages*

| | News context (1) | News event (2) | Autobiog. event (3) | Significance[a] (1) (2) | (1) (3) | (2) (3) |
|---|---|---|---|---|---|---|
| Element recall[b] | | | | | | |
| (score 0–4) | 2.37 | 2.66 | 2.84 | n.s. | *** | n.s. |
| Detail recall | | | | | | |
| (score 0–4) | 1.17 | 2.09 | 2.47 | *** | *** | * |
| Detail recognition | | | | | | |
| (percent) | 32.7 | 65.4 | 80.1 | *** | *** | *** |

*Note*: * $p < .05$; ** $p < .01$; *** $p < .001$.
[a] Separate ANOVAs with retention time grouped in five 2-month intervals as the second main factor (see text).
[b] What, Who, or Where element of events, Source element of news contexts.

2. *Recall of details.* Answers to questions about the unique details of events and, for news, reception contexts are probably much less subject to inferences and therefore more adequate measures of memory. This is supported by a strong effect of response mode on recall scores $(F(2, 314) = 42.90, p < .001)$ that did not interact with event type (news vs. autobiographical); answers from memory were superior, and guesses did not differ from inferences.

The difficulty of questions about autobiographical events, news events, and news contexts was similar, as judged from the probability of correct guesses (.13, .12, and .09, respectively) and accuracy scores for guesses (.93, 1.14, and .90 on the 0–4 scale, respectively).

3. *Recognition of details.* In contrast to the recall measures, the recognition ratings are not dependent on post hoc scoring of accuracy. There were no foils, however, so I could be absolutely certain that the information provided for recognition (after I had tried to recall it) was correct. This does not necessarily invalidate the measure (see Wallace, 1980), but the data should be interpreted with proper caution. Statistical analyses in the following are based on the 3-point recognition rating scale; however, in some cases results are given as percentages in which the two high scores, 1 = "vague recognition" and 2 = "vivid recognition," are counted as indicating recognition.

In summary, recall scores and recognition ratings of the "unique" details of events and reception contexts are preferable in terms of validity and reliability. These measures will receive primary attention in the following section.

### Memory of news reception contexts

It is seen from Table 3.2 that all memory measures show the same order:

News context < news event < autobiographical event.

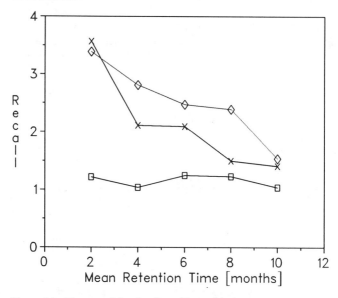

Figure 3.1. Memory of details of autobiographical events, news events, and news reception contexts as a function of retention time (2-month intervals, abscissa shows mean of each interval). Left panel: Recall (0–4 scale). Right panel: Recognition (0–2 scale).

Consider first memory of the reception context of news, which is the focus of flashbulb memory research. Reception context memory was compared with memory of the news event itself (a within-events factor) and with memory of autobiographical events (a between-events factor) in separate ANOVAs with retention time as the second factor (grouped into five 2-month intervals to obtain a minimum of 20 events per cell).

Recall of the context element Source ("Who informed me?") was clearly lower than recall of the Who element of autobiographical events, $F(1, 193) =$ 17.83, $p < .001$. The effect of retention time was insignificant. This was not unexpected in view of the contamination of this measure by guessing as discussed above.

The unique details should provide a cleaner indication of memory. In both recall and recognition, the reception context details were clearly inferior to the news event details; for recall, $F(1,308) = 29.70$, for recognition, $F(1,308) = 45.39$, both $ps < .0001$. It is evident from these results that the experience of hearing news events is not well remembered in ordinary cases; within the compound episode of news-reception-plus-news-event, the memory profile is strongly biased toward the news event itself, the "central event" of the episode. The difference is even more extreme when the reception context is compared to memory of the autobiographical events; for recall, $F(1,314) =$ 57.10, for recognition, $F(1,314) = 141.40$, both $ps < .0001$. It thus seems that

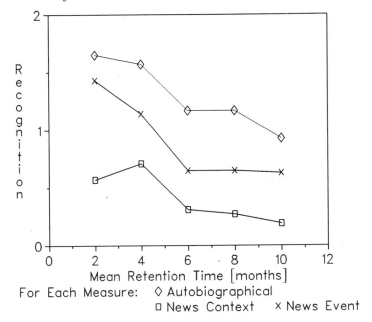

For Each Measure: ◊ Autobiographical
□ News Context    × News Event

if the memory of hearing news in certain cases, as in flashbulbs, could only achieve a level similar to everyday, mundate autobiographical events, this would be sufficient to consider them exceptional.

The influence of retention time in these analyses further supports the idea that news context information is unusually fragmentary and unstable. In recall of details, retention time was not significant as a main effect when the news context was involved, but it interacted significantly with type of detail (for news contexts vs. news events, $F(4,308) = 4.30$, $p < .01$; for news contexts vs. autobiographical events, $F(4,312) = 3.33$, $p < .05$). These interactions can be seen from the forgetting curves in the left panel of Figure 3.1.

No measurable forgetting of the reception context details is seen during the year of the experiment. Already at the shortest interval, 2 months (on the average), recall of reception context seemed to be at a floor level, around a score of 1, which is the level of guessing and inference noted earlier. Actually, I indicated that my answers to the context probes were based on pure guessing in two-thirds of the cases, and vivid recall occurred in only 6% of the cases. This is also evident in my very low confidence in reception context recall; at 2 months, confidence was .39 on a 0–2 scale, which is the same level as my confidence in recall of the news itself at 10 months. However, although recall accuracy for context did not deteriorate with time, my confidence in the answers kept sinking, finishing at a low of just .11 ($F(4, 154) = 4.42, p <$

.01). This significant decrease in confidence suggests that more information about the reception context was indeed available in the beginning than at the end of the retention period.

The recognition ratings, too, support the conclusion that the reception context of news was not completely absent from memory, although it was not picked up by the recall test. No interactions were observed in the recognition analyses, only strong main effects of retention time (see the right panel of Figure 3.1; for news contexts vs. news events, $F(4, 308) = 11.97$, for news contexts vs. autobiographical events, $F(4, 312) = 15.86$, both $ps < .0001$).

The forgetting rates shown in Figure 3.1 were further examined by regression analyses with raw retention time (i.e., not grouped in intervals) as the independent variable. Recall of news context details showed zero correlation with time, that is, no forgetting, whereas recognition of this context decreased linearly from an intercept of .75 on the 0–2 scale to zero at about 1 year. Memory of the "central" events, whether news or autobiographical, was also well described by linear regression curves. For recall, the forgetting rates were indistinguishable. For recognition, news was forgotten somewhat faster than autobiographical events (slopes of $-.4$ and $-.3$ per 100 days, respectively). For both measures, news events converged with news context after about 1 year.

It is of course inconceivable that forgetting can be linear in general, because at least a few events are remembered for years and years. In fact, logarithmic curves fitted the data equally well ($+/-2\%$ of the variance). The logarithmic functions raise another problem, however, because they have Y-intercepts well above the maximum score and thus imply that immediate memory is supramaximal and that it stays perfect during the first 20–30 days of retention for both types of central events.

Finally, the efficiency of mutual cueing between news event and reception context was investigated. In the context-last condition of memory testing, full information about the news event was provided before attempting recall of its reception context, similar to the usual procedure in flashbulb memory studies. However, the news event information did not significantly assist memory of the reception context, compared to the context-first condition. Mean recall scores for the news source increased from 2.01 to 2.59 ($t(158) = 1.90$, $p > .05$) and for the news context detail from 1.07 to 1.26 ($t < 1$). Similarly, providing full information of the context before the event recall task was completely inconsequential (all $t$ values $< 1$). The information available about the reception context seemed to be so poor, or so loosely associated with details of the news event itself, that it was worthless as an additional retrieval cue.

## Frequency, involvement, and rehearsal

As mentioned above, news was rated less frequent, less personally involving, and evaluated more negatively than autobiographical events. The contribution of these ratings toward explaining the variance of memory variables was examined by a series of 2-way ANOVAs, separately for the between-events (news vs. autobiographical) and within-events (news event vs. context) cases. If necessary, rating levels were pooled to get at least 20 observations per cell.

*Event frequency* predicted both recall and recognition of "central" event details ($F(2, 314) = 3.64$, $p < .05$ and $F(2, 314) = 13.21$, $p < .0001$, respectively) but not of news reception context ($F < 1$). Infrequent events were remembered better, as would be expected on the basis of distinctiveness. This should confer a memory advantage on the less commonplace news events. Notice that the frequency ratings concerned only the news itself, not the reception contexts that were mostly repetitive, of course.

Ratings of *personal involvement* were completely unrelated to recall, although they did predict recognition for both news events and contexts ($F(2, 312) = 11.11$, $p < .0001$, no interaction; higher involvement yielded better recognition), but not for autobiographical events (interaction with event type, $F(2, 314) = 5.34$, $p < .01$). Because of the generally low level of involvement, "moderate," "fair," and "strong" ratings were pooled in the analysis. With this heavily skewed distribution, it is possible that a floor effect was obscuring the influence of involvement on memory.

The ratings of event evaluation (good–bad) and same-day coverage of the news items did not have significant effects on memory.

Number of *rehearsals* (i.e., thinking or talking about the event in the retention period), rated after recall and recognition tests were completed, did not differ between news and autobiographical events ($X^2(3) = 3.74$), the most common rating being "1–2 times." However, rehearsal came out as the most powerful predictor of memory of unique details of the "central" events, news as well as autobiographical (recall, $F(3, 312) = 26.53$; recognition, $F(3, 312) = 62.57$; both $p$s $< .0001$, no interactions). On the other hand, memory of the details of news contexts – the potential flashbulbs – was significantly less affected by rehearsal (interaction with news event recall, $F(3, 310) = 4.32$, $p < .01$; interaction with news event recognition, $F(3, 310) = 6.78$, $p < .001$). These interactions are presented in Figure 3.2. The recall data in the left panel and the recognition data in the right panel show the same pattern. News events benefit from rehearsal to the same extent as autobiographical events whereas the recall of news context is totally unaffected ($F < 1$) and recognition of the context just barely (1-way ANOVA, $F(3, 155) = 3.31$, $p < .05$).

Because rehearsal was assessed after correct answers to the memory questions had been displayed, it is conceivable that my estimates were influenced

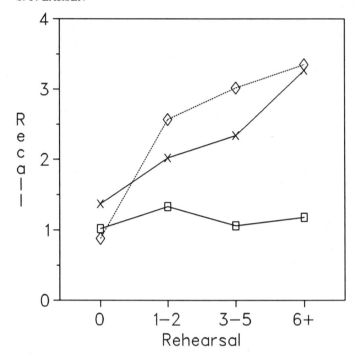

Figure 3.2. Memory of details of autobiographical events, news events, and news reception contexts as a function of estimated number of rehearsals. Left panel: Recall (0–4 scale). Right panel: Recognition (0–2 scale).

by knowledge of my success in recalling the event. This source of bias is unavoidable because rehearsal cannot meaningfully be rated unless the event is identified. Moreover, if an event was still completely unrecognizable when I read the original description, rehearsal was set to "never." This problem cannot be eliminated by removing events in which the unique details were not recognized, because the event as a whole might be identified (and rehearsal evaluated) even though particular details were not remembered. For these reasons, the data in Figure 3.2 might be artifactual to some extent. However, it is reassuring that the significant effects noted above were still present, though of course deflated, when events with zero recognition ratings were disregarded.

It is important to note that when the number of rehearsals was rated I did not attempt to distinguish rehearsal of the news itself from rehearsal of the context. Therefore, it might be suspected that the much smaller influence of rehearsal on memory of news context simply reflects the fact that I was disregarding rehearsal of the reception context. From my experience as the subject, however, I rather believe that the personal circumstances of this

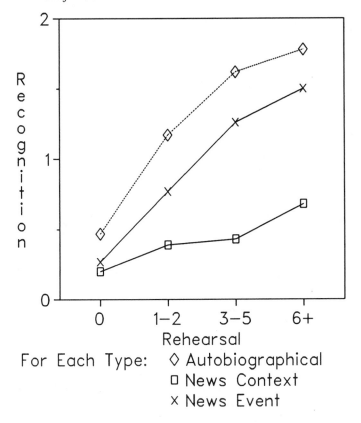

For Each Type: ◊ Autobiographical
□ News Context
× News Event

mundane news were not rehearsed to any significant extent even though the news itself was – with remarkable effect.

### *"Big news" and High Context Confidence memories*

Although the study was directed at ordinary news, by chance it offered data on two small sets of memories that are in different ways similar to classical flashbulb memories. First, several "big" news events occurred during the diary period in 1986, including a few that clearly had flashbulb proportions. Second, a handful of news events could be identified that had less than historical dimensions but still gave rise to memories with flashbulb-like properties. This is important because previous studies (with the exception of Rubin & Kozin, 1984) have only concerned "big" events, picked intuitively by the researcher to be important, consequential, and usually surprising. But for any given individual, "smaller" events might make an equal or even stronger impression.

Table 3.3. *Mean retention time, ratings, and memory scores of "Big" news, High Context Confidence (HCC) news, and ordinary news*

| News items | N | Rec. time ratings | | Retention time (days) | Rehearsal rating (0–3)[c] | Context confidence | | Context detail memory | | Event detail memory | |
|---|---|---|---|---|---|---|---|---|---|---|---|
| | | Frequency (1–5)[a] | Involvement (1–5)[b] | | | Source (0–2)[d] | Detail (0–2)[d] | Recall (0–4)[e] | Recogn. (0–2)[f] | Recall (0–4)[e] | Recogn. (0–2)[f] |
| Column # | | (1) | (2) | (3) | (4) | (5) | (6) | (7) | (8) | (9) | (10) |
| *First Big News* | | | | | | | | | | | |
| Palme | 1 | 5.00 | 4.00 | 157 | 3.00 | 2.00 | 1.00 | .00 | .00 | 3.00 | 2.00 |
| Chernobyl | 1 | 5.00 | 4.00 | 219 | 3.00 | 1.00 | 1.00 | .00 | .00 | 4.00 | 2.00 |
| *Challenger* | 1 | 5.00 | 1.00 | 188 | 3.00 | 2.00 | .00 | 1.00 | .00 | 4.00 | 2.00 |
| *Later Big News* | | | | | | | | | | | |
| Palme | 6 | 4.83 | 2.83 | 191 | 1.50 | .33 | .17 | .67 | .50 | 2.00 | 1.00 |
| Chernobyl | 12 | 4.75 | 2.92 | 142 | 1.83 | .58 | .17 | .50 | .33 | 2.83 | 1.33 |
| Soccer Cup | 15 | 4.33 | 2.00 | 120 | 1.67 | 1.07 | .13 | 1.07 | .53 | 2.87 | 1.00 |
| *Other news* | 118 | 4.04 | 1.64 | 196 | 1.08 | .47 | .19 | 1.21 | .32 | 1.86 | .71 |
| *HCC news* | 5 | 4.40 | 2.00 | 133 | 1.60 | 2.00 | 2.00 | 3.80 | 1.80 | 2.80 | 1.60 |

[a] 1 = Every day; 2 = Every week; 3 = Every month; 4 = Every year; 5 = Less than every year.
[b] 1 = None; 2 = Slight; 3 = Moderate; 4 = Fair; 5 = Strong.
[c] 0 = Never; 1 = 1–2 times; 2 = 3–5 times; 3 = 6 or more times.
[d] 0 = Pure guess; 1 = Uncertain; 2 = Certain.
[e] 0 = Nothing correct; 1 = Little correct; 2 = Half correct; 3 = Almost correct; 4 = Totally correct.
[f] 0 = No recognition; 1 = Vague recognition; 2 = Clear recognition.

According to my present intuitions, the most impressive news events were the assassination of Olof Palme (Case 1 in the introduction), the Chernobyl nuclear disaster (Case 2), and the soccer World Cup in Mexico (with apologies for the comparison). The first two were instantaneous and surprising events, as flashbulbs are commonly assumed to be. In addition, both were followed by a chain of succeeding news, thus making up an "extended event" (in some respects similar to the concept of Barsalou, 1988). In the Chernobyl case, full information was released gradually over several weeks, at the same time as the spread of radioactive pollution and protective measures in various countries were reported on. In the Palme case, later news was mostly about the unsuccessful police investigation. The soccer World Cup was also extended, consisting of many individual games, but each of them (including the first game) was entirely expected, although outcomes were often surprising.

These three "big events" were represented by several entries in the diary, as shown in Table 3.3. The top three lines of the table show the first times I heard news of the Palme and Chernobyl events, along with the explosion of the *Challenger* space shuttle (Case 3 in the introduction) for comparison with American data. The next three lines show the later, "follow-up" news items in the three event chains. The remaining 118 items of ordinary news (except the 5 "HCC news" discussed below) are in the next-to-bottom line.

Going across the table, columns 1–2 give means of the event frequency and personal involvement ratings made at the time of writing the diary; note that a high frequency score indicates low frequency. Mean retention time in days are in column 3, and the remaining columns (4–10) show measures obtained in the memory tests. Thus, column 4 gives the retrospective rehearsal ratings; columns 5–6 give separate confidence scores for my recall of the news source and the context detail (two parts of the reception context); column 7 shows recall accuracy scores and column 8 recognition ratings for the reception context detail (observe that a 5-point scale is used for recall, and a 3-point scale for recognition); and, finally, columns 9 and 10 present corresponding recall and recognition measures for the news event itself.

It is seen that my confidence in remembering the source and reception context of my first hearing of the big news was relatively high (columns 5–6), but that accurate recall and recognition of the context (columns 7–8) was almost nil. In contrast, memory of the big news events themselves (columns 9–10) was consistently good, far better than in the ordinary news items shown in the next-to-bottom line. The 33 relatively nonsurprising events later in the three big news chains are in between the first big news and the ordinary news in almost every respect. Most important, memory of the reception context of this unusual but not shocking news is slightly lower than in ordinary news, whereas memory of the news itself is somewhat higher. Altogether, the more intuitively impressive and emotionally involving the events are, the more memory of the event seemed to increase at the expense of memory of the context; that is, they behaved exactly opposite to what is expected from flashbulbs.

Although the three first-time cases in Table 3.3 would have satisfied Brown and Kulik's (1977) very lenient criterion of flashbulb memories – because I did recall one "canonical" feature, the source (or informant) – they hardly deserve the name: I did not remember the circumstances with the unwavering certainty of watching a photograph. If the flashbulb metaphor is taken at face value phenomenologically, flashbulb memories may rather be defined operationally as memories in which I felt completely certain to remember both the source and the reception context detail accurately. That is, both of these confidence scores should be at the maximum ( = 2). Only five news memories satisfied this High Context Confidence (HCC) criterion, of which the first one in the list below was a member of the "big news" chains:

1. The semifinal game between Brazil and France in the soccer World Cup, watched live on television. The context question was "Where and with whom did I watch it?" This event was the only one of the group to receive an involvement rating greater than "slight" and to be rehearsed more than 5 times. Memory was tested only 45 days after it occurred and it was the single news event in the diary that achieved top memory scores across the board.

2.  The television interview in Case 4 of the introduction, in which I knew the interviewee personally and was reminded of the occasion when I met him.
3.  A television news story commemorating Sweden's delivery of Baltic refugees from World War II to the Soviets 40 years ago. The context question concerned what it reminded me of, that is, a masterful book on these events that I read some years ago. After 190 days, I recalled the source and this reminding precisely.
4.  A newspaper story about a man beaten to death by three youngsters in a nearby small town. The context detail was the time and place where I read it. Both this event and the newspaper (which was not my ordinary paper) were recalled correctly after 107 days.
5.  A radio news story about the restoration from acid rain of a statue outside the Royal Theater in Copenhagen. The context detail was where I heard about it the second time, that is, in a television interview with the theater director. This was accurately recalled 82 days later.

The mean scores for these five HCC memories are also given in Table 3.3 (see the bottom line). Note that the HCC news was quite similar to the Later Big News in terms of frequency, involvement, and rehearsal, that is, in between the ordinary news and the First Big News. But then consider the memory scores in the four right-hand columns. It is striking that the relation between memory of the reception context (columns 7–8) and the news event (columns 9–10) is turned upside down in the HCC news. For every other category of news in the table, recall and recognition of the news itself is clearly higher than the context. For the five HCC memories, however, reception context memory is on top. Thus, my confidence was justified, and these five rather insignificant memories certainly look more like genuine flashbulbs than any of the big news items. Yet, it is hard to see any particular reason for this surprising finding from the available information.

At the time of this writing, almost 5 years later, I doubt that I would remember much about the HCC news (had I not worked on the data, that is). If they are accepted as flashbulbs at the time they were tested, they also exemplify the forgetting of flashbulbs. In contrast, I might still *believe* the first hearing of the Palme assassination and the Chernobyl explosion to be flashbulbs, because a rather clear image of the (incorrect) reception context still comes to my mind. In this respect, the two really sensational news items conform to the pattern found by Neisser and Harsch (this volume; Harsch & Neisser, 1989): Confidence has become dissociated from accuracy.

## Discussion

It is noteworthy that all news stories in the study were media reports. Generally, personal reports of public news seem very infrequent. Out of 246 news stories recorded by subjects in a parallel study (see Larsen, 1988b), 93% were media reports. Bohannon (1988) argued that media reports are unlikely to produce flashbulb memories because "media narrators are trained to be unemotional" (p. 182). He therefore focused on personal reports of the *Challenger* news. His results do not support this argument, however; for instance, media reports were rated somewhat higher in affect than personal reports both 2 weeks and 8 months after the event. But the distinction of personal and media reports could be important for other reasons. The social reception situations of personal reports, being both uncommon and unstereotyped, may easily be more distinctive than media situations. Moreover, personal reports are likely to involve social "rehearsal" in the form of talk and discussion about the news and one's reaction to it.

Because the contents of the present news and autobiographical events are by necessity so widely divergent, it is important to consider if systematic differences in their difficulty existed. Differences might arise from a biased selection of the two types of events and of the to-be-remembered details. Fortunately, the guessing probabilities and the stability of the results across the 6-month diary period suggest that such biases are unlikely. The level of remembering generally appears lower and the forgetting rate higher in this experiment than in Linton's (1978) and Wagenaar's (1986) diary studies, which also employed events selected to be remarkable. However, my ability to remember autobiographical events was close to that of White (1982) and my recognition data are very similar to the eight students in Brewer's (1988) study of events selected for memorability. The data may therefore be regarded as reasonably commensurate with those obtained in other naturalistic memory research.

### Discontinuity of ordinary news and flashbulbs

Since the publication of McCloskey et al.'s (1988) clear explication and refutation of the strong flashbulb mechanism hypothesis, researchers have agreed that flashbulb memories are neither complete and infallible nor immune to forgetting. The point of contention now is whether flashbulb memories are continuous with the characteristics of ordinary memories or if discontinuities exist that might be the products of a weaker special memory mechanism. It has been argued here that to decide if putative flashbulb memories are at all special, the most appropriate normal or ordinary memories to compare with concern the circumstances of hearing ordinary, mundane news. This is what flashbulb memories would have been like if special conditions had not turned them into flashbulbs.

As far as the properties of flashbulb memories are known from the available studies of a handful of extraordinary news events, it is apparently agreed that flashbulbs are at least as well remembered as ordinary autobiographical memories (far better remembered, special-mechanism proponents claim).

Therefore, if memories of ordinary news reception contexts are found to be discontinuous from autobiographical memories, similar or even greater discontinuities from flashbulb memories are implied.

*Source amnesia.* The present results indicate that memories of the circumstances in which ordinary news is learned are very different from memories of everyday autobiographical events as well as from the news events themselves. Unlike the "central" event information, the reception context of news was practically inaccessible to recall after 1 month. The reception context was occasionally recognized, however, but even the likelihood of this dropped to near zero before the end of a year. This massive loss of personal context is curiously similar to the "source amnesia" described by Schacter, Harbluk, and McLachlan (1984) in the autobiographical memory of amnesic patients. It confirms Brown and Kulik's (1977) and Pillemer's (1984) assumption that the circumstances of hearing news are normally lost from memory.

The findings give substance to the intuitive feeling that flashbulb memories are quite exceptional – beyond being infrequent, as shown by Rubin and Kozin (1984). It appears reasonable to consider memory of the ordinary news contexts as quantitatively discontinuous from the autobiographical memories and thus, by implication, from flashbulbs. Memories of the personal circumstances of news need neither be complete nor immune to forgetting to be regarded as special – apparently, any memory beyond a period of some 6 months is significant.

*Rate of forgetting.* Further indications of discontinuity come from the forgetting curves. Reception context information was essentially inaccessible to voluntary recall already at the earliest point of measurement, 1 month, whereas forgetting of the two kinds of central events followed a much slower course. The forgetting functions could be described as logarithmically decelerated, which is in accord with the evidence from laboratory as well as naturalistic research on autobiographical memory (cf. Rubin, 1982).

Because it can be assumed that all information could be accurately recalled immediately after the record was entered into the database, the extensive forgetting observed for the reception context must have taken place during the first month, that is, at a much faster rate than the central events. This very steep logarithmic decrease is conspicuously similar to the classical findings in verbal learning research with "nonsense" syllables and other unrelated materials. The rate of decrease for recognition was not particularly fast, however, suggesting that it is retrieval that poses a special problem for reception contexts, possibly due to a fast loss of associations with the content of the news.

*Cueing efficiency*. The cueing of recall of the reception context by full information about the news itself was ineffective and, symmetrically, information about the reception context was entirely incapable of cueing memory of the news event. The low level of cue efficiency seems to contrast with the apparent ease of cueing flashbulb memories. However, it supports the above interpretation of the forgetting data for ordinary news in terms of loss of content-to-context associations. This is in accordance with Larsen's (1988a) characterization of news reception circumstances as radically independent context information. On this basis, the generality of Brown's (1990) assumption of close links between autobiographical and historical knowledge is questionable.

*News/context profile*. Within the compound episode news-reception-plus-news-event, information about the news event itself was remembered far better. This heavily skewed memory profile is natural if the news is considered the "central event" of the episode and the circumstances are regarded as "peripheral" or irrelevant details. There is some truth to Brown and Kulik's (1977) assumption that memory of the news itself is not a big problem, it appears.

In flashbulbs the memory profile is more likely flat (i.e., equal memory of the two components as implied by Brown and Kulik's, 1977, "Now Print!" mechanism) or even biased in the direction of the reception context (as suggested by the results of Bohannon, 1988, this volume). Whatever the case may be, it seems impossible that this profile of flashbulb memories could be produced from ordinary news memories by any mechanism of indiscriminate, quantitative amplification. In this sense, it is reasonable to regard flashbulbs as qualitatively discontinuous. Further research on recall of the news information in flashbulb memories would be useful to clarify this issue.

Christianson (1989) noted an important discrepancy between flashbulb studies and laboratory research on memory of emotionally upsetting, traumatic material. In experiments with upsetting picture series, for instance, memory of peripheral details is impaired whereas central details improve, compared to neutral pictures. In upsetting news it is the peripheral, personal context that seems to enjoy an improvement of memory. The contradiction may be more apparent than real, however. Details of the personal context of news do not correspond to details of a picture one is watching, but rather to details of the circumstances in which the picture is seen (e.g., the looks of the experimenter or the furniture of the laboratory). Conversely, peripheral details of the picture correspond to peripheral details of the news event itself. Thus, the central–peripheral distinction may apply both to the news event and the reception context. The circumstances of hearing news are not necessarily peripheral, because under some conditions they might assume a central position. Such a reversal of central and peripheral may be the special thing about flashbulb memories.

*Conclusion.* These discontinuities imply that flashbulb memories are indeed exceptional among memories of the circumstances of hearing news. If the tenor of the studies by McCloskey et al. (1988) and Harsch and Neisser (1989; Neisser & Harsch, this volume) was to remove flashbulb memories from the research agenda, these results should put them back on.

### Determinants of memory

*Event frequency.* Although frequency ratings predicted memory of the central events, they did not affect memory of the reception context. Unfortunately, only frequency of the news items, not the reception context, was rated in the experiment. Therefore, the results merely show that the unusualness of a news event is insufficient by itself to make the circumstances of hearing it distinctive and memorable.

*Involvement.* Personal involvement is one aspect of affective response to information. Because this experiment dealt with everyday events, the ratings of personal involvement were generally very low, seldom exceeding "moderate involvement" (see exceptions in the next section). Probably due to a floor effect, involvement ratings only predicted recognition of news, including the reception context. It is still conceivable that extreme levels of personal involvement might have a share of producing the exceptional memory of context reported in flashbulbs (cf. Pillemer, 1984).

*Rehearsal.* The rating of rehearsal was the most potent determinant of memory in the study. Memory of news context was much less affected by rehearsal ratings than memory of the central events; recall was not affected at all and recognition of context only slightly ($p < .05$). The rating attempted to include talking to others and hearing about the event (overt rehearsal) as well as thinking about it (covert rehearsal). Unfortunately again, I did not distinguish between rehearsing the news itself and the reception context. Therefore, the very limited impact of rehearsal on the reception context probably reflects that this real-life rehearsal was largely concerned with the newsworthy event, which is usually the interesting thing to think and talk about. Although the news is "rehearsed," the circumstances of hearing it are not. The recognition data nevertheless suggest that the reception context occasionally does get some attention, even in ordinary news.

The rehearsal functions are not learning curves, of course. They do not show the acquisition of new information, but rather the role of rehearsal in maintaining the original information despite forgetting. Hence, the results indicate that information about both kinds of central events was basically maintained in the manner well known from the psychology laboratory, that is, by being rehearsed (and selectively elaborated in the process). The results suggest, furthermore, that the circumstances of hearing ordinary news are not remembered because they are not talked about and reflected upon later.

If it is assumed that the memory of every event is vivid like a flashbulb immediately after it has happened (Brewer, 1986; Rubin & Kozin, 1984), the phenomenon to be accounted for in flashbulb memories is not superior registration but rather superior maintenance: Why do these memories not · fade as quickly and completely as memories of learning about ordinary news events? The only study in which subjects were specifically asked to rate rehearsal of the reception context is Bohannon's (1988, this volume), which did find clear evidence that retelling of "the shuttle story" was important for memory of the circumstances but not of the news itself. With the open rehearsal questions employed by Brown and Kulik (1977), Winograd and Killinger (1983), and Pillemer (1984), it is understandable that inconsistent results have been reported. More detailed data on the everyday rehearsal of the components of ordinary as well as upsetting news events are obviously needed.

*Conclusion.* The study offers little direct evidence to show which variables might enhance reception context memory. A measure of event frequency, and thus distinctiveness, of news contexts was not obtained. Emotional involvement affected recognition memory only, but the influence was probably attenuated by a floor effect. Rehearsal (covert and overt) had a slight effect on context memory, and again only on recognition; however, the present measure of rehearsal did not allow the reception context to be separated from the news itself, so the results are inconclusive.

### Exceptional news memories

As another approach to the question of the causes of flashbulbs, some exceptional news memories were examined.

*Phantom flashbulbs.* There were two clear examples in the diary of the "big" news stories that have been selected for study in previous research, namely, the first Palme and Chernobyl reports. Both were perceived as personally very involving, in contrast to a third candidate item, the *Challenger* explosion. The Palme and Chernobyl memories might qualify as flashbulbs according to the classical criteria of confidence, imagery, and recall of at least one "canonical" feature. Nevertheless, memory of the reception context was mostly inaccurate – even worse than for the completely ordinary news. They were indeed "phantom flashbulbs" (Neisser & Harsch, this volume).

Consideration of other intuitively big news items suggested that as surprise and importance of the news increase, memory of the reception context may deteriorate while the news itself improves. This is analogous to the pattern known from laboratory studies of emotional material (cf. Christianson, this volume; Reisberg & Heuer, this volume), but opposite to the traditional picture of flashbulb memories.

*HCC news.* Among the seemingly quite ordinary news, five memories were found where I had the maximum confidence in recalling the source and the context detail accurately (HCC memories). Although the HCC items were not particularly important, unusual, or involving, the reception context was indeed remembered very well – much better than the news itself, that is, a reversal of the usual profile. The HCC news memories were in this sense better examples of flashbulbs than the sensational and shocking news. Still, my present impression is that the five HCC memories have failed to stay clear, so flashbulb status after several months does not guarantee against eventual forgetting.

The finding of superior memory of context in the five HCC memories may seem self-evident because they were selected on the basis of confidence of context recall in the first place. But it is not self-evident unless one is assuming that confidence in one's memory determines accuracy; among others, Neisser and Harsch (this volume; Harsch & Neisser, 1989) have shown that this is not the case. Moreover, high confidence in the accuracy of one's memory of the personal context is precisely the phenomenological quality that drew attention to flashbulbs originally and motivated interest in studying them. Alternative criteria, like surprise and consequentiality (McCloskey et al., 1988) or emotionality (Schmidt & Bohannon, 1988), really presuppose what should be proved, namely, that these variables are causes of the phenomenologically extraordinary quality of flashbulbs.

*Conclusion.* The two most impressive news items in the study provide additional examples of flashbulb-like memories in which the personal context is largely incorrect. More significantly, the HCC news showed the actual existence of memories that correspond to the classical description of flashbulbs: high confidence and very accurate memory of the reception context – plus better than average memory of the news story itself. What caused the observed reversal of personal circumstances and central event in memory is not clear. It is an important future task to investigate whether this reversal is also characteristic of "real" flashbulbs. The scant data available (Bohannon, 1988) suggest that it may be.

## A special flashbulb mechanism?

This study portrays the ordinary, everyday memory of two psychologically distinct components of news, namely, (a) the news event itself and (b) the personal circumstances, or reception context, in which this news is learned. When the fast and comprehensive "source amnesia" of this news is used as the baseline, flashbulb memories indeed appear to be an outstanding phenomenon, despite substantial incompleteness and forgetting.

Does this special phenomenon require the postulation of a special memory mechanism? If the big and impressive news items recorded in the study are considered, well-known (though not necessarily well-understood, cf. Reisberg & Heuer, this volume) mechanisms seem sufficient. In ordinary news, the news event itself was remembered better than the reception context. The more exceptional and impressive the news story, the greater became this bias, similar to the enhanced memory of central details at the expense of peripheral details produced by emotional arousal (Christianson, this volume).

If this were the whole truth, however, classical flashbulb memories (i.e., at least equally accurate memory of the reception context as of the central news event itself) simply would not exist. As memory of the central event is enhanced by impressiveness of the news, the reception context should decay even further (although the person might still be confident of remembering it). But the five High Context Confidence news examples in the present material show that such memories do exist. These quasi-flashbulbs actually exhibited a reversed memory profile, with facts about the news itself being recalled less well than the experience of hearing it.

The data give very limited insight into possible causes why the reception context was remembered so badly in ordinary news and so well in HCC news (and perhaps in flashbulbs generally), because distinctiveness and rehearsal of the context were not measured separately. However, there is some basis for speculation about the fact that rehearsal (overt *and* covert) was the most powerful predictor of memory of news events and autobiographical events alike, whereas news contexts were almost completely unaffected.

When people are thinking and talking about a piece of news in everyday situations, they probably do not (and cannot) cover the remembered information in its entirety; they have to be selective in response to what is individually and socially relevant and interesting. The circumstances in which the news is learned may be particularly unlikely to be brought up in such real-life rehearsal. Accordingly, they very soon become hard to remember, as it is seen in ordinary news. But rehearsal might be allocated very differently in flashbulb memories. Assume that rehearsal in flashbulbs were displaced away from the news event, either to be deployed evenly across the news and its reception context or to be directed mainly at the context. The position of news and personal context in memory would thereby be reversed, with the picture and the frame changing places, so to speak.

This "rehearsal displacement" hypothesis is almost entirely conjecture. As discussed earlier, the significance of rehearsal for flashbulbs has some support in the literature, but until rehearsal of the news itself and the reception context are distinguished the evidence is inadequate. Moreover, rehearsal has only been assessed retrospectively by relying on the tenuous assumption that instances of talking and thinking about even dimly recalled news events can themselves be remembered. Notice that inaccuracies and forgetting of flashbulbs are not in contradiction to rehearsal displacement, which predicts neither accuracy, nor permanence. On the contrary, with repeated rehearsals some changes are almost bound to creep in.

Rehearsal displacement may be seen as a weak "special flashbulb memory mechanism." But it employs a memory mechanism, namely rehearsal, which is the most familiar in existence. This familiar mechanism is used in a special way, however, reflecting the special structure of mass communicated information – the arbitrary relation between the impersonal, "central" event and the personal context.

The hypothesis locates the causal process behind flashbulb memories to the person's cognitive activity occurring during the period of retention ("poststimulus elaboration"; cf. Christianson, this volume). Cognitive activity is assumed to take a special, unusual direction in the case of flashbulbs, though not as an automatic, instantaneous, quasi-neurological process. The hypothesis also points to a large role for social communication processes in generating flashbulbs. The finding that the vast majority of memories of ordinary news events are based on media reports whereas most flashbulbs seem to originate in social, face-to-face reports (cf. Bohannon, 1988) is a suggestion in that direction.

Rehearsal displacement is not supposed to give a sufficient account of flashbulb memories. It is also necessary to identify the conditions that motivate rehearsal and direct the allocation of rehearsal to the personal context. Such conditions may involve a variety of complicated interactions among cognitive, social, and personality variables. For example, a strong emotional reaction to a piece of news is more than a physiological process – it is also a part of the personal circumstances, that is, information. This information may render the context more distinctive and become a target for later thought and conversation. In a related manner, if many individuals attribute great personal significance to a news event, it is likely to become a frequent topic of conversation. In addition, such exchanges may serve to confirm that one's personal feeling of the significance of the news is a shared, social feeling (Neisser, 1982). However, because everybody has heard almost the same facts about the event itself, the only new information to talk about may concern the individuals' personal circumstances when they learned these facts.

All of these speculations point to knowledge about flashbulbs and news memories that is simply not available. To me, perhaps the most important lesson to be learned from studying these matters is how little we know about the cognitive and social vicissitudes of information in everyday life.

## NOTE

This research was supported by grants from the Danish Research Council for the Humanities and the University of Aarhus Research Foundation. The author thanks Klaus Bærentsen for assistance with scoring the data, and Zehra Peynircioglu, David Rubin, and the editors for comments on earlier versions of the chapter.

## REFERENCES

Baddeley, A. (1982). Domains of recollection. *Psychological Review, 89,* 708–729.

Barclay, C. R., & DeCooke, P. A. (1988). Ordinary everyday memories: Some of the things of which selves are made. In U. Neisser & E. Winograd (Eds.), *Remembering reconsidered: Ecological and traditional approaches to the study of memory* (pp. 91–125). New York: Cambridge University Press.

Barsalou, L. W. (1988). The content and organization of autobiographical memories. In U. Neisser & E. Winograd (Eds.), *Remembering reconsidered: Ecological and traditional approaches to the study of memory* (pp. 193–243). New York: Cambridge University Press.

Bohannon, J. N. III. (1988). Flashbulb memories for the Space Shuttle disaster: A tale of two theories. *Cognition, 29,* 179–196.

Brewer, W. F. (1986). What is autobiographical memory? In D. C. Rubin (Ed.), *Autobiographical memory* (pp. 25–49). New York: Cambridge University Press.

Brewer, W. F. (1988). Memory for randomly sampled autobiographical events. In U. Neisser & E. Winograd (Eds.), *Remembering reconsidered: Ecological and traditional approaches to the study of memory* (pp. 21–90). New York: Cambridge University Press.

Brown, N. R. (1990). Organization of public events in long-term memory. *Journal of Experimental Psychology: General, 119,* 297–314.

Brown, N. R., Rips, L. J., & Shevell, S. K. (1985). Subjective dates of natural events in very-long-term memory. *Cognitive Psychology, 17,* 139–177.

Brown, R., & Kulik, J. (1977). Flashbulb memories. *Cognition, 5,* 73–99.

Christianson, S.-Å. (1989). Flashbulb memories: Special, but not so special. *Memory & Cognition, 17,* 435–443.

Christianson, S.-Å., & Loftus, E. F. (1987). Memory for traumatic events. *Applied Cognitive Psychology, 1,* 225–239.

Harsch, N., & Neisser, U. (1989, November). *Substantial and irreversible errors in flashbulb memories of the Challenger explosion.* Poster presented at meeting of the Psychonomic Society, Atlanta.

Larsen, S. F. (1988a). Remembering without experiencing: Memory for reported events. In U. Neisser & E. Winograd (Eds.), *Remembering reconsidered: Ecological and traditional approaches to the study of memory* (pp. 326–355). New York: Cambridge University Press.

Larsen, S. F. (1988b). Remembering reported events: Memory for news in ecological perspective. In M. M. Gruneberg, P. E. Morris, & R. N. Sykes (Eds.), *Practical aspects of memory: Current research and issues* (Vol. 1, pp. 440–445). London: Wiley.

Linton, M. (1978). Real world memory after six years: An in vivo study of very long term memory. In M. M. Gruneberg, P. E. Morris, & R. N. Sykes (Eds.), *Practical aspects of memory* (pp. 69–76). London: Academic Press.

McCloskey, M., Wible, C. G., & Cohen, N. J. (1988). Is there a special flashbulb memory mechanism? *Journal of Experimental Psychology: General, 117*, 336–338.

Neisser, U. (1982). Snapshots or benchmarks? In Neisser, U. (Ed.), *Memory observed: Remembering in natural contexts* (pp. 43–48). San Francisco: Freeman.

Pillemer, D. B. (1984). Flashbulb memories of the assassination attempt on President Reagan. *Cognition, 16*, 63–80.

Pillemer, D. B. (1990). Clarifying the flashbulb memory concept: Comment on McCloskey, Wible, and Cohen. *Journal of Experimental Psychology: General, 119*, 92–96.

Rubin, D. C. (1982). On the retention function for autobiographical memory. *Journal of Verbal Learning and Verbal Behavior, 21*, 21–38.

Rubin, D. C., & Kozin, M. (1984). Vivid memories. *Cognition, 16*, 81–96.

Schacter, D. L., Harbluk, J. L., & McLachlan, D. R. (1984). Retrieval without recollection: An experimental analysis of source amnesia. *Journal of Verbal Learning and Verbal Behavior, 23*, 593–611.

Schmidt, S. R., & Bohannon, J. N., III. (1988). In defense of the flashbulb-memory hypothesis: A comment on McCloskey, Wible, and Cohen. *Journal of Experimental Psychology: General, 117*, 332–335.

Thomson, D. M. (1988). Context and false recognition. In G. M. Davies & D. M. Thomson (Eds.), *Memory in context: Context in memory* (pp. 285–304). Chichester, UK: Wiley.

Tulving, E. (1972). Episodic and semantic memory. In E. Tulving & W. Donaldson (Eds.), *Organization and memory* (pp. 381–403). New York: Academic Press.

Wagenaar, W. A. (1986). My memory: A study of autobiographical memory over six years. *Cognitive Psychology, 18*, 225–252.

Wallace, W. P. (1980). On the use of distractors for testing recognition memory. *Psychological Bulletin, 88*, 696–704.

White, R. T. (1982). Memory for personal events. *Human Learning, 1*, 171–183.

Winograd, E., & Killinger, W. A. (1983). Relating age at encoding in early childhood to adult recall: Development of flashbulb memories. *Journal of Experimental Psychology: General, 112*, 413–422.

# 4

# Flashbulb memories:
# Confidence, consistency, and quantity

JOHN NEIL BOHANNON III AND
VICTORIA LOUISE SYMONS

*The event*

On January 28, 1986 at 11:38 a.m. EST, the Space Shuttle *Challenger* rose into the sky on a pillar of fire. It carried five men and two women aloft, including the first black astronaut, and the first teacher to go into space, Christa McAuliffe. Approximately 72 seconds into the flight, shortly after the astronauts had received and acknowledged the command to go to full throttle, the main external fuel tank exploded. The *Challenger* disintegrated, killing all on board before the horrified eyes of millions. A high-level executive for Morton-Thiokol, the company that made the solid rocket boosters, watched the vapor trail from the moment of launch and knew something was wrong. After the explosion the booster engines continued to burn and flew off on tangential trajectories. Ironically, his first thought was that at least the boosters that his company manufactured had performed well. He remembered wondering who was going to head the disaster investigation and who was to blame. Shortly thereafter, he was to receive another shock. The booster rockets were responsible for the explosion, and his company's executive decisions were shown to have been determined by expediency and characterized by a blatant disregard for safety.

If the man in question had been only one out of a few people with unusual memories for their personal discoveries of the *Challenger* disaster, there would be no reason for this book. The fact that a Morton-Thiokol executive had a particularly vivid set of personal memories for the context of this discovery and the facts about the disaster itself would not surprise anyone, let alone memory researchers. There are many well-understood memory mechanisms that would jointly contribute to this particular case, and all lead to long-lasting, consistent recall reports. Because the executive had considerable a priori knowledge of the shuttle program, facts about the shuttle explosion were especially meaningful to him at the time of exposure, enhancing processing at input (e.g., Bransford & Franks, 1972). The effects of the disaster on his company and his ongoing life were much more consequential than for the average person. His life and job literally changed from the

65

moment of the explosion, surely making the event quite distinctive (e.g., Eysenck, 1979; Schmidt, 1985; von Restorff, 1933) and facilitating reconstruction (e.g., Neisser, 1982). Lastly, the subsequent investigation into who and what were responsible for the disaster was particularly trying for the executives of Morton-Thiokol, who had to account for their actions repeatedly. Such constant rehearsal alone would enhance anyone's recall (Green, 1987; Tulving, 1966). Taken together, these memory functions could easily account for this performance. Few memory researchers would have worried about the extent and veridical nature of this particular executive's memories or question his high level of confidence in those recollections, those of both a personal/episodic and of a factual/semantic nature.

Queries into the role of Morton-Thiokol's booster engines were not the only investigations precipitated by the *Challenger* explosion. Within 2 weeks, over a thousand subjects were asked to recall their discoveries of the shuttle explosion (Bohannon, 1988; Warren & Swartwood, this volume; McCloskey, Wible, & Cohen, 1988; Neisser & Harsch, this volume). The reason for this flurry of psychological research is that vivid, extensive, and consistent memories of this event may be common to many people, few of whom have such a direct connection to the NASA shuttle program. It is the proliferation of these "flashbulb memories" (Brown & Kulik, 1977), that serves as the raison d'être for this volume.

### Issues and questions

Because few of those who report flashbulb memories had all the supportive mechanisms of the Morton-Thiokol executive, researchers have wondered how so many people could have: (1) such extensive personal memories about the episode, (2) such confidence in the vivid details of their memories, and (3) so little degradation of their reports, even with the passage of considerable time (Bohannon, 1988; Brown & Kulik, 1977; Colgrove, 1899; McCloskey, Wible, & Cohen, 1988; Winograd & Killinger, 1983). The unique and compelling nature of flashbulb reports suggested to some a new, or at least under-researched, memory mechanism related to emotion and arousal. Initially labeled the "Now-Print!" mechanism (Bohannon, 1988; Brown & Kulik, 1977; Gold, 1987), it is activated under conditions of arousal and surprise, which are supposed to make the current contents of consciousness more permanently accessible to recall. The "Now-Print!" proposal, in turn, raised further questions concerning how skeptical scientists under the gun of Lloyd Morgan's canon accept new and independent mechanisms within the field of memory research (see Cohen, McCloskey, & Wible, 1988, 1990; Pillemer, 1990; Neisser, 1982; Schmidt & Bohannon, 1988). Moreover, flashbulb memories are examples of "ecologically valid" data gathered in the field under conditions of poor or little experimental control. Some have suggested that the ecological study of memory as a whole is so confounded as to be bankrupt (Banaji & Crowder, 1989). In short, flashbulb memories seem to lie at the center of issues pertaining to: (1) the nature and identity of the mechanisms responsible for the unusual episodic reports, (2) the difference between episodic and semantic memory (see McKoon, Ratcliff, & Dell, 1986; Tulving, 1985), (3) the types of evidence and procedures necessary to support the existence of a novel memory mechanism, and (4) the value of ecological memory research in general. If that were not enough to account for all of this research interest, we further suggest that flashbulb memories allow researchers to question the very nature of the memory system itself.

The average person, and most theories of memory for that matter, assume that one's memory is a semiaccurate reflection of experience. Although we may not remember all the details of day-to-day life, it is assumed that what we do recall is veridically related to experienced reality in nontrivial ways. Many of our fundamental notions about ourselves and the world around us rely on an assumption of relatively reliable memory. Basic attitudes and attributions concerning the self may merely be the recorded sum of our behaviors and thoughts relevant to particular domains (Bem, 1972). For example, we assess the degree to which we are "politically active" by recalling all the behaviors we attribute to the category "politics." Some even feel that the quality of our lives in old age may depend on the quality of our autobiographical reminiscences (Butler, 1974, 1981; Molinari & Reichlin, 1984). Within the legal system, the testimony of witnesses about their memories for an event is an important source of evidence in the prosecution of justice (Loftus, 1979; Loftus & Doyle, 1987; Loftus & Fathi, 1988). We also naively think that we can assess the probability that our memories are veridical. The assumptions may be illustrated with the following example. Imagine that two people recall a shared event and their recollections differ. Assuming both reports are equally likely, whose version of the event should we believe? We tend to weigh more heavily the memory of the individual whose recollection: (1) contains more details (quantity), (2) is related with more confidence, and (3) is more consistent over time. As stated above, flashbulb memories seem to embody these very qualities.

Unfortunately, our faith in these aspects of memory may be partially misplaced. The issue of veridicality must be acknowledged. The fact that one subject reports more information than another does not necessarily mean that all those extra details are accurate. Experiments have shown that hypnotized subjects typically increase the amount of detail in their reports without a significant increase in accuracy (Laurence & Perry, 1983). High confidence does not necessarily guarantee accuracy either. In studies of eyewitness testimony, the most favorable estimates of the correlation between confidence and accuracy are about .40 (Bothwell, Deffenbacher, & Brigham, 1987; Smith, Kassin, & Ellsworth, 1989). The relationship between consistency and accuracy has not been investigated to our knowledge, but may also be less than perfect. Conceivably, subjects could report errors just as consistently as veridical information. Are flashbulb memories mere deceptive shadows that only resemble hypermnesic phenomena? There are surely cases where detailed, vivid errors are consistently reported with high confidence (for an example see Neisser, 1982, 1986; Neisser & Harsch, this volume; Thompson & Cowan, 1986). However, the issue is not the existence of idiographic exceptions, but whether the variables of confidence, consistency, and quantity of report are significantly related. A further issue is whether flashbulb memories compare favorably to other types of memory report (see Neely & Durongulu, 1985; Schmidt & Bohannon, 1988).

### Prior studies

Existing data on flashbulb memories are difficult to interpret. Those studies already published often measure the basic phenomena quite differently (see Table 4.1). To a certain extent this is understandable. Studies of people's discovery of shocking news, by their very nature, must be opportunistic and put together in a short period of time (Schmidt & Bohannon, 1988). A summary of the existing studies and their designs and measures is provided in Table 4.1. A perusal of the varied techniques employed in flashbulb assessment indicates a surprising variation in a relatively circumscribed arena. The number of "canonical" features (from Brown & Kulik, 1977) assessed in an open-ended free recall narrative often changed from study to study. Some studies (e.g., McCloskey, Wible, & Cohen, 1988) eschewed the free recall method altogether, and employed a probe recall technique where the subjects were directly queried about some subset of flashbulb features.

The information assessed in probe recall measures varied widely as well. Pillemer (1984) directly probed all of Brown and Kulik's (1977) canonical features, whereas Bohannon (1988) only included a single canonical feature (location of discovery) and asked for related but more detailed information concerning the subject's discovery context. The method of measuring affect or arousal also differed. McCloskey, Wible, and Cohen (1988) measured affect as just another memory feature, whereas others have used 5-point self-report scales (Bohannon, 1988; Pillemer, 1984) or 10-point scales (Christianson, 1989). Only one study (Christianson, 1991) found no significant relationship between self-rated affect and flashbulb memory, possibly because of the noise introduced by a scale with more than seven values. Few of the studies reviewed (Bohannon, 1988; Bohannon & Schmidt, 1989; Christianson, 1989; Larsen, this volume) probed any comparison memories at the time of flashbulb assessment. All studies that did employ such a measure reported superior recall of the flashbulb information compared to the control information.

Table 4.1. *Studies of flashbulb memories*

| Author | Event | Ss | Delays | Type | Measures | Results |
|--------|-------|-----|--------|------|----------|---------|
| Brown & Kulik (1977) | Assassination JFK, RFK, M. L. King | 80 | 13 yrs<br>8 yrs<br>8 yrs | Group test CS[a] | Free recall, consequentiality recounts | Racial differences, consequentiality, & rehearsal affect recall |
| Winograd & Killinger (1983) | JFK assassination | 338 | 17 yrs | Group test CS | Probed recall | Steep recall gradient in ages 1–7 years of exposure, good recall 6–11 years |
| Pillemer (1984) | Reagan assassination attempt | 83<br>44<br>38 | 1 mos<br>1 & 7 mos<br>7 mos | Take home CS & L[b] | Free recall, probed recall (affect & aftermath), recounts | Initial affect not consequentiality or rehearsals is primary determinant |
| McCloskey, Wible, & Cohen (1988) | *Challenger* explosion | 27<br>31 | 1 week &<br>9 mos<br>9 mos | Take home CS & L | Probed recall (location, activity, source, reaction | Memory became more vague and general over time, 7% inconsistent |
| Bohannon (1988) | *Challenger* explosion | 424<br>262 | 2 wks<br>8 mos | Group test CS | Arousal rating, rehearsals & exposures, free recall, probed recall (details), *Challenger* facts | Source of discovery (media vs. person) important, free recall and probed recall related to both arousal and rehearsal; *Challenger* facts unrelated. |
| Bohannon & Schmidt (1989) | *Challenger* explosion | 304 | 15 mos | Group test CS | Same as Bohannon (1988) | Arousal leads to no decline in free recall; rehearsal needed to maintain details in probed recall |
| Christianson (1989) | Olof Palme assassination | 40 | 6 wks &<br>1 yr | telephone interview L | probed recall affect, rehearsal, consequentiality | Arousal unrelated to memory |
| Neisser & Harsch (Ch 2) | *Challenger* explosion | 106<br>44<br>40 | next day<br>32 mos<br>38 mos | Group test, Individual test, Interview L | free recall (source, place, activity, time, others present) | Many gross errors; no recovery even with extensive cuing |

[a] Cross-sectional design with different subjects at different periods of delay from event.
[b] Longitudinal design with original subjects followed up after a specified delay.

With respect to the consistency of flashbulb memories, McCloskey, Wible, and Cohen (1988) found that about a third of the responses were altered in some way, but only 9 answers of more than 120 were actually inconsistent over the course of the study. Neisser and Harsch (this volume) found many gross memory errors (inconsistencies) over the course of 3 years. Further, many of the subjects were absolutely confident in their inconsistent reports despite confrontation with their original memory protocols. Unfortunately neither study employed a systematic measure of affect or a comparison memory measure. Thus the inconsistent responses could have originated from those subjects who did not react strongly to the news of the shuttle disaster. Because of the lack of comparison memory measures, it is also impossible to determine whether the flashbulb memories were more or less consistent than other memories. Pillemer (1984) found high consistency (about 70%) but used no control memory measures, which makes his results also difficult to interpret. We are still wondering whether flashbulb memories are any different from more mundane, episodic, or semantic recollections.

The investigations reported here were performed to assess subjects' flashbulb memories of the *Challenger* disaster. The *Challenger* explosion was grimly fortuitous with respect to flashbulb memory research. Not only did it stimulate a healthy number of investigations, but the *Challenger* explosion is a better flashbulb test event in some ways than the assassinations of world leaders. Few lives were irredeemably altered by the explosion of the shuttle, although it upset multitudes. In contrast, when a president is killed, new leaders are installed and new policies are put into effect that impinge on everyday life in ways that make Brown and Kulik's (1977) term "consequentiality" quite relevant. The very consequentiality of such an event can aid reconstructive recall as the lives of a country's citizenry take an abrupt turn toward a different future. The bombing of Pearl Harbor and the United States' entry into global conflict is an excellent example of such an event. One explanation for the common flashbulb experience is that people use distinctive world events to help plot the course of their episodic recall using reconstructive procedures (Neisser, 1982). For example, a man might easily recollect where he was on January 5, 1942 because he "dropped out of school to join the Navy within 3 weeks of Pearl Harbor." On the other hand, the strong empirical relationship between self-reported affect and the extent of flashbulb memories suggests a mechanism related to arousal at encoding (Bohannon, 1988; Brown & Kulik, 1977; Gold, 1987; Livingston, 1967; Pillemer, 1984, 1990; Rubin & Kozin, 1984). Although not all the details of the arousal/affect mechanism are well understood, the most likely hypothesis is that strong emotional reactions at the time of encoding lead to more durable, vivid memories. Using the technique of functional dissociation, Bohannon (1988) showed that episodic flashbulb information was related to affect, whereas the semantic memory information concerning details about the *Challenger* explosion was not. Unfortunately, the initial 1988 study from our lab was cross-sectional in design, and hence did not allow any estimate of consistency.

Below we report data from two studies. The first was a cross-sectional design with over a thousand subjects tested over 3 years (the first two groups were reported in Bohannon, 1988), and the second was a longitudinal design that followed up a subsample of our original subjects after 3 years. We used a multiple memory task procedure, attempting to measure as completely as possible the subject's flashbulb experience and an additional control memory measure. The subjects' memories for their discoveries of the disaster (i.e., how they first heard about it) were assessed in both a free and probed recall procedure (Bohannon, 1988; Brown & Kulik, 1977). The subjects were also asked to rate their confidence in the probed details. The control memory task asked about the details of the shuttle explosion itself, details that were repeatedly available from the media on the day of the explosion. The longitudinal study allowed an estimate of the consistency of the reports, both factual and episodic.

### Hypotheses

1. As Banaji and Crowder (1989) point out, one must be very careful in interpreting observational data gathered under conditions of poor control. Evidence must be provided to assess obvious, logical relations in the data. In the present study, we tested several such relations. For example, affect ratings of the initial responses to the *Challenger* news should not change over time, whereas estimates of cumulative recounts and exposures to news stories of the disaster ought to increase. Further, the Time 1 data from the longitudinal sample were compared to the original pool of subjects to assess its representativeness. The 36-month delay data from the longitudinal sample were compared to a new cross-sectional sample to assess the representativeness of the latter. Subjects in the new sample were exposed to the news of the *Challenger* in high school (age 15), whereas those in the longitudinal sample were exposed in college (age 19).

2. Assuming the data are not mere noise, we can examine the relationship between the extent of subjects' memories and their stability. Do people who do not change their stories over the course of 3 years also have the most extensive memories? Further, what are the relations among how upset subjects were at the news of the *Challenger* disaster (affect), how many times they overtly rehearsed the story of their discovery (recounts), and the extent and stability of their memories? Lastly, are the different types of memory measure (free vs. probed recall) and content (flashbulb/episodic vs. semantic/factual) dissociable with respect to affect, rehearsal, and consistency? According to Bohannon (1988), affect ought to be a better predictor of the flashbulb/episodic material than the semantic/factual material, although the pattern of consistency across these factors is as yet unknown.

3. What is the relationship between subjects' confidence in their recollective responses and the consistency of those responses? If the findings reported in the literature are supported, there ought to be a moderate but reliable tendency for subjects to relate consistent reports with more confidence than inconsistent ones. Further, we examined the relationship between affect, recounts and exposures, and the subjects' confidence and consistency.

## Method

### Subjects

The subjects were 990 undergraduates at Virginia Tech who were assessed at three different time lags. Four hundred twenty-four were tested within

2 weeks of the shuttle explosion, and 262 subjects were assessed after an 8-month delay (these two groups were reported in Bohannon, 1988), and 304 subjects with a delay of 15 months (reported in Schmidt & Bohannon, 1988). A further 264 undergraduate subjects from Butler University were tested after a 36-month delay. In addition to the cross-sectional data, the same questionnaire was mailed to the original 2-week subjects in the winter of 1989; 116 subjects returned the questionnaire, yielding a 28% response rate (10 packets were returned due to inaccurate addresses). With the exception of the longitudinal mail sample, all subjects were enrolled in introductory psychology classes, and tested in groups of 30 to 50. The testing of each delay group was completed within a single week. The experiment was introduced as a study of their memory for the shuttle explosion. All subjects were given questionnaire and allowed roughly 20 minutes to complete all of the items.

### Questionnaire

The questionnaire was divided into three sections. The first section ascertained: (1) the source of the subjects' shuttle discoveries (media or another person) (*source*), (2) an estimate of the number of times they retold the discovery story to another (*recounts*), (3) an estimate of the number of times they were exposed to information about the shuttle explosion from any source (person or media) (*exposures*), (4) an estimate of their emotional reaction to the shuttle news on a 5-point scale (1 = couldn't care less, to 5 = stunned speechless) (*affect rating*), and (5) their written account of their discovery of the shuttle event (including any particularly vivid details). The written account served as the basis for the free recall measure. The second section was a series of questions about the details surrounding their discovery of the shuttle accident (discovery probes). The subjects were also asked to estimate their confidence in each answer on a 5-point scale (1 = not sure at all, to 5 = absolutely sure). The questions were: (1) On which day of the week did you discover the *Challenger* news? (2) What was the weather like that day? (3) What were you wearing when you heard the news? and (4) Where were you when you heard the news? Subjects who heard about the shuttle from another person were asked two additional questions: (1) What was the name of the person who told you? and (2) What was your informant wearing?

The Discovery probes were related to the prototypic flashbulb categories previously reported (Brown & Kulik, 1977; Pillemer, 1984, 1990). One of the items was identical (Where were you when you heard?) to those previously studied, and the others probed additional details. Instead of "Who told you?" we asked the source's name and what they were wearing at the time of narration. The extent to which the immediate group included these details in their flashbulb memories 2 weeks after the event can provide a baseline with which to compare the memories of the other delay groups.

The last section of the questionnaire concerned recall of facts about the *Challenger* mission itself. These facts were available on the day of the explosion and serve as a memory control condition for nonflashbulb information learned at the same time as the discovery, and accessed by the same memory cue (i.e., *Challenger* explosion). The questions were: (1) What time of day did the shuttle explode (11:00 a.m. to noon)? (2) What was the date of the accident (January 28, 1986)? (3) What was the name of the shuttle (*Challenger*)? (4) How long into the flight was it before the explosion (60 to 90 seconds)? (5) What was the last voice communication between the shuttle and the ground (referring to "full throttle" or "throttle-up")? (6) How many men were on the shuttle (5 men)? and (7) How many women were on the shuttle? (2 women).

### Scoring

The free recall responses were scored for the presence of 6 features: (1) who told them (*source*), (2) where they were when they heard the news (*location*), (3) what they were doing when they heard (*activity*), (4) when did they hear (*time*), (5) What was the emotional reaction of those people surrounding the subject at the time of discovery (*others' emotion*), and (6) What did they do immediately after their discoveries (*aftermath*). Each category was scored relatively strictly. For *source*, specific reference to the source of the information must have identified the auditory or visual source. Example: "The *professor of my chemistry class* announced in class . . ." "As I was walking past the store, the *TV in the window* was turned on and I saw . . ." For *activity*, specific reference to some activity relating to the self had to be evident. Example: "I *was sitting* in class . . ." "I *was walking* past the store . . ." "I was in class . . ." (not scored as a *activity*, but scored as a *location*). *Location* had to include a specific reference to some geographical location. Example: "I was sitting *in class* . . ." "I was walking *past the store* . . ." *Time* included specific references to some chronological time. Example: "It was *during lunch* when . . ." "I was having lunch *between classes* when . . ." scored as both *activity* and *time*). *Others' emotion* was ascertained by reference to an emotional state of another, not necessarily including the subject's informant. Example: "All the guys on my floor were standing around the TV not saying anything. They *looked stunned* . . ." "Billy ran into my room and *he was crying*. I had never seen him cry before . . ." *Aftermath* was scored if a specific reference was made to an activity or experience that occurred postdiscovery. Example: "I was so upset, that *I went to the restroom to throw up* . . ." " . . . Then *we spent almost an hour trying to find a TV* to hear more . . ." Each category present was scored 1 and absent categories were scored zero. These scores were averaged to determine a proportion of the six categories present for each subject. The section on Discovery probes was similarly scored. If subjects wrote any answer at all, they received a 1 for that question. Only blank responses were scored as a zero. These scores were summed and divided by the number of questions. The confidence ratings for these answers were also averaged. The section on probes concerning the *Challenger* facts was scored as the proportion of questions correctly answered. A subsample of 40 protocols was scored independently by two raters and the average rate of agreement was 96%.

The longitudinal sample ($N = 116$) was scored slightly differently. The elaboration of the free recall protocols at both times of testing (2 weeks and 36 months) were scored on a scale ranging from zero to 3 (*elaborative free recall*). A zero was assigned if the category was absent. A 1 was assigned if the category was not explicitly stated but could be reconstructively inferred. Example: "I had just gotten out of bed and turned on the radio when . . ." Although only *activity* was explicitly stated (score of 2) both *location* (the student's room) and *time* (morning) could be inferred from this statement (each scored 1). A score of 2 was given if the category was explicitly stated according to the rules in the preceding paragraph (see also Bohannon, 1988). A score of 3 was assigned if a particular feature could be scored explicitly more than once in the protocol. For example, a 3 might be given if the subject referred to more than one *activity* of the self: "I *was sitting* at my desk, *studying* for the quiz when . . ." "I *was having lunch* with my buddies and *we were joking* about this economics professor . . ."

The protocols were also scored for consistency on a 3-point basis. If the two reports were contradictory either in detail or in implication, the feature was scored as *inconsistent* (0). Example: "*I heard of the accident from Bill*" (Time 1) and "*When Fred told me about it* . . ." (Time 2). If subjects reported more or less detail they were not necessarily scored as inconsistent unless the details or inferences drawn from the details differed. Example of inconsistent: "*I had just gone to brush my teeth when* . . ." (Time 1) and "*I was in my dorm room when* . . ." (Time 2). Features were further scored as inconsistent if the subjects remembered differently some detail about their feature like their informant's clothing or what their informant was doing at the time of report. Example: "*Bill told me and he was wearing his old high school jacket*" (Time 1) and "*Bill came into my room wearing his bathrobe when* . . ." (Time 2). Responses were rated as *consistent* (score = 1) if both the Time 1 and Time 2 reports agreed both in detail and by inference. Subjects were scored as unmeasurable (score = .5) if they failed to respond at either time of measurement. The total consistency scores for free recall were then divided by the number of features scored to obtain an average consistency score. The resultant consistency scale ranged from inconsistent (0) to consistent (1) and was independent of the number of items reported ($r = .04$). The Discovery probes and *Challenger* facts were similarly scored for consistency. Within the *Challenger* facts, responses could be scored both as "incorrect" and consistent, and frequently were for the question about the number of women on the shuttle. Many subjects said "1" at both times of measurement (consistency = 1) when the correct answer was 2 (Time 1 and Time 2 accuracy = 0). A sample of 30 longitudinal responses were scored independently by two raters. The average rate of agreement was 92%. Disagreements were settled by discussion.

In summary, each of the 1254 cross-sectional subjects contributed: (1) an emotion rating *affect*, (2) an estimate of the number of *recounts*, (3) an estimate of the number of *exposures* to stories about the shuttle, (4) the *source* of their initial discovery (media or a person), (5) an average free recall discovery score (hereafter called *free recall*), (6) an average probed recall discovery score (*Discovery probes*), (7) an average probed discovery *confidence rating*, and (8) an average control memory score for shuttle facts (*Challenger facts*). In addition, the 116 follow-up subjects had another, identical assessment of their memories with free recall scored for elaboration and an average consistency score for each of their memory test: *free recall consistency*, *Discovery probe consistency*, and *Challenger fact consistency*.

## Results and discussion

### Hypothesis 1: Initial methodological comparisons

With the methodological hypotheses in mind, the grouping variables of affect rating, recounts, and exposures were examined in the cross-sectional sample (hereafter the CS sample). If subjects at the time of the test are accurately estimating these variables we might expect stability over time in the affect rating and an increase in the other two variables. The affect rating was a self-estimate of the initial reaction and should not depend on the delay of the test. The number of recounts and exposures must have been higher for the subjects tested after longer delays because they had more opportunity to tell their discovery stories and to gather information from the media about the accident itself. The results clearly show that affect ratings did not significantly change over time [$F(3, 1221) = 2.201$, NS; Mean affect ratings: 2 weeks = 3.67, 8 months = 3.85, 15 months = 3.67, 36 months = 3.74]. In contrast, Figure 4.1 shows a significant increase in the average number of times subjects reported receiving information about the *Challenger* accident itself [$F(3, 1213) = 73.82, p < .001$] (plotted as *exposures* in Figure 4.1) and in their reported recounts [$F(3, 1221) = 17.23, p < .001$].

It has been suggested that subjects who have good flashbulb memories about a particular event mis-estimate their affect, recounts, and exposures (Neisser, 1982). The essence of this hypothesis is that subjects might bias their estimates dependent upon the quality of their memories (McCloskey, Wible, & Cohen, 1988). A person who vividly recalls the event may therefore conclude that they must have reacted strongly to the news, talked about it a lot, and sought out more information about it (see Neisser, 1982). Such a

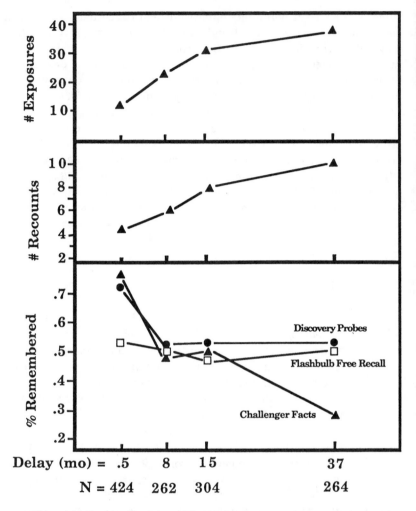

Figure 4.1. Cross-sectional data indicating increasing exposures to the news of the *Challenger* disaster and increasing recounts of the subjects' flashbulb stories to others. Bottom panel reflects differential forgetting of the three memory measures.

hypothesis is difficult to maintain in the face of the current data. As will be seen below, the memory measures generally show a decrease over time, whereas the grouping variable of affect remains steady and the self-estimates of recounts and exposures increase. The most likely explanation is that the subjects' responses were at least, in part, veridical. Other studies (Barclay & Wellman, 1986) that asked subjects to estimate the number of times they performed some acts over the span of several months found a reasonable

Table 4.2. *Initial sample and follow-up sample comparison*

| Dependent Measures | Bohannon (1988) N = 308 | | Bohannon & Symons N = 116 | |
|---|---|---|---|---|
| | X | SD | X | SD |
| Affect | 3.55 | 1.19 | 3.66 | .92 |
| Recounts | 4.65 | 8.23 | 3.84 | 3.02 |
| Exposures | 15.62 | 47.31 | 11.77 | 15.50 |
| Free recall | 0.51 | .32 | 0.48 | .45 |
| Shuttle facts | 0.79 | .25 | 0.68 | .29 |
| Discovery probes | 0.71 | .28 | 0.75 | .23 |
| Confidence | 3.37 | .74 | 3.49 | 1.32 |

*Note*: All comparisons were performed between the portion of the initial subjects who were not retested and the retested subjects. All *t* tests were nonsignificant.

correlation between the subjects' own diary reports written at the time of the acts and their self-estimates several months later. In short, the pattern of the effect, recount, and exposure measures resembles what we would expect from reality.

The longitudinal (L) sample was compared to the overall initial sample from which it was drawn to determine its representativeness. Although all further longitudinal comparisons will be within the L sample itself, the fact that the follow-up sample was obtained through the mail raises issues of self-selection. It is possible that only those people with good flashbulb memories of their discoveries of the *Challenger* disaster responded, limiting our ability to generalize from the sample. The results are shown in Table 4.2. None of the comparisons were significant (*t* test), suggesting that the follow-up sample was representative of the initial sample at least at the time of the initial measurement. It is still possible that the subjects who responded to the mailed questionnaire after a 3-year delay (L sample) were the subjects who, in 1989, had retained more information.

Another comparison was performed between the new 36-month group (N = 241) and the L sample (N = 116). The results are reported in Table 4.3. The L sample reported fewer recounts and exposures than the new sample, but recalled more Discovery probed details and *Challenger* facts. To examine this difference further, affect and recounts were converted into independent variables in 3-way ANOVAs with memory measures as the dependent variables. The subjects were grouped according to their affect ratings (calm vs. upset: ratings of 3 or less vs. ratings of 4 or 5; see Bohannon, 1988), their recount estimates (few vs. many: estimates of 4 or less vs. estimates of 5 or more) and their group membership (L or new). These groupings did not interactively predict any measure of memory.

Table 4.3. *Comparison of retest sample with a new sample, both gathered at a 36-month delay*

| Dependent measures | New sample $N = 241$ | Retest sample $N = 116$ | $F$ ratio $(1,343)$ | p < |
|---|---|---|---|---|
| Affect | 3.70 | 3.65 | .002 | ns |
| Recounts | 10.45 | 5.65 | 9.17 | .003 |
| Exposures | 37.55 | 15.07 | 59.40 | .001 |
| Elaborative free recall | 1.11 | 1.02 | 5.05 | ns |
| Discovery probes | .532 | .632 | 12.96 | .001 |
| *Challenger* facts | .279 | .388 | 15.251 | .001 |
| Probe confidence | .533 | .520 | .632 | ns |

The simple main effects of group probably reflect a cohort difference. The L sample subjects were generally freshmen and sophomores in college at the time of the *Challenger* disaster whereas the new sample subjects were in their first year of high school. The regimented high school environment may have produced more recounts and exposures through directed discussions in class and homework assignments than the less structured college environment of the L sample. But then it is puzzling that the new sample recalled fewer Discovery probed details as well as fewer *Challenger* facts. Another possibility is that the L sample had been required to recall all the tested information at least once before, suggesting a simple rehearsal effect. In any event, we should be very cautious in comparing the absolute levels of recall across cohorts and across groups.

There are several major trends in the cross-sectional sample. As already noted, affect, recounts, and exposures all show systematic patterns. Affect remained constant, whereas the estimates of recounts and exposures increased over time. Next, the three estimates of memory do not all have the same forgetting curve (see bottom panel of Figure 4.1). The semantic information tested in shuttle facts declined more quickly than the flashbulb probed responses. Further, both of the probed measures, episodic/discovery and semantic/factual, declined more rapidly than the probability of reporting the canonical flashbulb features in free recall. Lastly, the affect was more strongly related to the free recall measure than either of the other two assessments.

*Hypothesis 2: Accounting for consistency in the longitudinal data*

The major advantage of the L sample is that the consistency of the subjects' responses on all the memory measures can be addressed. Because we have no direct data on the veridical nature of these responses, the stability of the various responses over time will have to suffice, with the cautious assumption that memory responses that are inconsistent over time are probably less veridical than those responses that remain the same. Neisser and Harsch (this volume) obtained both probed and free recall protocols of the canonical features. In their coding, activity, location, and source were treated as "central" features. In the present study, only location was assessed in both a free and probed recall technique. In an effort to make the current study comparable to that of Neisser and Harsch, the L subjects were grouped according to their consistency on the question of location in both free and probed recall at both times of testing. If the subject's responses were consistent across all four points of measurement (free recall and Discovery probe at Time 1 and 2), they were consigned to the *Consistent* group. If any of the responses failed to agree, then the subject was placed in the *Inconsistent* group. Those subjects who failed to respond to the location probes or who had not mentioned location in their free recall protocols at one or the other time of testing were placed in a third group whose consistency was *Unknown*. There were no cases where the probed location was incompatible with the free recall response. The responses of the two main consistency groups (Consistent vs. Inconsistent) were then compared across all the other variables in a series of split-plot ANOVAs with consistency (2 levels) serving as a between-subjects effect and time of testing (2 levels) as a within-subject effect. The results are shown in Table 4.4.

The results of the analyses of the recount, affect, and exposure data are similar to the pattern of results from the CS sample and support the tentative conclusion that the measures are not random or simply correlated with the extent of the subjects' flashbulb reports. There is no significant change over time in the affect ratings, which is what we would expect if the subjects' ratings were an assessment of their initial emotional reaction to the news of the *Challenger* disaster. Further, the variables of recounts and exposures significantly increased over the 3-year delay. Again, this is the result we would expect, as the subjects had 3 more years of opportunity both to retell their discovery stories to others and to gather more information about the disaster itself (*Challenger* facts). The major finding within these initial three comparisons is that affect was significantly different across the consistency groups (see Table 4.4). The subjects who were consistent in their four reports of where they first heard about the *Challenger* disaster rated themselves as significantly more upset than those who were inconsistent. Another way of looking at the consistency/affect connection is to categorize the subjects in

Table 4.4. *Consistency group differences between original time of test (1986) and follow-up (1989)*

| Variable | | Inconsistent N=26 | | Consistent N=52 | | Effect | $F(1, 76)$ | $p<$ |
|---|---|---|---|---|---|---|---|---|
| | | 1986 | 1989 | 1986 | 1989 | | | |
| Affect | X | 3.27 | 3.27 | 3.83 | 3.83 | Group | 9.30 | .003 |
| | SD | 1.00 | 0.78 | 0.90 | 0.78 | Time | .01 | .99 |
| | | | | | | G * T | .01 | .99 |
| Recount | X | 3.77 | 6.31 | 4.31 | 5.83 | Group | .01 | .98 |
| | SD | 2.30 | 11.2 | 3.38 | 5.43 | Time | 4.98 | .03 |
| | | | | | | G * T | .31 | .58 |
| Exposures | X | 12.0 | 16.6 | 12.3 | 17.7 | Group | .03 | .86 |
| | SD | 18.2 | 23.2 | 16.7 | 16.1 | Time | 5.40 | .03 |
| | | | | | | G * T | .04 | .84 |
| Elaborative | X | 1.21 | 0.86 | 1.40 | 1.44 | Group | 17.60 | .0001 |
| free recall | SD | 0.57 | 0.62 | 0.44 | 0.44 | Time | 4.44 | .027 |
| | | | | | | G * T | 6.39 | .014 |
| Discovery | X | 0.85 | 0.65 | 0.78 | 0.64 | Group | 1.01 | .32 |
| probes | SD | 0.17 | 0.23 | 0.19 | 0.20 | Time | 45.68 | .0001 |
| | | | | | | G * T | 1.15 | .29 |
| Confidence | X | 0.75 | 0.51 | 0.68 | 0.53 | Group | .02 | .38 |
| in probes | SD | 0.16 | 0.17 | 0.14 | 0.13 | Time | 109.10 | .0001 |
| | | | | | | G * T | 2.87 | .093 |
| *Challenger* | X | 0.67 | 0.35 | 0.75 | 0.43 | Group | 3.02 | .09 |
| facts | SD | 0.25 | 0.19 | 0.26 | 0.25 | Time | 21.80 | .0001 |
| | | | | | | G * T | .01 | .93 |

*Note*: Consistency group was determined by matching flashbulb location feature in free recall and discovery probes across time. All responses had to match for a subject to be included in the consistent group. A mismatch of any location response placed the subject in the inconsistent group. A failure to report location at either time placed the subject in the unknown group, which was excluded from the analysis.

the three consistency groups into affect groups in a fashion identical to that used by Bohannon (1988). Subjects who rated themselves as very or extremely upset by the *Challenger* explosion (ratings of 4 or 5) were put into an *Upset* group. Subjects with lower affect ratings were placed in a *Calm* group. The distribution of the subjects in the 3(consistency groups) × 2(affect groups) matrix is shown in Figure 4.2. The subjects' ratings of their initial emotional reaction clearly predicts the consistency of their memories about where they first heard about the *Challenger* explosion. The vast majority of the subjects in the Upset group were consistent. Only seven subjects who rated themselves as upset at the news of the *Challenger* explosion were inconsistent with respect to where they first heard the news.

Some caution was taken in analyzing the memory consistency data. The

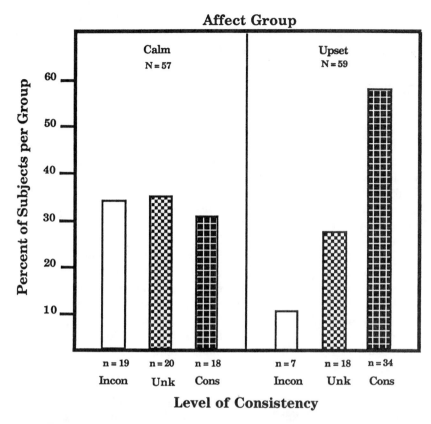

Figure 4.2. Relative distribution of subjects in the consistency groups (Incon = Inconsistent, Unk = Unknown, Cons = Consistent) by affect group.

Unknown group failed to respond to the location question at one or both of the times of test, so their flashbulb free recall and Discovery probe scores were lower by definition. Therefore, the data analyzed in Table 4.4 excluded the Unknown group. In the free recall measure, the significant group effect suggests that subjects who were inconsistent on the location feature were less likely to report the other features as well. The significant group by time interaction revealed that the Consistent group showed no decline in the extent of their flashbulb discovery stories with time, whereas the Inconsistent group's reports significantly decreased (see Table 4.4). This suggests that, at least within the free recall procedure, the extent of flashbulb reports over time is significantly correlated with their stability. Subjects with more extensive flashbulb stories, as measured by the proportion of features present in the recall narrative, were also more likely to tell the same narrative, even over the span of 3 years. The results of the more detailed, Discovery probe data and the subjects' confidence in their responses indicated only an effect of time. This suggests that the Discovery probe data is measuring something slightly different than the traditional flashbulb free recall narratives. The probability of the Discovery probe responses simply declined over time regardless of the subjects' consistency status, as did their responses to the *Challenger* facts.

### Consistency and recounts

Table 4.4 showed that the two consistency groups did not differ in overall recounts and exposures. This finding argues against one of Brown and Kulik's (1977) hypotheses. They suggested that overt rehearsal (in recounting one's flashbulb story) and covert rehearsal (through exposure to information about the flashbulb event) should lead to better memory. The apparent absence of any relation between consistency and recounts also argues against the opposite hypothesis, proposed by Loftus (1979): that ruminative recall may actually interfere with the original memory. To explore this issue further, we treated the consistency scores as dependent variables and asked whether increasing numbers of rehearsals in interaction with other variables might lead to higher consistency. The three memory measures (elaborative free recall, Discovery probes and *Challenger* facts) were included in this analysis together with affect and recounts, producing a $2 \times 2 \times 3$ split-plot ANOVA. The three-way interaction is shown in Figure 4.3. Clearly, the free recall measure was the most consistent followed by the probed recall measure, with the subjects' memories of the facts of the *Challenger* disaster being the least consistent [$F(2, 224) = 19.41, p < .001$]. The effect of affect was also significant; the Upset group was more consistent than the Calm group in all measures [$F(1, 112) = 5.99, p < .016$]. Both of these effects were moderated in interaction with each other [$F(2, 224) = 2.86, p < .059$] (see Figure 4.3). This last marginal interaction was due to the differential effect of recounts across the memory measures within the Upset group; only in *Challenger* facts did increasing rehearsal lead to greater consistency. In the Calm group, recounts had no effect on consistency. This may mean that the more one talks about the facts of the disaster, the more will one's errors be corrected by one's listeners. For one's memory of the discovery context, repeated retelling of the story is unlikely to lead to verification by one's listeners. In both the free recall measure and (more obviously) in the Discovery probe measure, increasing recounts were related to less consistency. Why only the Upset group showed this effect is not clear. It may be possible that affect potentiates the original memory in a way that makes it more susceptible to interference with other information, even that which is self-generated.

Another way to test the relationship between memory consistency and recounts is to employ recounts as a dependent variable while grouping the subjects on affect and consistency as described above. If increasing recounts

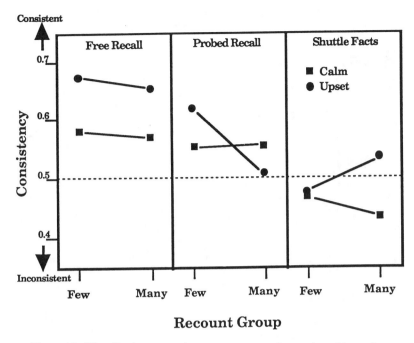

Figure 4.3. The affect by recount by memory measure interaction with consistency scores as a dependent variable.

in the Upset group leads to inconsistent reports, then the seven upset but inconsistent subjects (see Figure 4.2) ought to have the highest self-estimated number of rehearsals. The recounts estimates were analyzed by a 3(consistency group) $\times$ 2(affect group) $\times$ 2(time of testing) split-plot ANOVA. The significant three-way interaction [$F(2, 110) = 4.0$, $p < .021$] is shown in Figure 4.4. The inconsistent, Upset group estimated that they talked about their discoveries almost three times more over the course of 3 years than any other group at any time. The results are clear. If the event upset a subject and the subject talked about his or her discovery a lot, then the reports tended to be inconsistent. Loftus (1979) has shown many times that misleading information supplied by others can be incorporated into future memory reports. The current data suggests that the subjects themselves can supply the misleading information, but high affect seems also to be required if it is to be incorporated into a mutated flashbulb report.

### Hypothesis 3: Confidence and consistency

The last set of analyses addressed the relation of the subjects' confidence in their memories and the consistency of those memories. The only data on the subjects' confidence comes from their estimates in the Discovery probe

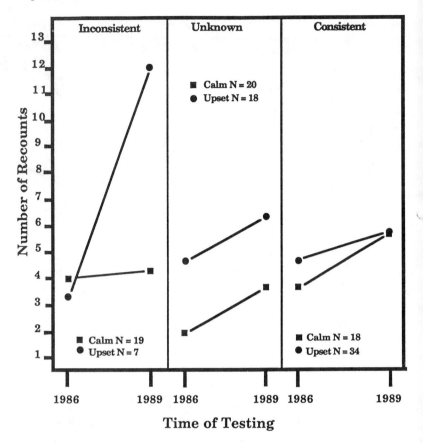

Figure 4.4. Affect by consistency group interaction with recounts as a dependent variable.

portion of the assessment. Subjects were asked to rate their confidence in the veridicality of their answers for each of the six probe questions. The data on consistency for each question was used to form consistency groups based on the stability of the subjects' reports for each question. Those subjects who failed to report, and whose consistency is indeterminate, were excluded from this analysis as before. The resulting consistency groups were then compared in a series of one-way ANOVAs. The results are shown in Table 4.5. The most consistent result in this analysis is that the subjects' rating of confidence in their responses was related to their consistency (see Table 5.5). For every question, those subjects who did not change their responses over 3 years were more confident in their memories than those subjects who were inconsistent. This supports prior work in the area of eyewitness testimony (Smith, Kassin, & Ellsworth, 1989). Confidence in one memory is not a

Table 4.5. *Discovery probe consistency relationship to mean affect, recounts, exposure, and confidence ratings*

| Memory measure | Consistency group | Dependent Variables | | | |
|---|---|---|---|---|---|
| | | Affect rating | No. of recounts | No. of exposures | Confidence ratings |
| Day of discovery | Inconsistent N=49 | 3.85 | 5.53 | 15.12 | 2.85 * |
| | Consistent N=25 | 3.58 | 4.77 | 14.81 | 3.19 |
| Weather that day | Inconsistent N=50 | 3.66 | 5.37 | 16.88 | 3.3 ** |
| | Consistent N=46 | 3.75 | 4.44 | 12.05 | 3.71 |
| Location of discovery[a] | Inconsistent N=18 | 3.31 ** | 5.81 ** | 11.17 | 4.53 *** |
| | Consistent N=93 | 3.75 | 4.72 | 14.11 | 4.83 |
| Own clothing | Inconsistent N=25 | 3.71 | 6.16 | 13.3 | 3.26 *** |
| | Consistent N=39 | 3.87 | 4.76 | 14.92 | 3.83 |
| Name of source | Inconsistent N=11 | 3.82 | 6.0 ** | 12.77 | 4.18 ** |
| | Consistent N=31 | 3.58 | 3.63 | 13.61 | 4.68 |
| Source's clothing | Inconsistent N=13 | 3.87 | 3.69 | 16.5 | 3.5 * |
| | Consistent N=14 | 3.64 | 4.54 | 13.46 | 4.14 |

*Note*: All significance levels determined by a series of separate one-way between-subject ANOVAs with consistency group the single variable. Consistency was determined by the agreement of the subjects' protocols for each specific probe question.
[a] The number of consistent and inconsistent subjects in the location featured in this table differs from that in Table 4.4 because it relies on a single criterion of comparing the Discovery probe location question at two times of testing. The consistency grouping in Table 4.4 was derived from the double criteria of consistency across both flashbulb free recall location and the Discovery probe location responses at two times of testing.
* $p < .10$.
** $p < .05$.
*** $p < .01$.

perfect predictor of veridicality, but it is clearly related in a fashion consistent with common assumptions.

## Summary: The good, the bad, and the ugly

We began this report with the promise that observation of flashbulb memories would allow the assessment of common assumptions about memory. It is generally assumed that more extensive memories, reported with more confidence and conviction, are more stable and accurate than memories that are deficient in any of these dimensions. Our data confirm these assumptions. The most consistent memories were also the most extensive, and they were associated with the highest levels of confidence. Moreover, the data suggest that memories of the discovery of shocking news are more resilient over time than semantic memories of the actual event, when both types of information are assessed using the same probe technique. Over the course of 3 years, flashbulb memories were more consistent than memories for the event of the *Challenger* disaster itself.

As we release our collective breath now that flashbulb memories have survived this test of their unusual character, we can turn to the candidate mechanisms responsible for the phenomenon. The features of such a mechanism can easily be delineated. First, it is clear that the degree of affective response to shocking news has pervasive effects. Those subjects who reported more shock to the news of the disaster had more consistent and extensive free recall reports than those who reported less emotional responses (see Figures 4.2 and 4.3). This agrees with prior reports (Bohannon, 1988; Brown & Kulik, 1977; Gold, 1987; Pillemer, 1984). Second, we might expect other mechanisms such as imagery and rehearsal to interact with the hypothetical flashbulb mechanism. In accord with this prediction, the data revealed an interaction between rehearsal and affect. Those subjects in the Upset group who were inconsistent in reporting where they were when they heard of the *Challenger* disaster also reported retelling their stories almost three times more often than any other subject. Lastly, although we expect our candidate mechanism to result in more durable, consistent, and extensive memories, there is no reason to expect these memories to be perfectly complete or unchanging. The data from both the cross-sectional and the longitudinal samples show evidence of forgetting and inconsistency. However, despite the evidence of decay in flashbulb memories, they do seem to be "better" in all the conventional estimates of quality than our comparison measure of semantic recall.

It is unfortunate that Brown and Kulik (1977) chose the name "flashbulb memories" to describe this phenomenon. It implied that at the moment of surprise and shock, an enduring "photograph" is taken of the current contents of consciousness. Clearly, that is not the case. Flashbulb memories are simply more extensive, more enduring, more consistent, and reported with more confidence than other memories. They are not perfect by any means. Further, the subjects who were strongly affected by the event and elected to talk about their experiences exhibited less consistency than those who remained calm (see Figure 4.4). Why such memories are more susceptible to change is unknown. Research on testimony (e.g., Loftus, 1979) suggests that eyewitness reports are quite liable to change given specific misleading information after initial exposure. The current study is the first report of such misleading information being generated by the subjects themselves.

The notion of instantaneous memory pictures can be discarded as a bad idea that does not fit any candidate mechanism. The most common errors reported by subjects seemed to be incorrect "time slices" (see Brewer, 1988). Subjects replace the "aftermath" feature with the context of previously reported discovery. Even the most likely physiological candidate mechanism, glucose regulation (see Gold, 1987, this volume), takes several minutes to function. If the subjects immediately move to a new context, as in the case of discovering the *Challenger* disaster from an overheard conversation and immediately running to a radio or television, it is possible that the aftermath of information gathering might replace the actual discovery engram. On the other hand, the current study suggests that this is more likely to occur in subjects that have a weaker emotional response to the news. It is possible that the candidate mechanism has an extensive exposure speed, to maintain the camera metaphor. Just as photographs that are taken with the shutter open too long are blurred images, flashbulb memories may be blurred in similar ways. Those aspects of such photographs that change during aperture opening are also blurred in the resulting picture, whereas unchanging features come out somewhat better. Maybe the glucose mechanism does take a "picture of the contents of consciousness," only the picture is several minutes or more in duration. Those contents of consciousness that remain the focus of the mind during this time are clear, enduring engrams, whereas those that change may be blurred. At least superficially, we might surmise that shocking news might stimulate just such concentration on the context of discovery, and further, that the more upset subjects might be, the more they concentrate during the critical interval. Thus, flashbulb memories may be the "sums over histories" of the objects of concentration and our processing of those objects following the discovery of shocking news.

Methodologically, some aspects of gathering data on such "ecologically valid" topics as flashbulb memory are downright ugly and messy. Subjects' discovery context cannot be controlled, nor, for the most part, verified. The data are extremely noisy! We recommend that if the reader plans on entering the field, he or she be prepared to gather reports from hundreds of subjects, be resigned to self-estimates of important variables such as affect and rehearsal and to dealing with facetious responses to important questions (e.g., How many times did you retell your discovery story? Response: "Billyuns and billyuns").

We hope that the current text will allow researchers to settle on a common method of testing flashbulb memories and comparing them appropriately to other types of memories. For example, future studies should begin within days of the flashbulb-inspiring event (e.g., Neisser & Harsch, this volume) and simultaneously employ an affect rating, a recount measure, and an exposure rating along with a comparison memory measure about the event itself. Without such complete and immediate assessment, the conclusions drawn will be quite limited. We further hope that probabilistic, nomothetic comparisons will be employed as the method of choice in contrast to idiographic examples. Some researchers have tried to dispute the unusual character of flashbulb memories with case report vignettes (e.g., McCloskey, Wible, & Cohen, 1988; Neisser & Harsch, this volume). We make the nomothetic claim that on the average, subjects with high emotion tend to possess flashbulb reports that are more extensive and consistent than subjects with less emotion. Relation of vignettes that counter this statement do not disprove the probabilistic position at all. In a similar way, one can accept the nomothetic fact that the average man is taller than the average woman despite the case that the center of the women's national basketball team of China is seven feet tall. We could have reported only the errors our subjects made, but it would not have helped to understand the basic phenomenon of flashbulb memory. The only mechanism disproved by such data would be one that required an absurdly strict set of criteria: 100% consistency, 100% completeness, and 100% durability in 100% of the subjects tested. As previously argued (see Pillemer, 1990; Schmidt & Bohannon, 1988), flashbulb memory researchers have rarely made such claims.

In conclusion, we seem to have a mechanism that improves the probability of recalling the personal context of the discovery of shocking news rather than the probability of recalling the news itself (see also Christianson & Loftus, 1991; Christianson, Loftus, Hoffman, & Loftus, 1991). As a biological mechanism this seems somewhat at odds with the goal of fitness in an evolutionary sense. Is not the news itself more important than the relatively meaningless context of discovery? Probably so in today's world, but this may not have been the case during the millennia necessary to evolve such a mechanism in humans. It is easy to speculate that the discovery of shocking information in prehistoric, hunter-gatherer groups might be all too personal and immediate. The tiger that jumped out and ate one's father would serve as both the context of discovery and the fact itself. Remembering the details of such events might well enhance the fitness of individuals. It is rather ironic that in today's world of multimedia news presentation of distant events, the same mechanism might impede memory for the relevant facts of the shocking event and improve recall of more meaningless details such as the jacket one's informant was wearing.

## NOTE

The authors would like to thank Dr. Amye Warren for her help in the setup of this study, Marjorie Hall, Wendy Basham, Jim Henon, Roberta Hull, and Nancy Dykstra for their assistance in gathering and coding the data. The first author would also like to thank Eugene Winograd, Ulric Neisser, and Amye Warren for their assistance in formulating the questions to be asked of our data set.

## REFERENCES

Banaji, M., & Crowder, R. (1989). The bankruptcy of everyday memory. *American Psychologist, 44*, 1185–1193.

Barclay, C., & Wellman, H. (1986). Accuracies and inaccuracies in autobiographical memory. *Journal of Memory and Language, 25*, 93–103.

Bem, D. (1972). Self-perception theory. In L. Berkowitz (Ed.), *Advances in experimental social psychology* (Vol. 6). New York: Academic Press.

Bohannon, J. N. (1988). Flashbulb memories of the space shuttle disaster: A tale of two theories. *Cognition, 29*, 179–196.

Bohannon, J., & Schmidt, S. (1989, March). Another look at flashbulb memories for the *Challenger* disaster. Paper presented at the meeting of the Southeastern Psychological Association, Atlanta.

Bothwell, R., Deffenbacher, K., & Brigham, J. (1987). Correlation of eyewitness accuracy and confidence: Optimality hypothesis revisited. *Journal of Applied Psychology, 72*, 691–695.

Bransford, J., & Franks, J. (1972). The abstraction of linguistic ideas: A review. *Cognition, 1*, 211–249.

Brewer, W. F. (1988). Memory for randomly sampled autobiographical events. In U. Neisser & E. Winograd (Eds.), *Memory reconsidered: Ecological and traditional approaches to the study of memory* (pp. 21–90). New York: Cambridge University Press.

Brown, R., & Kulik, J. (1977). Flashbulb memories. *Cognition, 5*, 73–99.

Butler, R. (1974). The life review: An interpretation of reminiscence in the aged. *Psychiatry, 26*, 65–75.

Butler, R. (1981). Successful aging and the role of life review. *Journal of the American Geriatrics Society, 22*, 529–535.

Christianson, S.-Å. (1991). Flashbulb memories: Special but not so special. *Memory and Cognition, 17*, 435–443.

Christianson, S.-Å., & Loftus, E. (1991). Remembering emotional events: The fate of detailed information. *Cognition and Emotion, 5*, 81–108.

Christianson, S.-Å., Loftus, E., Hoffman, H., & Loftus, G. (1991). Eye fixations and accuracy in detail memory of emotional versus neutral events. *Journal of Experimental Psychology: Learning, Memory and Cognition, 17*, 693–701.

Cohen, N., McCloskey, M., & Wible, C. (1988). There is still no case for a flashbulb-memory mechanism: Reply to Schmidt & Bohannon. *Journal of Experimental Psychology: General, 117*, 336–338.

Cohen, N., McCloskey, M., & Wible, C. (1990). Flashbulb memories and the underlying cognitive mechanisms: Reply to Pillemer. *Journal of Experimental Psychology: General, 119*, 97–100.

Colgrove, F. (1899). Individual memories. *American Psychologist, 10*, 228–255.

Eysenck, M. W. (1979). Depth, elaboration, and distinctiveness. In L. W. Cermak &

F. I. M. Craik (Eds.), *Levels of processing in human memory* (pp. 89–118). Hillsdale, NJ: Erlbaum.

Gold, P. (1987). Sweet memories. *American Scientist, 75,* 151–155.

Green, R. L. (1987). Effects of maintenance rehearsal on human memory. *Psychological Bulletin, 102,* 403–413.

Laurence, J., & Perry, C. (1983). Hypnotically created memory in highly hypnotizable subjects. *Science, 222,* 523–524.

Livingston, R. B. (1967). Brain circuitry relating to complex behavior. In G. C. Quarton, T. Melnechuck, and F. O. Schmitt (Eds.), *The neurosciences: A study program* (pp. 499–514). New York: Rockefeller University Press.

Loftus, E. (1979). *Eyewitness testimony.* Cambridge, MA: Harvard University Press.

Loftus, E. F., & Doyle, J. M. (1987). *Eyewitness testimony: Civil and criminal.* New York: Kluwer Law Book Publishers.

Loftus, E., & Fathi, D. (1988). Retrieving multiple autobiographical memories. *Social Cognition, 3,* 280–295.

McCloskey, M., Wible, C., & Cohen, N. (1988). Is there a special flashbulb memory mechanism? *Journal of Experimental Psychology: General, 117,* 171–181.

McKoon, G., Ratcliff, R., & Dell, G. (1986). A critical evaluation of the semantic episodic distinction. *Journal of Experimental Psychology: Learning, Memory, and Cognition, 12,* 295–306.

Molinari, V., & Reichlin, R. (1984). Life review reminiscence in the elderly: A review of the literature. *International Journal of Aging and Human Development, 12,* 15–26.

Neeley, J., & Durongulu, A. (1985). Dissociative episodic and semantic priming effects in episodic recognition and lexical decision tasks. *Journal of Memory and Language, 24,* 466–489.

Neisser, U. (1982). Snapshots or Benchmarks? In U. Neisser (Ed.), *Memory observed* (pp. 43–48). San Francisco: Freeman.

Neisser, U. (1986). Remembering Pearl Harbor: Reply to Thompson and Cowan. *Cognition, 23,* 285–286.

Pillemer, D. (1984). Flashbulb memories of the assassination attempt on President Reagan. *Cognition, 16,* 63–80.

Pillemer, D. (1990). Clarifying the flashbulb memory concept: Comment on McCloskey, Wible, and Cohen. *Journal of Experimental Psychology: General, 119,* 92–96.

Rubin, D., & Kozin, M. (1984). Vivid memories. *Cognition, 16,* 81–95.

Schmidt, S. R. (1985). Encoding and retrieval processes in the memory for conceptually distinctive events. *Journal of Experimental Psychology: Learning, Memory and Cognition, 11,* 565–578.

Schmidt, S. R., & Bohannon, J. (1988). In defense of the flashbulb Memory hypothesis. *Journal of Experimental Psychology: General, 117,* 332–335.

Smith, V., Kassin, S., & Ellsworth, P. (1989). Eyewitness accuracy and confidence: Within and between subjects correlations. *Journal of Applied Psychology, 74,* 356–359.

Thompson, C., & Cowan, T. (1986). Flashbulb memories: A nicer interpretation of a Neisser recollection. *Cognition, 22,* 199–200.

Tulving, E. (1966). Subjective organization and effects of repetition in multi-trial free recall. *Journal of Verbal Learning and Verbal Behavior, 5,* 193–197.

Tulving, E. (1985). *Elements of episodic memory.* Oxford: Oxford University Press.

von Restorff, H. (1933). Uber die Virkung von Bereichsbildungen im Spurenfeld. *Psychologie Forschung, 18,* 299–342.

Winograd, E., & Killinger, W. A., Jr. (1983). Relating age at encoding in early childhood to adult recall: Development of flashbulb memories. *Journal of Experimental Psychology: General, 112,* 413–422.

Yarmey, A., & Bull, M. (1978) Where were you when President Kennedy was assassinated? *Bulletin of the Psychonomic Society, 11,* 133–135.

*Part II*

# Developmental studies

# 5

# Developmental issues in flashbulb memory research: Children recall the *Challenger* event

AMYE RICHELLE WARREN AND
JEFFERY N. SWARTWOOD

Following the appearance of the now classic paper on "flashbulb" memory by Brown and Kulik (1977), Winograd and Killinger (1983) conducted a retrospective developmental study of the phenomenon. In reviewing Brown and Kulik's (1977) data, they noted that 24 of the 80 informants had been between 7 and 11 years of age at the time (1963) of the Kennedy assassination, yet their reports of the circumstances under which they discovered the news were no different from those informants who were adults at the time. A similar pattern was noted by Yarmey and Bull (1978), who found that only 15% of their subjects who had been between 6 and 10 years old in 1963 responded that they could *not* remember what they had been doing at the time they heard of Kennedy's assassination. Apparently, age at the time of encoding had little relation to subsequent recollections of the event's discovery. Winograd and Killinger (1983) thus set out to determine whether there were any differences between the memories of those who had been 7 or older at the time of the event versus those who had been younger. If age differences emerged, perhaps they could shed some light on both the development of autobiographical memory in general and the factors that contribute to flashbulb memories.

Winograd and Killinger (1983) collected questionnaires from 338 college students who had been 1 to 7 years old at the time of John F. Kennedy's assassination. They found that those subjects who had been older at the time of the event had more elaborate reports with more canonical features. Over 50% of those who had been 4½ years of age or older at the time could recall hearing the news, and also could provide at least one of five specific canonical details. More than half of the subjects who had been 6 or older at the time could provide at least four of the five core details.

The age differences observed by Winograd and Killinger (1983) may be interpreted in many ways. There are two competing explanations for adults' flashbulb memories, the first of which is Brown and Kulik's (1977) "Now Print!" hypothesis focusing on the extreme emotional arousal generated by the news of a consequential event. According to this theory, high levels of arousal not only produce physiological changes that permanently imprint

95

memories, but also engender more frequent rehearsal of the event. With frequent rehearsal, the "pure," unchanging core memory achieves an elaborate and easily accessible verbal narrative form. According to this view, developmental differences in flashbulb memories should result primarily from age differences in emotional arousal and only secondarily from age differences in rehearsal. Winograd and Killinger (1983) suggested that older children might have understood the consequentiality of JFK's assassination better and therefore had stronger emotional reaction to it, resulting in better encoding of the personal circumstances surrounding its discovery. However, it is well established that from infancy, children engage in "social referencing," a tendency to check the emotional reactions of significant others prior to acting or reacting themselves. The strong reactions among the adults (parents and teachers) from whom the children took their cues might serve to attenuate age differences in children's emotional reactions. Additionally, a current controversy in the developmental literature revolves around the extent to which emotional arousal hinders or facilitates children's event memory. Whereas Goodman and her colleagues (e.g., Goodman, Aman, & Hirschman, 1987) repeatedly find that children who are more aroused by medical procedures or other situations later better remember the events and their contents, Peters (1987) reports the opposite. Contemporary versions of Freudian theory (see White & Pillemer, 1979, or Pillemer & White, 1989, for reviews) also suggest that emotional events during childhood are likely to be repressed ("forgotten") or reinterpreted ("reconstructed").

The alternative explanation for flashbulb memories relies strongly on rehearsal. As proposed by Neisser (1982), this view holds that adults attach significance to events after the fact rather than at the time of encoding. Events later deemed important are rehearsed or reconsidered frequently, and narrative reports of these events are then reconstructed using a general schema for similar events. The schema most likely includes slots for some or all of the very core items described by Brown and Kulik (1977), such as who (told you), and what (were you doing). Thus, even though Brown and Kulik's (1977) subjects who had been children at the time of the event produced vivid, elaborate memories that were apparently no different from those of the other subjects, the commonalities may have arisen not from their shared emotional and physiological reactions, but from a socially shared narrative convention. In application to Winograd and Killinger's (1983) results, schema theory suggests that those who had been younger at the time of encoding had not sufficiently acquired this narrative convention, or had less well-developed schema. White and Pillemer (1979) state: "fragmentary memory traces are the raw material for the fully formed narrative memories that the child is only capable of constructing at older ages," and "memories in narrative form do not exist before 5, 6, or 8 years. It is not that they are not available. They are not there. What are available are nuclear memories of powerful and emotionally significant events" (p. 34).

How would the schema and narrative convention that Neisser (1982) describes develop? As with other schemata, the "historically important event schema" would develop through experience with like events. The work of Fivush and her colleagues (e.g., Fivush, 1984; Fivush, Hudson, & Nelson, 1984) suggests that even young children rapidly develop scripts for familiar events. Although little experience with any given event is necessary before an organized script emerges, older, more experienced children typically have more complex and elaborate scripts. However, Fivush and Slackman (1986) speculate that scripts may also be learned vicariously, by hearing others talking about or hearing stories about events, or watching television or movies. In fact, "Because children . . . have experienced fewer events than adults, they may depend to a larger extent on more vicarious avenues of event learning" (Fivush & Slackman, 1986, p. 74).

A complementary application of the script approach to flashbulb memory involves viewing important historical events as *atypical* events within the "everyday activity" script. Research has indicated that atypical events may be remembered better than typical or expected events. For example, Fivush, Hudson, and Nelson (1984) state that "memory for a particular episode can remain intact over a substantial period of time if the episode deviates from the expectations of the general event representation" (p. 313). The Kennedy assassination occurred within a background of routine school activities. Fivush (1984) has shown that normal "school day" scripts are formed fairly rapidly with experience (even by the second day of kindergarten). Winograd and Killinger (1983) found that the typical memory for their older subjects involved a normal school day being disrupted by news of Kennedy's shooting coming over an intercom or from someone bursting into the classroom. All normal activities ceased, teachers often cried, and children were sent home early from school. All of these factors enhanced the initial significance of the event itself. Winograd and Killinger (1983) have thus dubbed this potential explanation for the seemingly peculiar vividness and permanence of these memories the "disruption hypothesis."

Perhaps because of better established school day scripts, or more elaborate historical event scripts, older children attached more significance to the event afterward, and rehearsed the event more frequently thereafter. The more frequent reconsideration would lead to more elaborate narratives over time. But would these narratives be more accurate or complete reflections of the initial encoding? According to Reed (1979), ". . . the more an original event has been recalled (or reminisced about), the more modifications will have been introduced and therefore the weaker the fit between our current reconstruction and . . . the original" (p. 24). Reed also asserts that later recollections will be reordered, condensed, elaborated, or distorted.

Winograd and Killinger (1983) attempted to test a rehearsal explanation for their results by asking their subjects to rate how frequently they had talked about the event to someone else (on a 4-point scale), and by correlating this rating with the memory elaboration measure (number of core features reported). The resultant correlation of .23, although significant, was much weaker than the range of .77 to .89 reported by Brown and Kulik (1977). Winograd and Killinger (1983) thus concluded that "the case is not strong for attributing a causative role to overt rehearsal in determining the richness of early memories" (p. 418).

Such correlations are inadequate tests of the effects of rehearsal, however. Subjects' ratings of rehearsal may themselves be reconstructed or inaccurate. Even if they are accurate, the fact that the ratings do not correlate strongly with measures of unverifiable memories in no way proves that rehearsal is unrelated to changes that may have occurred to a memory report after the initial encoding. In addition, rehearsal takes many forms, only one of which involves talking about the event with others. Finally, the tendency to rehearse and the effects of rehearsal are known to vary with age; younger children rehearse less often and less efficiently.

The fact that Brown and Kulik (1977) and Winograd and Killinger (1983) assessed their subjects' memories for Kennedy's assassination only once many years after its occurrence renders it impossible for them to test the competing claims that these memories are permanent and unchanging or inconsistent and reconstructed. Only a study that reassesses memories at a later date, and therefore can measure consistency or change, can adequately address these major issues. Pillemer (1984) conducted just such a study concerning memories for the assassination attempt on President Reagan. He asked his subjects, all of whom were adults, to recollect their discovery of the news shortly after the event and then again 6 months later. He found that subjects were highly consistent in their reported memories over time, but second reports were often condensed relative to first reports. Although condensation could indicate forgetting, it may also reflect adoption of a narrative convention in which second reports to the same audience should be at least slightly different from first reports.

How would children compare to adults given repeated assessments? In January of 1986, the explosion of the Space Shuttle *Challenger* provided a tragic opportunity to answer this question. This disaster was thought to be particularly relevant to and therefore traumatic for children. The teacher Christa McAuliffe was among the crew on this mission, and many schools required students to study the mission in preparation for broadcasts of her lessons from space. Further, space travel is salient for many children, especially boys (Wright, Kunkel, Pinon & Huston, 1987). The accident occurred during school hours just before noon Eastern time and most students were informed of its occurrence during the school day. Some classes were even watching live television coverage of the shuttle launch; it is estimated that 25% of 5–8-year-olds, 48% of 9–13-year-olds, and 31% of 14–17-year-olds saw the *Challenger* launch at their school that day (Clymer, 1986). Others watched news of the accident in their classrooms or at home later that afternoon. A survey conducted for the National Science Foundation revealed that 57% of the population turned immediately to television for more news upon hearing of the disaster, and 95% had viewed some coverage by the end of the day (Miller, 1987). Finally, the accident was unexpected, as it was the nation's only space-related accident ever to occur in flight and its first fatal space accident since 1967 (Wright et al., 1987).

In January of 1986, the first author was teaching a cognitive psychology course and had assigned Neisser's (1982) *Memory Observed* as supplementary reading. Students had just completed the first few chapters, which coincidentally include an excerpt of Brown and Kulik's (1977) paper along with Neisser's commentary. Thus the stage was set for a class research project that became the basis for the present study. Being most interested in the effects of repeated assessments and the delay since the event on children's possible flashbulb accounts, we (quickly) designed an independent samples longitudinal study, utilizing an entire (and very cooperative) private school with kindergarten through eighth-grade classes. Within 2 weeks of the event, we had designed our procedures and questionnaires, and had obtained the reports of approximately half of the children from this school.

## Method

### Subjects and procedure

In February of 1986, 2 weeks following the *Challenger* explosion, 347 children in kindergarten through the eighth grade at a private school in Chattanooga, Tennessee were selected as subjects. Approximately half of the children were tested at both 2 weeks (Time 1) and 2 months (Time 2) after the event, the other half only at Time 2. This design was employed in order to examine the effects of delay and rehearsal (see Table 5.1). The subjects were first asked to report as much as they could remember about the first time they heard the news about the space shuttle explosion (free narrative report), then were given additional specific "prompting" questions relating to the canonical features found by Brown and Kulik (1977) in the reports of their adult subjects. These prompting questions included: "Where were you when you first heard about the space shuttle accident?" "What were you doing?" "How did you first find out about the space shuttle accident? Did someone tell you, or did you see it on TV or hear it on the radio?" and "How did you feel when you heard about it?" Children in kindergarten through the second grade were tested orally. Their responses were tape-recorded and later transcribed verbatim for scoring. All older children were tested in groups, and instructed to read the questions and answer in writing.

In January of 1988 (Time 3), just prior to the second anniversary of the

Table 5.1. *Number of subjects by age group and number of times tested*

|  |  | Three tests | Two tests |  |  | One test |  |
|---|---|---|---|---|---|---|---|
| Grade | n | 3 | 1&2[a] | 2&3[b] | 1&3[c] | 2 | 3 |
| KG[d] to 2nd | 152 | 37 | 12 | 42 | 1 | 12 | 48 |
| 3rd to 5th | 180 | 45 | 18 | 49 | 1 | 15 | 52 |
| 6th to 8th | 170 | 30 | 26 | 30 | 2 | 27 | 55 |
| Total = 502 |  | 112 | 56 | 121 | 4 | 54 | 155 |

*Note*: The first time of testing occurred 2 weeks after the shuttle accident; the second time of testing occurred two months after the shuttle accident; and the third time of testing occurred 2 years after the shuttle accident.
[a] Refers to testing at times 1 & 2.
[b] Refers to testing at times 2 & 3.
[c] Refers to testing at times 1 & 3.
[d] KG = Kindergarten

*Challenger* explosion, as many of the original participants as possible were located and assessed again. A new comparison sample of the same ages at similar private schools was also located and tested. This Time 3 assessment again included a free narrative report and the specific questions, but added a rating scale for emotional reaction to the *Challenger* event (from 1 – "I didn't really care," to 5 – "I was shocked and stunned").

The final sample thus consists of 502 children ranging in age from approximately 5 years (kindergartners at the original Time 1 assessment) to 15 years (tenth graders at the final time of testing), who were questioned regarding their memories for the circumstances in which they first discovered that the Space Shuttle *Challenger* had explored. Of these 502 subjects, 112 were questioned all three times, 181 were tested twice, and the remaining 209 were tested only once (see Table 5.1).

Not only are subjects divided into three "rehearsal" groups according to the number of times they were questioned, but they are also divided into three roughly equivalent age groups as follows. The Young group consists of 152 children who were in kindergarten through the second grade at the time of the *Challenger* accident. All were tested orally, and are considered to be in the primary grades. Within the Young group, 37 children were tested all three times, 12 were tested at Times 1 and 2, 42 were assessed at Times 2 and 3, and 1 child was tested only at Times 1 and 3. Sixty of the youngest children were tested only once, 12 at Time 2, and 48 at Time 3.

The Middle age group consists of 180 children who were in the third through fifth grades at the time of the event. Of these, 45 were assessed all three times. The 68 twice-tested children included 18 at Times 1 and 2, 49 at Times 2 and 3, and 1 at Times 1 and 3. Sixty-seven "middle" children were tested only once; for 15 of these the assessment occurred at Time 2; for the remaining 52, it occurred at Time 3.

The Old age group consists of 170 children who were enrolled in the sixth through eighth grades in January of 1986. This group consists of 30 children tested all three times, 26 twice-tested at Times 1 and 2, 30 more assessed at Times 2 and 3, and 2 children seen only at Times 1 and 3. Eighty-two children in this older group were assessed only once, 27 of these at Time 2, and 55 at Time 3.

### Scoring

The free narrative reports in response to "Please tell me everything you can remember about when you first heard about the space shuttle exploding" were scored for elaboration/length by counting the total number of words in the reports (excluding conversational placeholders such as "well" or "um" in the orally given reports). The narratives were also scored according to Brown and Kulik's (1977) guidelines in order to determine the extent to which children report the canonical features observed in adult narratives. The six canonical features were: informant (source of the *Challenger* news), location, activity, affective reaction, others' reactions, and aftermath. One point was given for each of the six core items mentioned in a free narrative. During the scoring process, we noticed that many narratives were worded in such a manner that the presence of one feature implied the presence of another, though it might not be explicitly stated. For example, if a child reported, "I was watching TV at home when the program was interrupted and I heard the news," we felt safe in assuming that the informant was television (implied by the activity). Also, if a child stated, "I was in the cafeteria," we assumed the child was also eating lunch, so we credited that subject with reporting location and activity. Although this might appear too lenient, from all the other information we have about the activities at the school that day from the other child subjects and teachers, it seems clear that the only activity that occurred in the cafeteria was lunch. In contrast, if a child reported, "I was watching TV," we could not assume that he or she was either at home or at school, or if the child said, "I was in class," we could not assume his or her activity. Once we had established the number of canonical features present in a narrative report, we converted the scores to percentages by dividing each by 6, the total possible score. Following Brown and Kulik's (1977) example, this measure is termed "content elaboration."

The answers to all questions for the subjects who were tested at least twice were then examined for consistency over time. In our first measure of consistency, labeled "gist consistency," if the fundamental content of the narrative report was the same at both times being compared, the report was said to be consistent, regardless of whether the second report contained additional or fewer canonical features. For example, if at Time 1 a subject reported being at home watching TV with his mother when he heard the news, then at Time 2 said only that he had been at home watching TV, we scored the reports as consistent. Moreover, to receive a point for consistency, the subject had to have provided an answer at both times (in other words, lack of response at both times was not scored as consistent). If, for example, a child stated at Time 1 that she was at home, then reported nothing at Time 2, she was categorized as "unscorable" for consistency. Finally, a child who reported any contradictory information (even a single discrepant feature) across times of assessment was scored as inconsistent. For example, if at Time 2 a child claimed to be at school in the cafeteria when his teacher announced the news, then at Time 3 reported being in the classroom after lunch, we scored his reports as inconsistent.

Another measure of consistency was termed "feature type consistency." For example, a child who reported her location and activity at Time 1, then her informant and emotional reaction at Time 2 would be consistent in the amount of information reported, even though the two features she reported were completely different on the two occasions. To examine feature type consistency, we developed three separate feature consistency scores for every two times of assessment being compared. The first is "features added," meaning the number of features reported at a later time of testing that were not reported at the earlier time. Because children who reported many or all of the six features at an earlier time simply could not add many (or any) at the later time, this score was converted to a percentage, taking the actual number added divided by the number it was possible to add (6 minus the number reported at the earlier time). The second feature consistency score was "features deleted," defined as the number of features reported at an earlier time that were not reported subsequently (divided by the number it was possible to delete – or the total number reported at the prior testing). Finally, we examined the number of "features retained" over time, which again was divided by the number of features that had been reported at the prior testing. To facilitate comprehension of this consistency scoring system, consider the following sample reports compared at Times 2 and 3.

> Time 2: I was sitting in class doing my math when the teacher told us. (Features reported: location, activity, informant.)
>
> Time 3: The teacher told us and nobody could believe it. I was really sad. (Features reported: informant, others' affect, own affect.)

In comparing the above reports, this subject would receive a score of 1 for features retained (informant was common to both reports), divided by 3 for features reported at the earlier assessment (or .33). She would receive a score of 2 for features deleted (having failed to report location or activity at Time 3 after reporting them at Time 2), again divided by 3 (the number it was possible to delete), or .67. She would also be credited with adding 2 features (her own and others' affect), which would be divided by 3 (the maximum that she could possibly have added to her Time 2 report), or .67, for features added.

For all the previously described measures, intercoder reliability was determined by independent scoring of 10% of the subjects' reports. Intercoder agreement was calculated to be 90%, which closely matches the reliability of 90% reported by Brown and Kulik (1977) and of 89% reported by Winograd and Killinger (1983). With satisfactory reliability achieved, all responses were scored subsequently by one coder (the second author) to further insure reasonable consistency across subjects.

## Results

In examining our results, it should be kept in mind that the number of subjects included in any particular analysis varied greatly depending on the time(s) of testing and dependent variable(s) under consideration. We have tried to ease the reader's task by confining our references to sample size and other details (e.g., standard deviations) to tables rather than text. In the interest of space, we have omitted actual significance levels ($p$ is less than .05 for all effects reported as significant) and the numerical outcomes of statistical tests (such as $F$ values), but these are available upon request. Further, where possible, we have limited our discussion to representative rather than exhaustive analyses.

### Report elaboration and age

Our preliminary analyses were aimed at comparing our results to those of Brown and Kulik (1977), and thus we used measures based on, or identical to, their measures of the free narrative reports of subjects in response to "Please tell me everything you can remember about the first time you heard about the space shuttle exploding." The first measure is termed "content elaboration," defined previously as the percent of canonical features of the six possible reported in the narrative, and the second is "length elaboration," the number of words in the narrative.

First, we examined these measures by age group in separate analyses of variance for each time of testing. In these separate analyses, all children who had been assessed at that particular time of testing were included, regardless of how many other times they had been or would be assessed. At each time of testing, the age effect was significant with older children scoring significantly higher on content elaboration than either of the younger two groups (who did not significantly differ from each other at Time 1 or 2). The same pattern was observed for report length elaboration with significant effects of age at each

Table 5.2. *Content elaboration and report length over time by age groups*

| Grade | Time 1 | | Time 2 | | Time 3 | |
|---|---|---|---|---|---|---|
| | Content[a] | Length[b] | Content | Length | Content | Length |
| KG to 2nd (n = 37) | | | | | | |
| M | .42 | 49.8 | .37 | 27.7 | .23 | 21.5 |
| SD | .19 | 54.7 | .15 | 22.2 | .23 | 22.4 |
| 3rd to 5th (n = 44) | | | | | | |
| M | .40 | 34.5 | .36 | 25.0 | .30 | 23.4 |
| SD | .19 | 22.6 | .13 | 16.4 | .20 | 14.9 |
| 6th to 8th (n = 30) | | | | | | |
| M | .67 | 75.5 | .53 | 46.3 | .54 | 39.4 |
| SD | .18 | 48.3 | .21 | 20.8 | .22 | 22.2 |

*Note*: Only data from subjects tested at all three times are included.
[a] Content is the proportion of Brown and Kulik canonical features out of six possible reported in the recall narrative.
[b] Length is the number of words in the recall narrative.

time of testing, and older children having significantly longer reports than the two younger groups, who did not differ from each other except at Time 3.

Next, content elaboration was examined in a repeated measures analysis using only subjects tested all three times. There were significant age and time effects, and a time-by-age trend. Essentially, all age groups reported fewer canonical features over time, but this tendency was somewhat greater early on in the oldest group (who had the most to forget). Moreover, although the oldest children tended to level off in their content elaboration at Time 2, the younger children's scores continued to decline at Time 3. These data are displayed in Table 5.2. A repeated measures analysis of variance for length elaboration across all three times of testing revealed significant main effects of age and time, and a significant interaction of the two. The oldest children's average reports showed the most precipitous drop in length from Times 1 to 3, followed by the youngest group and lastly the Middle age group. In general, older children had more elaborate reports in terms of both content and length, as earlier reports were more elaborate than later reports, and older children's scores declined the most over time.

As may be seen from these results, length elaboration and content elaboration are related but not perfectly. Although more words are required to report more features, some lengthy reports contain largely irrelevant or redundant information and thus do not necessarily possess more features than other, shorter reports. Pearson correlation coefficients were computed between length and content elaboration scores at each time of testing. All the correlations were significant, ranging from .53 to .60. Considering the fact that older children score higher on both measures, the contribution of age to the relation of these two variables must be removed for a more accurate picture. When age was controlled, the correlations were slightly reduced (ranging from .48 to .54), but all were still significant. It should also be noted that these correlations are moderate in comparison to the .79 to .93 range reported by Brown and Kulik (1977) for their adult subjects.

### Report elaboration and emotion

Before discussing the possible effects of emotional reaction on report elaboration, we must first consider that emotion was rated only at Time 3, 2 years after the event, and that observed age differences in emotional reaction may be partially attributed to age differences in understanding the emotion rating scale. When emotion rating was examined as a dependent variable using age as the grouping variable in a one-way analysis of variance on all children with Time 3 assessments, we found that older children had significantly *lower* emotion ratings (averaging 3.8 on the 5-point scale, as compared to the Middle age group's 4.1 average and the mean of 4.3 for the youngest children). This effect was only exaggerated when the analysis was limited to the children tested more than once. In this analysis, the average emotion ratings for the oldest, middle, and youngest children were, respectively, 3.8, 4.0, and 4.5. Thus, the results of our analyses of emotion effects on elaboration, or other measures, especially those taken from Time 1 or 2 assessments (prior to the Time 3 administration of the emotion rating scale) should be interpreted with extreme caution.

In subsequent analyses of emotion effects, we grouped children both by age, as previously described, and by emotion. The emotion groups were formed after examining observed frequencies for each point along the 5-point emotion rating scale (with 5 representing "I was shocked" and 1 "I didn't care"). Fairly equal groups could be formed within each age group if those who rated themselves as "shocked" were separated from all others (i.e., subjects rating themselves as 1 through 4 in emotional reaction were pooled into a "low" emotion group).

Using content elaboration as the dependent measure and age and emotion as grouping measures, a repeated measures analysis of variance was performed on the data from Times 1, 2, and 3. No significant main effect of emotion on content elaboration was observed at any time of testing, nor were there any significant interactions of emotion with age. However, when report length was the dependent measure, significant effects of emotion and interactions of emotion with age and time of testing were found. In a repeated measures analysis of variance across all three times of testing, the emotion main effect was significant, as were the age and time of testing main effects. There were also significant two-way interactions between age and emotion, time and age, and time and emotion, yet the three-way interaction of time,

Table 5.3. *Emotion effects on report length over time by age*

| Grade | n | Time 1 | | Time 2 | | Time 3 | |
|---|---|---|---|---|---|---|---|
| | | Low | High | Low | High | Low | High |
| *KG to 2nd* | | | | | | | |
| M | 29[a] | 35.4 | 49.6 | 26.2 | 30.8 | 23.8 | 24.5 |
| SD | | 45.5 | 51.5 | 18.2 | 25.5 | 14.7 | 29.8 |
| *3rd to 5th* | | | | | | | |
| M | 44[b] | 33.2 | 36.3 | 27.5 | 21.7 | 23.7 | 22.9 |
| SD | | 20.5 | 25.5 | 17.4 | 14.8 | 15.3 | 14.7 |
| *6th to 8th* | | | | | | | |
| M | 29[c] | 61.7 | 119.0 | 41.0 | 62.7 | 36.0 | 50.0 |
| SD | | 28.1 | 72.3 | 19.3 | 17.0 | 19.9 | 27.2 |

*Note*: Only data from subjects tested at all three times are included. Emotion was rated at the third time of testing only.
[a] Low emotion ($n = 12$); High emotion ($n = 17$).
[b] Low emotion ($n = 25$); High emotion ($n = 19$).
[c] Low emotion ($n = 22$); High emotion ($n = 7$).

age, and emotion was not significant. In general, the interactions may be interpreted as follows: The role of emotion is strongest in the oldest children (higher emotion is related to longer reports), and at the earlier times of testing (the effect is most pronounced at Time 1). Examining each time of testing separately, starting with Time 3 (when emotion was actually rated), we find that in the Old age group, children with higher self-rated emotion had longer narratives, whereas there were no differences in the Middle or the Young age groups. The Time 2 analysis revealed an interesting pattern of emotion effects across age groups, in that the oldest and youngest children exhibited the expected longer reports with higher emotion, whereas the opposite held true for the Middle age group. Finally, at Time 1, the effect of emotion was most pronounced, with all three age groups demonstrating the predicted effect. The effect was most striking in the Old group, followed by the Young group, and the Middle age group. These results are illustrated in Table 5.3.

### Report elaboration and repeated testing

In the next set of analyses, children who had been repeatedly tested were compared to those who had been tested less often or only a single time. These comparisons enabled us to examine the effects of prior testing on subsequent reports. Looking first at content elaboration at Time 2, we conducted an analysis of variance that compared those children who had been tested earlier at Time 1 with those who had not. Significant main effects of age and

Table 5.4. *Effects of repeated testing on proportions of content elaboration and report length (in words) over time by age groups*

| Grade | | Time 2 | | Time 3 | |
|---|---|---|---|---|---|
| | | Content | Length | Content | Length |
| *KG to 2nd* | | | | | |
| all 3 | M | .38[a] | 30.1 | .24 | 21.5 |
| 2 & 3 | M | .34[b] | 21.4 | .24 | 19.7 |
| 3 only | M | | | .20 | 18.2 |
| *3rd to 5th* | | | | | |
| all 3 | M | .35 | 24.1 | .30 | 23.4 |
| 2 & 3 | M | .36 | 27.0 | .28 | 26.2 |
| 3 only | M | | | .39 | 30.8 |
| *6th to 8th* | | | | | |
| all 3 | M | .53 | 45.4 | .54 | 39.4 |
| 2 & 3 | M | .44 | 38.9 | .40 | 28.4 |
| 3 only | M | | | .47 | 35.6 |

[a] At Time 2, the "all 3" group also contains subjects tested at Times 1 & 2 only.
[b] At Time 2, the "2 & 3" group also contains subjects tested at time 2 only.

testing were observed, as well as a trend toward an interaction of the two. Retesting seemed to enhance the reporting of canonical features, at least for the oldest and youngest children (see Table 5.4). In a similar analysis of length elaboration at Time 2, a significant main effect of age and trends for a retesting effect and an interaction of age and testing were revealed. The youngest and oldest children who were retested had longer reports at Time 2 than those whose first report occurred at Time 2, but no difference was found in the Middle age group (see Table 5.4).

At Time 3, there were three testing groups: those tested twice before (at Times 1, 2, and 3), those tested once before (at Times 2 and 3), and those never before tested (Time 3 only). Using retesting and age as grouping variables and Time 3 content elaboration as the dependent measure, a significant main effect of age and an interaction of age and retesting were found. The results are displayed in Table 5.4. Essentially, retesting (but only at Times 1 and 2, not just Time 2) led to better performance at Time 3 only for the oldest children. For the Middle age group, the once-tested children actually had higher scores than those who had been retested, and no differences among testing groups were found for the youngest children. A similar analysis conducted on length elaboration scores at Time 3 essentially mirrored these effects, although the interaction was weaker and only the age effect was significant. Again, as Table 5.4 illustrates, the oldest children appeared to benefit from the testing at Time 1, whereas the youngest children exhibited no testing effects and the Middle age group displayed opposite tendencies (with less frequent testing producing the longest reports).

*Age and consistency over time*

The earlier defined measures of consistency were examined for possible relations to age at the time of the event. The first such consistency measure was gist consistency, or the tendency for a child to retell essentially the same event discovery story over time. Narrative pairs were coded as either consistent, inconsistent, or unscorable, which occurred when a child did not have a narrative at one of the times of testing under scrutiny. Chi-square analyses were conducted on these categorical data, with age and consistency codes as the factors. Comparison of Time 1 and 2 reports showed significant age differences, with fewer of the oldest children categorized as inconsistent (5%) than either the Middle or Young age groups (16% and 21% respectively), whereas more older children were unscorable compared to their younger counterparts (29%, 18%, and 6% for old to young). However, there were no major age differences for consistency (oldest = 66%, middle = 67%, youngest = 73%). Overall, almost 70% of the children were consistent over this 6-week period, and the remainder were equally split into the inconsistent and unscorable categories (see Table 5.5). Moreover, when unscorable reports were excluded, 83% of the scorable reports were consistent over this time period (68% consistent/82% scorable as consistent or inconsistent).

Comparison of the gist consistency of reports from Time 2 to Time 3 revealed no significant age effects. Overall, only 30% of the children were clearly consistent in their reports, whereas 15% were inconsistent and the remainder (55%) were neither. However, it should be noted that 67% of all the scorable reports were consistent (30% consistent/45% scorable). For Time 1 and 3 comparisons, the overall pattern was similar, with no age effects and 36% consistency, 15% inconsistency, and 49% neither (see Table 5.5). Seventy-one percent of the scorable reports were consistent between Times 1 and 3.

To detect patterns across time in the percentages of children who were placed in these three categories, regardless of age, a Chi-square analysis was conducted with the times being compared (1 to 2, 2 to 3, and 1 to 3) and the consistency categories as grouping factors. In general, consistency decreased, unscorability increased, and inconsistency remained constant as the interval between the time of reports being compared increased. These results are displayed in Table 5.5.

*Age and changes over time in canonical features reported*

As mentioned previously, the quantitative measures of children's narratives do not always reflect the kinds of canonical features they report. Conceivably, a child can obtain the same content elaboration score at all three times of testing, yet no two reports when compared would contain the same

Table 5.5. *Consistency of report gist across paired times of testing*

| | Time | | |
|---|---|---|---|
| Consistency | 1 to 2 | 2 to 3 | 1 to 3 |
| Unscorable[a] | 18% | 55% | 49% |
| Inconsistent | 18% | 15% | 15% |
| Consistent | 68% | 30% | 36% |

*Note:* $X^2 = 38.1$, $p < .001$.
[a] Subjects that were rated as "unscorable" either did not answer or answered "I don't remember" for at least one time of testing.

combination of canonical features. Therefore, we examined every child's reports and compared them with regard to how specific features were retained, deleted, or added over time. Repeated measures analyses of variance were conducted separately for these three dependent measures (deletions, retentions, and additions). Recall that deletions and retentions are divided by the number of features reported at the earliest time of testing examined (e.g., Time 2 for a Time 2 to 3 comparison), whereas additions are divided by the number of possible reported features (6) subtracting the number actually reported at the earlier time. These proportions were computed in order to make age groups more comparable, as older children tended to report more features to begin with, and thus could add less, delete more, and retain more over time.

The repeated measures analysis of deletions revealed significant age and time effects, as well as a time-by-age interaction. Essentially, the interaction indicates that all children delete features at equal rates early on (averaging around .23 between Times 1 and 2), but younger children delete more features over the longer time intervals (averaging .5 features deleted between Times 2 and 3 or 1 and 3 as compared to the older children's average of .32). Further, if we examine deletions in terms of the number of children who engage in the process (who delete at least one feature), rather than the number of features deleted on average, we find time differences but no age differences. Between Times 1 and 2, approximately 50% of the children deleted at least one feature. This figure increases to 60% when comparing Times 2 and 3, and 70% for Times 1 and 3.

Analysis of the number of features retained over time by repeated measures analysis of variance revealed significant age and time main effects and a time-by-age interaction. Almost three-quarters (.73) of the features possible to be retained were retained by all age groups between Times 1 and 2 (and over 90% of all the children did retain at least one feature from Time 1 in their Time 2 narratives). Between Times 2 and 3 and Times 1 and 3, however, the younger two groups of children retained significantly fewer features (averaging approximately .39) than did the older children (still averaging around .66). The number of younger children retaining at least one feature between times also fell off dramatically to approximately 50% between Times 2 and 3.

Finally, the repeated measures analysis of additions revealed significant age and time effects, but only a trend toward their interaction. Older children added more features than younger children, and more features were added later (between Times 2 and 3 or Times 1 and 3) than earlier (Time 1 to 2). Further, whereas approximately 25% to 30% of all children added at least one feature between Times 1 and 2, over 80% of the older children added features between Times 2 and 3 and Times 1 and 3, compared to figures of 34% and 61% for the Middle age group, and 58% and 67% for the youngest children over those same time intervals.

### Emotion and consistency over time

To examine the relationship between emotion and consistency, we again performed analyses in which subjects were categorized as having either high (self-rated as shocked, or a 5) or low (any lower rating) emotional reaction to their discovery of the space shuttle accident. Recall that emotion was rated at Time 3 only. When we conducted a Chi-square analysis using this emotion rating and gist consistency between Times 1 and 2, we observed a weak effect. Of those reports classified as inconsistent, 69% came from low emotion children. Incomparable or unscorable reports also were more likely to be produced by low emotion children (79%), but consistent reports were provided equally often by the high and low emotion groups (51% and 49%). Similar analyses based on gist consistency between Times 2 and 3 or 1 and 3 revealed no effects.

When examining specific features reported in the narratives over time, there was a relation to emotion. Although there was no emotion effect in the analysis of Time 1 to 2 or Time 2 to 3 features deleted, a significant effect was found for Times 1 and 3. The higher emotion children tended to delete more features from their reports than the lower emotion children (.56 vs. .36, Time 1 to 3). The tendency to report the same features over time was only weakly related to emotion. Trends were observed for both Times 2 and 3 and Times 1 and 3 comparisons, but there simply was no effect for Times 1 and 2. The trend resulted from lower emotion children keeping more features constant in their reports over time. Analyses of features added over time also revealed trends for all three time–pair comparisons, in which lower emotion children tended to add more features than did high emotion children (approximately .20 vs. .10, respectively).

## Repeated testing and consistency over time

The effects of overt rehearsal (retesting) on consistency were also examined. First, gist consistency from Time 2 to Time 3 was compared for those children tested all three times (in this case, having one additional testing) versus those only tested at Times 2 and 3. A Chi-square analysis revealed no effects. Additional testing did not decrease inconsistency (16% in those thrice tested vs. 13% in twice tested), and produced only slightly greater consistency (35% vs. 25%) and less unscorability (49% vs. 62%). Moreover, this type of rehearsal did not remarkably affect children's tendencies to delete, add, or report the same specific canonical features over time.

# Discussion

## Memory and age at encoding

We found significant relations with age for almost every measure over the entire age range we studied (approximately 5 to 13 years). Our older subjects not only provided more elaborate reports containing more canonical features, but their reports changed over time in ways that differed from younger subjects. Older children tended to retain more features from their original reports in their subsequent reports, and to add more features to their later reports.

In attempting to account for the apparent discrepancies between our findings and those of Brown and Kulik, we must note three major discrepancies in the studies themselves. First, the "flashbulb provoking" events were different. Perhaps the assassination of a president is more unexpected or emotional than an explosion involving a space mission, or perhaps children of various ages have more equivalent comprehension of presidents and shootings than of space exploration (a possibility we discuss further in the following section). Second, the delay following the event before testing occurred was different. In our study, the retention interval ranged from 2 weeks to 2 years, whereas the interval for Brown and Kulik's study was almost 15 years. Third, our subjects were children at all times of testing, whereas Brown and Kulik's were all adults at the only time of assessment. It is possible that our subjects' memories for this event will grow more similar over time, such that by the year 2000, when all of our subjects are technically adults, their narratives will be virtually indistinguishable from one another. Of course, whether the changes that occur in their narratives render them more or less complete and more or less accurate remains to be seen.

*Memory, age, and knowledge at encoding*

Although many possible explanations exist for developmental differences in autobiographical memories, we will limit our focus in the present discussion to the mechanisms of most concern in the adult flashbulb literature, namely, emotional reaction and rehearsal. Before considering either of these factors separately, however, we must first examine the potentially interactive or mediating role of children's age and knowledge base for historical events in general and this event in particular. We alluded earlier to the idea that children of differing ages might have differential understanding of potential flashbulb provoking events. Such differential understanding might result in differential levels of emotional reaction, rehearsal, or both.

Two recent studies lend support to the contention that school-aged children have differing levels of knowledge of space exploration and the space shuttle explosion. First, Monaco and Gaier (1987) assessed the responses of children aged 5 to 15 to presentations made the day following the space shuttle explosion. Teachers spoke with their classes for approximately 20 minutes about where the shuttle was launched, some background information about the crew including teacher Christa McAuliffe's role in the mission, and what was currently known about the cause of the explosion. Following these presentations, children were encouraged to ask questions and discuss the event, and these discussions were audiotaped. Monaco and Gaier (1987) examined the children's comments for reflections of Piagetian levels (i.e., pre-operational, concrete, and formal). They found that younger children were more likely to attribute animistic causes and features to the shuttle's explosion, despite what their teachers had told them (e.g., "The rocket died" and "Somebody shoudda moved the clouds," p. 94). Even more telling, the younger children frequently appeared unable to clearly distinguish this event from fantasy, referring to other explosions on He-Man, Shera, and Gobot cartoons, and failing to appreciate the event's (and death's) permanence and significance (e.g., "Does this mean we don't get the space lessons?" p. 88). The oldest children, on the other hand, not only demonstrated greater understanding of the shuttle explosion through their discussions, but they also frequently mentioned other tragedies such as assassinations, perhaps indicating the basis for a general tragic event script. For example, one 14- or 15-year-old stated, "This reminds me of when the president was shot and the whole country was shocked" (Monaco & Gaier, 1987, p. 95).

In the second related study, Wright, Kunkel, Pinon, and Huston (1987) interviewed children in the fourth through sixth grades on the sixth day following the *Challenger* explosion. The older children reported that they had watched more television concerning space prior to the event, and had greater predisaster space program knowledge. Overall, knowledge about the shuttle program was positively related to the perceived distinctiveness between "space reality and space fantasy" (although none of the children expressed any major doubts that the explosion was real). Of course, with a wider age range, such as that of our own study, we speculate that greater differences would exist in the ability to distinguish fantasy from reality. Some anecdotal evidence along these lines is found in the previous discussion of Monaco and Gaier's (1987) study, and from our study as well. One of our kindergarten subjects reported that he had been playing outside and looked up in the air and saw the explosion, and another reported that his father had been on the shuttle. Finally, Wright et al. (1987) found that almost all children continued to seek more information following their discoveries of the disaster, and that final knowledge of the *Challenger* mission was high for all age groups.

Neither the Wright et al. study nor our study directly assessed the relation between prior knowledge of the space program or the *Challenger* mission and subsequent memory, either factual or autobiographical, for the *Challenger* event. Nonetheless, much previous developmental research has clearly documented a positive relation between domain specific knowledge and memory (e.g., Chi, 1978, 1982; Chi & Koeske, 1983). Thus, we feel safe in saying that differential knowledge of the space program in general or the *Challenger* mission resulted in differential memory for the event. However, we are hesitant at this point to speculate further on the nature of the kinds of memory differences that may have resulted from knowledge differences. Although logically it would seem that a greater quantity of prior knowledge would yield a greater quantity of details in subsequent memory reports, differential prior knowledge might also affect the qualitative aspects of subsequent reports such as their organization without significantly changing their quantitative features.

### Memory and emotion

Age and differential knowledge of the space program or the shuttle accident may not only affect memory of the shuttle accident directly but indirectly as well, by mediating emotional reaction to the *Challenger* disaster. Contrary to our initial expectations and Winograd and Killinger's (1983) speculations, older (and more knowledgeable) children actually had lower self-rated affect, both in our study and that of Wright et al. (1987). In fact, in the Wright et al. study, younger children (fourth- and fifth-graders) not only reported greater negative affect but also reported greater physical and behavioral effects (e.g., cried once or more, had trouble sleeping) than the older, sixth-grade subjects. Younger children indicated more personal involvement in the tragedy (e.g., feeling sad for the teacher's family), whereas older children indicated more impersonal regret (feeling sorry that the shuttle program was now in trouble). There were also sex differences in the Wright et al. study that were consistent with the age differences found. Boys demonstrated greater space shuttle knowledge and more frequent space TV viewing prior to the accident than girls, yet less negative affect or emotional upset than girls. Girls were more similar to younger children in having less prior knowledge but greater personal involvement in the tragedy.

The results of Wright et al.'s study suggest that our own findings of age differences in ratings of emotional reaction to the *Challenger* event reflect true differences in emotional reaction rather than simply artifacts of the rating scale. It is interesting to note that Wright et al. made their measurements of emotion only 6 days following the disaster, yet their findings parallel ours from 2 years following the event. Also, Wright et al. found age differences similar to ours even within a restricted age range.

Older children might appear to be *more* emotionally affected than younger children if one examines only their verbal narratives rather than numerical ratings. This possibly deceiving appearance may be due to older children's greater facility with spoken and written language, and to more extensive vocabularies of emotional terms. Monaco and Gaier (1987) suggested that younger (pre-operational) children typically have a limited range of vocabulary in which words such as happy or sad are used to express a broad range of emotions. Their results reflected this narrow range of expressed emotions, in that their younger subjects were likely to say that they were "sad" after the event, and expressed intensity by adding "very," sometimes repeatedly, rather than by using another adjective. Along those same lines, our younger subjects almost without exception responded with either "bad" or "sad" to the question "How did you feel (when you first found out about the space shuttle accident?), whereas terms such as "shocked" did not emerge until around the fifth grade.

We had also speculated previously that because children of all ages looked to adults for their reactions (social referencing), and because most adults expressed similar emotional reactions, age differences in emotion might be small. It is possible, however, that the same adult's emotional reaction would be interpreted differently by children of different ages. Perhaps younger children would be more surprised by the sight of an adult crying than older children, for example. Certainly, others' reactions seemed to play a role in children's emotional reactions to the event. In the Wright et al. (1987) study, most children used others' emotional reactions both on and off television as a cue that the event was real rather than fictional. Children mentioned adults' and specifically newscasters' uncharacteristic emotional displays. In the Monaco and Gaier (1987) study, one of the youngest (5–6-year-old) children stated, "Even my Dad said it was sad" (p. 94), one 9–10-year-old stated, "Even the Russians felt bad," and one of the 14–15-year-olds said, "The children watching must have been shocked" (p. 95). In our own study many children mentioned others' reactions, which is not surprising given that Brown and Kulik (1977) included "others' affect" as a core feature because so many of their adult subjects mentioned it. However, a quick review of our data indicated that younger children were more likely to mention their teachers' or parents' reactions whereas older children more often reported peers' reactions. Older children also appeared more likely to report their original source of the *Challenger* news as a peer rather than an adult, and tended to report that they thought their peer-informants were joking with them. Thus, younger children may have had greater emotional reaction due to the greater likelihood that their original source of the news was a believable, emotional adult.

What, then, are we to make of the relations in our data between emotion and memory? First, unlike adults (e.g., Bohannon, 1988, this volume), emotion did not significantly increase children's reports of canonical features. In other words, children who reacted more strongly to the event did not receive higher flashbulb memory scores than those with weaker reactions. However, emotion did play a significant role in the narrative's length, particularly at the earliest time of assessment. High emotion children of all ages responded with significantly more words to the request "Tell me everything you remember about the first time you heard about the space shuttle explosion" at Time 1. Two years later, this was true only for the oldest children. Emotional reaction was also related to the changes over time in children's reports. Slightly fewer high than low emotion children had clearly inconsistent reports, and low emotion children appeared to be adding more canonical features into their narratives over time (reconstructing?), whereas high emotion children were deleting more features (forgetting?). These latter results thus lend some support to an affect-based theory of flashbulb memories.

*Memory and rehearsal*

With regard to the hypothesis that greater rehearsal leads to more elaborate but possibly inaccurate memories, we are again compelled to point out that prior knowledge of the shuttle program, of disasters in general, and age level may all interact with rehearsal to produce changes in reports of memories for the *Challenger* accident. Given that flashbulb producing events are rare by definition, few of the children are likely to have had any direct experiences with such surprising, nationally significant, tragic events (with the possible exception of the assassination attempt on President Reagan). However, we expected that older children would have better developed scripts for this event, and thus we hypothesized that older, and/or more knowledgeable children would rehearse or reconsider the event more frequently.

For reasons delineated below, we did not report these data earlier, but we in fact (in the Time 2 and 3 surveys) asked children to rate, on a scale of 1 to 100, how many times they had both talked about the event to others, and seen or heard about the event. In all cases, older children had higher average ratings. However, just as we had some misgivings about the affect rating scale, we were reluctant to interpret age differences in rehearsal ratings as reflections of true difference in amount of rehearsal, given younger and older children's differential understanding of number. We ultimately decided therefore to focus on our one objective measure of rehearsal, which is the number of times the children recounted their stories to us (the number of times they were tested). Although retesting and rehearsal are traditionally considered to be separate, when it comes to autobiographical memory their distinction becomes blurred. For the purposes of the present study, the times of testing were regarded as opportunities for rehearsal, because there could be neither any feedback on the accuracy of the report, nor any "further study" of the event.

The rehearsal or schema position adopted by Neisser (1982) and Reed (1979) led us to expect that those children who were tested more frequently might have more elaborate accounts over time, but that those accounts might be inaccurate or inconsistent. However, there were also compelling reasons for us to adopt the opposite stance, namely, that such rehearsal might increase accuracy and consistency. For example, Howe, Brainerd, and their colleagues (e.g., Brainerd, Reyna, Howe, & Kingma, 1990; Howe & Brainerd, 1989; Howe, Kelland, Bryant-Brown, & Clark, in press) have found that subjects repeatedly asked to recall word lists show enhanced recall compared to those assessed fewer times, despite equal opportunities for study. Brainerd and Ornstein (1991) state that repeated questioning following an event or "repeated testing after a lengthy forgetting interval may have positive effects on the recovery of information" (p. 15). Further, Fivush and Hamond (1989) presented 2-year-olds with novel events in the laboratory, then assessed their recall through reenactment of the events either 2 weeks or 3 months later, or at both times. Children who were repeatedly tested recalled more information than those once tested. The children were also very consistent in the type of information they accurately recalled over time, but the youngest, repeatedly tested children also made the most errors. Fivush and Hamond (1989) concluded that reexperiencing an event after a relatively brief time interval "seems to guard against forgetting over longer time intervals" (p. 272).

Thus we came to the examination of our results with two possibly contradictory views of the potential effects of rehearsal or reconsideration. Keeping in mind Reed's (1979) caution that the longer the series of recollections the more inaccurate the memories would become, and Fivush and Hamond's (1989) findings that repeated reenactments increased both children's accurate and, to a lesser extent, inaccurate recall, we predicted that children tested more frequently would have longer narratives containing more canonical features, but that they would also tend to be more inconsistent and to add more (perhaps false) features over time. Repeated assessment did, in fact, enhance children's tendencies to report canonical features and to provide longer narratives. This was particularly true at the second time of testing and for the oldest children. However, the interaction with age was in the opposite direction from that we had predicted. Considering that youngest children should be least knowledgeable about, and have less well-developed scripts for the event, we thought they would benefit most from retesting, but the reverse was true. Retesting played only a minor role in the consistency of children's reports over time. Although it appeared that additional rehearsal produced slightly greater consistency in the "gist" of the reports (from 2 months to 2 years), it did not produce any greater consistency in the types of canonical features reported over time. Taken together, these results suggest that repeated assessments do produce more information (longer narratives containing more canonical features), but contribute little to the accuracy of that information.

### Accuracy

Given that one of the major differences between the rehearsal and emotion explanations for flashbulb memories revolves around accuracy, it is unfortunate that these memories are not objectively verifiable by experimenters. Like other researchers facing this dilemma, we found it necessary to use consistency as a barometer of accuracy. Only 15% of the children in our study were clearly inconsistent over time in their reports of how they had discovered the news of the shuttle accident. Although the reports of many children could not be compared over time (i.e., they reported nothing at one or both times), of those children who provided scorable reports more than 80% were consistent over the 6-week interval, and 70% were consistent over the entire 2-year period studied. It is unclear whether this high, yet imperfect, level of consistency sufficiently meets the standards for permanent and unchanging memories required to support the "Now-Print!" hypothesis. However, these figures are comparable to those obtained from adult samples by Pillemer (1984) and Bohannon (this volume). Further, older children were no more consistent than younger children over the 2-year span. If consistency can be construed as accuracy, then we may conclude that younger children simply recalled less than, but were as accurate as, adults or older children. This conclusion is in keeping with the results of most studies on children's event and eyewitness memory, in which children typically provide impoverished but generally accurate free recall accounts (see Cole & Loftus, 1987, for a review).

*Conclusions*

Although experimental and statistical manipulations may eventually allow us to estimate separately the influences of emotion, rehearsal, and other factors on memories for the *Challenger* accident and similar events, we have become convinced over the course of this study that they are in fact naturally inseparable. It is apparent throughout this volume that neither the colorful "Now-Print!" hypothesis nor its more modest rehearsal competitor can alone adequately explain the occurrence or nonoccurrence of vivid and lasting memories for the *Challenger* event. Their failure is even more evident when attempting to account for age differences in these memories. Rather than continuing to argue the predominance of one factor over the other in producing consistency or change in memories over time, a more fruitful approach might be to combine these and other factors into interactive models that may be tested for their adequacy in accounting for various memory measures. We need not wait, however, for another national disaster to occur in order to develop such models. There are many naturally occurring, emotional, socially shared events that should give us insight into interactions of the myriad of factors that do and do not produce lasting and vivid memories. Moreover, many of these events will be experienced by adults and children differently, thus allowing us to explore further the ways in which such memories originally develop and then evolve over time.

## NOTE

Portions of this chapter were presented originally at the Conference on Human Development, Charleston, SC, April 1988 and the Southeastern Psychological Association Convention, New Orleans, March 1988. The authors gratefully acknowledge the assistance of the following students: Clara Bradley, Rick Curvin, Ivy Hinton, Charles Johnson, Therese Porter, Melissa Ross, and Michael Springfield.

## REFERENCES

Bohannon, J. N. III. (1988). Flashbulb memories for the space shuttle disaster: A tale of two theories. *Cognition, 29*, 179–196.

Brainerd, C. J., & Ornstein, P. A. (1991). Children's memory for witnessed events: The developmental backdrop. In J. L. Doris (Ed.), *The suggestibility of children's recollections: Implications for eyewitness testimony* (pp. 10–20). Washington, DC: APA.

Brainerd, C. J., Reyna, V. F., Howe, M. L., & Kingma, J., (1990). The development of forgetting and reminiscence. *Monographs of the Society for Research in Child Development, 55* (3–4, Serial No. 222).

Brown, R., & Kulik, J. (1977). Flashbulb memories. *Cognition, 5*, 73–99.

Chi, M. T. H. (1978). Knowledge structures and memory development. In R. S.

Siegler (Ed.), *Children's thinking: What develops?* (pp. 73–96). Hillsdale, NJ: Erlbaum.

Chi, M. T. H. (1982). Knowledge development and memory performance. In M. Friedman, J. P. Das, & N. O'Connor (Eds.), *Intelligence and learning* (pp. 221–229). New York: Plenum.

Chi, M. T. H., & Koeske, R. D. (1983). Network representation of a child's dinosaur knowledge. *Developmental Psychology, 19,* 29–39.

Clymer, A. (1986, Feb. 2). Poll finds children remain enthusiastic on space flight. *New York Times,* pp. 1, 15.

Cole, C. B., & Loftus, E. F. (1987). The memory of children. In S. J. Ceci, M. P. Toglia, & D. F. Ross (Eds.), *Children's eyewitness memory* (pp. 178–208). New York: Springer-Verlag.

Fivush, R. (1984). Learning about school: The development of kindergartners' school scripts. *Child Development, 55,* 1697-1709.

Fivush, R., & Hamond, N. (1989). Time and again: Effects of repetition and retention interval on 2 year-olds' event recall. *Journal of Experimental Child Psychology, 47,* 259–273.

Fivush, R., Hudson, J., & Nelson, K. (1984). Children's long-term memory for a novel event: An exploratory study. *Merrill-Palmer Quarterly, 30,* 303–316.

Fivush, R., & Slackman, E. (1986). The acquisition and development of scripts. In K. Nelson (Ed.), *Event knowledge: Structure and function in development* (pp. 71–96). Hillsdale, NJ: Erlbaum.

Goodman, G., Aman, C., & Hirschman, J. (1987). Child sexual and physical abuse: Children's testimony. In S. J. Ceci, M. P. Toglia, & D. F. Ross (Eds.), *Children's eyewitness memory* (pp. 1–23). New York: Springer-Verlag.

Howe, M. L., & Brainerd, C. J. (1989). Development of long-term retention. *Developmental Review, 9,* 301–340.

Howe, M. L., Kelland, L., Bryant-Brown, A., & Clark, S. (in press). Measuring the development of children's amnesia and hypermnesia. In M. L. Howe, C. J. Brainerd, & V. F. Reyna (Eds.), *Development of long-term retention.* New York: Springer-Verlag.

Miller, J. (1987). *The impact of the Challenger accident on public attitudes toward the space program.* Report to the National Science Foundation, Public Opinion Laboratory, Northern Illinois University.

Monaco, N., & Gaier, E. (1987). Developmental level and children's responses to the explosion of the space shuttle Challenger. *Early Childhood Research Quarterly, 2,* 83–95.

Neisser, U. (1982). Snapshots or benchmarks? In U. Neisser (Ed.), *Memory observed: Remembering in natural contexts* (pp. 43–48). New York: W. H. Freeman Co.

Peters, D. P. (1987). The impact of naturally occurring stress on children's memory. In S. J. Ceci, M. P. Toglia, & D. F. Ross (Eds.), *Children's eyewitness memory* (pp. 122–141). New York: Springer-Verlag.

Pillemer, D. B. (1984). Flashbulb memories of the assassination attempt on President Reagan. *Cognition, 16,* 63–80.

Pillemer, D. B., & White, S. H. (1989). Childhood events recalled by children and adults. In H. W. Reese (Ed.), *Advances in child development and behavior* (Vol. 21, pp. 297–340). Orlando, FL: Academic Press.

Reed, G. (1979). Everyday anomalies of recall and recognition. In J. F. Kihlstrom & F. J. Evans (Eds.), *Functional disorders of memory* (pp. 1–28). Hillsdale, NJ: Erlbaum.

White, S. H., & Pillemer, D. B. (1979). Childhood amnesia and the development of a socially accessible memory system. In J. F. Kihlstrom & F. J. Evans (Eds.), *Functional disorders of memory* (pp. 29–73). Hillsdale, NJ: Erlbaum.

Winograd, E., & Killinger, W. (1983). Relating age at encoding in early childhood to adult recall: The development of flashbulb memories. *Journal of Experimental Psychology: General, 112,* 412–422.

Wright, J., Kunkel, D., Pinon, M., & Huston, A. (1987, April). Children's affective and cognitive reactions to televised coverage of the space shuttle disaster. Paper presented at the Biennial Meeting of the Society for Research in Child Development, Baltimore, MD.

Yarmey, A. D., & Bull, M. P., III. (1978). Where were you when President Kennedy was assassinated? *Bulletin of the Psychonomic Society, 11,* 133–135.

# 6

# Preschool children's memories of personal circumstances: The fire alarm study

DAVID B. PILLEMER

Several years ago, the teacher of a preschool class in the Boston area held a morning meeting to announce a sad occurrence: The mother of one of the children had died following a long illness. As the teacher began to talk, several children anticipated the topic: "K's mom died"; "I know, K's mom died." Some children also spontaneously described their own personal circumstances when they originally heard the news: "My mom told me at the hospital"; "My mom told me at breakfast"; "My mom was making orange juice"; "My mom and dad told me"; "My mom said, 'You won't be able to realize this.'" The teacher explained that K was fine, that K's mother had been sick for a long time, that the event was very unusual, and that it made people feel very sad. The discussion then turned to the general topic of death and the children's fears and misconceptions.

Preschool personnel observed and recorded the emotionally charged discussion, but had they not been aware of the author's interest in memories of personal circumstances, they might well have overlooked the children's comments about how they had "heard the news." The target event itself – the death of a parent of a young classmate – was terrifying, and needed to be presented and discussed in a supportive context. On the other hand, the children's memories of their *own* circumstances upon hearing the news evoke the same sense of "mystery" first identified by Brown and Kulik (1977) with respect to adults' "flashbulb" memories of public tragedies. For example, one would expect an adult to remember that President Kennedy had been shot by an assassin, but why should Kulik have vividly recalled that he was seated in a sixth-grade music class when he heard the news over the school intercom? Similarly, why should a 4-year-old remember that her mother was making orange juice when she provided the tragic information about K's mother's death?

According to Brown and Kulik (1977), whenever a surprising and consequential event is encountered, concomitant circumstances are encoded. Flashbulb-triggering events can be experienced directly (e.g., witnessing a fatal automobile accident) or only indirectly (e.g., hearing the news of a presidential assassination on the radio). The initial registration in memory of

121

concomitant circumstances is presumed to be automatic. Flashbulb memory *narratives* are subsequently constructed from the basic, imagistic memory through covert rehearsal and overt retellings. The automatic encoding of shocking events would have survival value because the memories may contain information about how to act, or survive, when experiencing similarly threatening circumstances in the future. Neisser (1982) questioned Brown and Kulik's emphasis on automatic encoding of shocking events; he argued instead that flashbulb memories exist and persist because of the enduring social and personal functions that they serve.

Analyses of flashbulb memory function can be extended to young children. From Brown and Kulik's (1977) perspective, flashbulb memories would presumably serve a directive function for children as well as for adults: A vivid memory of how one encountered a shocking event could potentially inform future actions in similar situations. In addition, remembering and recounting detailed personal memories can serve important psychodynamic and communicative functions (Pillemer, this volume), and these functions may be observable in children's as well as in adults' memory activities. For example, the preschool children's spontaneous recounting of how they had learned about the death of K's mother may have enabled direct emotional expression and release, in the same way that college students' talking with a psychologist about how they learned of the Kennedy assassination apparently offered emotional benefits (Greenstein, 1966). Memory sharing also communicated to others the child's active, albeit indirect, participation in K's tragedy: Fear, shock, and sadness became a shared, collective experience.

In this chapter I describe and analyze preschool children's memories of personal circumstances accompanying another unexpected, naturally occurring event – a building evacuation in response to a fire alarm. Previous research on flashbulb memories has with one exception (Warren & Swartwood, this volume) used adult informants, and no study has included preschoolers. The research focus on adults' flashbulb memories may be attributable to Brown and Kulik's (1977) emphasis on shocking and consequential *public* events; learning that President Kennedy had been assassinated was identified by Brown and Kulik as the "prototype case" (p. 73). This and other attacks on public figures – the attempted assassination of President Reagan (Pillemer, 1984), the assassination of Swedish prime minister Olof Palme (Christianson, 1989) – certainly were more shocking, consequential, newsworthy, and understandable to school-age children and adults than to preschoolers. Although the space shuttle disaster (Bohannon, 1988; McCloskey, Wible, & Cohen, 1988; Neisser & Harsch, this volume; Warren & Swartwood, this volume) was probably somewhat more meaningful to young children, developmental differences exist in children's understanding of space exploration and disasters that could influence memory for this event (Warren & Swartwood, this volume).

Because the term flashbulb memory is associated with learning about shocking *public* events, the broader concept *memory of personal circumstances* may be preferable (Pillemer, 1990), especially in research with young children. Adults' memories of momentous events experienced first-hand appear to be structurally similar to memories of learning about public tragedies (Pillemer, Koff, Rhinehart, & Rierdan, 1987). In research with preschoolers, it is necessary to expand the research agenda to include events experienced directly. Most 4-year-olds do not have a coherent concept of the president of a country or of space exploration. Consequently, studies of how children learned about impersonal, newsworthy events may say little about very young children's memory per se.

Research on young children's memories of directly experienced, emotionally salient events can inform theory and, ultimately, practice. Psychologists have shown considerable interest in the phenomenon of *childhood amnesia* – the difficulty that many adults experience when attempting to recall specific episodes from their first several years of life (Freud, 1905/1953; Neisser, 1962; Nelson, 1989; Pillemer & White, 1989; Schachtel, 1947; Wetzler & Sweeney, 1986; White & Pillemer, 1979). Direct studies of young children's memories of specific episodes are a necessary complement to studies demonstrating adults' impoverished long-term recall (Nelson, 1989; Pillemer & White, 1989). If young children have difficulty locating memories of recent events, or if the memories appear disorganized or distorted from an adult's perspective, then one would hardly expect adults' very long-term retrieval efforts to be successful.

Research on memories of personal circumstances could provide important clues to the childhood amnesia puzzle. Memory for personal circumstances accompanying a momentous target event is more than a mere side effect of emotional arousal: It appears to be a defining characteristic of personal memory (Pillemer, this volume). When an adult is asked if he or she remembers the Kennedy assassination, the first day of school, or the birth of a younger sibling, the response does not depend primarily on the retrieval of relevant but impersonal facts. Rather, it depends on whether the remember can mentally activate or "relive" some component of the concomitant circumstances as personally experienced: one's own location when the event occurred, expressed feelings, or ongoing activities. If vivid images of personal circumstances persist, then a presidential shooting is preserved as a personal event memory as well as an impersonal semantic record of the newsworthy happening. Should preschool children's memories of personal circumstances differ in important ways from memories recounted by older individuals, these differences could point to a viable cognitive developmental explanation for childhood amnesia.

From an applied standpoint, children's memories of emotional events, including memories of personal and peripheral details, are a potentially important component of legal testimony. Nevertheless, relatively little is known about children's memories of naturally occurring episodes. According to Ceci, Ross, and Toglia (1987), "this absence of knowledge is especially serious in the legal arena, where young children are increasingly being called upon by courts to provide eyewitness accounts of naturalistic events" (p. 38). Research on the organization and persistence of memories laid down in early childhood is directly relevant to courtroom proceedings. For example, in one recent trial a 13-year-old boy was asked to give an account of a brutal attack on his aunt, an event that he witnessed more than 10 years earlier (Langner, 1990, p. 26).

In the present study, 3- to 5-year-old children were interviewed about an unexpected preschool evacuation following a fire alarm. This study is the first to describe preschoolers' memories using the categories of personal information commonly found in adults' flashbulb memories. The overarching research issue has potential theoretical and practical significance: Does the organization of memories of personal circumstances undergo developmental change in the preschool years?

## Previous research

### Adult studies

A primary impetus for the present research was Winograd and Killinger's (1983) ingenious study of adults' flashbulb memories of newsworthy events experienced in childhood. Winograd and Killinger questioned high school students and adults about the 1963 assassination of President Kennedy; respondents were between 1 and 7 years of age in 1963. Participants answered five questions about their own personal circumstances upon learning about the tragedy: location, activity, source of information, aftermath, and "any additional details." Several age-related changes in memory were apparent. Most subjects who were younger than age 3 in 1963 had no recollection whatever of learning about the assassination, and very few subjects who were younger than age 5 had an elaborate memory (i.e., at least four of the five informational categories were represented in memory). Additional analyses were conducted for only those respondents who had some memory of the event. The amount of information in memory accounts given by respondents who were between 1 and 4 years of age in 1963 was uniformly low, but there was a clear age-related increase in memory complexity beginning with respondents who were 5 years old in 1963. The memory shift between ages 4 and 5 is especially relevant to the present study, where memories recounted by 3- to 5-year-old children were examined directly.

Sheingold and Tenney (1982) questioned college students about their early memories of a salient personal (as opposed to a newsworthy) event: the birth of a sibling. Respondents answered 20 direct questions, some of which tapped personal circumstances (e.g., "Who told you that your mother was leaving to go to the hospital?"). Virtually no college students who were younger than age 3 at the time of the birth remembered the event, but almost all students who were at least 4 years old at the time of the birth provided some information. Sheingold and Tenney did not provide fine-grained analyses of age-related changes in the informational complexity of memories of personal circumstances, so that it was not possible to determine if memories of a sibling birth show the 4- to 5-year-old "shift" identified by Winograd and Killinger (see the commentary by Pillemer & White, 1989, p. 310).

The relative inaccessibility of very early memories of personal circumstances found by Winograd and Killinger (1983) and by Sheingold and Tenney (1982) is consistent with reviews of research on childhood amnesia (Pillemer & White, 1989; Wetzler & Sweeney, 1986; White & Pillemer, 1979). The absence or incompleteness of memories given by respondents who were very young at the time of a salient event points to a possible cognitive developmental basis for childhood amnesia. College students who were either 3 or 5 years old in 1963 had the same adult capacity for reconstructing early memory fragments of the Kennedy assassination, yet people who were 5 years old when the assassination occurred were more likely than people who were 3 years old to report personal memories, and their memories were more elaborate.

### Child studies

Systematic studies of preschool children's memories of unexpected, emotionally salient events are scarce. The paucity of data is probably attributable to several factors (Pillemer & White, 1989): Momentous events rarely happen to large numbers of preschoolers under known circumstances; gaining research access under such circumstances is problematic; staging emotional events poses ethical and logistical problems; and very young children are not always able or willing to respond to the queries of a strange investigator.

Although no previous study has focused directly on preschool children's flashbulb memories, a sizable body of research exists on children's personal memories. Pillemer and White (1989) reviewed and synthesized this rapidly expanding research literature; their conclusions lead to two general expectations for children's memories of the fire alarm in the present study. First, specific questions should be more successful than general, open-ended probes in eliciting personal memories from young preschoolers. Second, developmental differences are likely to exist in the richness and coherence of verbal reports: "Memory narratives of 3-year-olds tend to be loose and somewhat disorganized, and they may be connected by associations that are understandable only to familiar adults. As children approach school age, their event descriptions more closely adhere to the organization and logic of adults' memories" (Pillemer & White, 1989, pp. 325–326). Winograd and Killinger's (1983) study of adults' flashbulb memories and Pillemer and White's (1989) review of the developmental literature on personal memory both identified ages 3 to 5, the age span of children in the present study, as a potential transition point of particular interest and significance from the perspective of research on and theories of childhood amnesia.

## Method

### Participants

The children were enrolled at the Wellesley College Child Study Center, a private preschool located in a middle class suburb of Boston. The 28 children attended either a younger ($n = 12$; mean age = 44 months; age range = 39–50 months) or an older ($n = 16$; mean age = 55 months; age range = 51–62 months) classroom. Four additional children in the younger classroom were not included: Two children were absent on the day of the fire alarm, and two children did not respond directly to the interviewer's questions. There were 7 girls and 5 boys in the younger group, and 8 girls and 8 boys in the older group.

### Event

Three children from the younger group and an assistant teacher were making popcorn in the school's basement, away from their classroom. The popcorn burned, setting off a fire alarm. The classroom teachers initially were unaware of the cause of the alarm and followed emergency procedures for evacuating the building. The children had never experienced a fire alarm at the school. Children and teachers exited the building and gathered in the adjoining playgrounds, where children were instructed to sit by the sandboxes. A police car drove up a footpath with lights flashing, and firefighters entered the building and turned off the alarm (the fire station is next door to the preschool). Teachers and children then reentered their classrooms. Once inside, the children were told that there was no real fire, and that burning popcorn in the basement had set off the alarm. Discussions turned to the general topics of smoke detectors, fire, and firefighters.

### Interviews

Approximately 2 weeks after the event, the author interviewed each of the 28 children. Individual interviews were conducted in a quiet room at the preschool. Children were first asked an *open-ended* question: "A few days ago there was a very loud noise at school. It was the fire alarm. What happened when you heard the fire alarm? What else happened?" The open-ended question was followed by six *direct* questions, five of which corresponded to categories of information commonly found in adults' flashbulb memories (Brown & Kulik, 1977): location, ongoing event, own feelings, others' feelings, and aftermath. For example, the question about location was "Where were you when you heard the fire alarm?" The extra direct question asked about the source of the noise ("What did you think it was?").

## Results

### Open-ended memories

Open-ended memory narratives were coded for the presence of the 5 categories of information elicited by the direct memory questions (location, ongoing event, own affect, others' affect, aftermath). Two individuals independently coded all 28 narratives. Intercoder agreement was at least 93% for all categories except location (50%). Considerable disagreement existed for the location category because one coder required an explicit mention of location, whereas the other coder required that location be implied by the response (e.g., "We went outside" implies that the child was inside the school when the alarm sounded). Because the interviewer stated in his introductory remarks to the children that the noise had occurred at school, the children may have assumed that location was known to the interviewer and that it did not need to be identified directly and specifically. For this reason, implied locations were coded as positive responses.

A majority of both 3 1/2-year-olds (75%) and 4 1/2-year-olds (88%) provided codable information in response to the open-ended prompts. The types of information represented in children's open-ended memories are shown in Table 6.1. Clearly, most of the information concerned location and aftermath. The mean open-ended memory total score for all 28 children, summing across the five categories, was approximately two informational categories per narrative ($M = 1.93$). Although the mean total score for 4 1/2-year-olds ($M = 2.19$) was higher than for 3 1/2-year-olds ($M = 1.58$), neither age nor sex differences were statistically significant. When only those children who provided codable information in their open-ended accounts ($n = 23$) were included, the difference in memory content between 4 1/2-year-olds ($M = 2.50$) and 3 1/2-year-olds ($M = 2.11$) still did not approach statistical significance.

### Cued memories

All 28 children answered some direct questions. The types of information represented in cued memories are shown in Table 6.1. The proportion of

Table 6.1. *Information contained in memories of the fire alarm*

| | Type of question | |
|---|---|---|
| Type of information | Open-ended | Direct |
| Location | 75 | 96 |
| Ongoing event | 25 | 89 |
| Own affect | 7 | 68 |
| Others' affect | 4 | 25 |
| Aftermath | 82 | 86 |

*Note*: The values represent proportions of all 28 children who provided each type of information.

children who provided information in response to a direct question was higher than the proportion of children who provided information in their open-ended memories for all five content categories. The mean cued memory total score ($M = 3.64$) was almost twice as high as the mean open-ended memory total score ($M = 1.93$), paired $t = 7.68$.[1] The pattern of responses to the direct memory questions indicated that children were not simply complying with the interviewer's request for information: Children rarely answered the direct question about others' affect ("How did other people feel?"). The mean cued total score of 4 1/2-year-olds ($M = 3.81$) was slightly higher than the mean cued total score of 3 1/2-year-olds ($M = 3.42$), but neither age nor sex differences in cued memory scores were statistically significant.

### Qualitative characteristics of memory

Although quantitative indices demonstrated only minor age differences in memory, a striking qualitative age difference was apparent even as the interviews were being conducted. In response to the direct question about location ("Where were you when you heard the fire alarm?"), almost all (15/16) of the 4 1/2-year-olds placed themselves inside the school, as an adult might have done, whereas over one-half (6/11) of the 3 1/2-year-olds placed themselves outside at the time (one 3 1/2-year-old did not specify location). Although this age difference was statistically significant (chi-square = 7.92), it may actually underestimate the size of the age effect. Two of the 3 1/2-year-olds who placed themselves inside the building were downstairs making popcorn, and hence were in touch with the causal event.

The young children who located themselves outside on the playground were not wrong in a technical sense, because the alarm could still be heard after they had converged outside. Nevertheless, the story is very different depending on whether the central activity takes place inside or outside.

Memories provided by two children, one from the older group (56 months old) and one from the younger group (44 months old), illustrate this qualitative difference:

*4 1/2-year-old*:

E: Where were you when you heard that loud noise? Do you remember that?

C: I was at the blue corner making something.

E: You were at the blue corner making something. So, do you remember what you were making?

C: Yeah.

E: What was it?

C: A necklace.

E: A necklace. Ah, that's very nice. When you heard that loud noise, though, what did you think that it was?

C: The fire alarm.

E: You knew it was the fire alarm. Oh, that's good. How did you feel when you heard that loud noise?

C: Very kind of frowned.

E: Frowned.

C: Yeah.

E: Were you scared? Or were you . . .

C: No, just frowned.

E: Just frowned. How did other people feel, do you remember how other people felt?

C: No.

E: Do you remember how Mary [teacher] felt or how the other children felt?

C: No.

E: No? What did you do after you heard that big noise?

C: We went back in.

*3 1/2-year-old*:

E: Where were you when you heard that fire alarm?

C: We were sitting on the sandbox.

E: On the sandbox. Uh huh. And what were you doing there?

C: We were singing songs.

E: You were singing songs. When you heard that loud noise, what did you think it was?

C: The alarm clock.

E: The alarm clock. Uh huh. And how did you feel when you heard that loud noise?

C: I feeled sort of scared . . . but I don't feel scared . . . just feeled sort of scared.

E: Sort of scared. How did other people feel . . . do you remember how Dorothy [teacher] . . .

C: They feeled happy.

E: They all felt happy? Why did they feel happy?

C: They just did because they thought that noise was great.

E: It was great, they thought the noise was great? What did you do after you heard the noise?

C: After I heard the noise I just . . . um . . . my mommy . . . my mommy came and bringed me home.

The older child's answers to direct questions resemble adults' flashbulb memories in that immediate circumstances upon receiving the "news" are the focus of the story. Similarly, other 4 1/2-year-olds described classroom locations and activities that just happened to co-occur with hearing the alarm – gluing at the round table, playing with the hollow blocks, washing hands, and so on. In contrast, many 3 1/2-year-olds focused on outside locations and activities rather than on circumstances accompanying the initial sounding of the alarm.

One possible explanation for the age differences in location, and the corresponding differences in memory content, is that the younger and older children had different levels of understanding about what had transpired. If the younger children did not have a firm grasp of the causal and temporal sequence of events, it would not be so surprising that their narratives focused on salient playground activities. Additional qualitative analyses explored developmental differences in event understanding or awareness. Two individuals coded all open-ended memories for the presence of information suggesting that it was *necessary* to evacuate the building (e.g., "I had to rush outside without my coat on"; "We had to run out"). Intercoder agreement was 84%. Most (75%) of the 4 1/2-year-olds but only one-third (33%) of the 3 1/2-year-olds described a sense of urgency in evacuating the building (chi-square = 4.86). Entire interviews were also coded for any mention of "popcorn" or "smoke" as the *cause* of the alarm. Intercoder agreement was 100%. Only one 3 1/2-year-old (8%) but almost one-half (44%) of the 4 1/2-year-olds mentioned the cause (chi-square = 4.21). The one 3 1/2-year-old who identified the cause had been in the basement making popcorn and had had direct contact with the causal event.

Consistent with the age group comparisons, children whose responses to the direct question about location focused on events occurring inside rather than outside the school showed higher apparent levels of understanding. A majority (65%) of children who located themselves inside but only 29% of children who located themselves outside indicated in their open-ended memories that it was necessary to evacuate the building. With respect to causal influences, 40% of children who located themselves inside identified popcorn or smoke as the cause, whereas none of the children who located themselves outside identified the cause (chi-square = 3.98).

## Discussion of empirical findings

All 28 children interviewed in the present study were able to describe some aspects of their personal circumstances during a building evacuation that had occurred 2 weeks earlier. Responses to open-ended prompts were sketchy and for the most part limited to two informational categories: location and aftermath. In contrast, direct questions usually elicited specific information about location, ongoing activities, own affect, and aftermath. The superiority of cued over free recall is consistent with both naturalistic and experimental research on children's memory (Pillemer & White, 1989).

Although most memory accounts appeared to be plausible, it was not possible to definitively assess memory accuracy for this unanticipated, naturally occurring event. It is possible that children felt obligated to answer direct questions posed by the adult interviewer, and therefore constructed reasonable but potentially inaccurate responses. The use of direct questions rather than free recall can increase the incidence of inaccurate responding by children (King & Yuille, 1987, p. 27). Nevertheless, most of the preschoolers in the present study did not answer the direct question about others' feelings, suggesting that children were not answering solely to comply with the interviewer's direct requests for information.

Another possible explanation for the superiority of cued over free recall is that the preschool children had not yet internalized the process of generating memory cues in order to facilitate their own construction of memory narratives (Pillemer & White, 1989). For very young children, talk about the past is heavily structured by adult conversational partners (Fivush, 1991; Nelson, 1989). If the children did not spontaneously employ cues related to the categories of information commonly found in adults' flashbulb memories (e.g., What was I doing when the alarm sounded?), then the paucity of information provided without adult guidance would be expected.

Although older preschoolers provided somewhat more information than younger preschoolers in response to both direct questions and open-ended probes, the age differences did not reach statistical significance in this relatively small sample. In contrast, there was a striking qualitative difference in memory content. In response to the direct question about one's location when the alarm was heard, almost all of the 4 1/2-year-olds placed themselves inside the school, whereas a majority of 3 1/2-year-olds located themselves outside. Neither type of response was implausible, because the alarm could be heard on the playground after the evacuation as well as inside the school. Yet as the narrative examples demonstrate, stories were sometimes so discrepant that a naive adult would assume that older and younger children were describing different happenings.

It seems certain that 3 1/2-year-old children knew that they began the day inside, but detailed descriptions of personal circumstances while inside the building often were not part of the memories they recounted. Some of the youngest children's open-ended memories briefly described leaving the building (e.g., "We went outside"), even though their responses to direct questions focused on activities occurring outside. Whether these children could have produced detailed descriptions of inside activities if explicitly pressed to do so is not known. It was not possible to determine from the protocols whether the lack of information about preevacuation circumstances was attributable to the comparative salience of outside activities, or to the absence or inaccessibility of relevant information in memory.

What are possible explanations for the age differences in location of the primary action contained in memory descriptions? At first glance, the younger children's memories appear to resemble what Freud (1899/1962) termed "screen memories," in which the emotional core of a past event is displaced, leaving only a banal representational shell in memory. The impetus for evacuating the building is missing in some of the 3 1/2-year-olds' accounts. Nevertheless, activities occurring inside the school prior to and accompanying the evacuation are highly unlikely targets for displacement of unacceptable affect. The alarm was startling, but there was neither disaster nor chaos: Adults and children left the building in a timely and orderly fashion.

A more plausible explanation for the age differences in memory involves differences in children's understanding of what exactly had transpired. The event was unfamiliar for all children and it violated expectations about school routines: The alarm sounded unexpectedly and the children were rushed outside at an unusual time; rather than playing freely, they were asked to sit by the sandboxes; teachers and firefighters acted with a sense of urgency, and yet there was no real fire.

Research in several different domains has identified important shifts in causal reasoning and temporal sequencing during the 3-to-5-year age range. Unfamiliar events appear to pose a particular challenge to young preschoolers' reasoning capacities. Sophian and Huber (1984) identified a developmental shift in preschool children's ability to identify causes, especially in novel contexts: "Early causal reasoning appears to be primarily empirical and based on concrete features of the events in question, whereas later reasoning may be more logical and involve greater reliance on abstract causal principles that enable children to interpret even unfamiliar events" (p. 512). Fivush and Mandler (1985) found that preschool children have more difficulty sequencing unfamiliar than familiar events, because sequencing unfamiliar events requires that children "understand and infer the logical relations linking actions together. Either the understanding of these relations, or the ability to make inferences about them, presents some difficulty for young children" (p. 1,444).

Bullock's (1985) review of developmental changes in causal reasoning during the preschool years is especially illuminating. Bullock observed a shift in causal reasoning between ages 3 and 4. The 3-year-old's understanding of (or attention to) the "mechanism principle" – the principle that "causes must literally do something to bring about their effects" (p. 172) – is quite limited, whereas "adult-like causal principles are available by the time a child is 4 or 5 years old" (p. 182). Older preschoolers are surprised and troubled by an apparent lack of mechanism, but 3-year-olds are unruffled by such an absence:"Whereas older children (and adults as well) seem to assume that causal events must, part and parcel, include a mechanism, and use that consideration to constrain their attributions, 3-year-olds evidence no such constraint. If a potential mechanism is available they sometimes can use it. If not, they are not particularly concerned about its absence" (pp. 181–182).

Preschoolers' stories often are similarly devoid of overarching causal and temporal relationships. Berman (1988) asked children to tell a story based on a series of pictures. She observed that preschool children "are unable to embed occurrences in a network of background circumstances and to relate them explicitly to the situations that lead up to and result from them . . . [they] tend to report each event as having equal, independent status, rather than as logically or temporally interconnected to what precedes or follows" (p. 492). The stories of 3-year-olds were "pregrammatical" with respect to narrative exposition, because "they fail on just about every count to sustain a narrative thread" (p. 491). In contrast, 4- and 5-year-olds were "more clearly en route to 'structure-dependent' storytelling" (p. 491).

Whether constructing narratives or solving logical problems, 3-year-olds do not appear to be disturbed by the absence of an underlying causal mechanism or structure that ties together events and outcomes. The findings of these experiments have implications for behaviors in naturalistic settings: Coppens (1985) found that preschool children's level of causal reasoning was related to their ability to differentiate between safe and unsafe situations. In the fire alarm study, a significantly higher proportion of 4 1/2-year-olds than 3 1/2-year-olds described a sense of urgency when leaving the school building, implying that a potentially dangerous cause prompted their actions. In addition, almost one-half of the 4 1/2-year-olds but only one 3 1/2-year-old mentioned the actual cause of the alarm (popcorn or smoke) in the course of the interview. Consistent with the performance of 3-year-olds described by Bullock (1985), some 3 1/2-year-olds' fire alarm narratives neither specified nor implied a causal mechanism, and the children appeared unperturbed by its absence.

## Implications for theories of childhood amnesia

How might the qualitative age differences in memory content inform theoretical explanations of childhood amnesia? Memories of the fire alarm themselves appear to be unlikely candidates for persistence into adulthood, because the evacuation proceeded without incident. Nevertheless, it may be useful to speculate about how the memory representations would fare over long time spans. The narrative memories of 4 1/2-year-olds would appear to be potentially identifiable later on as a building evacuation prompted by a fire alarm: An alarm sounded, ongoing classroom activities were abruptly halted, and the children left the building with a sense of urgency or necessity.

In contrast, the narrative memories of some 3 1/2-year-olds, focusing as they do on outside activities, do not fully represent an emergency building evacuation in response to a fire alarm. If memories of playground activities happen to contain fire-related information, then an older child or adult might be able to reconstruct the preceding events – "That must have been a fire alarm!" – but the impetus for the activities is not inherent in the narratives.

This analysis can be extended to events for which the long-term forgetting curve is known. Winograd and Killinger (1983) demonstrated that very young preschool children were less likely than older children to remember their personal circumstances at the time of the Kennedy assassination, and that younger children's memories contained less information. The assassination of a president is an unfamiliar and highly abstract event. The statement "The president of the United States has been shot!" cannot mean much to a 3-year-old, but adults' reactions to the news – emotional upset, attention and behaviors directed away from children's needs and concerns – would be very salient. How would the central event from the child's perspective (adults' emotional reactions to the tragedy) be tied in memory to the incomprehensible newsworthy event (the Kennedy assassination)?

Research on children's understanding of causality and temporal sequence with respect to unfamiliar events, and the fire alarm data, suggest that older preschoolers would be better able than younger preschoolers to forge conceptual links between the aftermath of hearing the news and the precipitating event, and that they would be more likely to search actively for such links. In contrast, children under age 4 would focus on the salient outcome – the parents' reactions themselves – rather than urgently attempt to identify potential causal mechanisms. Older children would have been more likely to ask "Why is Mommy crying?" and to have integrated their limited understanding of the cause into their event narratives. For these children, the memory cue "Do you remember hearing about the Kennedy assassination?" could potentially be successful. For younger children, the memorable but mysterious personal experiences would be disassociated from an adult's conception of the tragedy, in the same way that 3 1/2-year-olds' description of outside activities following the fire alarm often seemed disassociated from the precipitating event. Wolfenstein and Kliman (1966) offered a similar analysis with respect to the long-term persistence of young children's memories of the Kennedy assassination:

We would predict that for young children, to the extent that their personal experience survives, it will be remembered as an isolated event of an uncanny nature . . . Of course much was explained to them. They got some organized idea of the sequence of events, varying with their age and health of mind. But if some twinges of their own feelings from that time are revived later they will evoke something strange, something that intruded into the usual round of life and could not be quite assimilated. (pp. 232–233)

Whenever important differences exist between young children's and adults' understanding of an event, purposeful long-term recall of childhood experiences should be impaired (Pillemer & White, 1989). The recovery of very early memories is likely to be especially difficult when event sequences and underlying causal relationships were complex and unfamiliar to the child. Adult memory cues, either generated internally or provided by an interviewer in a memory study, would be unsuccessful in locating early memories. If images of very early events come to mind spontaneously, they may not be easily recognized by the adult as reactions to the Kennedy assassination or as the aftermath of an emergency building evacuation.

## Conclusions

The analysis of preschool children's memories of their personal circumstances during a fire alarm has several implications for research, theory, and practice. First, direct questions were more effective than open-ended probes in eliciting memories of personal circumstances, a finding that concurs with previous developmental research on other types of memory. Second, important age differences in memory may be qualitative (involving what is remembered) rather than quantitative (involving how much is remembered). Nelson's (1989) conclusion that "memories do exist in early childhood, and so far as we have been able to tell they do not differ in organization in any major way from later memories" (p. 146) should be reassessed by examining qualitative differences in narrative descriptions of unanticipated, unfamiliar, causally complex events. Third, the systematic age differences in memory content observed in the fire alarm study appear to be related to age differences in causal and temporal understanding, or in the child's propensity to forge conceptual links between the precipitating event and the subsequent outcome. Developmental differences in cognitive processing of salient episodes could impair long-term recall: When a substantial mismatch exists between an event representation laid down in early childhood and the adult's conception of the same event, purposeful retrieval efforts should suffer accordingly.

## NOTES

This research was supported by a grant from the Spencer Foundation. Lynn Goldsmith helped code and analyze data, and Trase Rourke transcribed the interviews. Marian Blum, Mary Ucci, and Dorothy McDonald of the Wellesley College Child Study Center provided essential information and invaluable insights.
1 Reported test statistics are significant at the .05 level, two-tailed.

## REFERENCES

Berman, R. A. (1988). On the ability to relate events in narrative. *Discourse Processes, 11*, 469–497.

Bohannon, J. N. III. (1988). Flashbulb memories for the Space Shuttle disaster: A tale of two theories. *Cognition, 29*, 179–196.

Brown, R., & Kulik, J. (1977). Flashbulb memories. *Cognition, 5*, 73–99.

Bullock, M. (1985). Causal reasoning and developmental change over the preschool years. *Human Development, 28*, 169–191.

Ceci, S. J., Ross, D. F., & Toglia, M. P. (1987). Suggestibility of children's memory: Psycholegal implications. *Journal of Experimental Psychology: General, 116*, 38–49.

Christianson, S-Å. (1989). Flashbulb memories: Special, but not so special. *Memory & Cognition, 17*, 435–443.

Coppens, N. M. (1985). Cognitive development and locus of control as predictors of preschoolers' understanding of safety and prevention. *Journal of Applied Developmental Psychology, 6*, 43–55.

Fivush, R. (1991). The social construction of personal narratives. *Merrill-Palmer Quarterly, 37*, 59–82.

Fivush, R., & Mandler, J. M. (1985). Developmental changes in the understanding of temporal sequence. *Child Development, 56*, 1437–1446.

Freud, S. (1953). Three essays on the theory of sexuality. In J. Strachey (Ed.), *The standard edition of the complete psychological works of Sigmund Freud* (Vol. 7, pp. 135–243). London: Hogarth Press. (Original work published 1905)

Freud, S. (1962). Screen memories. In J. Strachey (Ed.), *The standard edition of the complete psychological works of Sigmund Freud* (Vol. 3, pp. 303–322). London: Hogarth Press. (Original work published 1899)

Greenstein, F. I. (1966). Young men and the death of a young president. In M. Wolfenstein & G. Kliman (Eds.), *Children and the death of a president* (pp. 193–216). Garden City, New York: Anchor Books.

King, M. A., & Yuille, J. C. (1987). Suggestibility and the child witness. In S. J. Ceci, M. P. Toglia, & D. F. Ross (Eds.), *Children's eyewitness memory* (pp. 24–35). New York: Springer-Verlag.

Langner, P. (1990, October 27). Boy recalls to jury what he saw at age 2, on day his aunt was slain. *Boston Globe*, p. 26.

McCloskey, M., Wible, C. G., & Cohen, N. J. (1988). Is there a special flashbulb-memory mechanism? *Journal of Experimental Psychology: General, 117*, 171–181.

Neisser, U. (1962). Cultural and cognitive discontinuity. In T. E. Gladwin & W. Sturtevant (Eds.), *Anthropology and human behavior* (pp. 54–71). Washington, DC: Anthropological Society of Washington.

Neisser, U. (1982). Snapshots or benchmarks? In U. Neisser (Ed.), *Memory observed* (pp. 43–48). San Francisco: Freeman.

Nelson, K. (1989). Remembering: A functional developmental perspective. In P. R. Solomon, G. R. Goethals, C. M. Kelley, & B. R. Stephens (Eds.), *Memory: Interdisciplinary approaches* (pp. 127–150). New York: Springer-Verlag.

Pillemer, D. B. (1984). Flashbulb memories of the assassination attempt on President Reagan. *Cognition, 16*, 63–80.

Pillemer, D. B. (1990). Clarifying the flashbulb memory concept: Comment on McCloskey, Wible, and Cohen (1988). *Journal of Experimental Psychology: General, 119*, 92–96.

Pillemer, D. B., Koff, E., Rhinehart, E. D., & Rierdan, J. (1987). Flashbulb memories of menarche and adult menstrual distress. *Journal of adolescence, 10*, 187–189.

Pillemer, D. B., & White, S. H. (1989). Childhood events recalled by children and adults. In H. W. Reese (Ed.), *Advances in child development and behavior: Vol. 21* (pp. 297–340). Orlando, Florida: Academic Press.

Schachtel, E. (1947). On memory and childhood amnesia. *Psychiatry, 10,* 1–26.

Sheingold, K., & Tenney, Y. J. (1982). Memory for a salient childhood event. In U. Neisser (Ed.), *Memory observed* (pp. 201–212). San Francisco: Freeman.

Sophian, C., & Huber, A. (1984). Early developments in children's causal judgments. *Child Development, 55,* 512–526.

Wetzler, S. E., & Sweeney, J. A. (1986). Childhood amnesia: An empirical demonstration. In D. C. Rubin (Ed.), *Autobiographical memory* (pp. 191–201). New York: Cambridge University Press.

White, S. H., & Pillemer, D. B. (1979). Childhood amnesia and the development of a socially accessible memory system. In J. F. Kihlstrom & F. J. Evans (Eds.), *Functional disorders of memory* (pp. 29–73). Hillsdale, NJ: Erlbaum.

Winograd, E., & Killinger, W. A., Jr. (1983). Relating age at encoding in early childhood to adult recall: Development of flashbulb memories. *Journal of Experimental Psychology: General, 112,* 413–422.

Wolfenstein, M., & Kliman, G. (1966). Conclusion. In M. Wolfenstein & G. Kliman (Eds.), *Children and the death of a president* (pp. 217–329). Garden City, New York: Anchor Books.

*Part III*

# Emotion and memory

# 7

# A proposed neurobiological basis for regulating memory storage for significant events

PAUL E. GOLD

## Introduction

The goal of this chapter is to describe the biological systems that appear to promote the formation of memories for especially important information. The findings discussed here suggest that the most direct extrapolation from the evidence currently available is that "flashbulb" memories are not unique but represent a special case of more general neuroendocrine regulation of the biological processes responsible for storing information. It is also important to note that the same physiological processes appear to regulate not only memory systems but also a wide range of nonmemory neural and behavioral measures. Thus, at a neurobiological level, the findings suggest a more broadly based behavioral conception of what is regulated – including, but going beyond, memory.

The major point is that information comes in and is acted upon in retrograde fashion by neuroendocrine responses to the experience to promote the storage of recent information. The chapters included in this volume consider the viability of the view that there are unusually complete memories for ancillary information surrounding significant events. These firm memories are usually tested for events important to a large segment of a society, but presumably also apply to individually based significant events as well. It is only the latter case – individually specific memories – that is addressed directly by the neurobiological data.

At a biological level, there are two interacting processes that must be considered to gain a full understanding of the biological bases of memory storage. One consists of the neurobiological substrate mechanisms themselves. These mechanisms might include: anatomical changes such as the reorganization of fine anatomy of brain systems (e.g., Greenough & Bailey, 1988), biochemical changes such as increases and decreases in the activity of brain enzymes and protein synthesis (e.g., Crow, 1988), or neurophysiological changes such as those seen during classical conditioning (Weinberger et al., 1990; Thompson, 1988) or as represented in the analog of memory, long-term potentiation (Lynch & Baudry, 1987; McNaughton & Morris, 1987; Linden & Routtenberg, 1989).

It is likely that the substrates of memory are continually active, with specificity defined by the particular neural elements activated by particular events. However, these processes do not exist in isolation from other processes that regulate the magnitude and even the form these changes might take. It is these other processes that may have the greatest relevance for flashbulb memories, and these are the processes that I term regulators (also known as modulators) of memory storage.

What might these processes be? On the basis of early animal studies of memory consolidation, it is quite clear that memory storage can be manipulated by a host of treatments administered shortly after a training experience (for review, see McGaugh & Herz, 1972). The same treatment administered at some later time has no effect on memory. The predominant older interpretation of such findings was based on views of the duration of or the formation time for short- or long-term memory. I will not detail here those results suggesting that a time constant for memory formation is not what these experiments studied; this issue has been considered before (Gold & McGaugh, 1975). The focal question for this chapter is: Why does the brain retain memory in a state susceptible to perturbation for some time after an experience? In terms of biological theories of evolutionary adaptation, memory systems modifiable after the experience is over would appear to be a design destined to lead to uncertain memory storage unless – and this is the crux of the matter – the brain uses postexperiential consequences of an experience to determine whether it was worthwhile to store the specific information provided by each experience.

According to this view, it is possible that memory storage is susceptible to modification so that there is time for these relatively nonspecific (in an informational sense) consequences of an experience to promote the storage of important events and to lose – perhaps passively – the information contained in unimportant events. So, the next question is to identify rather global physiological responses to experiences that might contribute to memory storage. One candidate is arousal level. Conceptually, there is nothing wrong with this idea. However, at a practical level in behavioral neuroscience, arousal is a difficult dimension to apply to studies of memory because there is no general agreement on how one ought to measure arousal, let alone how to manipulate it. Essentially, this view would use one theoretical construct – arousal – to explain another – memory. In contrast to this ambiguity, hormonal responses to experience can be defined crisply and can be manipulated easily.

Considerations such as these led to some of the first examinations of the possibility that some hormonal responses to an experience might control memory storage. (In describing the basic design of such an experiment, I will leave it to the reader to decide whether these experiments represent demonstrations of flashbulb memories in animals.) One task often employed to study hormonal regulation of memory is a one-trial inhibitory (or passive) avoidance task. This task provides a relatively easy way to present the logic of the experiments. The apparatus is a two-compartment alley. A rat is placed in the well-lit start compartment and allowed to enter a dimly lit compartment containing a grid floor through which footshock is administered when the animal crosses. Memory is assessed later, usually 24 hours or more after training, by noting the latency of the rat to cross into the shock compartment on the test trial. Not surprisingly, retention latencies increase as a function of footshock intensity during training. In large part, this is a simple consequence of the increased sensory qualities of the aversive stimulus. Similarly, hormonal and other physiological consequences of training also increase at higher footshock intensity. The salient issue here is whether the hormonal consequences of an experience contribute to the later memories of the experience. To address that question, rats are trained with a relatively mild footshock, one that itself results in minimal hormonal responses at the time of training and in weak retention on later test trials. Shortly after receiving the mild shock, the rats receive an injection intended to mimic the consequences of a stronger shock. This is a "posttraining" design in which all animals are in a comparable state during training and, later, at testing, thus obviating potential confounds of arousal or sensory responsivity. This design also mimics the natural sequence of events, in which the hormonal consequences of an experience generally follow that experience by a relatively short time. When rats receive an injection of an appropriate hormone and dose, as described in the next section, their memory is enhanced: The animals avoid the shock compartment as if they had received a more intense footshock.

## Epinephrine effects on memory

Like other stressors, footshock releases a wide range of hormones, for example including many pituitary, adrenal, and gonadal hormones (Levine, Coe, & Wiener, 1989). But few of these hormones appear to enhance or impair memory storage. Of those hormones tested, the most robust memory enhancement is seen with posttraining injections of adrenocorticotrophic hormone (ACTH) and epinephrine, and perhaps vasopressin (McGaugh, 1989; McGaugh & Gold, 1989). Like most other treatments with retroactive effects on memory (Gold, 1989), epinephrine enhances memory in an inverted-U dose-response curve; the results of one such experiment are shown in Figure 7.1. Consistent with evidence obtained with other treatments testing retrograde actions on memory, epinephrine is most effective when administered close to the time of training; injections delayed by an hour or more after training do not affect later memory. Thus, the effects of epinephrine are dose- and time-dependent. The dose-dependency appears to be closely related to

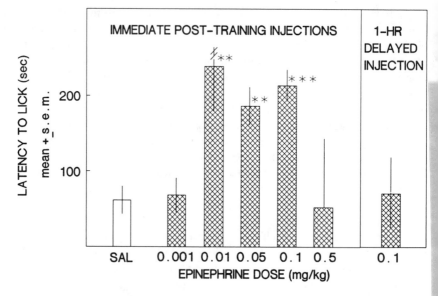

Figure 7.1. Effects of epinephrine on memory for inhibitory avoidance training. Note that when injected immediately after training, intermediate doses of epinephrine enhanced retention performance tested 24 hr after training and treatment. A memory-enhancing dose of epinephrine injected 1 hr after training had no effect on later retention. (** P < 0.02, *** P < 0.001 vs. saline.) [From Gold & van Buskirk, 1975.]

the magnitude of the increases in circulating epinephrine observed as normal responses to training. As shown in Figure 7.2, avoidance training results in an 8-fold increase in circulating epinephrine levels within 5–10 minutes of a training footshock. This magnitude is comparable to that seen after injection of a memory-enhancing dose of epinephrine.

## From epinephrine to glucose

Posttraining epinephrine injections enhance memory for a wide range of behavioral tasks, including inhibitory avoidance, discriminated avoidance, and appetitive learned responses (reviewed in: McGaugh & Gold, 1989; McGaugh, 1989; McGaugh & Herz, 1972). These broadly defined effects of epinephrine on memory are surprising in light of the evidence that epinephrine apparently does not itself cross the blood–brain barrier to act directly on the central nervous system (Axelrod, Weil-Malherbe, & Tomchick, 1959). Because transfer of epinephrine from blood to brain is minimal at best, it is reasonable to conclude that epinephrine effects on brain function involve a peripheral action (i.e., a transduction mechanism) by which epinephrine release can modify brain function. During the past few years, we

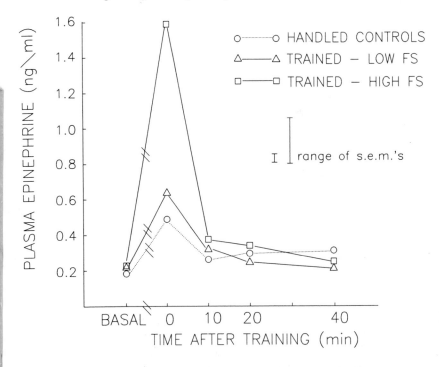

Figure 7.2. Effects of training on plasma epinephrine levels. Animals that were handled (placed in the training apparatus without footshock) or that received low footshock had significant 2–3-fold increases in epinephrine levels. Training with a stronger footshock resulted in an 8-fold increase in circulating epinephrine levels. Epinephrine doses that enhance memory for low footshock training (as in Figure 7.1) result in plasma epinephrine levels comparable to those of high footshock alone. [From Gold & McCarty, 1981.]

have identified one such process as an intermediate mechanism: the classic increase in circulating glucose levels after release or injection of epinephrine (Ellis, Kennedy, Eusebi, & Vincent, 1967). Like epinephrine, posttraining glucose administration enhances memory storage processing in an inverted-U dose-response manner (Messier & White, 1984, 1987; Messier & Destrade, 1988; White & Messier, 1988; Gold, 1986; cf. Gold, 1990), with glucose doses, epinephrine doses, and footshock intensities that lead to good retention resulting in comparable blood glucose levels shortly after training and treatment (Hall & Gold, 1986). The increase in blood glucose levels optimal for enhancing memory storage is about 25–50 mg/dl above a baseline of approximately 120 mg/dl (see Figure 7.3). Most important, the increases in blood glucose levels that enhance memory are well within normal physiological values.

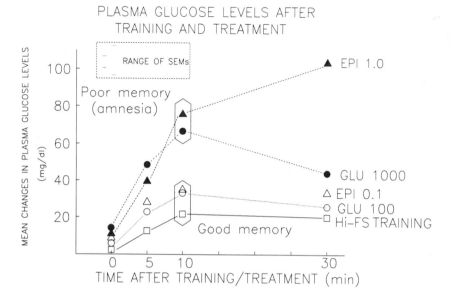

Figure 7.3. Blood glucose levels after training and after injections of epinephrine or glucose. The lower cluster of lines illustrate the extent of the increase in blood glucose levels that predict enhanced memory on later tests. The upper two lines illustrate the extent of increases in blood glucose levels that are associated with amnesia on later test trials. [From Hall & Gold, 1986.]

Thus, relatively small changes in blood glucose levels regulate memory storage processing and increases in blood glucose subsequent to epinephrine release or injection appear to contribute to the hormone's effects on memory. Two sets of findings are especially relevant to this conclusion. First, pretreatment with peripherally (but not centrally) administered adrenergic receptor antagonists blocks the effects of epinephrine on memory (cf. Gold, 1989) but does not block the effects of glucose on memory (Gold, Vogt, & Hall, 1986). These findings suggest that the relevant peripheral adrenergic receptor activation precedes the glucose step. In addition, central (lateral ventricle) glucose injections enhance memory at low doses in an inverted-U dose-response manner (Lee, Graham, & Gold, 1988). Although the central nervous system normally receives glucose via a facilitated transport mechanism from blood to brain and not from the ventricular system (Gjedde, Hansen, & Silver, 1980; Hochwald, Gandhi, & Goldman, 1983; Hochwald, Magee, & Ferguson, 1985), the finding that ventricular glucose enhances memory supports the view that glucose actions on memory and other functions are mediated by direct central actions of circulating glucose.

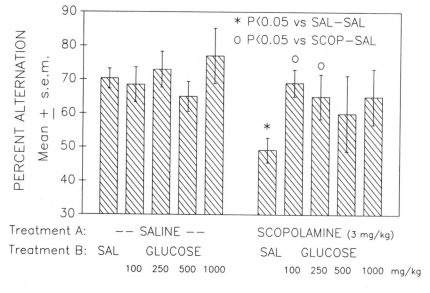

Figure 7.5. Consistent with the model in Figure 7.4, glucose injections reverse the impairment of spontaneous alternation performance induced by the cholinergic antagonist, scopolamine. Similar results have been obtained using glucose to reverse the effects of other cholinergic antagonists and also of opiate agonists. [From Stone, Walser, Gold, & Gold, 1991.]

receive other pharmacological treatments. However, glucose administration did enhance 2-DG uptake in young animals pretreated with scopolamine (reversing scopolamine-induced decreases in 2-DG uptake) (Stone & Gold, 1990a) and in 2-year-old mice. These findings suggest that, under some conditions (old age, scopolamine), blood glucose may contribute importantly to brain 2-DG uptake. One explanation of glucose attenuation of scopolamine-induced reduction of 2-DG uptake is that scopolamine depresses cholinergic control of cerebral blood flow (Honer, Prohovnik, Smith, & Lucas, 1988; Dam & London, 1984; Scremin, Allen, Torres, & Scremin, 1988), and that glucose augments cholinergic function here as in other cases.

In each case tested thus far, the evidence indicates that glucose injections attenuate the effects of cholinergic antagonists and augment the actions of cholinergic agonists. In a manner also likely to be related to cholinergic functions, glucose injections attenuate the actions of opioid agonists. The pharmacological pattern of results is redundant when assessing a broad range of measures – inhibitory avoidance memory, spontaneous alternation performance, activity, sleep, tremors, and brain 2-DG uptake. The repeated pharmacological patterns suggest that glucose acts as a functional cholinergic agonist and/or opiate antagonist. In this context, "functional" need not mean direct actions but includes possible effects on other systems that influence the activity of cholinergic and opiate systems. The mechanisms responsible for the effects of glucose on memory and other behavioral and neurobiological measures are as yet unclear. However, as noted above, the profile does fit well with past reports regarding the effects of cholinergic and opioid effects on memory and the effects of circulating glucose on cholinergic and opioid biological functions.

It should be noted that the possibility that physiologically relevant changes in blood glucose levels regulate brain functions is not one predicted by the traditional view that brain metabolism is invulnerable to such changes, although increases in glucose utilization in some brain areas appear to accompany increases in blood glucose levels (Orzi et al., 1988). Given the robust and varied consequences of increases in blood glucose for brain functions, it will be important to characterize more fully the underlying pharmacological mechanisms. Because these are new findings, there are of course many hypotheses that can be substituted or added to Figure 7.4 (e.g., other neurotransmitters such as glutamate and glycine that can be derived from glucose [Wenk, 1989], or glucose receptors [e.g., Oomura, 1983]). Also, under some conditions – particularly at higher glucose doses – peripheral actions of glucose may contribute to the treatment's effects on memory (Messier & White, 1987). Evidence that glucose injected directly into the lateral cerebral ventricle also enhances memory (Lee, Graham, & Gold, 1988), as well as evidence for interactions of circulating glucose with cho- linergic and opioid functions (Gibson & Blass, 1976; Gibson, Jope, & Blass, 1975; Gibson & Peterson, 1981; Brase & Dewey, 1988; Lee & McCarty, 1990), suggests that direct central actions may contribute to the effects of glucose on the varied range of measures we have tested. Whether the primary site(s) of glucose action prove to be peripheral or central (and these are not mutually exclusive possibilities in any case), the ultimate action is of course on the brain.

### Glucose amelioration of age-related memory deficits: Animal studies

The ability to retain recently acquired information also declines with age in many animal species. The memory deficit is often expressed as rapid forget- ting; retention performance is good soon after training but decays sooner in aged than in young subjects (Kubanis & Zornetzer, 1981; Gold & Stone, 1988; Winocur, 1988). The substantial evidence suggesting that neuroendo- crine systems are important regulators of memory storage processing opens the possibility that neuroendocrine dysfunctions may contribute to age- related memory impairments (Gold & Stone, 1988).

Increased rates of forgetting have been observed in aged rodents on a wide range of measures, including avoidance, appetitive, and spatial tasks (e.g.,

Zornetzer, Thompson, & Rogers, 1982; Barnes, 1988; also as reviewed in Kubanis & Zornetzer, 1981; Gold & Stone, 1988). In some cases, memory deterioration is seen for several memory measures within the same individual subjects (Gallagher & Burwell, 1989). Of related interest is that although the initial induction of the physiological model of memory, long-term potentiation (LTP) is comparable in young and old rats, old rats show substantially accelerated rates of decay compared to those seen in young rats (Barnes, 1979; Barnes & McNaughton, 1985). Other findings that may be relevant here are demonstrations that although both young and old rabbits and humans acquire classically conditioned responses with delay or very short trace conditioning paradigms, there is an age-related deficit observed with longer (> 500 ms) CS-US trace intervals (Solomon, Beal, & Pendlebury, 1988).

The evidence supporting age-related deficits appearing as a function of train-test intervals is quite clear in many tasks. The specific train-test interval required to reveal age-related deficits varies with specific task demands. For example, impaired retention after inhibitory avoidance training in aged rats can be seen at about 6 hrs after training (Gold, McGaugh, Hankins, Rose, & Vasquez, 1981). In a spontaneous alternation task, a 1-min intertrial interval is sufficient to observe deficits in 2-year-old mice as compared to 70-day-old mice. Thus, the general rule seems to be that performance is impaired at shorter intervals after training in old compared to young animals, although the train-test interval at which this deficit is evident varies with task.

The relationship of glucose to memory in aged organisms melds three biological hypotheses of age-related cognitive dysfunctions: central cholinergic functions (e.g., Coyle, Price & Delong, 1983; Drachman, 1981; Kesner, 1988), neuroendocrine functions (Meites, Goya, & Takahashi, 1987), and glucose metabolism (Cerami, 1985; Mooradian, 1988). Of specific relevance to this chapter, aged rats exhibit reduced release of epinephrine in response to mild stressors (McCarty, 1981, 1985); the effects of minor stressors on blood glucose levels have not yet been assessed in aged rodents.

The age-related deficit in release of peripheral epinephrine to a mild acute stressor observed in rats suggests that impaired functioning of this neuroendocrine system may contribute to the age-related deficits in memory. To examine this possibility, we tested the effects of posttraining epinephrine injections on memory storage after inhibitory avoidance (Figure 7.6) and appetitive maze training. In both tasks, and in both rats and mice, a posttraining injection of epinephrine enhanced memory and attenuated the rapid rate of forgetting observed in the aged rats (Sternberg, Martinez, McGaugh, & Gold, 1985). The single posttraining epinephrine injection effectively enhanced later retention performance in aged animals to a level comparable to that of young adult animals. The doses necessary for enhanced memory result in plasma levels that approximate those obtained after

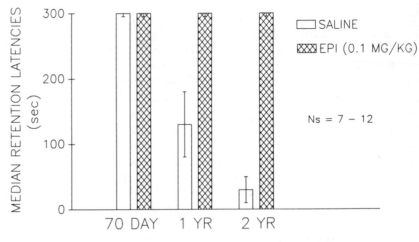

(200 uA, 0.4 sec FS; 1 week retention interval)

Figure 7.6. Epinephrine enhancement of memory in 1- and 2-year-old rats. Note that the saline control groups demonstrate an age-related deficit in retention of the learned response. A posttrial epinephrine injection enhanced retention of the learned response as tested 1 week after training and treatment. [From Gold, McGaugh, Hankins, Rose, & Vasquez, 1981.]

a training footshock in young adult rats. Thus, the results obtained with aged rats suggest that memory is impaired in rodents and that, in part, the memory deficits may result from decreased peripheral release of epinephrine, impairing this component of a system that modulates memory storage processing.

We also examined the effects of glucose administration on spontaneous alternation behavior. Glucose, injected (IP) 30 min prior to testing, enhanced performance of 2-year-old mice tested with a 1-min intertrial interval; the performance after glucose was comparable to that of young (3-month-old) mice (Figure 7.7). Like the findings described above of examinations of glucose interactions with neurotransmitter functions, glucose effects in aged animals are not restricted to measures of memory. Glucose also augments paradoxical sleep in aged rats, returning these levels to those of young rats (Stone, Wenk, Stone, & Gold, 1992).

## Effects of glucose on human memory, particularly during aging

Elderly humans also exhibit more rapid forgetting of new information than do young adult subjects, with such age-related changes often seen on tests of

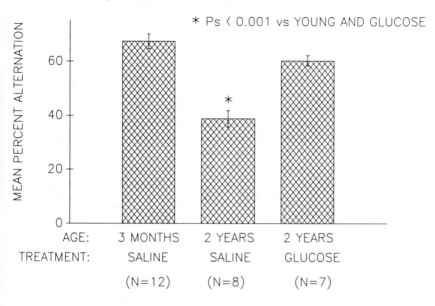

Figure 7.7. Glucose enhancement of spontaneous alternation performance in 2-year-old mice.

declarative memory (e.g., Craik, 1977; Huppert and Kopelman, 1989; Cullum et al., 1990). The relative safety of glucose as a treatment opened the possibility of examining glucose regulation of memory in humans. The findings of several experiments indicate that, as in rodents, glucose also enhances performance on some memory tasks in generally healthy elderly (60–75 years old) humans.

These experiments used a blind, crossover, counterbalanced design that enabled within-subject comparisons of performance on the measures taken. The results of the first experiment of this type (Hall et al., 1989) are shown in Figure 7.8. On two consecutive mornings, the subjects received a fruit drink prepared with either saccharin or glucose prior to several tests from the Wechsler (1981) memory scale. The findings indicate that glucose administration (ingestion in fruit drink) shortly before testing results in enhanced performance (primarily on the logical memory test) as compared to the subjects' performance under the saccharin control condition.

As shown in Figure 7.9, the results of a second experiment (Manning, Hall, & Gold, 1990) replicated the glucose enhancement of performance on the logical memory test. Glucose also significantly enhanced performance on an additional verbal selective reminding test (Buschke & Fuld, 1974), but did not affect performance on attention, motor, short-term memory, or overall cognitive function (Ammons' Quick Test; Ammons & Ammons,

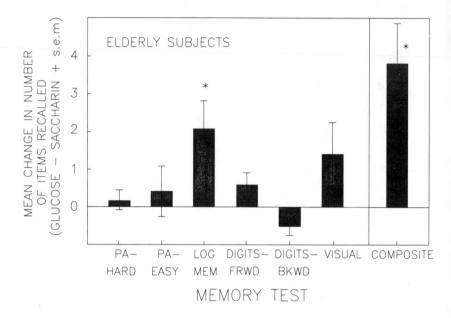

Figure 7.8. Difference scores (glucose day - saccharin day) for performance on tests of the Wechsler (1981) memory scale. On the basis of within-subject comparisons, glucose enhanced performance on the composite score, primarily reflecting the improved performance on the logical memory (narrative passage) test. (PA = paired associates, LOG MEM = logical memory; * Ps < 0.05, matched *t* tests vs. saccharin.) [From Hall et al., 1989.]

1962) tests. A further characteristic of the effects of glucose on memory is that, as in animals, the dose-response is an inverted-U function (see Figure 7.10; Parsons & Gold, in press), with the optimal glucose dose resulting in peak increases in postingestion blood glucose levels of about 40–50 mg/dl, a value remarkably similar to that observed in rodents. In addition, with modification of the logical memory test to include a 24-hr retention test, glucose enhances memory when given shortly after the material is presented, that is, in a posttraining design.

The parallels between the effects of glucose on memory in animals and humans are striking. The findings of the experiments with elderly humans, derived directly from research on rodents, support the utility of animal models of age-related memory loss for determining appropriate therapies to ameliorate memory loss in humans. Furthermore, the findings indicate that age-related impairment of memory may be subject to pharmacological control, a conclusion that supports the hypothesis that brain mechanisms responsible for memory storage are adequate but are not optimally regulated by neuroendocrine systems, resulting in memory impairments susceptible to improvement with pharmacological treatments.

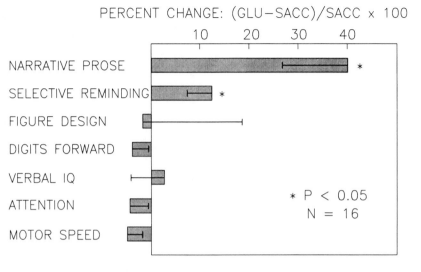

GLUCOSE EFFECTS ON PERFORMANCE OF ELDERLY HUMANS

PERCENT CHANGE: (GLU−SACC)/SACC × 100

Figure 7.9. Percent change in memory scores on several neuropsychological measures. Glucose enhanced performance on two verbal declarative memory tests, but not on measures of IQ (Ammons & Ammons, 1962), attention (letter cancellation test) or motor speed (finger tapping). (* Ps < 0.05 matched *t* tests vs. saccharin.) [From Manning, Hall, & Gold, 1990.]

The findings of the experiments with elderly humans suggest some interesting possibilities for aging research in terms of flashbulb memories. There are two quite opposite predictions here. The first is that the age-related memory deficits, associated with impaired neuroendocrine responses to emotion-laden events, will not exhibit flashbulb memories because the systems that regulate memory storage in young subjects are deficient. The second possibility is that elderly subjects will exhibit better formation of flashbulb memories, that is, the elevated threshold for appropriate neuroendocrine responses is surpassed, and that such memories will stand out even more in elderly subjects against a relatively impoverished state of memory abilities.

## Conclusions

The evidence presented here shows that: (1) Normal, endogenous neuroendocrine responses to training regulate the storage of information contained in an experience. The relationship between the magnitude of activation of this system and the magnitude of effects on memory follows an inverted-U

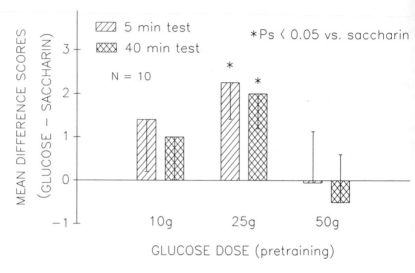

Figure 7.10. Dose-response curve for glucose effects on performance on the logical memory test (Wechsler, 1981). Note that the form of the dose-response is an inverted U, as seen regularly in animal studies of pharmacological enhancement of memory. [From Parsons & Gold, 1990.]

function. (2) This memory regulating system has considerable generality, extending from memory for avoidance training in animals to verbal declarative memory tests in humans. (3) The memory regulating system shows deficiencies in aging that may be associated with age-related memory deficits and experimental replacement of the functions attenuates age-related memory deficits.

One implication from the results reported in this chapter is that the neuroendocrine processes that regulate memory storage may contribute to the storage of information near the time of intensely emotional events. It would appear that such a system would be somewhat selective in time but not in the specific memories for which storage is enhanced. This fits well with the idea that seemingly irrelevant information received near the time of an emotional experience is stored well. If such findings reveal a neurobiological basis for flashbulb memories, then one additional feature is likely to be shared as well: The unusual storage of information at the time of the emotional event is not mechanistically unique but reflects a near-maximal instance of physiological enhancement of memory.

**NOTE**

Research described in this chapter from the author's laboratory was supported by grants from ONR (N0001489-J-1216), NIA (AG 07648), and NSF (BNS-9012239).

**REFERENCES**

Ammons, R. B., & Ammons, C. H. (1962). The Quick Test (QT): Provisional manual. *Psychological Reports, 11,* 39–69.

Axelrod, J., Weil-Malherbe, H., & Tomchick, R. (1959). The physiological disposition of $^3$H-epinephrine and its metabolite metanephrine. *Journal of Pharmacology and Experimental Therapeutics, 127,* 251–256.

Baratti, C. M., Introini, I. B., & Huygens, P. (1984). Possible interaction between central cholinergic muscarinic and opioid peptidergic systems during memory consolidation in mice. *Behavioral and Neural Biology, 40,* 155–169.

Barnes, C. A. (1979). Memory deficits with senescence: A neurophysiological and behavioral study in the rat. *Journal of Comparative and Physiological Psychology, 93,* 74–100.

Barnes, C. A., & McNaughton, B. L. (1985). An age comparison of the rates of acquisition and forgetting of spatial information in relation to long-term enhancement of hippocampal synapses. *Behavioral Neuroscience, 99,* 1040–1048.

Barnes, C. A. (1988). Spatial learning and memory processes: The search for their neurobiological mechanisms in the rat. *Trends in Neurosciences, 11,* 163–169.

Brase, D. A., & Dewey, W. L. (1988). Glucose and morphine-induced analgesia. In J. E. Morley, M. B. Sterman, & J. H. Walsh, (Eds.), *Nutritional modulation of neural function* (pp. 263–268). New York: Academic Press.

Buschke, H., & Fuld, P. A. (1974). Evaluating storage, retention, and retrieval in disordered memory and learning. *Neurology, 24,* 1019–1025.

Cerami, A. (1985). Hypothesis: Glucose as a mediator of aging. *Journal of the American Geriatric Society, 33,* 626–634.

Coyle, J. T., Price, D. L., & Delong, M. R. (1983). Alzheimer's disease: A disorder of cortical cholinergic innervation. *Science, 219,* 1184–1190.

Craik, F. I. M. (1977). Age differences in human memory. In J. E. Birren & K. W. Schaie (Eds.), *Handbook of the psychology of aging* (pp. 384–420). New York: Van Nostrand Reinhold.

Crow, T. (1988). Cellular and molecular analysis of associative learning and memory in Hermissenda. *Trends in Neurosciences, 11,* 136–142.

Cullum, C. M., Butters, N., Troster, J., Conant, J., & Cairns, P. (1990). Age effects and preliminary elderly norms for the Wechsler Memory scale-revised. *Archives of Clinical Neuropsychology, 5,* 23–30.

Dam, M., & London, E. D. (1984). Glucose utilization in Papez circuit: Effects of oxotremorine and scopolamine. *Brain Research, 295,* 137–144.

Drachman, D. A. (1981). The cholinergic system, memory, and aging. In S. J. Enna, T. Samarajski, & B. Beer (Eds.), *Aging, Vol. 17: Brain neurotransmitters and receptors in aging and age-related disorders.* New York: Raven Press.

Ellis, S., Kennedy, B. L., Eusebi, A. J., & Vincent, N. H. (1967). Autonomic control of metabolism. *Annals of the New York Academy of Science, 139,* 826–832.

Flood, J. F., & Cherkin, A. (1986). Scopolamine effects on memory retention in mice: A model of dementia? *Behavioral Neural Biology, 45,* 169–184.

Gallagher, M. (1984). Neurochemical modulation of memory: A case for opioid peptides. In L. Squire & N. Butters (Eds.), *The neuropsychology of memory* (pp. 579–587). New York: The Guilford Press.

Gallagher, M., & Burwell, R. D. (1989). Relationship of age-related decline across several behavioral domains. *Neurobiology of Aging, 10,* 691–708.

Gibson, G. E., & Blass, J. P. (1976). Impaired synthesis of acetylcholine in brain accompanying mild hypoxia and hypoglycemia. *Journal of Neurochemistry, 27,* 37–42.

Gibson, G. E., Jope, R., & Blass, J. P. (1975). Deceased synthesis of acetylcholine accompanying impaired oxidation of pyruvic acid in rat brain minces. *Biochemistry Journal, 148,* 17–23.

Gibson, G. E., & Peterson, C. (1981). Aging decreases oxidative metabolism and the release and synthesis of acetylcholine. *Journal of Neurochemistry, 37,* 978–984.

Gjedde, A., Hansen, H. J., & Silver, I. A. (1980). The glucose concentration of brain interstitial fluid is low. *Proceedings of the International Union of Physiological Sciences, 14,* 434.

Gold, P. E. (1986). Glucose modulation of memory storage processing. *Behavioral and Neural Biology, 45,* 342–349.

Gold, P. E. (1989). Neurobiological features common to memory modulation by many treatments. *Animal Learning and Behavior, 17,* 94–100.

Gold, P. E. (1990). An integrated memory regulation system: From blood to brain. To appear in R. C. A. Frederickson, D. L. Felten, and J. L. McGaugh (Eds.), *Peripheral signaling of the brain.* Toronto: Hogrefe & Huber Publishers.

Gold, P. E., & McCarty, R. (1981). Plasma catecholamines: Changes after footshock and seizure-producing frontal cortex stimulation. *Behavioral and Neural Biology, 31,* 247–260.

Gold, P. E., & McGaugh, J. L. (1975). A single-trace, two process view of memory storage processes. In D. Deutsch & J. A. Deutsch (Eds.), *Short-term memory* (pp. 355–390). New York: Academic Press.

Gold, P. E., Vogt, J., & Hall, J. L. (1986). Posttraining glucose effects on memory: Behavioral and pharmacological characteristics. *Behavioral and Neural Biology, 46,* 145–155.

Gold, P. E., McGaugh, J. L., Hankins, L. L., Rose, R. P., & Vasquez, B. J. (1981). Age dependent changes in retention in rats. *Experimental Aging Research, 8,* 53–58.

Gold, P. E., & Stone, W. S. (1988). Neuroendocrine effects on memory in aged rodents and humans. *Neurobiology of Aging, 9,* 709–717.

Gold, P. E., & van Buskirk, R. B. (1975). Facilitation of time-dependent memory processes with posttrial epinephrine injections. *Behavioral Biology, 13,* 145–153.

Gold, P. E., & Zornetzer, S. F. (1983). The mnemon and its juices: Neuromodulation of memory processes. *Behavioral and Neural Biology, 38,* 151–189.

Greenough, W. T., & Bailey, C. H. (1988). The anatomy of memory: Convergence of results across a diversity of tests. *Trends in Neurosciences, 11,* 142–147.

Hall, J. L., & Gold, P. E. (1986). The effects of footshock, epinephrine, and glucose injections on plasma glucose levels in rats. *Behavioral and Neural Biology, 46,* 156–176.

Hall, J. L., Gonder-Frederick, L. A., Chewning, W. W., Silveira, J., & Gold, P. E. (1989). Glucose enhancement of performance on memory tests in young and aged humans. *Neuropsychologia, 27,* 1129–1138.

Hochwald, G. M., Gandhi, M. S., & Goldman, S. (1983). Net transport of glucose from blood to cerebrospinal fluid in the cat. *American Journal of Physiology, 212,* 1199–1204.

Hochwald, G. M., Magee, J., & Ferguson, V. (1985). Cerebrospinal fluid glucose: Turnover and metabolism. *Journal of Neurochemistry, 44,* 1832–1837.

Honer, W. G., Prohovnik, I., Smith, G., & Lucas, L. R. (1988). Scopolamine reduces frontal cortex perfusion. *Journal of Cerebral Blood Flow and Metabolism, 8,* 635–641.

Huppert, F. A., & Kopelman, M. D. (1989). Rates of forgetting in normal ageing: A comparison with dementia. *Neuropsychologia, 27,* 849–860.

Introini, I., & Baratti, C. M. (1984). The impairment of retention induced by B-endorphin in mice may be mediated by reduction of central cholinergic activity. *Behavioral and Neural Biology, 41,* 152–163.

Introini-Collison, I., & McGaugh, J. L. (1988). Modulation of memory by post-training epinephrine: Involvement of cholinergic mechanisms. *Psychopharmacology, 94,* 379–385.

Izquierdo, I. (1984). Endogenous state dependency: Memory depends on the relation between the neurohumoral and hormonal states present after training and at the time of testing. In G. S. Lynch, J. L. McGaugh, & N. M. Weinberger (Eds.), *Neurobiology of learning and memory* (pp. 333–350). New York: Guilford Publications.

Kesner, R. P. (1988). Reevaluation of the contribution of the basal forebrain cholinergic system to memory. *Neurobiology of Aging, 9,* 609–616.

Kubanis, P., & Zornetzer, S. F. (1981). Age-related behavioral and neurobiological changes: A review with emphasis on memory. *Behavioral and Neural Biology, 31,* 115–172.

Lamour, Y., & Epelbaum, J. (1988). Interactions between cholinergic and peptidergic systems in the cerebral cortex and hippocampus. *Progress in Neurobiology, 31,* 109–148.

Lee, J. H., & McCarty, R. (1990). Glycemic control of pain threshold in diabetic and control rats. *Physiology and Behavior, 47,* 225–230.

Lee, M., Graham, S., & Gold, P. E. (1988). Memory enhancement with posttraining intraventricular glucose injections in rats. *Behavioral Neuroscience, 102,* 591–595.

Levine, S., Coe, C., & Wiener, S. G. (1989). Psychoneuroendocrinology of stress: A psychobiological perspective. In R. Brush & S. Levine (Eds.), *Psychoendocrinology* (pp. 341–377). New York: Academic Press.

Linden, D. J., & Routtenberg, A. (1989). The role of protein kinase C in long-term potentiation: A testable model. *Brain Research Reviews, 14,* 279–296.

London, E. D., Dam, M., & Fanelli, R. J. (1988). Nicotine enhances cerebral glucose utilization in central components of the rat visual system. *Brain Research Bulletin, 20,* 381–385.

Lynch, G., & Baudry, M. (1987). Brain spectrin, calpain and long-term changes in synaptic efficacy. *Brain Research Bulletin, 18,* 809–815.

Manning, C. A., Hall, J. L., & Gold, P. E. (1990). Glucose effects on memory and other neuropsychological tests in elderly humans. *Psychological Science, 1,* 307–311.

Martinez, J. L., Weinberger, S. B., & Schulteis, G. (1988). Enkephalins and learning and memory: A review of evidence for a site of action outside the blood-brain barrier. *Behavioral and Neural Biology, 49,* 192–221.

McCarty, R. (1981). Aged rats: Diminished sympathetic-adrenal medullary response in acute stress. *Behavioral and Neural Biology, 33,* 204–212.

McCarty, R. (1985). Sympathetic-adrenal medullary and cardiovascular responses to acute old stress in adult and aged rats. *Journal of the Autonomic Nervous System, 12,* 15–22.

McGaugh, J. L. (1989). Involvement of hormonal and neuromodulatory systems in the regulation of memory storage. *Annual Review of Neuroscience, 12,* 255–287.

McGaugh, J. L., & Gold, P. E. (1989). Hormonal modulation of memory. In R. Brush & S. Levine (Eds.), *Psychoendocrinology* (pp. 305–339). New York: Academic Press.

McGaugh, J. L., & Herz, M. J. (1972). *Memory consolidation.* San Francisco: Albion.

McNaughton, B. L., & Morris, R. G. (1987). Hippocampal synaptic enhancement and information storage within a distributed memory system. *Trends in Neurosciences, 10,* 408–415.

Meites, J., Goya, R., & Takahashi, S. (1987). Why the neuroendocrine system is important in aging processes. *Experimental Gerontology, 22,* 1–15.

Messier, C., & Destrade, C. (1988). Improvement of memory for an operant response by post-training glucose in mice. *Behavioural Brain Research, 31,* 185.

Messier, C., & White, N. M. (1984). Contingent and non-contingent actions of sucrose and saccharin reinforcers: Effects on taste preference and memory. *Physiology and Behavior, 32,* 195.

Messier, C., & White, N. M. (1987). Memory improvement by glucose, fructose and two glucose analogs: A possible effect on peripheral glucose transport. *Behavioral and Neural Biology, 48,* 104–127.

Mooradian, A. D. (1988). Tissue specificity of premature aging in diabetes mellitus. *Journal of the American Geriatrics Society, 36,* 831–839.

Moroni, F., Cheney, D. L., & Costa, E. (1977). Inhibition of acetylcholine turnover in rat hippocampus by intraseptal injections of B-endorphin and morphine. *Naunyn-Schmiedeberg's Archives of Pharmacology, 299,* 149–153.

Oomura, Y. (1983). Glucose as a regulator of neuronal activity. *Advances in Metabolic Disorders, 10,* 31–65.

Orzi, F., Lucignani, G., Dow-Edwards, D., Namba, H., Nehlig, A., Patlak, C. S., Pettigrew, K., Schuier, F., & Sokoloff, L. (1988). Local cerebral glucose utilization in controlled graded levels of hyperglycemia in the conscious rat. *Journal of Cerebral Blood Flow and Metabolism, 8,* 346–356.

Parsons, M. W., & Gold, P. E. (in press). Glucose enhancement of memory in elderly humans: An inverted-U dose-response curve. *Neurobiology of Aging.*

Piercy, M. F., Vogelsang, G. D., Franklin, S. R., & Tang, A. H. (1987). Reversal of scopolamine-induced amnesia and alterations in energy metabolism by the nootropic piracetam: Implications regarding identification of brain structures involved in consolidation of memory traces. *Brain Research, 424,* 1–9.

Rush, D. K. (1986). Reversal of scopolamine-induced amnesia of passive avoidance by pre-and post-training naloxone. *Psychopharmacology, 89,* 296–300.

Scremin, O. U., Allen, K., Torres, C., & Scremin, A. M. (1988). Physostigmine enhances blood flow – metabolism ratio in neocortex. *Neuropsychopharmacology, 1,* 297–303.

Solomon, P. R., Beal, M. F., & Pendlebury, W. W. (1988). Age-related disruption of classical conditioning: A model systems approach to memory disorders. *Neurobiology of Aging, 9,* 535–546.

Sternberg, D. B., Martinez, J., McGaugh, J. L., & Gold, P. E. (1985). Age-related memory deficits in aged mice and rats: Enhancement with peripheral epinephrine. *Behavioral and Neural Biology, 44,* 213–220.

Stone, W. S., Cottrill, K. L., & Gold, P. E. (1987). Glucose and epinephrine attenuation of scopolamine-induced increases in locomotor activity in mice. *Neuroscience Research Communications, 1,* 105–111.

Stone, W. S., Cottrill, K., Walker, D., & Gold, P. E. (1988). Blood glucose and brain function: Interactions with CNS cholinergic systems. *Behavioral and Neural Biology, 50,* 325–334.

Stone, W. S., Croul, C. E., & Gold, P. E. (1988). Attenuation of scopolamine-induced amnesia in mice. *Psychopharmacology, 96,* 417–420.

Stone, W. S., & Gold, P. E. (unpublished manuscript). Glucose effects on scopolamine-induced and age-induced deficits in spontaneous alternation behavior and in regional brain [3H]-2-deoxyglucose uptake.

Stone, W. S., Rudd, R. R., & Gold, P. E. (1990). Glucose and physostigmine effects on morphine- and amphetamine-induced increases in locomotor activity in mice. *Behavioral and Neural Biology, 54,* 146–155.

Stone, W. S., Rudd, R. R., & Gold, P. E. (unpublished manuscript). Glucose injections attenuate atropine-induced sleep and memory deficits: Possible effects of atropine on peripheral glucose regulation.

Stone, W. S., Walser, B., Gold, S. D., & Gold, P. E. (1991). Scopolamine- and morphine-induced impairments of spontaneous alternation performance in mice: Reversal with glucose and with cholinergic and adrenergic agonists. *Behavioral Neuroscience, 105,* 264–271.

Stone, W. S., Wenk, G. L., Stone, S. S., & Gold, P. E. (1992). Glucose attenuation of paradoxical sleep deficits in old rats. *Behavioral and Neural Biology, 57,* 79–86.

Thompson, R. F. (1988). The neural basis of basic associative learning of discrete behavioral responses. *Trends in Neuroscience, 11,* 152–155.

Wechsler, D. (1981). *WAIS-R manual.* New York: Psychological Corporation.

Weinberger, N. M., Ashe, J. H., Metherate, R., McKenna, T. M., Diamond, D. M., & Bakin, J. (1990). Retuning auditory cortex by learning: A preliminary model of receptive field plasticity. *Concepts in Neuroscience, 1,* 91–132.

Wenk, G. L. (1989). An hypothesis on the role of glucose in the mechanism of action of cognitive enhancers. *Psychopharmacology, 99,* 431–438.

White, N. M., & Messier, C. (1988). Effects of adrenal demedullation on the conditional emotional response and on the memory improving action of glucose. *Behavioral Neuroscience, 102,* 499–503.

Winocur, G. (1988). A neuropsychological analysis of memory loss with age. *Neurobiology of Aging, 9,* 487–494.

Wood, P. L., Cheney, D. L., & Costa, E. (1979). An investigation of whether septal g-amino-butyrate-containing interneurones are involved in the reduction in the turnover rate of acetylcholine elicited by substance P and B-endorphin in the hippocampus. *Neuroscience, 4,* 1479–1484.

Zornetzer, S. F., Thompson, R., & Rogers, J. (1982). Rapid forgetting in aged rats. *Behavioral and Neural Biology, 36,* 49–60.

# 8

# Remembering the details of emotional events

DANIEL REISBERG AND FRIDERIKE HEUER

How well does one remember the emotional events in one's life? Many studies indicate a strong correlation between the *vividness* with which an event is recalled, and the *emotionality* of the event, at the time it occurred (Bohannon, 1988; Brown & Kulik, 1977; Christianson & Loftus, 1990; Conway & Bekerian, 1988; Pillemer, 1984; Rubin & Kozin, 1984). Interestingly, this correlation seems independent of the type of emotion at stake (Reisberg, Heuer, McLean, & O'Shaughnessy, 1988; Robinson, 1980; White, 1989). Thus, in general, the stronger the emotion, the greater the vividness of subsequent recall. In this regard at least, "flashbulb" memories are continuous with remembering in general; that is, flashbulb memories simply represent the extreme of this affect–vividness relationship.

But how *accurate* are these vivid and detailed memories? If emotional events are recalled with great detail, is this evidence for some encoding or retrieval advantage associated with emotionality? Or, alternatively, is this evidence for high levels of construction and confabulation associated with emotion? In the former case, emotional memories would be both vivid and also veridical; in the latter case, emotional memories might be filled with errors and intrusions.

This question about accuracy is fueled by several concerns. As we describe below, several studies have documented conspicuous errors in the recall of emotional events. At the least, this implies that neither emotionality nor memory vividness provides any guarantee of memory accuracy. Moreover, these documented errors lead us to wonder what further inaccuracies lie undetected. In addition, laboratory research has directly examined emotion's impact on learning and memory, and the results generally indicate that emotionality works against accurate and detailed remembering. This all seems to lead to a remarkable suggestion – namely, that emotionality is positively associated with memory vividness, but negatively associated with memory accuracy. In this case, it may turn out to be our most vivid, most detailed memories that are most prone to error!

In this chapter, we will examine the warrant for this striking claim. As we will see, three lines of evidence point to the conclusion that emotion does

162

work against memory, and, indeed, there is something close to consensus in the literature that this is the case (e.g., Kassin, Ellsworth, & Smith, 1989; Yarmey & Jones, 1983). We will argue, however, that this consensus is unwarranted. We will argue that the evidence is at best ambiguous, and, in fact, we believe that a case can be made that emotion systematically *improves* memory for some types of material. To anticipate the argument to come, we will end up arguing that the interaction between emotion and memory is a complex one, with emotion having several different effects on remembering, with each of these in turn moderated by other factors. Nonetheless, we will develop an optimistic claim – that we can largely trust our vivid memories of emotional events.

## Naturalistic studies

A growing number of studies have examined subjects' recollection of actual emotional events in their lives; many of these studies have focused on potential flashbulb events. In these procedures, subjects are interviewed, immediately after the event, about how the event unfolded – what happened, how they heard the news, who was with them when they heard the news, and so on. Comparable reports are then collected from the same subjects months or, in some cases, years later.

In these naturalistic studies, subjects' immediate and delayed reports often agree on many details, but it is easy to find deviations in the delayed report, and some of these deviations are rather large (Christianson, 1989; Larsen, this volume; Linton, 1975, pp. 386–387; McCloskey, Wible, & Cohen, 1988; Neisser, 1982; Wagenaar & Groeneweg, 1990). This obviously suggests that the delayed report, as vivid as it might seem, does contain mistakes. A particularly striking case of this sort comes from a study by Neisser and Harsch (this volume). They interviewed subjects 1 day after the space shuttle explosion, and then again 3 years later. In many of the reports, there was remarkably little agreement between the immediate and delayed versions, even with regard to such major details as who delivered the news, where the subject was when the news arrived, and so forth. At the same time, most of the subjects were completely confident in the accuracy of their delayed reports! Here we have an example, then, where accuracy levels were near floor, and confidence levels near ceiling, in remembering an emotional event.

## Easterbrook's hypothesis

These findings converge with a theoretical claim that has been in the literature for several decades, namely, the so-called Easterbrook hypothesis. Easterbrook (1959) proposed that arousal leads to a "narrowing of attention," that is, a decrease in the range of cues to which an organism is sensitive. At low levels of arousal, this mechanism would improve performance in many tasks, as the proposed narrowing would prevent distraction. At high levels of arousal, though, attention would be narrowed to such a degree that even task-relevant information would be excluded, and so performance would be undermined.

A number of studies have examined the Easterbrook claim, with evidence coming from tasks as diverse as the memorization of word lists, visual search tasks, and a variety of animal-model evidence, much of it from discrimination tasks (Bruner, Matter, & Papanek, 1955; Easterbrook, 1959; Eysenck, 1982; Mandler, 1975). Arousal has been manipulated in these studies in various ways, including severity of shock, presentation of noxious noise, and varying levels of food deprivation. Across these procedures, the evidence is broadly consistent with the Easterbrook claim: With increasing arousal, organisms seem sensitive to a decreasing range of stimulus cues.

Given that arousal typically accompanies emotion, the Easterbrook claim leads directly to a prediction about memory for emotional events: If one witnesses a very emotional event, one will attend only to a restricted range of information, and encode correspondingly few details. If many details are subsequently recalled, therefore, they are likely to be reconstructions, and so open to error. No wonder, then, that researchers easily document cases of inaccuracy in memories of emotional events, including flashbulb events.

Thus the laboratory investigations of the Easterbrook hypothesis, like the naturalistic studies, suggest that emotionality works against memory. But how persuasive is all this? Although naturalistic studies of emotional memory document many errors, it is striking just how much subjects do seem to retain about emotional events. For example, both Pillemer (1984) and Bohannon (this volume) have reported that emotional memories are, in fact, relatively consistent over time. That is, subjects who report more affect associated with the target event also show a greater degree of concordance between their immediate and delayed descriptions of the event. Likewise, McCloskey, Wible, and Cohen (1988) report many errors in their subjects' recall, but we can equally well focus on how much their subjects did remember. After a 9-month delay, 81% of their subjects either reported the same information, or more specific information, about where they were when they heard the emotional news about the space shuttle explosion; 70% of their subjects reported the same or more specific information about who had told them the news. Summing across categories of information, 67% of subjects' responses at 9 months matched (or were more specific than) their responses immediately after the emotional event.

Comparable data are reported by Yuille and Cutshall (1986). These researchers interviewed 13 witnesses to an actual crime 4 to 5 months after the event. The crime was clearly an emotional one, inasmuch as subjects were on the scene during a shooting in which one person was killed and another wounded. Yuille and Cutshall had available to them the police interviews and a variety of forensic evidence, all of which could be used in assessing the veracity of the subjects' memories. The data indicate impressive accuracy in subjects' reports. Even with reasonably strict scoring criteria, subjects were correct, after a 4–5 month delay, in 83% of the details reported about the action itself within the episode, 76% of their descriptions of people, and 90% of their descriptions of objects in the scene.

It is not clear, however, what to make of findings like these. Should we be impressed by the high levels of retention in these studies? Or should we instead focus on the substantial numbers of errors, often large errors? In asking whether performance in these studies is to be praised or lamented, we need to ask, "compared to what?" For example, consider the Neisser and Harsch data, described earlier. These subjects clearly did forget a great deal, but we have no way to know if they would have forgotten even more, or forgotten more quickly, if the target event had been unemotional for them. This robs the Neisser and Harsch data of none of their interest, particularly the striking contrast in their results between memory accuracy and memory confidence. However, it is not obvious what to conclude from these data about the remembering of emotional events.

Likewise, Bohannon (this volume) also examined subjects' memories for the space shuttle explosion. He reports data seemingly at odds with the Neisser and Harsch findings, namely, that subjects did remember the event, even at a 3-year delay. That is, Bohannon reports strong concordance between subjects' recollections of the event, 1 week after its occurrence, and then again, 3 years later. This by itself makes both the Bohannon and Neisser and Harsch data difficult to interpret. In addition, though, Bohannon reports that the stability of subjects' memory was linked to emotionality: Those subjects who were most upset by the space shuttle disaster turn out to be the subjects whose 3-year reports are most in line with their reports shortly after the event occurred. But how should we interpret this? Our main concern here is that we do not know *why* some subjects were more upset by the disaster than others. Could it be that some subjects were more interested in the space program, or better informed about the event? Could it be that some subjects heard the news in a dry and factual manner, whereas others heard it in a more vivid fashion? If so, it could be factors like these, and not the emotionality itself, that is influencing memory. These possibilities make it difficult to interpret Bohannon's findings.

Given all this, it is unclear what lessons to draw from these naturalistic studies. The huge advantage of these studies, needless to say, is that subjects are remembering actual events in their lives, events accompanied by genuine and strong emotion. But this external validity is purchased at a stiff price, namely, a lack of several desirable controls. Memory in these studies is far from perfect, and so we can certainly conclude that such memories are vulnerable to error. This is a valuable point for evaluating some hypotheses, in particular strong claims that one might make about flashbulb memories (cf. McCloskey et al., 1988; see also Bohannon, 1988; Cohen, McCloskey, & Wible, 1988, 1990; Pillemer, 1990; Schmidt & Bohannon, 1988). At the same time, this still leaves us asking what impact (if any) emotionality has on memory.

In a sense, we encounter the converse problem in trying to evaluate the second category of evidence described earlier, namely, evidence relevant to the Easterbrook claim. In this case, the relevant data come from well-designed laboratory studies, and so problems of control or comparison are not an issue. However, it is difficult to know how to generalize from these experiments to the questions of interest here. We will discuss below several of the considerations and parameters relevant to human memory for complex emotional events. These considerations are largely incommensurate (or inapplicable) to procedures involving animal learning, or memorization of word lists, and so on. As a result, translating between these domains seems difficult at best, and it certainly seems premature (for example) to apply laboratory evidence supporting the Easterbrook claim to cases like flashbulb memories.

## Simulation studies

Thus we have mirror-image concerns about the evidence sketched so far: On the one side, the naturalistic studies are clearly relevant to the issues under scrutiny, but lack desirable controls. On the other side, laboratory studies of arousal's effects are rigorously controlled, but are of uncertain application to cases like flashbulb memories. Given this pattern of concerns, it seems appropriate to seek studies that are positioned midway, so to speak, between the naturalistic studies and the laboratory studies of arousal. In particular, what we seem to need is experimentally controlled research in which subjects are asked to remember emotional events similar to the complex events one remembers in day-to-day life. This brings us, at last, to the third line of evidence pertinent to emotion's impacts on memory, namely, the "simulation" studies.

Many simulation studies exist, due in part to an increasing interest in eyewitness testimony (for reviews of this literature, see Heuer & Reisberg, in press; Loftus, 1979). In these studies, subjects are exposed to a complex, contrived situation designed to manipulate emotion or arousal; control subjects are exposed to a comparable situation, but one lacking the arousal manipulation. Memory can then be compared for these two groups.

Many of the studies in this category are concerned with the phenomenon of "weapon-focus." This term refers to an effect often cited by lawyers in which witnesses to crimes involving a weapon seem to attend exclusively to the weapon, to the exclusion of all else. Thus the weapon is remembered well, but little else is, making the witness a poor source of information about such things as, say, the perpetrator's identity. The weapon-focus claim shares with the Easterbrook hypothesis an assertion that attention is narrowed under circumstances of emotional arousal. If correct, the weapon-focus claim will once again lead us to the prediction that emotional events create relatively impoverished memories. What, therefore, is the empirical status of the weapon-focus claim?

Early studies of the weapon-focus claim suggested that the claim is indeed correct, but these studies were unpersuasive. For example, Kuehn (1974) surveyed a number of police reports, and found that victims of robberies provided much fuller descriptions of their assailant than did victims of rapes or physical assaults. This is consistent with the weapon-focus claim, but we have no way to assess the accuracy of these victims' reports. In addition, we have no way to determine if victims remember less about a rape or assault, or if they are just unwilling to report what they remember. Likewise, there are several early experimental demonstrations of the weapon-focus pattern, but these are for various reasons difficult to interpret (for discussion, see Egeth & McCloskey, 1984; Heuer & Reisberg, in press; Loftus, 1979; McCloskey & Egeth, 1983).

More recent evidence, though, is more persuasive, as several well-controlled studies have now documented the weapon-focus phenomenon. As one example, Maass & Köhnken (1989) had their subjects sitting in a laboratory, taking various tests, when an assistant appeared in the room, conspicuously carrying a hypodermic needle. The sight of this "weapon" clearly influenced subjects' memory, and subjects had better memory for the hypodermic needle (and details of the hand itself) than the control subjects. By the same token, subjects who saw the hypodermic needle remembered less about the assistant's face than the control subjects. (For further evidence, see Cutler, Penrod, & Martens, 1987; Kramer, Buckhout, & Eugenio, 1990; Loftus, Loftus, & Messo, 1987; Tooley, Brigham, Maass, & Bothwell, 1987.)

The weapon-focus studies thus seem to imply that emotional events do lead to "narrower" memories. (As it turns out, there is reason to believe that it may not be emotionality itself that produces the weapon-focus effect, but some other feature of these events. We return to this point shortly.) These studies are joined by several others in the literature that are not specifically concerned with weapon-focus, but compare subjects' memories for emotional and (otherwise comparable) unemotional episodes. For example, Loftus and Burns (1982) presented their subjects with a brief film clip depicting a bank robbery. For half of the subjects, the film showed the robber run out of the bank with two men pursuing him. The robber then turned and shot a small boy in the face. For the remaining subjects, the film was the same up until the shooting, but then cut back to the inside of the bank, where the manager is telling everyone to remain calm. Immediately after viewing the films, subjects' memories were tested for the *early* part of the film (i.e., for the portion of the film that was identical for the two groups). Subjects who had seen the neutral version remembered more of the details, a finding that emerged with both recognition and recall testing.

Similar findings are reported by Clifford and Hollin (1981) and Clifford and Scott (1978). Half of their subjects viewed a videotaped violent event (a thief grabs a woman's purse and flees); the other half viewed a neutral event (a man approaches a woman and asks her for directions). Immediately after viewing this videotape, subjects were questioned about the event, including such details as the height, weight, and clothing of the perpetrator. The results showed poorer performance from subjects who had seen the violent event, and this effect became more pronounced with a greater number of perpetrators involved in the event. (This latter point fits well with the Easterbrook claim: If arousal narrows attention, then arousal's impact should be most visible with complex events, as these would be particularly difficult to encode under circumstances of a narrow attentional focus.)

These studies broadly indicate that emotion works against accurate remembering (see also Christianson, 1984; Christianson & Loftus, 1991; Deffenbacher, 1983; Kebeck & Lohaus, 1986). The data in these studies are reasonably consistent; the experiments in question are well controlled. The to-be-remembered materials in these studies are sufficiently realistic to support generalizations outside of the laboratory. Thus perhaps it is the case that emotionality does undermine memory accuracy.

## The effect of retention interval

Even with these advantages, however, we suggest that caution is needed in interpreting the evidence cited so far. As one prominent concern, most of the laboratory studies in this area have assessed memory immediately after the to-be-remembered event occurred. Yet it is obvious in one's day-to-day remembering that one remembers events from months or years back. Does this matter? A suggestion that retention interval is crucial comes from studies of subjects' memories for emotion-laden words, such as "rape" or "vomit" (e.g., Kleinsmith & Kaplan, 1963, 1964). To be sure, we have already urged caution about generalizing from studies of word lists. Nonetheless, the Kleinsmith and Kaplan data provided an early indication that retention interval interacts with emotion's memory effects. In their study, memory was tested after various intervals. At short intervals, memory was poorer for emotional words. At longer intervals (1 week), this pattern reversed, with better retention for emotional materials.

The Kleinsmith and Kaplan results have been replicated many times (Baddeley, 1982; Butter, 1970; Farley, 1973; Kaplan & Kaplan, 1969;

McLean, 1969; Osborne, 1972; Walker & Tarte, 1963; for reviews, see Craik & Blankstein, 1975; Eysenck, 1976; Hockey, 1978). Each of these studies has shown a beneficial effect of arousal on memory, *provided that* memory is tested at longer retention intervals. But all of these studies have employed word lists, or nonsense syllables, or numbers, as the to-be-remembered materials. One study in this literature did employ richer materials (a 10-minute film; Levonian, 1967), but memory was only globally assessed (via a brief yes–no questionnaire). Thus none of these studies can speak directly to the question of emotion's impact on memory for complex materials.

A few studies in the literature have examined the relation between emotion, retention interval, and event memory, but the data are difficult to interpret. First, Kebeck and Lohaus (1986) tested their subjects immediately after seeing an emotional event, and then retested the same subjects 1 week later. They found that arousal worked against memory in both the immediate and delayed tests. However, it is difficult to interpret their delayed tests, because we do not know what impact there might have been from the repeated testing itself. Hence we hesitate to draw conclusions from this study.

Likewise, Christianson (1984) tested memory for an emotional event both immediately and after a 2-week delay. He found that arousal hurt memory with immediate test, but, on several measures, improved memory with a delayed test. Thus his data are broadly consistent with the Kleinsmith and Kaplan pattern. However, a subsequent study did not replicate the Christianson (1984) results: Christianson and Loftus (1987) employed the same stimuli and the same memory tests as those in the earlier Christianson study, but obtained very different results. In this later study, Christianson and Loftus found poorer performance for the emotional materials in both immediate and delayed testing. We note, though, that these two studies differed in how subjects were instructed to attend to the slides. In the Christianson (1984) study, subjects were simply asked to concentrate carefully on each of the slides shown. In the Christianson and Loftus study, subjects were required, as they viewed each slide, to write down a word or phrase identifying the slide's most distinctive features. Although this instruction difference seems a plausible explanation of the contrasting data from these studies, we have no direct evidence on this point. Thus, this pair of studies is difficult to interpret.

To summarize, then, many studies have examined memory for (simulated) complex emotional events. These studies are consistent in their finding that emotion works against memory, particularly memory for details of the events. However, most of these studies have employed retention intervals of less than 1 hour, quite unlike the retention intervals at stake in flashbulb memories, or autobiographical memory in general. A few studies have employed longer retention intervals, but the evidence from these studies is contradictory, and, as discussed, there are problems in interpreting these studies.

## The Heuer and Reisberg slide-sequence study

All of this provided a large part of the motivation for a series of studies run in our laboratory. In particular, how does retention interval shape emotion's effects on remembering? In one of our early procedures (Heuer and Reisberg, 1990), memory performance was compared for two groups of subjects. (This procedure was modeled after the Christianson, 1984, design.) Each group saw a story, depicted in a slide sequence. The story began in the same way, and ended in the same way, for both groups. The middle sequence of the story showed a boy and his mother visiting father at his workplace, and watching the father at work. In the neutral version, the father was a mechanic, and the boy watched him perform a car repair. For the arousal group, the father was a surgeon, and the boy observed him performing surgery on an accident victim. These slides were matched as much as possible for lay-out, number of people shown, and so on. Both groups were told only that we were interested in "measuring physiological arousal to different types of material," in this way hoping to ensure that learning would be incidental.

The material presented to subjects, and the subsequent test items, had been categorized by a panel of judges into "central" and "detail" information. In this early experiment, central information was defined as everything directly relevant to plot, and which could not be changed without changing the gist of the story. Detail information was everything else. For example, central information was whether the boy visited his father at the hospital or at a garage. An example of detail information would be the color of clothing people in the slides were wearing.

Memory was tested after a 2-week interval, with both a recall and a recognition test. (For now, we concentrate on the recognition data; we return to the recall data below.) Subjects who saw the arousing version of the story showed a clear memory advantage. The two groups did not differ in their memory for phase 1 of the presentation (i.e., before the two stories diverged). The arousal group showed a clear advantage, however, in remembering the story's phase 2, where the arousing manipulation was actually introduced. This advantage then continued into the story's final phase, which was, again, identical for the two stories.

Figure 8.1 shows the data for remembering *central* information, broken down according to the individual slides in the presentation. Note, first, that the profile of performance is roughly the same for both groups. This suggests that we succeeded in producing matched neutral and arousal stories. More important, arousal subjects have a clear memory advantage, particularly for the materials at the story's center, where the arousal manipulation took place.

Figure 8.2 shows the comparable slide for *detail* information. Arousal subjects have no advantage in remembering the early slides; this is not

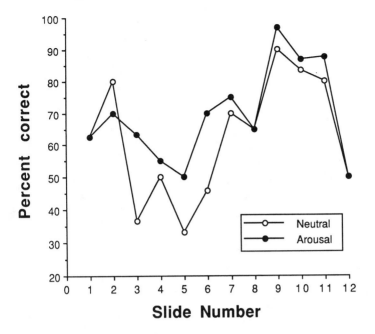

Figure 8.1. Slide-by-slide recognition performance for *central* information, from Heuer & Reisberg (1990).

suprising, because these were the same slides for both groups. However, arousal subjects have a consistent advantage across the latter half of the presentation. This advantage in remembering details is of course critical for present purposes, because this finding is seemingly contrary to the Easterbrook or weapon-focus claims. That is, it is precisely the detail information that should be excluded by the hypothesized narrowing of attention central to these claims.

This first study thus indicated that emotional arousal might have a beneficial effect on memory *if* memory is tested at a sufficiently long delay. We obviously cannot rest this claim, however, on a single study. In addition, one might worry about whether we truly succeeded in matching the arousal and neutral materials. It might be, for example, that the arousal material somehow provided a more cohesive or structured tale; if true, this would obviously influence the pattern of results.

### Remembering popular movies

To address these questions, Dorman (1989) compared memory for two versions of a film clip, taken from a horror movie, *Rosemary's Baby*.[1] The clip

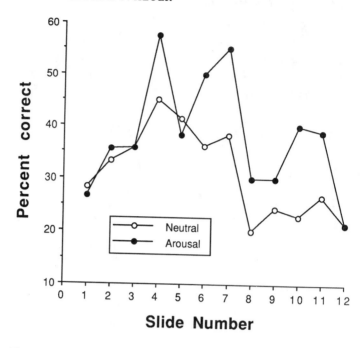

Figure 8.2. Slide-by-slide recognition performance for *peripheral* information, from Heuer & Reisberg (1990).

begins with some moments of dialogue, and then shows Rosemary sneaking into a neighbor's apartment. Subjects in the arousal group were first given a summary of the film up to that point, then they saw the film clip, including its frightening background music. Subjects in the neutral group were given a cover story of Rosemary suffering from the flu, and were told that she was entering the neighbor's apartment to locate the source of an annoying noise. They were then shown a carefully edited version of the film clip. The visual track was left untouched, as was the dialogue at the start of the clip, which concerned Rosemary drinking her milk, the weather, and so on. All that was changed was the soundtrack that accompanied the latter part of the clip, replacing the frightening music with some light-hearted Mozart.

Subjects saw the film (ostensibly as part of a study on physiological effects of visual stimuli), and then were tested 2 weeks later. To put the results briefly, Dorman replicated the earlier Heuer and Reisberg findings. With this delayed testing, emotional arousal improved memory both for central materials and for details. And in this case it seems clear that we do have matched stories – in particular, visually identical stories.

One might still be concerned, however, about the artificial nature of these laboratory events. In particular, does the level of arousal created in these studies match anything people experience in their day-to-day lives? Likewise, subjects were at best passive witnesses to these to-be-remembered events. How (if at all) does this influence performance?

As a step toward addressing these issues, Andrews (1990) examined memory for scenes selected from several commercially successful movies (*Fatal Attraction, Dangerous Liaisons*, etc.). Unlike the Dorman study, however, in which an isolated movie scene was observed in a laboratory setting, Andrews tested memory for scenes observed in far more natural circumstances – that is, scenes observed as part of an entire film viewed in a movie theater. Andrews argued that to-be-remembered materials of this sort seem likely to stir viewers' emotions to a considerable degree – far more than the stimuli created by laboratory psychologists. In addition, it seems clear that movie viewers often become quite involved in the film, and so are not "passive witnesses" to the filmed event.

Subjects were identified who had seen these films 6 months or more prior to the memory study; memory was tested for several target scenes within each film. Andrews selected target scenes matched as far as possible for duration, placement within the film, and also relevance to plot. Each scene, in addition, had been assessed by a panel of judges as being either bland and unemotional, or as highly emotional.

As Figure 8.3 shows, most subjects remembered the emotional scenes from these movies more accurately than they remembered the neutral scenes. (Note that chance-performance in this 4AFC procedure would be 25%; subjects are comfortably above this level.) Andrews also assessed memory separately for gist and memory for plot-irrelevant detail. Gist questions generally probed the plot of the scenes; detail questions focused on details relevant to both emotional and neutral scenes. For example, subjects were asked about the color of the actors' clothing in each of the scenes, or objects in the background of the two scenes, or about the exact phrasing of dialogue. This ensured that the detail questions were comparably difficult for both the emotional and neutral scenes.

Even at these long delays, memory for gist was quite good for both the emotional and neutral scenes (71.8% vs. 70.4%, respectively). There is little effect of emotionality here, perhaps reflecting near-ceiling performance. (Subjects were asked only three or four gist questions per scene; hence they were, on average, merely making one error on the gist questions.) However, memory for plot-irrelevant detail did show the expected pattern, with performance consistently better for the emotional scenes (40.4% correct) than for the neutral scenes (29.6%).

Subjects in this study had also filled out a separate measure, roughly assessing how "arousable" they were, at least according to self-report. This measure, developed by Mehrabian (1977a; 1977b), asks subjects how bothered they are by changes in weather, or how long after a fight they

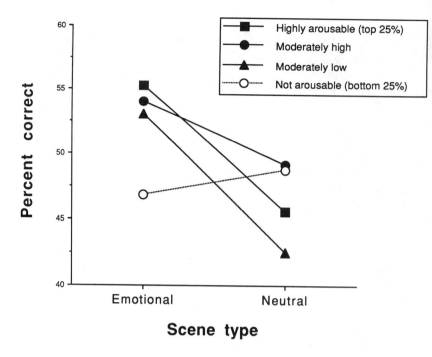

Figure 8.3. Memory for movie scenes, by type of scene and by arousability of the subjects (according to self-report), from Andrews (1990). The data were partitioned at the quartiles to define the four groups shown. The least arousable subjects showed no effect of scene type; all other subjects showed a robust effect of scene type.

remain angry, and so on. As Figure 8.3 shows, this variable interacted with the type of to-be-remembered material. Our "least arousable" subjects (by self-report, divided at the quartiles) were unaffected by the emotionality of the scenes, and remembered the emotional and neutral scenes equally well. (The slight trend in this group for better memory for the neutral scenes is nowhere near reliable.) The remaining subjects showed a substantial effect of scene type, reliably remembering more of the emotional scenes than of the neutral scenes. This interaction between scene type and arousability implies that emotionality is indeed the key factor in distinguishing the neutral and emotional scenes. That is, one might be concerned that the emotional scenes in these movies differed in some other way from the neutral scenes – perhaps being longer, or more relevant to the plot, or some such. However, it is not obvious why these factors would interact with the individual-difference variable.

In a follow-up study, Andrews compared memory for three types of movie scenes – happy scenes from movies, sad scenes from the same movies, and

then, for comparison, emotionally neutral scenes. The data largely repro-
duced the pattern just described, although the effects were stronger for sad
scenes than for happy ones. This may reflect the fact that the sad scenes were
more emotional, more involving, than the happy ones. In any event, memory
for both of these was reliably different from memory for neutral scenes.

## The Burke, Heuer, and Reisberg study

At short delays, study after study has found a detrimental effect of emotion
on memory (Christianson, 1984; Christianson & Loftus, 1991; Clifford &
Hollin, 1981; Clifford & Scott, 1978; Deffenbacher, 1983; Kebeck & Lohaus,
1986; Loftus & Burns, 1982; Siegel & Loftus, 1978). If we were to consider
only these studies, the conclusion would be clear: Emotion undermines
memory, and, in particular, undermines memory for detail. This is clearly
consistent with the Easterbrook hypothesis, or the weapon-focus claim. But
other data show the reverse pattern: Several studies, all using longer retention intervals, have shown that emotion seems to help memory for detail,
contrary to the Easterbrook or weapon-focus claims (Andrews, 1990, Study 1
and Study 2; Christianson, 1984; Dorman, 1989; Heuer & Reisberg, 1990;
Snyder, 1989).

This pattern of evidence suggests an important role for retention interval
in moderating emotion's effects. However, note that this is a pattern of
evidence *across diverse studies*, indicating a need for caution in interpreting this
pattern. We have emphasized that the various studies just cited differed with
regard to retention interval, but they also differed in other ways, including
their stimulus materials, the instructions to subjects, their test procedures
and so on. These various studies provided subjects with different to-be-
remembered materials, and probed subjects' memories for rather different
sorts of details. Indeed, these studies differ with regard to how "details" were
defined, and thus with regard to how the data were analyzed. In the Heuer
and Reisberg study, for example, the contrast between central materials and
detail hinged on whether the information was or was not pertinent to the
plot. In other studies, though, materials have been considered "central" if
they are associated with visually central elements (e.g., Christianson &
Loftus, 1991) and detail otherwise; in this categorization, some plot-
irrelevant material would be considered central, some as detail. This
obviously makes comparisons across studies immensely difficult.

In clarifying these issues, what seems needed is a study that looks simultaneously at emotion, retention interval, and type of remembered material.
Such a study was recently completed by Burke, Heuer, and Reisberg (in
press). Burke et al. once again employed the stimuli from the Heuer and
Reisberg (1990) procedure – that is, a slide sequence in which a boy visits his
father at work, with the father being either a car mechanic or a surgeon.

Subjects were shown these slides and merely instructed to watch them carefully, without knowing that memory would be subsequently tested. Four groups of subjects were tested: Half of the subjects saw the neutral story; half saw the emotional story. Within each group, some subjects were tested immediately after the presentation, and the remaining subjects were tested after a delay (1 or 2 weeks in their first experiment, 1 week in their second experiment).

Burke et al. also wanted to take a closer look at how emotion shapes memory for different types of material, beyond the relatively crude categorization of "central" materials and "details" used in previous studies. To make this possible, independent judges categorized the to-be-remembered material (and the test items) into four different categories of information. The first two categories subdivided what we had previously called central materials. The first category contained items pertaining to the gist or plot of the story, essentially items one could ask for by the question "What happened next?" The second category concerned the materials that were visually central to the slide. These were materials that would be the "basic-level" answer to the question "What does the slide show?" (cf. Rosch, 1978; also Morris & Murphy, 1990; Rifkin, 1985; Vallacher & Wegner, 1987).

The third and fourth categories were designed to subdivide what we had been calling detail – that is, material not relevant to the plot. The third category included those details that were attached to the visually central materials; for example, if a slide centrally depicted the father working, a question about whether he was wearing gloves, or the color of his hat, would fall into this category. Finally, a fourth category was concerned with truly peripheral detail, that is, details from the backgrounds of the slides, or plot-irrelevant details from the taped narrative accompanying the slides.

These distinctions among types of to-be-remembered materials turned out to be crucial in the Burke et al. data. In their results, emotion generally improved memory for the plot-relevant information (gist and basic-level visual information). Emotion's effects on detail memory, though, were more complex. Consider first the plot-irrelevant details that happen to be associated with central characters in the story. For these materials, Burke et al. found that emotion *improved* memory in the middle phase of the presentation (the phase in which the arousing materials themselves were presented), but worked *against* memory for materials in the third (final) phase of the story. The pattern was quite different for plot-irrelevant details that happened to concern "background." For these, emotion undermined memory accuracy, with this effect being most visible in the story's middle phase.

Broadly put, the pattern of these data is that emotion aided memory for materials tied to the "action" in the event. Plot and basic-level visual information are tied to the event by virtue of defining what the story itself is, and arousal improved memory for information in these categories. But what about plot-irrelevant detail? Details associated with central characters are *spatially* tied to the action, but that does not seem to be enough. Emotion had a positive effect on memory in this category only when the to-be-remembered details were also *temporally* tied to the action, that is, in phase 2 of the presentation. When that temporal connection was broken, as in phases 1 and 3, emotion worked against memory for information in this category. Finally, when the spatial connection was also broken – as it is for "background" detail – emotion again worked against accurate remembering.

The Burke et al. results therefore yield a consistent (albeit complex) pattern with regard to type of to-be-remembered material. Unfortunately, though, their data are less clear-cut with regard to retention interval. Their first experiment yielded no reliable interactions between interval and emotionality; their second experiment showed the predicted interactions in some measures, but not in all. This is reminiscent of the contrast between the Christianson (1984) and Christianson and Loftus (1987) studies, with the former showing an effect of interval, but not the latter. Given all of this, we can only offer tentative conclusions about retention interval's role. The data do imply that retention interval matters: Several interactions between emotion and interval were observed, and these were quite consistent in direction. But these effects are plainly not robust, and further data are needed to determine why retention interval seems to play a role in some studies but not in others.

Against this backdrop of caution, we emphasize that the interval effects, where observed by Burke et al., were consistent in direction. As noted above, some categories of information yielded a memory advantage associated with emotion, and these advantages tended to grow over time, so that larger advantages were observed with delayed testing. Other categories of information, however, yielded a memory *dis*advantage associated with emotion, and these disadvantages tended to shrink over time, so that the disadvantage was diminished (or reversed) in delayed testing. An obvious reading of all of this is that emotion served to slow the rate of forgetting, so that initial advantages gradually grew, and initial disadvantages were gradually offset.

Finally, the Burke et al. procedure also examined one further issue. Subjects who were tested immediately after viewing the to-be-remembered materials were also *re*tested 1 week later, allowing us to examine the effects of repeated testing. Overall, the immediate test seemed to act as a rehearsal, and, as a result, subjects *re*tested after a week performed better than those tested for the first time after the same delay. But this rehearsal seemed also to have frozen a memory pattern in place: That is, the effects of arousal in the 1-week second test clearly resemble those from the *immediate* test far more than they resemble those from the 1-week *first* test.

Thus the Burke et al. study indicates a strong influence on later memory tests by earlier ones. Whatever emotion's effects with longer retention intervals, therefore, these effects may not be detected if subjects' memories had also been tested at shorter intervals. To put it differently, the immediate test seems to serve as a strong source of memory interference, with an effect reminiscent of that obtained when subjects receive postevent information (cf. Loftus, 1979; Loftus & Hoffman, 1989; Loftus & Palmer, 1974). In many studies, postevent information seems to merge with memory for the event itself, so that memory for the original event (without the postevent information) is difficult to detect. In the Burke et al. procedure, the postevent information is, in essence, provided by the subjects' own responses on the memory test (cf. Bartlett, 1932; Belbin, 1950). For research purposes, this means we need to be extremely cautious about studies that compare immediate and delayed test with the same subjects tested at both intervals (e.g., Buckhout, Alper, Chern, Silverberg, & Slomovits, 1974; Cutler et al., 1987; Kebeck & Lohaus, 1986).

## Emotion and the rate of forgetting

How should we think about all these findings? We would suggest that the data, both in the Burke et al. study and in the literature overall, can be understood as reflecting two basic effects. First, as we have already mentioned, emotion appears to *slow forgetting*. Of course, emotional events are gradually forgotten, just as any events are. This forgetting is revealed in the main effect of retention interval in the Burke et al. data; it is also consistent with studies cited above in which errors are documented in the recall of emotional events. The key, though, is that emotional events are forgotten more slowly than (otherwise comparable) neutral events. This is clearly implied by the pattern across studies in the literature; it is also directly shown in the Christianson (1984) data; it also emerges in many measures in the Burke et al. data.

The literature contains two results seemingly in conflict with this claim of slowed forgetting, but these results are easily accommodated: Christianson and Loftus (1987), as we discussed early on, failed to find an emotionality x interval interaction, but their study included an explicit manipulation of subjects' attention. For the reasons described below, it seems likely that this manipulation counteracted at least some of emotion's effects. Second, Kebeck and Lohaus (1986) also found no emotionality x interval interaction, but their comparison between immediate and delayed tests was *within-subjects*. The Burke et al. data make it plain that we need to be cautious in interpreting these data, given the likelihood of contamination from the early test on the later one.

The suggestion that emotionality slows forgetting has been anticipated by a number of authors, and, in fact, several mechanisms may contribute to this effect. (See Heuer & Reisberg, in press, for a review.) First, Gold's (this volume) evidence indicates that arousal may directly lead to stronger memory encoding, via its effects on glucose metabolism. Second, it seems likely that emotional events are more distinctive, and more interesting, than neural events. This may lead subjects to pay more attention to these events, and also to think about these events more afterward. This is tantamount to extra rehearsal devoted to emotional events and thus would contribute to slowed forgetting.

Once again, though, we emphasize that this "slowed forgetting" of emotional events is not always observed, and this fact needs to be explained. Perhaps emotion, via the mechanisms just mentioned, retards forgetting by providing long-lasting but diffuse retrieval cues. This would provide a retrieval advantage at long delays, accounting for the interval effects we have described. However, this retrieval path would benefit subjects only when other, more specific retrieval cues were not available; if other cues were available, then the "slowed forgetting" pattern would not be observed.[2] And, of course, the availability of other cues will depend on many features of the to-be-remembered materials, and of the retrieval context. As a result, emotion's interaction with interval will be observed only intermittently. However, this conjecture is surely in need of further test.

### Emotion and selectivity

Whatever the mechanisms of slowed forgetting, however, this will not be enough to account for all of emotion's impact on memory, and this brings us to the second of emotion's effects. Emotion seems also to cause a selectivity in memory, presumably as a result of selectivity in both encoding and postevent elaboration. This selectivity is directly revealed in the Burke et al. studies; it is also the pattern of the weapon-focus data in the literature.

Several mechanisms are likely to contribute to this selectivity. First, physiological arousal itself, according to the Easterbrook claim, will lead to a narrowing of attention during emotional events. In addition, the narrowing of attention evident in weapon-focus demonstrations seems *not* to derive from arousal, but instead from the informativeness or distinctiveness of the weapon (cf. Maass & Köhnken, 1989; Kramer et al., 1990). Finally, the nature of an emotional event seems certain to shift one's "informational priorities." That is, when experiencing an emotional event, one has neither the resources nor the inclination to "enjoy the scenery." This also will serve to rivet one's attention on the central action, effectively leading, once again, to narrowed attention.

These mechanisms are all consistent with evidence that emotion promotes memory for materials tied to an event's center, and works against memory for materials at the event's edge. Note, though, that information can be "tied" to an event in several ways: Information about gist is semantically tied to an event. Plot-irrelevant information, on the other hand, can be tied to an event by virtue of spatial and temporal contiguity. The Burke et al. data carry the interesting implication that these very different forms of association may have equivalent impact on how emotional events are remembered.

The selective mechanisms just described all concern selectivity in *encoding* emotional events. In addition, there is also selectivity inherent in how one thinks about emotional events. In particular, one thinks about emotional events in more personal, more psychological terms, and less in schematic or abstract ways, relative to how one thinks about neutral events. (For further discussion of this, including the relevant evidence, see Christianson & Loftus, 1991; Heuer & Reisberg, in press; Hockey, 1978.) This would, on the one hand, aid memory, due to the extra attention and rehearsal given to emotional events. At the same time however, this pattern of thought will contribute to the selective nature of what is remembered – pulling away attention from either abstractions or remote details, but emphasizing memory for the event itself.

The selectivity in how one thinks about emotional events is likely to emerge in one further way: Whether or not an experienced event was emotional, one's memory for the event is certain to be incomplete, certain to contain gaps. However, the selectivity just described will result in rather different sorts of gaps in remembering emotional events than in remembering neutral ones. This is likely to lead to a distinctive pattern of confabulations and intrusions in the recall of emotional events. In addition, subjects' post-event elaborations will be very different for emotional events than for neutral ones – different associations will come to mind, different aspects of the event will be contemplated. This also should be reflected in the pattern of confabulations and intrusions.

Evidence relevant to these points comes from Heuer and Reisberg (1990). In their procedure, subjects' memories were tested both via recall and recognition. (We described their recognition data earlier in this chapter.) The recall data were scored both for number of correct propositions recalled, and also for number of intrusion errors – aspects of the event that were reported, but that actually had not taken place. Their data indicate that, at a 2-week delay, the arousal and neutral stories led to comparable numbers of intrusion errors. However, the two stories led to very different types of intrusions. Subjects who saw the neutral story made many errors about plot – for example, whether the mother brought the child to school or to the garage; whether she went grocery shopping afterward and so on. In general, these subjects seemed to be reconstructing sensible but false aspects of the tale, as if to fill gaps in the sequence of what they remembered.

In contrast, arousal subjects made very few plot errors. Instead, they tended to make up things about the story's protagonists' motives or reactions. Subjects often exaggerated what the story had said about these, and sometimes falsified what the story had said. For example, subjects reported vivid recollections of hearing the mother was upset that the child saw the medical procedure, or that the mother was angry that the father allowed his son to view the surgery. Neither of these points was mentioned in the story. In these cases, subjects seem to have projected their own emotions into the memory, or, in the words of Bartlett (1932), they seem to have remembered an "attitude" toward the event, and were working in their recollections to "justify" this attitude.[3]

In summary, it appears that several mechanisms together lead to slower forgetting for emotional events. When emotion initially creates a memory advantage, the slowed forgetting causes this advantage to increase over time. When emotion initially produces a memory *dis*advantage, slowed forgetting causes a gradual erosion of this disadvantage. Likewise, several mechanisms together lead to a bias in how subjects attend to, and think about, and later talk about, emotional events. This bias emerges in the data in several ways. It is manifest, for one, in a selectivity in what is remembered and what is forgotten, as clearly can be seen in the Burke et al. findings. This bias also emerges in the pattern of intrusion errors, as we have just seen. Finally, and perhaps most directly, this bias can be detected if we simply ask subjects, immediately after an emotional event, what they are thinking about (Christianson & Loftus, 1991).

This still leaves us to ask, however, how these claims apply to remembering outside of the laboratory, and, in particular, to flashbulbs and other very vivid memories of emotional events. Before we can address this, one seeming discrepancy in the laboratory data needs to be examined.

## Weapon focus revisited

As we have discussed, the selective remembering of emotional events is clearly reflected in demonstrations of the weapon-focus effect. In these data, memory is improved for the weapon and details of the hand holding the weapon, but this improvement is at the expense of memory for other aspects of the scene, including the face of the person wielding the weapon (Christianson, Loftus, Hoffman, & Loftus, 1991; Kramer et al., 1990; Maass & Köhnken, 1989). Note, though, that in the Burke et al. classification scheme, details of the *hand* and details of the *face* would both count as "central" details, because both are details associated with a central character. Hence both should, according to this categorization, be affected similarly by emotion. Yet this is not what the weapon-focus data show.

One might attribute this discrepancy to a contrast between *emotion's* effects (critical for the Burke et al. procedure) and the effects of *seeing a weapon* (obviously crucial for the weapon-focus studies). That is, perhaps emotion improves memory for all details associated with central characters, whereas the sight of a weapon leads to more selective effects. The sight of the weapon, in this view, might favor memory for some central details at the expense of others. However, the evidence speaks against this suggestion, and indicates, in particular, that emotionality and sight of a weapon have similar memory effects. For example, in a study by Peters (1988), subjects were confronted with a "weapon" (a hypodermic needle) and, consistent with other data in the literature, this led to poorer memory for the face of the "weapon-carrier" (i.e., the person wielding the needle). Critically, this effect was largest in those subjects who were most upset by the injection (as revealed by heart rate). Similar data were reported by Kramer, Buckhout, & Eugenio (1990). In their procedure, the weapon effect was most pronounced in subjects who were made anxious (according to self-report) by the stimulus sequence. In both of these studies, therefore, the weapon effect (better memory for the weapon, poorer memory for other details) is predictively related to emotion. Apparently, emotion is pertinent to the weapon-focus effect, just as it is to the Burke et al. findings.[4] And this leaves in place the discrepancy between the weapon-focus effect and the Burke et al. claims.

## The role of attention

All of this indicates to us that the Burke et al. classification scheme is not quite right. Burke et al. distinguished between details associated with central characters, and those not; central characters were in turn defined by virtue of their relevance to the episode's plot. Thus "plot relevance" clearly plays a critical role in this scheme. As an alternative, however, one could identify central characters in terms of their centrality to subjects' *attention*, rather than relevance to plot. On this definition, "central" details would be those details associated with material central to attention, independent of whether the details were also associated with material central to the event's plot. (Cf. Christianson & Loftus, 1991.)

This alternative categorization of to-be-remembered materials strikes us as enormously plausible. If one fails to pay attention to details associated with plot-relevant materials, these details will probably not be remembered. Likewise, if one happens to pay attention to details *not* associated with plot-relevant materials, it seems sensible that these details *would* be remembered. In either case, it would be relevance to attention, rather than relevance to plot, that is essential for memory.

To be sure, these categorization schemes overlap heavily, because one tends to pay attention to information pertinent to plot. Given this overlap, the Burke et al. data are consistent with either classification scheme. However, these classification schemes will diverge on some points. It seems plausible, in situations involving a weapon, that attention will be caught by the weapon itself, and not by the face of the weapon-holder (this is consistent with eye movement data reported by Christianson et al., 1991), despite the fact that both are associated with a plot-relevant character. If attention is deployed in this manner, then details of the weapon-holder's face should not be remembered; this is of course what the data show. Hence we would urge reframing the Burke et al. claims in this way – in terms of subjects' attention. Once reframed, the classification scheme meshes with both the Burke et al. data and with the weapon-focus evidence.

We believe it is useful to make this same point in a slightly different fashion: Perhaps emotion does improve memory for details associated with plot-relevant characters, and impairs memory for other details. The twist, however, is that we must interpret "plot" in this context to mean *plot as the subject understands it*. Consider two concrete cases: In the Burke et al. stimuli, the narrative of the to-be-remembered materials focused on a family visit. Subjects saw a boy's father who was a surgeon, and the father was wielding a scalpel. In this case, the plot might be construed as "*father* is carrying a scalpel." In contrast, in a weapon-focus study, subjects see some anonymous character wielding a weapon with unknown target and unknown intentions. In this case, the plot might sensibly be construed as "a weapon is being carried by someone," or, better still, "a weapon is being carried."

Thus these two situations are superficially similar. Moreover, both might be emotional situations. However, the situations clearly have different meanings in several relevant ways. In the eyes of subjects, these situations have different plots, and therefore different "central characters." Thus each situation will require its own classification of which details are or are not associated with central characters, with appropriate consequences for how these details are (or are not) remembered.

## Flashbulb memories reconsidered

We have dwelt on this issue because we believe it to be essential to the questions with which we began this chapter, questions about the accuracy of memories of emotional events, and the accuracy of flashbulb memories. The laboratory evidence makes it plain that emotion aids memory for some sorts of material within an event, but undermines memory for other sorts of material. How should we apply these findings to remembering outside of the laboratory? Obviously the first step would be to categorize the to-be-remembered material, outside the lab, in terms similar to those we have used with the laboratory materials. But this is not a straightforward matter. The original Burke et al. categorizations depended heavily on an assessment of an event's plot, and a corresponding determination of what information about the event was tied to that plot. However, in complex events in "real life," it is often difficult to say exactly what the plot of an event is. For example, many flashbulb events are "reported events" rather than "experienced events" (cf.

Larsen, this volume). In these cases, there is, so to speak, an event within an event – for example, an episode in Florida in which a space shuttle exploded, and an episode somewhere else in which the subject learned about this explosion. To apply the Burke et al. analysis to cases such as this, we would need to determine which of these episodes (the explosion itself, or the report of the explosion) constitutes the event's "plot," and then categorize information about the event accordingly. But it is not obvious to us, in cases such as this one, how to make or justify this determination. (For relevant discussion of this theme, and the problem of defining an "event," see Brewer, 1986; Christianson & Loftus, 1991; Heuer & Reisberg, in press; Neisser, 1986.)

The point of the previous pages' discussion, however, is that, for present purposes, we may be able to avoid these complex theoretical issues. As we have seen, laboratory data on event memory may best be understood in terms of how subjects deployed their attention, quite independent of plot. Thus rather than trying to define an event's plot, we should focus instead on the task of determining how subjects' attention was distributed across the event. This is a difficult empirical problem, but a tractable one, and tackling this matter seems essential if we are to apply the laboratory evidence on emotional remembering to cases outside of the lab.

It should be said, though, that we know remarkably little about how attention is deployed during complex emotional events, and so clearly there is work to be done here. Despite this ignorance, one can still offer some speculations that are open to empirical test. Here is one such speculation: In experiencing an emotional event, the deployment of attention is likely to be influenced enormously by the social surround, both during the event and immediately afterward. In particular, one seems very likely, in emotional events, to pay attention to *other people* on the scene. This seems probable for two reasons. First, in an emotional situation, people in one's surround are themselves likely to become emotional, and it seems to us that others' emotion is an attention-grabbing stimulus of great force. Second, a considerable amount of "social referencing" is likely to take place in emotional settings, as one seeks information in other faces – information about the event itself, and also about how one should react.

This line of reasoning leads to the following predictions. In an emotional situation involving other people, one attends to these other people, and this implies attention to a great many episodic particulars. Hence one will remember many details about the people, including where they were, what they said, and so forth. In the case of "reported events," this would entail more attention to the "reception context," and correspondingly less to the reported event itself. In emotional events *not* involving other people, one's attention is likely to be caught by other aspects of the event – less by the reception context, and more by the gist of the reported event. As a result, the event will be remembered rather differently. If, in the latter case, one later remembers details of the reception context, we suspect that these are likely to be sketchier, and more open to error, than memories for social events. We intend this speculation to be read at two levels. Specifically, we suspect that the social surround is indeed a variable of great importance in influencing attention and therefore memory, yet this is a variable that has received little attention in the memory literature. Hence we concretely intend our speculation as a source of testable hypotheses.

We also offer this speculation as an illustration of a larger theme, namely, how one might investigate emotional remembering within the framework we have sketched. If memory for emotional events is shaped by subjects' attention, then one research strategy would be to track subjects' attention (perhaps via eye movements) during emotional events (cf. Christianson et al., 1991). This strategy, although addressing key issues, is obviously cumbersome. A different strategy would be to examine factors likely to play a role in guiding attention, and to ask how these "attention magnets" influence memory. It is this latter strategy that we have tried to illustrate here.

To summarize our discussion, the answer to the question "What does emotion do to memory?" seems to be a *list*. Emotion improves memory for some sorts of material and undermines memory for other material. Emotion seems to slow forgetting. Emotion creates an interesting species of intrusion errors in recall testing. Emotion creates state-dependency effects, that is, mood-congruent recall (cf. Blaney, 1986; Ellis & Ashbrook, 1989). Under some circumstances, though, emotion can lead to mood-*in*congruent recall (Parrott & Sabini, 1990). We also would suggest that emotionality by itself can impede memory retrieval. Finally, emotion seems likely to create in subjects expectations about how they will remember emotional events; these expectations emerge, for example, in the sharp dissociation between memory confidence and memory accuracy observed by Neisser and Harsch (this volume).

This is, to be sure, a complex picture, but it is a picture that seems appropriate, given the complexities of emotion, the complexities of memory, and their interaction. Critically, though, the laboratory evidence makes it plain that we must find the appropriate categorization of the to-be-remembered material. Emotion has different effects on different sorts of information, and we will miss these effects unless we partition the to-be-remembered material appropriately. Moreover, it seems that we will make little progress, in understanding emotional memories, if we look merely at singular or global assessments of remembering, because these seem certain to lump together information for which memory is aided by emotion and information for which memory is impeded. The problem, of course, is that we do not know exactly which is the right partition; we do not know, in essence, how to "carve nature at the joints." It is clear that this is an issue on which further work is needed, and, in our view, may be the issue of key importance if we are to understand how accurately we remember emotional events.

## NOTES

1 The stimulus materials for this study had been prepared as part of an earlier study by Burke, Wessler, Heuer, and Reisberg (ms.).
2 The unreliability of these interval effects is reminiscent of the replication concerns that plague the "mood and memory" literature; for reviews, see Blaney (1986); Eich and Metcalfe (1989); Ellis and Ashbrook (1989). Within that literature, Eich and Metcalfe (1989) have offered an account that anticipates the conjecture we are offering in this paragraph.
3 People seem often to remember their emotions as having been more intense than they actually were (Thomas & Diener, 1990). When this happens it may make intrusion errors particularly likely, as subjects seek to "justify" their (exaggerated) "attitudes"!
4 Note that we need to keep separate two claims about the weapon-focus effect. First, several researchers have argued that this effect can be documented in the *absence* of emotional arousal; in this case, the effect derives from the informational priority of the weapon, and not from emotionality. Second, weapon-focus effects seem to be accentuated when emotion is on the scene, as in the Peters or Kramer et al. procedures. The obvious reading of these data is simply that sight of the weapon and emotionality have similar (and additive) effects, at least in creating the selectivity that is the heart of the weapon-focus phenomenon. See also Maass and Köhnken (1989).

## REFERENCES

Andrews, K. (1990). *The effects of emotion on memory accuracy.* Unpublished bachelor's thesis, Reed College, Portland, OR.

Baddeley, A. (1982). *Your memory: A user's guide.* New York: MacMillan Publishing Co.

Bartlett, F. C. (1932). *Remembering: A study in experimental and social psychology.* Cambridge: Cambridge University Press.

Belbin, E. (1950). The influence of interpolated recall upon recognition. *Quarterly Journal of Experimental Psychology, 2,* 163–169.

Blaney, P. H. (1986). Affect and memory: A review. *Psychological Bulletin, 99,* 229–246.

Bohannon, J. N. (1988). Flashbulb memories of the space shuttle disaster: A tale of two theories. *Cognition, 29,* 179–196.

Brewer, W. (1986). What is autobiographical memory? In D. C. Rubin (Ed.), *Autobiographical memory* (pp. 25–49). New York: Cambridge University Press.

Brown, R., & Kulik, J. (1977). Flashbulb memories. *Cognition, 5,* 73–99.

Bruner, J. S., Matter, J., & Papanek, M. L. (1955). Breadth of learning as a function of drive level and mechanization. *Psychological Review, 42,* 1–10.

Buckhout, R., Alper, A., Chern, S., Silverberg, G., & Slomovits, M. (1974). Determinants of eyewitness performance on a lineup. *Bulletin of the Psychonomic Society, 4,* 191–192.

Burke, A., Heuer, F., & Reisberg, D. (in press). Remembering emotional events. *Memory and Cognition.*

Burke, Wessler, Heuer, & Reisberg. (unpublished ms.). *Memory and Emotion.*

Butter, M. J. (1970). Differential recall of paired associates as a function of arousal and concreteness-imagery levels. *Journal of Experimental Psychology, 84,* 252–256.

Christianson, S.-Å. (1984). The relationship between induced emotional arousal and amnesia. *Scandinavian Journal of Psychology, 25*, 147–160.

Christianson, S.-Å. (1989). Flashbulb memories: Special, but not so special. *Memory & Cognition, 17*, 435–443.

Christianson, S.-Å., & Loftus, E. (1987). Memory for traumatic events. *Applied Cognitive Psychology, 1*, 225–239.

Christianson, S.-Å., & Loftus, E. (1990). Some characteristics of people's traumatic memories. *Bulletin of the Psychonomic Society, 28*, 195–198.

Christianson, S.-Å., & Loftus, E. (1991). Remembering emotional events: The fate of detailed information. *Cognition & Emotion, 5*, 693–701.

Christianson, S.-Å., Loftus, E., Hoffman, H., & Loftus, G. R. (1991). Eye fixations and accuracy in detail memory of emotional versus neutral events. *Journal of Experimental Psychology: Learning, Memory, and Cognition, 17*, 693–701.

Clifford, B., & Hollin, C. (1981). Effects of the type of incident and the number of perpetrators on eyewitness memory. *Journal of Applied Psychology, 66*, 364–370.

Clifford, B., & Scott, J. (1978). Individual and situational factors in eyewitness testimony. *Journal of Applied Psychology, 63*, 352–359.

Cohen, N., McCloskey, M., & Wible, C. (1990). Flashbulb memories and underlying cognitive mechanisms: Reply to Pillemer. *Journal of Experimental Psychology: General, 119*, 97–100.

Cohen, N. J., McCloskey, M., & Wible, C. G. (1988). There is still no case for a flashbulb-memory mechanism: Reply to Schmidt and Bohannon. *Journal of Experimental Psychology: General, 117*, 336–338.

Conway, M., & Bekerian, D. (1988). Characteristics of vivid memories. In M. M. Gruneberg, P. Morris, & R. Sykes (Eds.), *Practical aspects of memory: Current research and issues* (pp. 519–524). New York: John Wiley & Sons.

Craik, F., & Blankstein, K. (1975). Psychophysiology and human memory. In P. H. Venables & M. J. Christie (Eds.), *Research in psychophysiology* (pp. 389–417). London: John Wiley & Sons.

Cutler, B., Penrod, S., & Martens, T. (1987). The reliability of eyewitness identification. *Law and Human Behavior, 11*, 233–258.

Deffenbacher, K. (1983). The influence of arousal on reliability of testimony. In S. Lloyd-Bostock & B. Clifford (Eds.), *Evaluating witness evidence* (pp. 235–252). New York: John Wiley & Sons.

Dorman, C. (1989). *The effects of emotional arousal on memory*. Unpublished bachelor's thesis, Reed College, Portland, OR.

Easterbrook, J. A. (1959). The effect of emotion on cue utilization and the organization of behavior. *Psychological Review, 66*, 183–201.

Egeth, H., & McCloskey, M. (1984). Expert testimony about eyewitness behavior: Is it safe and effective? In G. L. Wells & E. F. Loftus (Eds.), *Eyewitness testimony: Psychological perspectives*, (pp. 283–303). New York: Cambridge University Press.

Eich, E., & Metcalfe, J. (1989). Mood dependent memory for internal versus external events. *Journal of Experimental Psychology: Learning, Memory and Cognition, 15*, 443–455.

Ellis, H. C., & Ashbrook, P. W. (1989). The "state" of mood and memory research: A selective review. *Journal of Social Behavior and Personality, 4*, 1–21.

Eysenck, M. (1976). Arousal, learning and memory. *Psychological Bulletin, 83*, 389–404.

Eysenck, M. W. (1982). *Attention and arousal: Cognition and performance*. Berlin: Springer Verlag.

Farley, F. (1973). Memory storage in free recall learning as a function of arousal and time with homogeneous and heterogeneous lists. *Bulletin of the Psychonomic Society, 1*, 187–189.

Heuer, F., & Reisberg, D. (1990). Vivid memories of emotional events: The accuracy of remembered minutiae. *Memory & Cognition, 18,* 496–506.

Heuer, F., & Reisberg, D. (in press). Emotion, arousal and memory for detail. In S.-Å. Christianson (Ed.), *Handbook of emotion and memory.* Hillsdale, NJ: Erlbaum.

Hockey, G. (1978). Arousal and stress in human memory: Some methodological and theoretical considerations. In M. Gruneberg, P. Morris, & R. Sykes (Eds.), *Practical aspects of memory* (pp. 295–302). New York: Academic Press.

Kaplan, R., & Kaplan, S. (1969). The arousal-retention interval interaction revisited: The effects of some procedural changes. *Psychonomic Science, 15,* 84–85.

Kassin, S., Ellsworth, P., & Smith, V. (1989). The "general acceptance" of psychological research on eyewitness testimony: A survey of the experts. *American Psychologist, 44,* 1089–1098.

Kebeck, G., & Lohaus, A. (1986). Effect of emotional arousal on free recall of complex material. *Perceptual and Motor Skills, 63,* 461–462.

Kleinsmith, L., & Kaplan, S. (1963). Paired-associate learning as a function of arousal and interpolated interval. *Journal of Experimental Psychology, 65,* 190–193.

Kleinsmith, L., & Kaplan, S. (1964). The interaction of arousal and recall interval in nonsense syllable paired-associate learning. *Journal of Experimental Psychology, 67,* 124–126.

Kramer, T., Buckhout, R., & Eugenio, P. (1990). Weapon focus, arousal and eyewitness memory: Attention must be paid. *Law and Human Behavior, 14,* 167–184.

Kuehn, L. (1974). Looking down a gun barrel: Person perception and violent crime. *Perceptual and Motor Skills, 39,* 1159–1164.

Levonian, E. (1967). Retention of information in relation to arousal during continuously presented material. *American Educational Research Journal, 4,* 103–116.

Linton, M. (1975). Memory for real-world events. In D. A. Norman & D. E. Rumelhart (Eds.), *Explorations in cognition* (pp. 376–404). San Francisco: Freeman.

Loftus, E. F. (1979). *Eyewitness testimony.* Cambridge, MA: Harvard University Press.

Loftus, E., & Burns, T. (1982). Mental shock can reproduce retrograde amnesia. *Memory & Cognition, 10,* 318–323.

Loftus, E., Loftus, G., & Messo, J. (1987). Some facts about "weapon focus." *Law and Human Behavior, 11,* 55–62.

Loftus, E. F., & Hoffman, H. G. (1989). Misinformation and memory: The creation of new memories. *Journal of Experimental Psychology: General, 118,* 100–104.

Loftus, E. F., & Palmer, J. C. (1974). Reconstruction of automobile destruction: An example of the interaction between language and memory. *Journal of Verbal Learning and Verbal Behavior, 13,* 585–589.

Maass, A., & Köhnken, G. (1989). Eyewitness identification. *Law and Human Behavior, 13,* 397–408.

Mandler, G. (1975). *Mind and emotion.* New York: John Wiley & Sons.

McCloskey, M., & Egeth, H. (1983). Eyewitness identification: What can a psychologist tell a jury? *American Psychologist, 38,* 550–563.

McCloskey, M., Wible, C. G., & Cohen, N. J. (1988). Is there a special flashbulb-memory mechanism? *Journal of Experimental Psychology: General, 117,* 171–181.

McLean, P. D. (1969). Induced arousal and time of recall as determinants of paired-associate recall. *British Journal of Psychology, 60,* 57–62.

Mehrabian, A. (1977a). Individual differences in stimulus screening and arousability. *Journal of Personality, 45,* 237–250.

Mehrabian, A. (1977b). A questionnaire measure of individual differences in stimulus screening and associated differences in arousability. *Environmental Psychology and Non-Verbal Behavior, 1*, 89–103.

Morris, M., & Murphy, G. (1990). Converging operations on a basic level in event taxonomies. *Memory & Cognition, 18*, 407–418.

Neisser, U. (1982). *Memory observed.* San Francisco: W. H. Freeman and Company.

Neisser, U. (1986). Nested structure in autobiographical memory. In D. C. Rubin (Ed.), *Autobiographical memory* (pp. 71–81). New York: Cambridge University Press.

Osborne, J. (1972). Short- and long-term memory as a function of individual differences in arousal. *Perceptual and Motor Skills, 34*, 587–593.

Parrott, W. G., & Sabini, J. (1990). Mood and memory under natural conditions: Evidence for mood incongruent recall. *Journal of Personality and Social Psychology, 59*, 321–336.

Peters, D. (1988). Eyewitness memory and arousal in a natural setting. In M. Gruneberg, P. Morris, & R. Sykes (Eds.), *Practical aspects of memory: Current research and issues* (pp. 89–94). New York: John Wiley & Sons.

Pillemer, D. (1990). Clarifying the flashbulb memory concept: Comment on McCloskey, Wible and Cohen. *Journal of Experimental Psychology: General, 119*, 92–96.

Pillemer, D. B. (1984). Flashbulb memories of the assassination attempt on President Reagan. *Cognition, 16*, 63–80.

Reisberg, D., Heuer, F., McLean, J., & O'Shaughnessy, M. (1988). The quantity, not the quality, of affect predicts memory vividness. *Bulletin of the Psychonomic Society, 26*, 100–103.

Rifkin, A. (1985). Evidence for a basic level in event taxonomies. *Memory & Cognition, 13*, 538–556.

Robinson, J. (1980). Affect and retrieval of personal memories. *Motivation and Emotion, 4*, 149–174.

Rosch, E. H. (1978). Principles of categorization. In E. Rosch & B. B. Lloyd (Eds.), *Cognition and categorization* (pp. 27–48). Hillsdale, NJ: Erlbaum.

Rubin, D. C., & Kozin, M. (1984). Vivid memories. *Cognition, 16*, 81–95.

Schmidt, S. R., & Bohannon, J. N. III. (1988). In defense of the flashbulb-memory hypothesis: A comment on McCloskey, Wible, and Cohen (1988). *Journal of Experimental Psychology: General, 117*, 332–335.

Siegel, J., & Loftus, E. (1978). Impact of anxiety and life stress upon eyewitness testimony. *Bulletin of the Psychonomic Society, 12*, 479–480.

Snyder, N. (1989). *An empirical approach to answer what emotion might be doing for memory.* Unpublished bachelor's thesis, Reed College, Portland, OR.

Thomas, D., & Diener, E. (1990). Memory accuracy in the recall of emotions. *Journal of Personality and Social Psychology, 59*, 291–297.

Tooley, V., Brigham, J., Maass, A., & Bothwell, R. (1987). Facial recognition: Weapon effect and attentional focus. *Journal of Applied Social Psychology, 17*, 845–859.

Vallacher, R., & Wegner, D. (1987). What do people think they're doing? Action identification and human behavior. *Psychological Review, 94*, 3–15.

Wagenaar, W. A., & Groeneweg, J. (1990). The memory of concentration camp survivors. *Applied Cognitive Psychology, 4*, 77–88.

Walker, E., & Tarte, R. (1963). Memory storage as a function of arousal and time with homogeneous and heterogeneous lists. *Journal of Verbal Learning and Verbal Behavior, 2*, 113–119.

White, R. T. (1989). Recall of autobiographical events. *Applied Cognitive Psychology, 3,* 127–136.

Yarmey, A., & Jones, H. (1983). Is the psychology of eyewitness identification a matter of common sense? In S. Lloyd-Bostock & B. Clifford (Eds.), *Evaluating witness evidence: Recent psychological research and new perspectives* (pp. 13–40). New York: John Wiley & Sons.

Yuille, J. C., & Cutshall, J. L. (1986). A case study of eyewitness memory of a crime. *Journal of Applied Psychology, 71,* 291–301.

# 9

# Do flashbulb memories differ from other types of emotional memories?

SVEN-ÅKE CHRISTIANSON

One field of research that is pertinent to the relationship between emotion and memory, and that most consistently demonstrates high memory performance for negative emotionally arousing events, is research on so-called "flashbulb memories" (see Brown & Kulik, 1977). Since the publication of the original study by Brown and Kulik (1977), numerous studies have shown an impressive concordance in subjects' remembering of shocking national events, such as assassinations, and so forth (see e.g., Bohannon, 1988; Christianson, 1989; Colgrove, 1899; Pillemer, 1984; Rubin & Kozin, 1984; Winograd & Killinger, 1983). Not only does such emotionally shocking news itself appear to be well preserved, but so too do the subjects' memories of the specific detail information associated with the circumstances under which they heard the news. In this chapter, I will discuss how these so-called flashbulb memories compare with memories of other types of emotional events such as personal traumatic events and laboratory-induced emotional events. In this comparison, I will focus on how detailed and persistent these memories are over time. I will also discuss whether a special memory mechanism is involved in remembering flashbulb events as well as other types of emotional events. Before moving on with a discussion of flashbulb memories, I will briefly discuss research concerning memory for negative emotional events. In discussing this research, I use the term "negative emotional events" to refer to scenes or experiences that have very unpleasant features, and that have the potential to evoke strong negative emotional feelings in a victim or a witness.

## Research on memory for negative emotional events

During the last few decades, there has been some confusion in the literature as to whether negative emotional events are poorly or well retained. Whereas laboratory research shows mixed results concerning memory for emotional events (see Christianson, 1984; Clifford & Hollin, 1981; Clifford & Scott, 1978; Heuer & Reisberg, 1990; Loftus & Burns, 1982; see also Christianson, 1992 and Deffenbacher, 1983 for reviews), research on real-world events usually shows that details of emotional events are relatively well retained in memory (e.g., Bohannon, this volume; Brown & Kulik, 1977; Rubin & Kozin, 1984; Yuille & Cutshall, 1986, 1989). For example, in an often cited laboratory study by Loftus and Burns (1982), it was found that subjects who had been presented with a violent version of a video film remembered certain detail information presented prior to the emotion-eliciting event less accurately than subjects who saw a nonviolent version of the film. Similar detrimental effects on memory for information associated with emotional events have been demonstrated in other simulation studies (e.g., Christianson & Nilsson, 1984; Christianson, Nilsson, Mjörndal, Perris, & Tjelldén, 1986; Kramer, Buckhout, Fox, Widman, & Tusche, 1991). In these studies, color slides depicting neutral or emotionally stressful scenic motifs (e.g., victims of crimes and accidents) have been presented to subjects. In the emotional condition, the slides have been embedded in the middle of the series, whereas in the control condition subjects have been presented with *neutral* slides in the same positions. In subsequent memory tests, the performance of subjects in the emotional condition has been found to be worse than the performance in the control condition.

These findings are contradicted by results obtained in studies of emotional events in real-world settings. For example, in a field study, Yuille and Cutshall (1986) found that witnesses to actual traumatic events (e.g., shootings, knifings) showed a high degree of accuracy of memory and little decline over time. Furthermore, by simply asking people about their most negative emotional or traumatic memories (Reisberg, Heuer, McLean, & O'Shaughnessy, 1988), we see a similar pattern: People claim that they remember these events quite well, and the more intense the emotional event the higher confidence in the memory. Real-world studies also purport to show that details of traumatic events are remarkably consistent and accurate over longer retention intervals (e.g., Wagenaar & Groeneweg, 1990; Yuille & Cutshall, 1986).

Still other studies demonstrate interactions between type of event (emotional/nonemotional) and (a) whether the detail information is central or peripheral (Burke, Heuer, & Reisberg, in press; Christianson, 1984; Christianson & Loftus, 1987, 1990, 1991; Christianson, Loftus, Hoffman, & Loftus, 1991), (b) whether the test is recall or recognition (Christianson & Nilsson, 1984; Christianson & Larsson, 1990; Davis, 1990; Wagenaar, 1986), and (c) whether the test is immediate or delayed (Christianson, 1984; Levonian, 1967).

What then can we conclude on the basis of the apparent contradictions between these studies? On the surface, it appears that, for example, the field studies lead to different conclusions from the laboratory simulations. However, in many instances it seems that this contradiction has to do with what particular researchers focus upon. The common pattern has been that researchers using a field study approach focus on the accuracy of memory and its persistence over time (e.g., Yuille & Cutshall, 1986), tending to ignore or explain away the data on errors and inconsistencies. In contrast, in many laboratory studies, the researchers focus on errors in memory (e.g., Loftus & Burns, 1982). However, in recent simulation studies (e.g., Christianson, 1984; Heuer & Reisberg, 1990), other researchers have drawn attention to the persistence of emotional memories. Thus, these approaches are not as inconsistent or incompatible as they appear; the data in both interview and simulation studies show both good and poor recall.

In summing up findings in recent research on memory for negative emotional events, we see a pattern such that highly emotional events are relatively well retained, both with respect to the emotional event itself, and the central, critical detail information of the emotion-eliciting event, that is, the information that elicits the emotional reaction (see Burke et al., in press; Christianson, 1984; Christianson & Loftus, 1987, 1990, 1991; Christianson et al., 1991; Yuille & Cutshall, 1986, 1989; see also studies on weapon focusing by Loftus, Loftus, & Messo, 1987; Kramer, Buckhout, & Eugenio, 1990). Furthermore, it seems that detail information for negative emotionally arousing events and some circumstantial information are less susceptible to long-term forgetting compared with corresponding neutral detail information (see Bohannon, 1990; Brown & Kulik, 1977; Burke et al., in press; Christianson, 1984; Christianson & Loftus, 1987; Heuer & Reisberg, 1990; Pillemer, 1984; Wagenaar & Groeneweg, 1990; Winograd & Killinger, 1983; see also studies on arousal and memory reviewed by Eysenck, 1982).

Memory for information *associated* with negative emotional events, that is, information preceding and succeeding such events, or peripheral, noncentral information within an emotional scenario, is found to be less accurately retained – especially when tested after short retention intervals (see Christianson & Nilsson, 1984, 1989; Kramer et al., 1991; Loftus & Burns, 1982). This detrimental effect may recede, however, with strong retrieval support (see Christianson & Nilsson, 1984; Davis, 1990; Wagenaar, 1986), if delayed testing is employed (Christianson, 1984; Levonian, 1967; see also studies on repression, e.g., Erdelyi, 1990), or after repeated memory testing (Scrivner & Safer, 1988; Davis, 1990; Erdelyi, 1990; Erdelyi & Goldberg, 1979). Taken together, recent research in the field of emotion and memory, independent of the approach used, shows that emotion and memory interact in a very complex manner. The implication of the interactions described is that the Yerkes–Dodson law (1908) – proposing an inverted relation between arousal and performance – does not constitute an appropriate description of the relationship between emotion and memory performance (see also Egeth, 1990; McCloskey & Egeth, 1983; Näätänen, 1973; Neiss, 1988, for a discussion of the inadequacy of the Yerkes–Dodson law in this context, but see also Deffenbacher, 1983).

*Flashbulb memories*

How does research on flashbulb memories compare to research findings on memory for negative or traumatic events? The flashbulb studies represent another variation of the interview approach used in various field studies. The term flashbulb memories refers to the phenomenon that a person who experiences a traumatic newsworthy event (e.g., being told about the assassination of one's president) not only often reports a vivid memory for the emotionally shocking news itself, but also about the specific circumstances under which the unpleasant news was told. This is, of course, what subjects believe that they remember. The question is whether these flashbulb memories are as accurate and persistent in detail as claimed by Bohannon, Brown and Kulik, and others.

Although it is clear that people remember these sorts of public negative emotional events better than ordinary events that occurred equally long ago, by no means do these flashbulb memories seem to be completely accurate. Empirical evidence indicating that we do not retain flashbulb events and attendant circumstances as "photographically" complete memories – as we sometimes believe we do – has been shown in a number of studies (see Christianson, 1989; McCloskey, Wible, & Cohen, 1988; Neisser, 1982; Neisser & Harsch, this volume).

One critical problem in flashbulb studies, as in most other studies of real-life events, is that these studies do not include a baseline measure, for example a comparable salient everyday control event. In an attempt to include such a control event, Christianson (1989) found a higher recall performance for the flashbulb event as compared with the salient control event. However, the method of measuring the control event was far from perfect in the Christianson study. For example, the flashbulb questions concerned circumstances surrounding a known (cued) event, whereas the control event question did not. Thus, the comparability between the flashbulb event and the ordinary event was rather low.

Larsen (this volume) collected news events and everyday personal experiences in a diary over 9 months. In this study, both extremely upsetting and ordinary public events as well as personal events were included. By this procedure, Larsen was able to provide an appropriate baseline against which flashbulb-type events could be evaluated. At least two flashbulb-type events in fact occurred during Larsen's data collection period: the murder of Prime Minister Palme and the nuclear accident in Chernobyl. In an evaluation of the impact of emotion in remembering these events, Larsen found no appreciable effect of arousal on memory of the ordinary news contexts. However, the probability of recalling the *central* events was consistently predicted by factors related to emotional arousal, such as perceived excitement and activity.

Although Larsen's study is an important contribution in comparing flashbulb memories with memories of other types of emotional events, no clear pattern emerged, and the design itself includes some problems (see also McCloskey, this volume, for a discussion of Larsen's study). For example, besides the difficulties involved in including a comparable control event, there are also the problems of knowing what actually happened at the time when the shocking information was acquired, and the consistency in a subject's recollection of these circumstances. One way to verify the consistency of flashbulb memories is to compare the coherence between the recollections reported on the two occasions. That is, one can ask people a series of questions about the circumstances in which they first learned about the shocking event, and then ask the same questions again later on. This double assessment technique has been employed in several studies (e.g., Bohannon, 1990; Christianson, 1989; McCloskey et al., 1988; Pillemer, 1984). The results of these studies indicate fairly good consistency in recollections over longer retention intervals; however, it is far from perfect.

Another problem with this technique is that we cannot tell how accurate people really are in their initial descriptions of the flashbulb event and its concomitant circumstances. Unlike laboratory studies, there is often no way of knowing what subjects were actually doing, wearing, and so forth, when they were first exposed to the shocking information. The initial recalls may not have been truthful or accurate observations of the original situation. They may very well be reconstructive, and presumably contain some erroneous information, as do most other types of memories. What proportion of the initial memories or what particular details are of this sort? It is likely that a second attempt to remember the event and its concomitant circumstances produces the same memory for some *core* elements, while many details will be added or constructed that fit the most plausible memories (see also Loftus, 1979 and Winograd & Killinger, 1983, for a discussion of influences on peoples' original recollections).

The flashbulb memory studies obviously suffer from many of the usual validation problems associated with studies of real-life situations. However, although flashbulb memories are subject to forgetting and distortion effects, the overall loss of clarity and detail over time seems to be far less when compared to the forgetting curves typically found in basic memory research on ordinary, neutral events (cf. Murdock, 1974). One can then ask if this is a pattern specific to flashbulb memories, such that flashbulb memories constitute a separate category of emotional memories. In the next section, I will discuss memory for detail information in flashbulb studies in comparisons with findings obtained in laboratory simulations of negative emotional events.

*Flashbulb findings versus laboratory findings*

Using a laboratory approach, there are some studies (e.g., Christianson, 1984; Christianson & Loftus, 1987, 1991; Christianson et al., 1991; Heuer & Reisberg, 1990) that parallel in some respects the observed amount of detail of flashbulb memories, and that also show that emotional detail information is very well preserved over time. As noted, laboratory research that has compared memory for central and peripheral details in emotional and neutral events demonstrates that information about central details of emotional events is retained better than corresponding details in nonemotional events; the reverse pattern is seen for information about peripheral details. Moreover, the gist of the emotional event (i.e., the sum of the central aspects of the event) is well retained in memory over longer retention intervals, whereas a considerable loss is seen for peripheral aspects, or details surrounding the emotion-eliciting event. Before discussing this research in depth, it is important to define what is meant by central and peripheral detail information of emotional versus neutral events. First, it is difficult to determine what is central and what is peripheral information in advance, especially outside the laboratory. However, laboratory studies have an advantage over real-life situations because normative data can be collected to assist in the definition of centrality of detail. Second, the issue of centrality, as well as the definition of "associated" information (i.e., preceding and succeeding events), should be viewed as instances located on a continuum, and not as absolute distinctions. In my own research, central and peripheral details are distinguished as differentially remembered detail information within an emotional scenario. Thus, the statements here about memory for central and peripheral emotional information refer to a distinction between information that is a part of the source of the emotional arousal (i.e., the emotion-eliciting event and its central details) and information that is irrelevant and/or spatially peripheral to the source of the emotional arousal (i.e., peripheral details within an emotional scenario).

Memory for details of negative emotional events versus neutral events has been investigated in a series of recent studies (Burke et al., in press; Christianson, 1984; Christianson & Loftus, 1987, 1990, 1991; Christianson et al., 1991; Heuer & Reisberg, 1990; Reisberg et al., 1988). In a study by Christianson (1984), subjects viewed a slide sequence depicting two different versions of the same type of event. Both versions began by showing a mother and son walking through a downtown area. In the middle section, the emotional version shows the boy being hit by a white car and lying on its hood bleeding heavily from an eye injury, and then being transported to a hospital where the mother leaves him for care. The middle section in the neutral version shows the boy walking beside the same white car, and then taking a cab to school where the mother leaves him. Both versions end by showing the mother on her way back home. In comparing recall performance of either version of the slide sequence, it was found that subjects who had watched the emotional version recalled the main features and the theme of the pictures better than subjects who had watched the neutral version. However, when subjects were given a recognition test in which the main features of each picture were held constant and only the peripheral, surrounding information varied, no difference was obtained between conditions.

In a follow-up study by Christianson and Loftus (1987) using the same slide sequence, subjects were instructed to select and write down the most distinguishing detail of each slide and were then tested for recall of these details, and recognition of the pictures themselves. It was found that subjects were better able to recall central features selected from emotional pictures; however, they were less able to recognize the specific pictures that they had seen (i.e., testing of peripheral detail information).

There are other studies showing a similar pattern of results. Kebeck and Lohaus (1986) presented subjects with either an emotional or a nonemotional version of a film depicting an argument between a teacher and a student. Results showed that subjects in the two conditions were equal in recall of central details of the film; however, subjects who had seen the emotional version were at the same time less able to remember peripheral detail information of the film.

Heuer and Reisberg (1990) also used a simulation approach in their study that presented subjects with a series of slides depicting either a neutral or an emotional version of a story where a mother and her son visit the father at his workplace. The neutral version shows the father as a garage mechanic fixing a car, whereas the emotional version shows the father as a surgeon operating on a victim of an accident. Subjects were tested after a 2-week interval via a recognition test that included questions about central information of each slide (i.e., information pertaining to the basic story) or about peripheral details (i.e., specific details in a particular slide). The results replicated the Christianson (1984) finding in showing that subjects presented with the emotional version of the story remembered more of the central information than subjects who saw the neutral version. However, in contrast to results obtained by Christianson (1984) and Christianson and Loftus (1987, 1991), the Heuer and Reisberg study also showed that the peripheral details were better retained in the emotional condition.

In a subsequent study by Burke, Heuer, and Reisberg (in press), a closer investigation was made with respect to memory for central and peripheral detail over time (immediate testing vs. testing after one week). Using the same stimulus slides used by Heuer and Reisberg (1990), it was found that detail information that was spatially and temporally associated with the central characters in the slides was better retained in the emotional condition than in the neutral condition. But more important, the memory advantage for central details at immediate testing increased at delayed testing (i.e., after one week). Furthermore, the disadvantage obtained at early testing for the peripheral details in the emotional condition decreased at delayed testing. Thus, the results of Burke et al. (in press) indicate that not only is central information better retained from emotional events, but detail information of emotional events in general also seems to be more resistant to long-term forgetting compared with details of neutral events.

*Equating of detail information*

It can be argued that people remember details from emotional events differently than details from neutral events because of inadequate equating of the detail information of the two events. For example, the depiction of emotional events often differs from that of neutral events in more than the presumed elements (e.g., the complexity of the scene, the centrality of the to-be-remembered (TBR) information, the background information, etc.). This issue was addressed in a study by Christianson and Loftus (1991), in which subjects were presented with a thematic series of slides where the emotional valence of one critical slide in the series was varied, although the TBR details of the critical slide were identical in the emotional and neutral versions of this slide. In the neutral version, the critical slide showed a woman riding a bicycle. In the emotional version, the same woman was lying injured on the street near the bicycle. In both versions, a peripheral car was seen in the distant background. The results from a series of experiments with this stimulus material demonstrated that the central detail information was retained better in the emotional condition, but that the peripheral detail information (a car seen in the background) was retained better from the neutral condition (see also Christianson et al. 1991).

Critics of this attempt to compare these two groups of studies may argue that flashbulb memories do not concern details of the emotion-eliciting event itself, but rather surrounding or associated details (cf. peripheral detail information), and thus that the relationship between flashbulb memories and the laboratory findings of enhanced memory for central details of emotional events is indirect. For example, Larsen (this volume) points out the distinction between memory for the event per se and the reception context. He argues that flashbulb memories can only be compared to memory for the reception context, or peripheral details of autobiographical memories or laboratory-induced emotional events – not to central detail information of the emotion-eliciting event itself. In discussing research on memory for central and peripheral details of emotional events, Larsen states that the laboratory results (e.g., Christianson & Loftus, 1987) suggest the opposite bias compared with flashbulb memories: Memory for comparable peripheral event details are less well remembered in laboratory simulations.[1] Although this argument is basically relevant, there are still some laboratory findings that mirror the flashbulb findings. For example, in the study by Christianson and Loftus (1991) it was found that 66% to 73% of the subjects who had viewed an emotional event (a woman lying injured on the ground), correctly recalled nonemotional detail information associated with the central character of the emotionally provoking event (i.e., the color of the woman's coat). The corresponding proportion of correct recall for the neutral event (the same woman riding a bicycle) was 25% to 27%. Interestingly, this is about the same level of recall performance for color of clothing that was demonstrated in a field study by Yuille and Cutshall (1986), in which the accuracy of memory for colors of clothing of the central character was quite high and varied between 66% and 83%. Although it is most probably coincidental that the figures for color information were very close in these two types of studies, the high levels of memory performance indicate that memory for detail information not inherent in the emotional event itself can be relatively high in both real-life studies and laboratory-induced emotional events, and thus are comparable with the performance level seen in flashbulb memory studies. These results remedy to some extent the criticism that memory for emotional events in laboratory experiments is not comparable to memory for real-life experiences (see Neisser, 1978; Yuille & Cutshall, 1989).

In an attempt to develop a laboratory analogue of flashbulb memories, that is, to study more directly memory for the "reception context" (cf. Larsen, this volume) in laboratory-induced emotional events, one of my students, Jonas Berndtsson, conducted an experiment in which subjects were presented with an emotional or a neutral event, and where their memory was tested on the reception context. In short, the subjects were presented with a sequence of slides that in one condition included an emotionally arousing event, and in another condition included a neutral event (the same stimulus material that was used in the Christianson, 1984 study). Immediately after the presentation of the slides the subjects were asked to rate their emotional reactions evoked by watching the slides. About 1 week after viewing the slides, the subjects were contacted by telephone for an interview. Each call began with some introductory information. The subjects were then asked questions about one critical picture they had seen in the experiment (the last picture in the sequence of the slides), and they were also asked questions about the circumstances surrounding the presentation of the slides. For example, they were asked about the name of the experimenter and asked to describe what clothes he was wearing, the name of the building where they saw the slides, the exact time and date when they saw the slides, and asked to describe in as much detail as possible the clothes they were wearing at the time of presentation, and the number of subjects who saw the slides at the same time. The results of this study showed that subjects in the Emotional condition were significantly more emotionally aroused by the slides, and also reported that they had thought about the experimental event more often when asked 1 week later. It was also found that some of the specific circumstances under which the slides were presented were better retained by subjects in the Emotional condition. This work is, however, very preliminary, and is mentioned here primarily to suggest a design for studying flashbulb effects in a laboratory situation.

Although studies on flashbulb memories, studies on real-world events, or laboratory studies on emotional events may show some divergence as to which details are remembered, or the degree of accuracy in remembering detail information, they all indicate a similar pattern: Some critical aspects of emotional events are very well retained over time. Why is this so? Why are certain aspects of emotional events less susceptible to forgetting compared with ordinary, more neutral events? Is there a special mechanism involved; the type of "Now Print!" mechanism advocated by some researchers (e.g., Bohannon, 1988, this volume; Brown & Kulik, 1977) in the flashbulb literature? Or is there some other mechanism, based on factors that are especially critical when we are exposed to emotional situations in general? The possibility of a special flashbulb mechanism or some alternative critical factors will be discussed in the last part of this chapter.

### Is there a special mechanism?

Interpretations of the flashbulb phenomenon vary from those who advocate biological–evolutionary factors (e.g., Brown & Kulik, 1977; Bohannon, 1988; Gold, 1986, this volume) to those who emphasize psychological mechanisms, such as reconstructive processes (e.g., Neisser, 1982), or ordinary memory mechanisms (McCloskey et al., 1988; McCloskey, this volume). Among those advocating biological mechanisms (Brown & Kulik, 1977; Schmidt & Bohannon, 1988), Bohannon (this volume) maintains the position that we have an inherent special mechanism that is triggered when an event is highly emotionally arousing, surprising, and consequential. This mechanism is considered to be of great importance for our survival and has been referred to as a neuropsychological "Now Print!" mechanism (see Livingston, 1967), which is supposed to preserve a photographic image of the critical event in our brain. This interpretation has been disputed, for example, by McCloskey et al. (1988; see also Cohen, McCloskey, & Wible, 1988; McCloskey, this volume), who claim that postulation of a special memory mechanism that is triggered when we experience an emotional event is warranted only if there is evidence that these memories cannot be products of our ordinary memory mechanisms.

Although it seems clear that we do not preserve emotional events in exceptional detail as expressed in the idea of a "Now Print!" mechanism, it may still be the case that some kind of selective mechanism or factor is ritical when we retain emotional events. This alternative mechanism – which is not meant here as a separate memory mechanism that generates specific memories – could affect factors critical to memory at *early perceptual processing* (e.g., factors related to arousal and affect, attentional or preattentive factors), or *late conceptual processing* (e.g., the distinctiveness or the unusualness of a certain event, poststimulus elaboration). In discussing such an alternative mechanism or underlying factors, note that the factors involved are not only triggered by a flashbulb-type situation (cf. the special-mechanism account held by Bohannon and others), but also in ordinary remembering. However, it is argued here that emotional events, like hearing about national shocking news events, are remembered for reasons beyond the rehearsal hypothesis, which does not fully explain the results obtained in various studies of emotional events. A sample of factors, such as affect, attention, distinctiveness, and poststimulus elaboration that could be critical to remembering emotional events will be discussed in turn. Consider first factors at early perceptual processing such as affect or arousal, and attention.

### Affect and arousal

Of specific interest in flashbulb studies is the issue of level of affect as a predictor for flashbulb memories. It has been claimed that the more intense the emotional reaction to the discovery of the shocking event, the better retention of flashbulb details over time (see Bohannon, 1988; Pillemer, 1984). That is, high levels of emotional arousal are associated with persistence of a broad spectrum of detail information, both central and peripheral. Similar claims have been made by Yuille and Cutshall (1989) using a field study approach, and by Heuer and Reisberg (1990) using a laboratory-simulation approach.

In advocating an arousal explanation, Gold (1986, this volume) has proposed a biological system that promotes the formation of memories for individually based important events, a system that also applies to flashbulb events. In short, the neurobiological mechanism suggested by Gold is that stressors will release epinephrine (adrenaline), which in turn increases circulating glucose levels. The increase in blood glucose levels has been found by Gold and others (Gold, 1986; Manning, Hall, & Gold, 1990; Messier & Destrade, 1988) to enhance memory storage processing in animals and humans in an inverted-U dose-response curve. By way of extrapolation, we can assume on the basis of Gold's data (this volume) that high arousal events, like flashbulb events, are well retained because of increased levels of blood glucose.

From the flashbulb studies at hand, however, this correlation between arousal and memory is not consistently supported. For example, in Bohannon's studies on the *Challenger* explosion, there were no significant main effects of affect on memory. A significant interaction was only seen for subjects who had been told the news from another person and not for those who were told via media. (It should be noted that there was a nonsignificant difference between levels of self-rated affect between groups of subjects.) A lack of significant effect of affect on memory was also seen in the Christianson (1989) study. This may, however, be explained by ceiling effects of emotionality.

Although there seems to be a tendency that high levels of affect are associated with higher levels of overall recall, this is far from well established, and it is not justified to assume that *all* details are well retained because they occurred within an emotional scenario. As noted earlier in this chapter, several recent laboratory studies have shown that peripheral details do not persist in emotional memories. Furthermore, arguing against the notion of a *general* benefit of affect on detail memory are results from a survey study of peoples' most traumatic memories by Christianson and Loftus (1990). In this study, subjects were asked to report their most traumatic memory and to answer questions about their chosen memory. A major result was a significant relationship between rated degree of emotion and the number of central details, but not peripheral details, that the subjects believed they remembered. Moreover, results from a series of studies by Christianson and colleagues (see Christianson & Nilsson, 1984; Christianson & Mjörndal, 1985; Christianson et al., 1986) indicate a general increase in emotional arousal is significant as an intervening variable only when the source of emotional arousal is directly associated with the to-be-remembered (TBR) event; that is, when the emotional reaction is an inherent property of the TBR event (see also Yuille & Tollestrup, in press).

These findings, along with the laboratory findings reported earlier in this chapter, challenge the view that affect, or a general increase in arousal, promotes memory for a broad spectrum of details. At the same time there is no case for the view that memory is generally impaired during states of high affect. Rather, the studies discussed here show complex interactions between type of event, type of detail information, time of test, and type of retrieval information.

### Attention

It could be argued that differential distribution of attention at the time of stimulus processing promotes memory for central details of emotional events, but impairs processing of peripheral details. To more closely investigate the role of attention in memory for emotional versus neutral events, Christianson et al. (1991) conducted an experiment in which subjects were presented with an emotional or neutral event (using the same stimulus material that was used by Christianson & Loftus, 1991), and in which the number of eye fixations was limited to only one per slide. This was accomplished by presenting the slides for 180 ms/slide and by having each slide preceded by a fixation point that was directed to the critical detail information (which was exactly the same in the two conditions) tested in the subsequent memory test. This procedure assured that all subjects at the time of encoding paid attention to the same critical information and for the same amount of time.[2] Despite the fact that subjects in both the Emotional and the Neutral conditions were equated with respect to the detail information attended to during stimulus presentation, the central detail information of the Emotional condition was retained better than the corresponding detail information of the Neutral condition. This pattern of results was also found in a second experiment using the same procedure but different stimulus material.

In a third experiment of the same study, subjects were allowed to fixate normally on an emotional or a neutral critical slide while their eye movements were monitored. Subjects in the Emotional condition fixated more often on the central detail information compared with subjects in the other two conditions, yet they fixated on this detail information for shorter durations. Subjects who fixated 3, 4, 5, or 6 times on the central detail information in the two conditions were then compared with respect to memory accuracy. The results showed that even when subjects were equated with respect to number of eye fixations, subjects in the Emotional condition remembered the detail information associated with the central part of the picture better than subjects in the Neutral condition. Thus, although number of eye fixations and other attentional factors do matter, they are not the entire explanation as to why we retain certain detail information better from emotional than from neutral events.

An interesting aspect of the results from the Christianson et al. (1991) study was that the level of memory performance for subjects presented with emotional stimuli at very short exposures was almost the same as that found for subjects presented with the same emotional stimuli at long exposures (cf. Christianson & Loftus, 1991). Similarly, in a study by Christianson and Fällman (1990), it was found that very unpleasant scenic pictures (e.g., pictures of victims of traffic accidents, war, malady, or famine) shown for very brief durations (50 ms followed by a mask slide) were better recognized than neutral scenic pictures (e.g., pictures of people in everyday situations), or very positive scenic pictures (e.g., sexual pictures of nudes, very sensual summer scenes). It may be – I admit that this is a very speculative interpretation of the above findings – that we are, in some way, predisposed to retain certain characteristics of emotional information, a sort of "hardwired" process (cf. Steiner, 1973). Phrased somewhat differently, the findings by Christianson and colleagues (see also Zajonc, 1980, 1981, 1984; but see also Mandler, Nakamura, & Van Zandt, 1987) suggest that certain characteristics of emotional events are perceived and retained in an automatic fashion. Thus, it is possible that emotional events are perceived by a preattentive mechanism (cf. Neisser, 1967), which does not involve consciously controlled processes (cf. Pillemer, this volume; but also cf. perceptual priming; Tulving & Schacter, 1990), and which, of course, interacts with phylogenetically and ontogenetically more sophisticated memory mechanisms (cf. Tulving, 1972; see also Tulving, 1987, for a review). It is, however, for future research to show empirically whether this is an advantageous interpretation for some of the differences seen between memory for emotional events, such as shocking news events, and memory for ordinary, neutral events.

### Distinctiveness

It may be argued that the unusualness or distinctiveness of emotional details or events is the critical factor that explains why emotional events are remembered differently than ordinary, neutral events. The critical question is, then: Are emotional events remembered differently because they are unusual, or is it because emotion affects memory for reasons that go beyond the unusualness or distinctiveness of the emotional situation?

From weapon-focus studies (Kramer, Buckhout, & Eugenio, 1990; Loftus et al., 1987; Maass & Köhnken, 1989), it seems that the weapon-focus effect may also appear with nonemotional items, such as surprising or unusual objects instead of weapons. Thus, distinctiveness may account for the narrowing of attention in the weapon-focus situation, but is this also a critical factor in remembering emotional events in general?

In the study by Christianson and Loftus (1991) described earlier, memory for an unexpected emotional event (a woman lying in a street beside a bicycle and bleeding from a head injury) was compared with memory for an unexpected *unusual* event (a woman walking in a street, carrying a bicycle on her shoulder). It was found that peripheral detail information (a car seen in the distant background in both versions) was remembered equally well (or poorly) in both the Emotional and the Unusual conditions. However, with respect to detail information associated with the woman (the color of the woman's clothes), memory performance for the emotional event was superior to that for the unusual event. It could be argued that the central information in the Unusual condition was less distinctive and less attention-catching than the corresponding central information in the Emotional condition and therefore less well retained. On the other hand, the unusual event was far more distinctive and attention-catching than the neutral event, but without any accompanying differences between these conditions in memory for the central detail information. Thus, it seems unlikely that the unusualness of emotional details explains the difference in memory obtained for emotional neutral events. However, more research is warranted to evaluate the role of unusualness and distinctiveness in remembering emotional events.

## Poststimulus elaboration

We know that rote rehearsal is not very efficient for memory performance in general compared to elaborative processing (Craik & Lockhart, 1972; Craik & Tulving, 1975). There are also indications that the degree of self-reported frequency of rehearsal does not correlate with degree of memory performance in some studies of emotional events (e.g., Bohannon, 1988; Christianson & Loftus, 1990; Larsen, this volume). Perhaps differential poststimulus elaboration (i.e., elaboration just after encoding) occurs when subjects are exposed to emotional events as compared with neutral events, thus contributing to the different pattern seen in studies of emotional versus neutral events. For example, subjects presented with emotion-provoking content, such as an accident or a crime, might be more concerned with what they have just seen - about the injuries of the victim, and so forth - which will lead to increased poststimulus elaboration. Related ideas about elaboration of emotional thought content have been presented by Heuer (1987), who argues that the recall pattern for emotional events and associated details is different from that of neutral events. According to Heuer, emotional memories center around the causes of the emotions - the thoughts, feelings, and reactions of the subject - and thus cause the subject to personalize a narrative account around the central elements of the emotional experience. This "personalization" could imply that "arousal at the time of encoding enhances long-term memory both for the 'gist' of an event and also for detail information peripheral to the event" (Heuer, 1987).

Heuer and Reisberg (1990) present results indicating that subjects think more and in a different way about emotional events compared with neutral events. That is, they think of the emotional events in more personal, more psychological, and less schematic or abstract ways. For example, subjects presented with emotional slides are likely to be engaged by certain critical details in the slides, and are likely to think about these specific details. Heuer and Reisberg also found that the pattern of how subjects attend to and rehearse emotional events shows up in the pattern of intrusion errors made by the subjects when recalling the emotional events: They made fewer errors about the emotional event itself, but tended to confabulate about information associated with motives or reactions in the story.

Further support for differences in poststimulus elaboration of emotional versus neutral events is presented by Christianson and Loftus (1991), in which one experiment was conducted to gather thoughts that were evoked in the minds of the subjects while viewing either a critical emotional, unusual, or neutral picture in a series of slides. Analyses of these thoughts revealed that subjects' descriptions in the Emotional condition were more likely to contain expressions of affect and also more likely to make reference to the central character and the central action of the event. On the other hand, descriptions given by subjects in the Neutral condition were more likely to make reference to the environment or peripheral details. Subjects in the Unusual condition produced descriptions that were similar to those of the emotional subjects: That is, they were concerned about the main action and were less likely to refer to the environment. However, in comparison with the emotional group, the subjects in the Unusual condition were less explicit about the central detail information of the event.

Even if these results are far from conclusive, we do see indications that emotional events are remembered differently for reasons that go beyond attentional distribution and the unexpected, unusual characteristics of the emotional content. Thus, it may be that poststimulus elaboration is one critical factor in flashbulb memories or remembering emotional events in general.

The poststimulus elaboration hypothesis is consistent with Easterbrook's (1959) theory in the sense that there is increased cue selectivity and restriction of attentional span in emotionally arousing situations. However, at the same time, the attentional narrowing during the processing of emotional events seems to be associated with more elaborative processing of the information attended to. Thus, when people are exposed to emotional events, fewer aspects of the total event are properly attended to. This enhances processing for central details, but is detrimental to processing of peripheral or surrounding information of the emotional event.

The fact that subjects remember central detail information better from emotional events than from neutral events even when the detail information is shown only for 180 ms, as in the Christianson et al. (1991) study, suggests that an elaboration mechanism may interact with a preattentive mechanism, which does not involve consciously controlled processing. It is then assumed that critical characteristics of emotional events may be extracted and processed by a preattentive and automatic mechanism, which will act as an emotional prime, and thus trigger attentional selectivity and controlled memory processing. Thus, the specific pattern of better central and poorer peripheral detail may result from the interaction between preattentive processes that alert people to orient to emotional information, and more consciously controlled processes (e.g., poststimulus elaboration), that causes them to process preferentially central versus peripheral details.

To answer whether a mechanism based on affect or arousal, attentional or preattentive factors, distinctiveness, or poststimulus elaboration, or a combination of these factors, is critical in remembering emotional events, we definitely need more research and must combine different methodological approaches. This endeavor is under way in many research groups, and hopefully we will soon have a better understanding of how and why we remember emotional events in the way we do when we are exposed to shocking news events.

## Conclusions

This chapter discusses flashbulb memories in the context of other types of negative emotional memories. It is clear that people remember public negative emotional events (i.e., flashbulb events) better than they remember ordinary events, but these flashbulb memories are, by no means, completely accurate. Thus, instead of suggesting that the individual remembers emotionally arousing (or traumatic) events in exceptional detail, current research findings in the flashbulb literature and the literature on emotion and memory in general indicate that some central details are retained quite well from experiences of intense, negative emotional events, whereas some peripheral detail information is remembered less well.

Note, however, that these emotional events and the associated detail information are unusually well preserved at very long retention intervals, even 1 year or longer after the occurrence of the event. Thus, although flashbulb memories are subject to forgetting and distortion effects, the loss of clarity and detail over time seems to be far less for these emotional events than for ordinary, neutral events. This is also a pattern typically observed in laboratory studies of emotional events.

It should be clear then that flashbulb memories are not treated here as a unique category of memories. I prefer to interpret the flashbulb memory phenomenon in terms of the same mechanisms that are involved in other experiences of emotionally arousing events, but, at the same time, also raise the possibility that a selective mechanism or factor might be involved in emotional memories. As I emphasized, however, such a mechanism does not need to be unique for flashbulb events. This mechanism may affect memory at both early perceptual processing (e.g., effects of arousal or attentional/preattentive factors) or late conceptual processing (e.g., the distinctiveness of emotional events or poststimulus elaboration). Future research has to show which of these mechanisms or factors is most critical to why we retain negative emotional events differently from ordinary or unusual events. The findings at hand cast serious doubts on the hypothesis that the only reason why some detail information is better retained in emotional events is that subjects rehearse them more.

## NOTES

The preparation of this manuscript was supported by Grant B 31: 16–28/90 from Th↔ Swedish Council for Crime Prevention (BRÅ) and by Grant 89/9:2 from the Bank c Sweden Tercentenary Foundation.

1  It should be noted, that in a diary study of news memories, Larsen (this volume found that as surprise and importance of the news increased, memory of th reception context detoriated, whereas memory for the news itself improved. Thi finding is analogous to the pattern obtained in many laboratory studies of emotior al events (see Christianson, 1992), but opposite to the traditional picture c flashbulb memories.

2  Although attention and fixation location can, under some circumstances, be dis sociated, research by Posner (see Posner, 1980; Posner, Cohen, Choate, Hocke↔ and Maylor, 1984) indicates that in real-world situations, attention usually r↔ orients to the fovea with the eye movements, thus keeping coordinated the center c acute vision with the direction of attention.

## REFERENCES

Bohannon, J. N. (1988). Flashbulb memories for the space shuttle disaster. A tale c two theories. *Cognition, 29*, 179–196.

Brown, R., & Kulik, J. (1977). Flashbulb memories. *Cognition, 5*, 73–99.

Burke, A., Heuer, F., & Reisberg, D. (in press). Remembering emotional event↔ *Memory & Cognition*.

Christianson, S.-Å. (1984). The relationship between induced emotional arousal an amnesia. *Scandinavian Journal of Psychology, 25*, 147–160.

Christianson, S.-Å. (1989). Flashbulb memories: Special, but not so special. *Memo↔ & Cognition, 17*, 435–443.

Christianson, S.-Å. (1992). Emotional stress and eyewitness memory: A critic↔ review. *Psychological Bulletin*.

Christianson, S.-Å., & Fällman, L. (1990). The role of age on reactivity and memor for emotional pictures. *Scandinavian Journal of Psychology, 31*, 291–301

Christianson, S.-Å., & Larsson, M. (1990). Implicit and explicit memory c laboratory-induced emotional events. Manuscript.

Christianson, S.-Å., & Loftus, E. F. (1987). Memory for traumatic events. *Appli↔ Cognitive Psychology, 1*, 225–239.

Christianson, S.-Å., & Loftus, E. F. (1990). Some characteristics of people's trauma tic memories. *Bulletin of the Psychonomic Society, 28*, 195–198.

Christianson, S.-Å., & Loftus, E. F. (1991). Remembering emotional events: The fat of detailed information. *Cognition & Emotion, 5*, 81–108.

Christianson, S.-Å., Loftus, E. F., Hoffman, H., & Loftus, G. R. (1991). Eye fixation and memory for emotional events. *Journal of Experimental Psychology: Learning Memory, and Cognition, 17*, 693–701.

Christianson, S.-Å., & Mjörndal, T. (1985). Adrenalin, emotional arousal, an↔ memory. *Scandinavian Journal of Psychology, 26*, 237–248.

Christianson, S.-Å., & Nilsson, L.-G. (1984). Functional amnesia as induced by ↔ psychological trauma. *Memory & Cognition, 12*, 142–155.

Christianson, S.-Å., & Nilsson, L.-G. (1989). Hysterical amnesia: A case of aversive↔

motivated isolation of memory. In T. Archer & L.-G. Nilsson (Eds.), *Aversion, avoidance, and anxiety: Perspectives on aversively motivated behavior* (pp. 289–310). Hillsdale, NJ: Erlbaum.

Christianson, S.-Å., Nilsson, L.-G., Mjörndal, T., Perris, C., & Tjelldén, G. (1986). Psychological versus physiological determinants of emotional arousal and its relationship to laboratory amnesia. *Scandinavian Journal of Psychology, 27,* 302–312.

Clifford, B. R., & Hollin, C. R. (1981). Effects of the type of incident and the number of perpetrators on eyewitness memory. *Journal of Applied Psychology, 66,* 364–370.

Clifford, B. R., & Scott, J. (1978). Individual and situational factors in eyewitness testimony. *Journal of Applied Psychology, 63,* 352–359.

Cohen, N. J., McCloskey, M., & Wible, C. G. (1988). There is still no case for a flashbulb-memory mechanism: Reply to Schmidt and Bohannon. *Journal of Experimental Psychology: General, 117,* 336–338.

Colgrove, F. W. (1899). Individual memories. *American Journal of Psychology, 10,* 228–255.

Craik, F. I. M., & Lockhart, R. S. (1972). Levels of processing: A framework for memory research. *Journal of Verbal Learning and Verbal Behavior, 11,* 671– 684.

Craik, F. I. M., & Tulving, E. (1975). Depth of processing and the retention of words in episodic memory. *Journal of Experimental Psychology: General, 104,* 268–294.

Davis, P. J. (1990). Repression and the inaccessibility of emotional memories. In J. L. Singer (Ed.), *Repression and dissociation: Implications for personality theory, psychopathology, and health* (pp. 387–403). Chicago: The University of Chicago Press.

Deffenbacher, K. A. (1983). The influence of arousal on reliability of testimony. In S. M. A. Lloyd-Bostock and B. R. Clifford (Eds.), *Evaluating witness evidence* (pp. 235–251). Chichester: Wiley.

Easterbrook, J. A. (1959). The effect of emotion on cue utilization and the organization of behavior. *Psychological Review, 66,* 183–201.

Egeth, H. E. (1990). Expect Testimony. Paper presented at the annual meeting of the American Psychological Society, Dallas, Texas.

Erdelyi, M. H. (1990). Repression, reconstruction, and defense: History and integration of the psychoanalytic and experimental frameworks. In J. L. Singer (Ed.), *Repression and dissociation: Implications for personality theory, psychopathology, and health* (pp. 1–31). Chicago: The University of Chicago Press.

Erdelyi, M. H., & Goldberg, B. (1979). Let's not sweep repression under the rug: Toward a cognitive psychology of repression. In J. F. Kihlstrom and F. J. Evans (Eds.), *Functional disorders of memory* (pp. 355–402). Hillsdale, NJ: Lawrence Erlbaum.

Eysenck, M. W. (1982). *Attention and arousal: Cognition and performance.* Berlin: Springer-Verlag.

Gold, P. (1986). Glucose modulation of memory storage processing. *Behavioral and Neural Biology, 45,* 342–349.

Heuer, F. (1987). *Remembering detail: The role of emotion in long-term memory.* Unpublished dissertation. New School for Social Research, New York.

Heuer, F., & Reisberg, D. (1990). Vivid memories of emotional events: The accuracy of remembered minutiae. *Memory & Cognition, 18,* 496–506.

Kebeck, G., & Lohaus, A. (1986). Effects of emotional arousal on free recall of complex material. *Perceptual and Motor Skills, 63,* 461–462.

Kramer, T. H., Buckhout, R., & Eugenio, P. (1990). Weapon focus, arousal, and eyewitness memory: Attention must be paid. *Law and Human Behavior, 14,* 167–184.

Kramer, T. H., Buckhout, R., Fox, P., Widman, E., & Tusche, B. (1991). Effects of stress on recall. *Applied Cognitive Psychology, 5,* 483–488.

Levonian, E. (1967). Retention of information in relation to arousal during continuously-presented material. *American Educational Research Journal, 4,* 103–116.

Livingston, R. B. (1967). Reinforcement. In G. C. Quarton, T. Melnechuck, and F. O. Schmitt (Eds.), *The neurosciences: A study program* (pp. 568–576). New York: Rockefeller University Press.

Loftus, E. F. (1979). *Eyewitness testimony.* Cambridge, MA: Harvard University Press.

Loftus, E. F., & Burns, T. (1982). Mental shock can produce retrograde amnesia. *Memory & Cognition, 10,* 318–323.

Loftus, E. F., Loftus, G. R., & Messo, J. (1987). Some facts about "Weapon Focus." *Law and Human Behavior, 11,* 55–62.

McCloskey, M., & Egeth, H. E. (1983). Eyewitness identification: What can a psychologist tell a jury? *American Psychologist, 38,* 550–563.

McCloskey, M., Wible, C. G., & Cohen, N. J. (1988). Is there a special flashbulb-memory mechanism? *Journal of Experimental Psychology: General, 117,* 171–181.

Maass, A., & Köhnken, G. (1989). Eyewitness identification: Simulating the "weapon effect." *Law and Human Behavior, 13,* 397–408.

Mandler, G., Nakamura, Y., & Van Zandt, B. J. (1987). Nonspecific effects of exposure on stimuli that cannot be recognized. *Journal of Experimental Psychology: Learning, Memory, and Cognition, 13,* 646–648.

Manning, C., Hall, J., & Gold, P. (1990). Glucose effects on memory and other neuropsychological tests in elderly humans. *Psychological Science, 1,* 307–311.

Messier, C., & Destrade C. (1988). Improvement of memory for an operant response by post-training glucose in mice. *Behavioural Brain Research, 31,* 185.

Murdock, B. B. (1974). *Human memory: Theory and data.* Hillsdale, NJ: Erlbaum.

Näätänen, R. (1973). The inverted-U relationship between activation and performance: A critical review. In S. Kornblum (Ed.), *Attention and performance* (Vol. 4). New York: Academic Press.

Neiss, R. (1988). Reconceptualizing arousal: Psychological states in motor performance. *Psychological Bulletin, 103,* 345–366.

Neisser, U. (1967). *Cognitive psychology.* New York: Appleton.

Neisser, U. (1978). Memory: What are the important questions? In M. M. Gruneberg, P. E. Morris, and R. N. Sykes (Eds.), *Practical aspects of memory.* London: Academic Press.

Neisser, U. (1982). Snapshots or benchmarks? In U. Neisser (Ed.), *Memory observed* (pp. 43–48). San Francisco: Freeman.

Pillemer, D. B. (1984). Flashbulb memories of the assassination attempt on President Reagan. *Cognition, 16,* 63–80.

Posner, M. I. (1980). Orienting of attention. The VII Sir Frederic Bartlett Lecture. *Quarterly Journal of Experimental Psychology, 32,* 3–25.

Posner, M. I., Cohen, Y., Choate, L., Hockey, G. R. I., & Maylor, E. (1984). Sustained concentration: Passive filtering or active orienting? In S. Kornblum and J. Requin (Eds.), *Preparatory states and processes* (49–65). Hillsdale, NJ: Erlbaum.

Reisberg, D., Heuer, F., McLean, J., & O'Shaughnessy, M. (1988). The quantity, not the quality, of affect predicts memory vividness. *Bulletin of the Psychonomic Society, 26,* 100–103.

Rubin, D. C., & Kozin, M. (1984). Vivid memories. *Cognition, 16,* 81–95.

Schmidt, S. R., & Bohannon, J. N. III. (1988). In defense of the flashbulb-memory hypothesis: A comment on McCloskey, Wible, and Cohen (1988). *Journal of Experimental Psychology: General, 117,* 332–335.

Scrivner, E., & Safer, M. A. (1988). Eyewitnesses show hypermnesia for details about a violent event. *Journal of Applied Psychology, 73,* 371–377.

Steiner, J. E. (1973). The gustofacial response: Observation on normal and on encephalic newborn infants. In J. F. Bosma (Ed.), *Fourth symposium on oral sensation and perception.* Bethesda, MD: US Department of Health and Human Services.

Tulving, E. (1972). Episodic and semantic memory. In E. Tulving and W. Donaldson (Eds.), *Organization of memory* (pp. 381–403). New York: Academic Press.

Tulving, E. (1987). Multiple memory systems and consciousness. *Human Neurobiology,* 6, 67–80.

Tulving, E., & Schacter, D. L. (1990). Priming and human memory systems. *Science,* 247, 301–306.

Wagenaar, W. A. (1986). My memory: A study of autobiographical memory over six years. *Cognitive Psychology, 18,* 225–252.

Wagenaar, W. A., & Groeneweg, J. (1990). The memory of concentration camp survivors. *Applied Cognitive Psychology, 4,* 77–87.

Winograd, E., & Killinger, W. A., Jr. (1983). Relating age at encoding in early childhood to adult recall: Development of flashbulb memories. *Journal of Experimental Psychology: General, 112,* 413–422.

Yerkes, R. M., & Dodson, J. D. (1908). The relation of strength of stimulus to rapidity of habit-information. *Journal of Comparative Neurology of Psychology, 18,* 459–482.

Yuille, J. C., & Cutshall, J. L. (1986). A case study of eyewitness memory of a crime. *Journal of Applied Psychology, 71,* 291–301.

Yuille, J. C., & Cutshall, J. L. (1989). Analysis of the statements of victims, witnesses and suspects. In J. C. Yuille (Ed.), *Credibility assessment.* Dordrecht: Kluwer Academic Publishers.

Yuille, J. C., & Tollestrup, P. A. (in press). A model of the diverse effects of emotion on eyewitness memory. In S.-Å Christianson (Ed.), *The handbook of emotion and memory.* Hillsdale, NJ: Erlbaum.

Zajonc, R. B. (1980). Feeling and thinking: Preferences need no inferences. *American Psychologist, 35,* 151–175.

Zajonc, R. B. (1981). A one-factor mind about mind and emotion. *American Psychologist, 36,* 102–103.

Zajonc, R. B. (1984). On the primacy of affect. *American Psychologist, 39,* 117–123.

# 10

# Why do traumatic experiences sometimes produce good memory (flashbulbs) and sometimes no memory (repression)?

ELIZABETH F. LOFTUS
AND LEAH KAUFMAN

"The past is a foreign country . . . they do things differently there." So begins L. P. Hartley's classic book, *The Go-Between* (1953). In thinking about "flashbulb" memories, specifically about the match between their present character and the past experience that gave rise to them, it is tempting to ask a similarly phrased question: Did they do things differently there?

There is no doubt that present memories about past traumatic episodes persist in the minds of most of us. But were things different then (in reality) than they are now (in our minds)? It turns out that some aspects of traumatic experiences do apparently persist quite accurately, whereas other aspects get altered along the way. These persisting flashbulbs, dotted with error, raise a question about the kind of memory system that can accommodate both persistence and error. What functions would such a system serve, asks Pillemer (this volume)? Equally intriguing is why some traumatic events get transformed into persisting flashbulbs, whereas other traumatic events are entirely repressed in memory for long periods of life?

## Persisting flashbulbs that resemble the past

Clearly, we remember details from the traumatic events of our past. We remember the circumstances in which we first learned about shocking public or private tragedies. Take the first major eruption of Mount Saint Helens, which occurred on May 18, 1980. This shocking public event was well known to residents of the northwestern United States. The eruption began about 8:30 in the morning, and continued late into the night, sending more than 150 square miles of mountain thousands of feet into the air. Fifty-seven people were reported missing and are assumed dead.

Ten years later, I remember that on the morning of the eruption, I was flying from Seattle to San Francisco. Ten years later, Dixy Lee Ray, former

Washington governor remembers: "I was notified within a moment or two of the eruption. I quickly got onto a state plane and flew to the Chehalis area. My most vivid recollection of watching from the air was the enormous sense of power generated by the eruption. The huge gray cloud reached miles into the stratosphere; . . . It was seething and it looked like massive heads of dirty cauliflower being tossed about. I could see flashes of lightning in the clouds . . . (I worried about) people being caught too close to the mountain, concern for mudflows, and the anxiety of getting rescue operations underway." (*Pacific Northwest Magazine*, 1990, p. 35). Ann Wilson, lead singer of Seattle's most famous rock group, Heart, remembers: " . . . we were on the road in West Virginia. After we got over the initial shock and worry for our loved ones, we cracked up . . ." Wayne Cody, Seattle sportscaster, remembers: "I slept through it. I got up about 11 a.m. and went out on my back porch. I saw some dark clouds and thought to myself that we were in for some rain. Then I went out to Longacres, and someone told me the mountain had blown."

These recollections are both remarkable and unremarkable. They are remarkable in that they have survived – in some form – for so long. When compared to what we have retained in memory about the more mundane events of the same week, the apparent reality of these flashbulb memories is special. That flashbulbs have this advantage in memory over their more mundane counterparts has been amply documented (cf. Larsen, this volume).

## Persisting flashbulbs, dotted with error

Despite the remarkable persistence of subjective memory, there is a way in which flashbulbs are unremarkable. A casual reading of Brown and Kulik (1977), particularly the "Now Print!" idea, might have led to the expectation that flashbulbs would possess near-perfect accuracy (although Brown and Kulik did not claim they should be mirror images of the original experiences that launched them). Brown and Kulik explicitly emphasized the relative permanence of flashbulbs in claiming that they are "fixed for a very long time, and conceivably permanently, varying in complexity with consequentiality but, once created, always there, and in need of no further strengthening" (p. 85). Despite claims that a representation could be modified by rehearsal, Brown and Kulik would probably not have doubted Ann Wilson's claim that she was on the road in West Virginia. Nor Wayne Cody's memory that he went to Longacres. Nor Dixy Lee Ray's description that she saw something that resembled massive heads of dirty cauliflower being tossed about. But are these recollections accurate? Potentially we could verify part, but not all, of the details of these recollections. If we had the capability of verifying every aspect, we would undoubtedly find they were fraught with error. We infer a reasonable likelihood of error because the literature provides clear examples. Take the example of one of the worst public/personal tragedies in the history of baseball (Anderson, 1990). It occurred on August 18, 1967 in Fenway Park. It involved player Tony Conigliaro, who at the age of 20 led the American League with 32 home runs. By 22 he had accumulated 100 home runs. But at age 23, Tony C's career in essence ended that Friday night in August, when Jack Hamilton, then with the California Angels, crushed the outfielder's face with a first-pitch fastball.

More than 20 years later, Hamilton (now over 50) can't forget: "I've had to live with it; I think about it a lot . . . Watching baseball on TV, anytime a guy gets hit, I think about it." Hamilton remembered how it happened: "It was like the sixth inning when it happened. I think the score was 2–1, and he was the eighth hitter in their batting order. With the pitcher up next, I had no reason to throw at him."

It turns out that Hamilton's memory wasn't even close. It wasn't the sixth inning. The score wasn't 2–1. Tony C. wasn't the eighth hitter. Quite the contrary: It was the fourth inning, no score, two out, nobody on. Tony C. was batting sixth, right behind Reggie Smith. Hamilton remembered that it was a day game because he recalled trying to see Tony C. in the hospital later that afternoon. The truth is different: The game took place at night.

Errors like those of Jack Hamilton's will not surprise many contributors to the flashbulb literature (e.g., McCloskey, Wible, & Cohen, 1988; Neisser & Harsch, this volume). The prevalence of errors is one way in which flashbulb memories are like "ordinary" memories – in this way they are unremarkable. If evidence is produced that flashbulb memories are not exceptionally accurate, then there is no need to posit a special mechanism or remarkable mechanism to explain them (McCloskey et al., 1988). Most of the studies of flashbulb memories reveal that errors abound. Even when verification of the actual event details is not possible, inconsistencies from one telling to the next provide the evidence needed to know that flashbulb memories are far from highly accurate (e.g., McCloskey et al., 1988; Warren & Swartwood, this volume). McCloskey et al. obtained memories of learning about the January, 1986 space shuttle disaster on two occasions: 1 week and 9 months after the explosion. Warren and Swartwood examined memories for the same disaster 2 weeks, 2 months, and 2 years later. Both sets of investigators found substantial evidence of forgetting and inaccuracy. Clearly, although they may be relatively persistent, flashbulbs are not immune to forgetting (Pillemer, 1990).

## The function of persisting flashbulbs

In a refreshing way, Pillemer (chapter 12, this volume) asks us to shift away from an exclusive focus on the veridicality of flashbulb memories and instead consider their functions. Of course he is not the first researcher to remind us that our memories are not simply a passive storehouse for representations of past experience, but these memories serve various social functions, and they satisfy needs and desires (Neisser, 1988). But Pillemer broadens the discussion by identifying and then developing some of the social and personal activities that might be enhanced by remembering and recounting flashbulbs. Pillemer's arguments, ironically, lead us to the view that flashbulbs, rather than being specially adept at preserving accurate information, might possess just the opposite character – that is, they might be a breeding ground for errors.

Why should Dixy Lee Ray remember her trip in the state plane and the look of dirty cauliflower? For one thing the recounting of this memory has a communicative function. She gets to share her memory with others, and to hear about their memories of that fateful day in May, 1980. Now what she decides to share will undoubtedly depend on the relationship between her and her listener. But at least in some circles, she might have an interest in telling a good story. Reacting to a public tragedy as governor of the state makes a good story.

What details Dixy Lee Ray includes in her "story" will depend on her listener. In talking to the writer for *Pacific Northwest Magazine*, she undoubtedly provided a different version from the one she would tell an intimate friend. The longer, more intimate story could have included where she slept that night, what were her first words – aspects too awkward or trivial for the magazine.

In recounting her flashbulb, Dixy Lee Ray could have a hidden agenda. She might want to impress her listeners with her important position at the time – someone so important as to be taken by state airplane to view the wreckage of the blast. In the words she chose for her recounting, she may have wanted to impress. Consistent with a self-image of literary capability, she describes having seen something that looked like dirty cauliflower. The hidden agendas inherent in the sharing of flashbulbs made personal sense to me. Since the early 1960s I have been telling the story of where I was when I learned about the assassination of President John F. Kennedy. I flew that November day from Los Angeles to New York to attend the Yale/Harvard football game. I heard the news on the car radio together with my date, Rich, as we drove from the airport to New Haven, or maybe Rich told me when he met me at the airport; I'm now not exactly sure which. I've told the story of my flashbulb many times; it's something cognitive scientists do together. But what other motives might I have had for my numerous retellings? Did a desire to impress people with the fact that I, a mere beginning college student at UCLA, had been invited to something so faraway and impressive as the Yale/Harvard game? Did this play some role in my repeated sharing of this flashbulb?

In my desire to tell a good story, I, like Dixy Lee Ray, would want my recounting to be detailed. Research confirms that details make good stories, and listeners are impressed with details (Bell & Loftus, 1989). Thus, I would tell you more about my visit to the East for the Yale/Harvard game, if you showed the least bit of interest. I would tell you how the game was postponed, and how I missed a week of school so I could attend the game that was eventually played a week later. I would tell you about conversations that I had late into the night with Yale students and their weekend dates – we were all trying to cope with our collective tragedy.

In recounting my flashbulb with fellow Americans, I, according to Pillemer, signal emotionality and intimacy. Armed with my detailed story, I can presumably evoke emphatic responses in my listeners. By sharing with those who have had a similar experience, I can move the relationship with my conversational partners to a more intimate level. These intimacy-enhancing functions become even clearer to me when I think about the flashbulbs I have surrounding the death of my mother.

Pillemer also considers the psychodynamic functions of a flashbulb memory. He speculates about the continuing psychological impact on the rememberer, and suggests that recounting flashbulbs might actually help us to master the emotions we feel and thereby lessen their negative effects. We reduce tension and anxiety when we share these experiences. Moreover, flashbulbs have "directive functions" – we extract lessons from them about how to behave in the future.

In illuminating the psychological functions that may be served by detailed memories of personal circumstances surrounding traumatic episodes, Pillemer would have us believe that these memories are valuable indeed. However, his analysis leads us to support the rather provocative suggestion (Neisser, this volume) that flashbulb memories might be especially prone to distortion. When we repeatedly recount the flashbulb, we do so in an everchanging environment. Our specific listeners change, and thus the type of information we include also changes. Our needs to impress people, or to gain their empathy, or to reduce tension is not the same from one occasion of retelling to the next. As the story changes, does the memory change with it?

Pillemer has identified the myriad ways in which flashbulbs are valuable, and in doing so he raises in my mind a critical question. If flashbulbs are so valuable, then why don't all memories for past traumas persist? Why are some traumatic memories completely repressed?

**Repression of traumatic memories**

In 1990, a landmark case went to trial in Redwood City, California. The defendant, George Franklin, Sr., 51 years old, stood trial for a murder that occurred over 20 years ago. The victim, 8-year-old Susan Kay Nason, was murdered on September 22, 1969. Franklin's daughter, Eileen, only 8 years old herself at the time of the murder, provided the major evidence against her father. What was unusual about the case is that Eileen's memory of witnessing the murder had been repressed for over 20 years.

Eileen's memory did not come back all at once. Her first flashback came one afternoon in January, 1989, when she was playing with her 2-year-old son, Aaron, and her 5-year-old daughter, Jessica. At one particular moment, Jessica looked up and asked her mother a question like, "Isn't that right, Mommy?" A memory of Susan Nason suddenly came back. Eileen recalled the look of betrayal in Susie's eyes just before the murder. Later, more fragments would return, until Eileen had a rich and detailed memory. She remembered her father sexually assaulting Susie in the back of the VW van. She remembered that Susie was struggling as she said, "No don't" and "Stop." She remembered her father saying, "Now Susie" and mimicked his actual intonation (Preliminary hearing testimony, 1990). Next, her memory took the three of them outside the van, where she now saw her father with his hands raised above his head with a rock in them. She remembered screaming. She remembered walking back to where Susie lay, covered with blood, the silver ring on her finger smashed. Interestingly media reports from 20 years before, December, 1969, when the body was found, were filled with some of these same details – skull fractured on the right side, silver Indian ring found on the body (*San Francisco Chronicle*, Dec. 3, 1969, p. 1); hand up to protect self; crushed ring (*San Jose Mercury News*, Dec. 6, 1969).

Eileen's memory report was believed not only by her therapist, but by several members of her family, and by the San Mateo County District Attorney's office, which chose to prosecute her father. It was also believed by the jury, which convicted George Franklin, Sr. of murder in December, 1990.

Is Eileen's memory experience of repression followed by reported recovery unique? The answer is no. Repression of early traumatic memories is a concept many psychotherapists readily accept (Mithers, 1990). For example, during therapy patients often "recover" early childhood memories of instances of sexual abuse that have been repressed for several decades. These anecdotal reports constitute the clinical "evidence" that patients do indeed manage to remember later on some earlier inaccessible painful experiences (Erdelyi, 1985). In Freud's way of putting it, repression begins when: "A hysterical subject seeks intentionally to forget an experience or forcibly repudiates, inhibits and suppresses an intention or idea" (Freud, 1892/1940, p. 153). (At least this was one of Freud's many definitions; he used the term repression differently on different occasions [Holmes, 1990]). Others prefer a definition of repression that suggests that the banishment is involuntary, not intentional (Holmes, 1990). Then, time passes, and sometimes the memory comes back. This is what Freud called "the return of the repressed" and the existence of anecdotal, clinical experiences constitute straightforward "proof" of the existence of repression (Erdelyi, 1985, p. 244). One powerful clinical example of such "proof," which bears a family resemblance to the recovered memory of murder that we have discussed, was reported in El Salvador in 1987 (Lopez-Guerra, 1987). Under hypnosis, a female university student regressed to the age of 3 years and recalled the murder of her father. In contrast to Eileen Franklin, the student firmly believed that the events she recalled under hypnosis were most likely a dream. Thus these two women are similar in that both allegedly witnessed the death of a cherished person and both repressed memory of the incident until it was revived later, with the help of a therapeutic session. Yet one woman asserted that the memory was veridical and the other contended that it was only a dream.

These clinical "proofs" remain unconvincing to many laboratory researchers, one of whom denounced these proofs as "impressionistic case studies" (Holmes, 1990, p. 97), and claimed they could not be counted as "anything more than unconfirmed clinical speculations." After reviewing 60 years of research and finding no controlled laboratory support for the concept of repression, Holmes (1990) suggested, only half jokingly, that any use of the concept should be preceded by: "Warning. The concept of repression has not been validated with experimental research and its use may be hazardous to the accurate interpretation of clinical behavior."

Amid this controversy, a jury in California is asked to decide whether Eileen Franklin's memory of her father committing murder before her very eyes is real. If it is, why did it disappear for 20 years, and why did it return? Clinicians would say that the essence of repression lies in rejecting and keeping something out of consciousness as a defense (Erdelyi & Goldberg, 1979); it is a way to eliminate or prevent psychic pain. The trauma inflicted by seeing a murder was so enormous, some would say, that in order to cope both Eileen and the university student repressed their painful memories.

Rofe (1989) explicitly describes repression of memories as a normal coping mechanism. Whenever we encounter something that is potentially harmful we make a conscious and deliberate effort to distract attention from the stress-provoking stimuli. The common theme in both of these explanations is that in order to maintain our health and happiness and hence, live day-to-day in a relatively satisfactory manner, events that disturb our emotional equilibrium may be repressed. Here is one way in which flashbulb memories may differ from repressed memories: flashbulb memories may not be as emotionally laden as repressed memories. For many people, although John F. Kennedy's death and the eruption of Mount Saint Helens were shocking, the events themselves precipitated few changes in daily life. By contrast, Eileen Franklin had to cope with her father's continued presence and the university student with her father's sudden absence. Of course this discussion emphasizing the differences in the types of memories that go on to be flashbulbs and the types that are repressed is less than satisfying when we are forced to acknowledge that sometimes memories of the very same type (e.g., sex abuse, murder, whatever) are repressed and sometimes they are not.

Given that some traumatic events are repressed, how do they return to consciousness? A number of psychoanalytic techniques are oriented to recovery of repressed memories. Traditionally, a neurosis arises from painful memories that have been blocked; by releasing the memories, the emotions associated are also released and the neurosis can be healed. But is it possible to retrieve accurately memories of events experienced at age 3? At age 8? White and Pillemer (1979) point out that between the ages of 6 to 8, a child undergoes dramatic changes in memory organization and possibly equally dramatic changes in how the world is perceived. If retrieval of memories before the ages of 6 to 8 depends on having the same perceptual and conceptual organization used for storing early childhood experiences, then memories of these experiences may become inaccessible. It is as if (pardon the computer analogy) a diskette formatted by an early version of a computer operating system could not be read by the latest and most sophisticated version of the same system. This point has been made before: Schachtel (1947; excerpted in Neisser, 1982) made the point over half a century ago that adults have trouble remembering things from early childhood because the categories and the organization of adult memory are so different.

The psychotherapist might say that the information was never really lost from memory; rather, the cues needed for retrieval have changed. Suddenly one day, Eileen Franklin's daughter looked at her in a particular way. That look was enough to render the repressed memory accessible. By regressing to the age of 3 via hypnosis, the undergraduate also regained access to cues for a repressed memory.

Whatever role retrieval cues may play in their recovery, we must still wonder: How reliable are these once-repressed memories? To answer this, it is useful to step back and think: How reliable is any memory? Usually cognitive psychologists talk about rehearsal as a mechanism for keeping memory alive. Flashbulb memories are rehearsed; they become ways of sharing an experience. Rehearsal is thought to be one mechanism for keeping these memories alive. But in the case of flashbulb memories, as we suggested earlier, rehearsal in a new context, where new motives and desires abound, might contribute to changes in the recollection, rather than to its preservation.

How shall we think about a memory that was not consciously rehearsed at all? Repressed memories are obviously not shared because they are buried. If rehearsal is an important ingredient for memories to persist for later recall, then perhaps repressed memories are mostly confabulation – skeletons filled in with plausibilities. On the other hand, one could just as easily suggest that the once-repressed memory springs to life in some pristine form because no opportunities for reconstructive, elaborative, or otherwise memory-altering rehearsal would have occurred.

Once sprung to life, repressed memories, like flashbulb memories, are often expressed with copious detail. And as in the case of the flashbulbs, it is difficult to determine if the repressed memory detail is merely reconstructed from bits and pieces of the past or if it actually stems from veridical storage of the event. Erdelyi (1985) raises the possibility that people who purportedly recover lost memories are in fact generating not memories of true events but "fanciful guesses, fantasies, or plain confabulations. Such data would then constitute evidence not of repression but of imagination." (p. 246). Despite this obvious possibility, and despite the proof by existence of recovered lost memories that contain errors, some clinicians and politicians remain impressed by the veracity of these once-lost memories. A belief that repressed memories, once revived, are real was apparently part of the basis for a new law in California that extends the statute of limitations in abuse cases from age 19 to 26, and in certain cases permits victims to bring a civil suit at whatever age they are when they "discover" the injury. Similar laws have already been passed in Alaska, Colorado, Maine, Washington, and several other states. The question raised by these policy changes has been aptly asked: "Does allowing incest survivors to sue up to 10, 20, even 30 years after the fact result in justice for the survivors – or injustice for those they accuse?" (Mithers, 1990, p. 44).

One interesting aspect of the new law is that it gives special status to one type of memory but not another. A "victim" can bring a law suit if he says that his memory for a molestation was repressed and then in therapy came back. He cannot bring a law suit if he says that he always remembered the molestation but only recently through therapy developed the courage to report it. Does the return of a repressed memory deserve this special status?

The answer to this question might depend in part on the validity of the recovered memory. The legal system begs for quick answers to the validity issue, and cognitive scientists are interested in validity, too, although perhaps they are content to search for answers more slowly. But as the search continues, cognitive scientists could suggest, as Pillemer does for the case of surviving flashbulbs, that we shift away from an exclusive focus on veridicality and spend part of our scientific time simultaneously exploring the functions of both repression, and recovery from repression. What social and personal activities are enhanced by recovering repressed memories? What communicative functions? What psychodynamic functions? What directive functions? Therapeutically speaking, it makes sense that a recovered memory gives one something on which to blame present anxieties, tensions, and maladaptive behaviors. Communicatively speaking, the recovered memories are often accompanied by strong affect, which could lead listeners to even more readily believe that the memories are real.

Why do some traumatic memories persist, albeit with some error in detail, whereas others are repressed? Speculations are freely given. One psychiatrist

(Terr, 1990) suggests that it depends on the nature of the traumatic event. With long-standing, repeated events, a series of defensive operations, such as denial and self-anesthesia, are set in motion. These defenses interfere with memory formation and retrieval. "The child may even develop blanket amnesia for certain years in the past." On the other hand, "when the defenses are completely overrun by one sudden, unanticipated terror, brilliant, overly clear verbal memories are the result." The quick traumas lead to "full, accurate memory" (p. 183).

This speculation fails when it comes face to face with the empirical obstacle that sudden, unanticipated tragedies do not reliably produce accurate memories. Terr (1990) herself provides such examples. One example involved a child patient of Terr's to whom she gave the pseudonym "Betsy Ferguson." Betsy was apparently 9 years old when her grandmother was strangled by Betsy's mother's boyfriend. Betsy never saw the murder, as she had left her grandmother's house after breakfast and the door was locked when she returned. When the police arrived, they found the body in the kitchen and covered it with a blanket. An officer told a shocked Betsy what had happened. Months later, Betsy "developed a bothersome, repeated visualization – a picture of Grandma being strangled. It was Betsy's imagination . . . She pictured . . . what she could not ever have seen" (p. 133). Did Betsy now have a false memory? Although it remains a bit unclear from Terr's description whether Betsy actually came to believe she witnessed her murdered grandmother, in later discussing Betsy's case, her therapist discussed it immediately after writing: "Most 'false traumatic memory' has nothing at all to do with lying or with suggestion. It stems directly, instead, from what was heard and felt during a traumatic occurrence" (p. 178). Although some ambiguity remains in the description of the Betsy Ferguson example, there is little ambiguity in some of Terr's other cases. "Natasha Dimmit," who was hit by a car, remembered the Caucasian driver as a "Japanese" man – possibly because she overheard the police talk about the car having been a Japanese model. "Winifred Harrison," whose sister was eviscerated in a freak pool accident, later formed a memory of seeing this happen. She hadn't seen it, but her memory became a composite of "everyone else's memories" (p. 179), fueled by family lore. "The tales became visual. The resultant memory sounded as clear and as real as if it had entered her brain down the optic tracts" (p. 179).

More can be said about the speculation that long-standing repeated events lead to repression. The speculation is incomplete in providing any sort of specification of how and when recovery of repressed memories occurs. We have a lot to learn about the myriad ways in which repression can be implemented, such as through displacement or projection. Perhaps a functional approach to the problem of repression, along the lines provided by Pillemer for the persisting flashbulbs, would provide the kinds of insights and suggestions for future research that could advance our thinking about traumatic memories and the varieties of forms that they take.

## Summary

Many strong claims exist about the accuracy of traumatic memories. In form, they resemble this one: ". . . memories of trauma remain quite accurate and true to the events that stimulated them" (Terr, 1988). In fact, traumatic memories take many forms: Sometimes they persist as flashbulbs, sometimes they are repressed, and sometimes they are repressed but return. In all cases, the memories appear to contain at least some elements of error. Error is, it seems, one thing that these varieties of memories have in common with one another, and with memories of more mundane events. It remains for further research to illuminate the ways in which traumatic memories – however they are expressed – are different from more mundane memories, and to document the varieties of functions they serve.

## REFERENCES

Anderson, D. (1990) Handcuffed in history to Tony C. *New York Times*, February 27, p. B9.

Bell, B. E., & Loftus, E. F. (1989). Trivial persuasion in the courtroom: The power of (a few) minor details. *Journal of Personality and Social Psychology, 56*, 669–679.

Brown, R., & Kulik, J. (1977). Flashbulb memories. *Cognition, 5*, 73–99.

Erdelyi, M. H. (1985). *Psychoanalysis: Freud's cognitive psychology*. New York: Freeman.

Erdelyi, M. H., & Goldberg, B. (1979). Let's not sweep repression under the rug: Toward a cognitive psychology of repression. In J. F. Kihlstrom & F. J. Evans (Eds.), *Functional disorders of memory* (pp. 355–402). Hillsdale, NJ: Erlbaum.

Freud, S. (1982). Sketches for the preliminary communication of 1893. (C) On the theory of hysterical attacks. In J. Strachey (Translator and Ed.), *The standard edition of the complete psychological works of Sigmund Freud*. London: Hogarth Press, (1966, original published in 1940).

Hartley, L. P. (1953). *The go-between*. London: Hamish Hamilton.

Holmes, D. A. (1990). The evidence for repression: An examination of fifty years of research. In J. Singer (Ed.), *Repression and dissociation: Implications for personality, theory, psychopathology, and health*. Chicago: University of Chicago Press.

Lopez-Guerra, O. (1987). Un grave caso di amnesia risolto in due sedute ipno-terapeutiche/A serious case of amnesia cured during two hypnotherapeutic sittings. *Rivista Internazionale di Psicologia e Ipnosi, 28* (1–2), 113–117.

McCloskey, M. Wible, C. G., & Cohen, N. J. (1988). Is there a special flashbulb-memory mechanism? *Journal of Experimental Psychology: General, 117*, 171–181.

Mithers, C. L. (1990). Incest and the law. *New York Times Magazine*, October 21, p. 44, 53–58, 62–63.

Neisser, U. (1982). *Memory observed: Remembering in natural contexts*. San Francisco: Freeman.

Neisser, U. (1988). Time present and time past. In M. M. Gruneberg, P. E. Morris, & R. N. Sykes (Eds.), *Practical aspects of memory: Vol. 2.* (pp. 545–560). Chichester: John Wiley & Sons.

*Pacific Northwest Magazine.* (1990, May). 10 Years After. Pp. 33–39.

Pillemer, D. B. (1990). Clarifying the flashbulb memory concept: Comment on McCloskey, Wible, & Cohen (1988). *Journal of Experimental Psychology: General, 119,* 92–96.

Rofe, Y. (1989). *Repression and fear: A new approach to resolve the crisis in psychopathology.* New York: Hemisphere Publishing.

*San Francisco Chronicle.* (1969, December 3). Susan Nason Body Found in a Dump. P. 1.

*San Francisco Examiner.* (1969, December 3). Police Hunt Clues to Susan's Killer. P. 1.

Schachtel, E. G. (1947). On memory and childhood amnesia. *Psychiatry, 10,* 1–26. (Excerpted in Neisser, 1982.)

Terr, L. (1988). What happens to early memories of trauma? A study of twenty children under age five at the time of documented traumatic events. *Journal of American Academy of Child and Adolescent Psychiatry, 27,* 96–104.

Terr, L. (1990). *Too scared to cry.* New York: Harper & Row.

White, S. H., & Pillemer, D. B. (1979). Childhood amnesia and the development of a socially accessible memory system. In J. F. Kihlstrom & F. J. Evans (Eds.), *Functional disorder of memory.* Hillsdale, NJ: Erlbaum.

*Part IV*

# Theoretical issues

# 11

# Special versus ordinary memory mechanisms in the genesis of flashbulb memories

MICHAEL McCLOSKEY

The chapters in this volume, as well as the discussions at the conference from which the volume emerged, illustrate clearly that the study of "flashbulb" memories raises a wide variety of difficult and often controversial issues. In commenting on the chapters by Larsen (this volume) and Neisser and Harsch (this volume), however, I will focus primarily on a single question: What are the implications of these studies for the hypothesis of a special flashbulb memory mechanism?

## The special-mechanism hypothesis

The special-mechanism hypothesis has dominated flashbulb memory research since Brown and Kulik's 1977 article. Larsen addresses this hypothesis directly in his chapter; and although Neisser and Harsch do not couch their discussion in terms of the special-mechanism hypothesis, the data they present are certain to figure prominently in any future discussions of the hypothesis.

The Larsen study and the Neisser and Harsch study report data that will be, and I think should be, taken as evidence against the special-mechanism hypothesis. However, both studies may attract an objection that has been raised against previous critiques of the special-mechanism hypothesis. Specifically, the objection may be that neither the Larsen study nor the Neisser and Harsch study definitively refutes the special-mechanism hypothesis, because neither study demonstrates clearly that ordinary memory mechanisms are sufficient to account for flashbulb memories. This objection deserves careful attention, because it is entirely valid, but at the same time entirely ineffective as a defense of the special-mechanism hypothesis.

*Ordinary and special memory mechanisms.* In developing these points let me begin by making clear what I mean by ordinary and special memory mechanisms, because these terms have been used in a number of different ways. By *ordinary memory mechanisms* I mean mental machinery that functions in the usual course of events to retain information about past experiences:

227

processes for generating internal representations of experienced events, storing these representations in memory, and retrieving them at a later time. In contrast, I use the term *special mechanism* to refer to cognitive machinery that is not involved in ordinary remembering, but instead is brought into play only when specific triggering conditions are met.

Given this use of terminology, two broad classes of interpretations for flashbulb memories may be defined. *Ordinary-mechanism* accounts interpret flashbulb memories in terms of cognitive machinery involved in ordinary remembering, perhaps referring to variables that affect the functioning of the ordinary mechanisms and hence the level of memory performance they support. On the other hand, *special-mechanism* accounts hold that flashbulb memories cannot be interpreted in terms of ordinary memory mechanisms, but instead require postulation of cognitive machinery not involved in ordinary remembering.

For example, although Larsen (this volume) refers to his *displacement of rehearsal* account as a weak special-mechanism interpretation, this account is an ordinary memory interpretation in my use of the term. In essence, the displacement of rehearsal account states

1. Rehearsal improves the retention of information by ordinary memory mechanisms.
2. In the case of flashbulb memories rehearsal effort is displaced from the news itself (e.g., the details of the space shuttle explosion) to the "news reception context" (i.e., the circumstances in which the news was learned). Thus, for flashbulb events the reception context is rehearsed more than is usually the case.
3. Consequently, in flashbulb memories the reception context is better remembered than for most news events.

Thus, Larsen's account interprets flashbulb memories in terms of variables affecting processes involved in ordinary remembering. Although on this account flashbulb memories are special in that they result from an unusual allocation of rehearsal effort, these memories are not special in the sense of involving cognitive machinery not implicated in ordinary remembering.

### The form of definitive arguments

Let us now consider what would constitute a well-fleshed-out, logically tight argument for or against the special-mechanism hypothesis. A definitive argument in favor of the hypothesis would take the following form:

1. Under a certain set of conditions $C$ (e.g., high levels of surprise and consequentiality, or strong emotional reaction) ordinary memory mechanisms would produce memories with properties $P$ (e.g., lacking in vividness, fragmentary, often inaccurate).
2. However, memories actually produced under conditions $C$ do not have

properties $P$, but instead have different properties $P'$ (e.g., vivid, relatively complete, long-lasting).

3. Therefore, the memories produced under conditions $C$ could not have been generated by ordinary memory mechanisms, and must instead have been created by a special mechanism that is triggered under these conditions.

In contrast, a well-articulated argument *against* the special-mechanism hypothesis asserts that ordinary memory mechanisms are adequate to explain flashbulb memories, and hence no appeal to a special mechanism is required:

1. Under conditions $C$, ordinary memory mechanisms would produce memories with properties $P$.
2. Memories produced under conditions $C$ do indeed have these properties.
3. Therefore, ordinary memory mechanisms are sufficient to explain the memories produced under conditions $C$, and postulation of a special mechanism is not warranted.

It is easy to see that a fully developed argument of either sort must include at least two elements: (1) A well-motivated estimate of the performance expected from ordinary memory mechanisms under the critical conditions $C$; (2) An assessment of the actual properties of memories generated under these conditions.[1] The objection that could be raised to the Larsen (this volume) and Neisser and Harsch (this volume) studies may now be stated more clearly: Neither study provides a strongly motivated estimate of the performance expected from ordinary memory mechanisms. This objection would, I think, be valid, although it speaks more to the current state of sophistication in the field than to flaws in these particular studies. Consider first the Larsen study.

### The Larsen study

A major strength of Larsen's work is that whereas most previous flashbulb memory studies have given short shrift to questions concerning the performance expected from ordinary memory mechanisms, Larsen confronts these questions squarely. This is not to say, however, that he is entirely successful in this endeavor. Estimating the performance expected from ordinary memory mechanisms under the critical conditions is perhaps the most vexing problem in attempts to evaluate the special-mechanism hypothesis. Consider what has to be done in order to make such an estimate.

*Control conditions.* Obviously, one cannot simply assess performance under the critical conditions, and take the results as measures of how ordinary mechanisms perform under these conditions – it is precisely the point at issue *whether* ordinary memory mechanisms are responsible for the performance observed under the critical conditions.

Nor can one simply assess memory performance under some noncritical control conditions, and assume that ordinary memory mechanisms would perform in exactly the same way under the critical conditions. For example, one cannot simply assess memory for learning about rather mundane news events, find that performance is poor, and assume that the same would be true for performance mediated by ordinary memory mechanisms under the critical conditions.

The reason such an approach would not be valid is that ordinary memory mechanisms may perform differently under the critical conditions than under whatever set of noncritical conditions one selects as a control. In the first place, the variables that define the critical conditions – such as emotional reaction, or consequentiality of the news event – may affect the functioning of the ordinary mechanisms. If, for example, strength of emotional reaction affects ordinary memory mechanisms, we would expect ordinary memory performance to be different under critical conditions defined by strong emotional reaction than under control conditions not involving strong emotion.

Also, ordinary memory mechanisms may be influenced by variables correlated with the critical variables. For example, on the hypothesis that a special mechanism is triggered by strong emotional reactions, the distinctiveness of an experience in which one learns of a shocking event is not important per se in triggering the special mechanism. However, distinctiveness may be correlated with the critical triggering condition – experiences that evoke strong emotional reactions may tend to be more distinctive than experiences that do not. As a consequence, distinctiveness may differ between the critical conditions one is interested in, and some noncritical control conditions under which one assesses the performance of ordinary memory mechanisms.

Thus, one cannot simply assume that noncritical conditions will be equivalent to the critical conditions with respect to the performance of ordinary memory mechanisms. What one must do instead is *extrapolate* from what is known about performance of ordinary memory mechanisms under some noncritical conditions to derive an estimate of how these mechanisms would perform under the critical conditions.

*Extrapolating from control to critical conditions.* In order to perform such an extrapolation, one needs to know three things: (1) the performance of ordinary memory mechanisms under some appropriate noncritical conditions; (2) the ways in which the observed conditions differ from the critical conditions on all variables that may affect the functioning of the ordinary mechanisms; and (3) *how* these variables affect the functioning of the ordinary mechanisms.

The first two requirements present a number of difficulties. However, the most serious problems center around the third requirement. Even if one knows how ordinary mechanisms perform under some set of noncritical conditions, and how the values of potentially relevant variables differ between the two sets of conditions, one cannot extrapolate from the noncritical to the critical conditions unless one also knows how the potentially relevant variables actually affect the functioning of ordinary memory mechanisms.

Unfortunately, for the most part we do not have this knowledge. We do not know exactly how distinctiveness, surprise, personal significance, emotional reaction, the nature of the to-be-remembered material, and so forth, affect the functioning of ordinary memory mechanisms. What we need but do not have is a well-developed theory specifying the structure and functioning of ordinary memory mechanisms, and hence the ways in which particular variables affect these mechanisms.

Thus, in attempting to determine the performance expected from ordinary memory mechanisms under flashbulb conditions, Larsen faces formidable obstacles, and falls somewhat short of the goal. First, although his assumption that reception contexts for flashbulb events are typically rehearsed more than reception contexts for more mundane events seems plausible, Larsen does not present strong evidence for this point. Further, even if one accepts the assumptions of enhanced rehearsal for flashbulb contexts, Larsen does not demonstrate that the enhanced rehearsal is sufficient to account for the differences between flashbulb events and mundane news events in memory for reception context. Although our understanding of ordinary memory is adequate to tell us that rehearsal generally improves retention, we do not know enough to assess whether any particular difference in rehearsal between flashbulb and mundane reception contexts would be sufficient to account for whatever the differences in memory performance may be under these two sets of conditions. Finally, Larsen's analysis of the potential effects of other variables that may differ between reception contexts for mundane and flashbulb events must be considered preliminary. For these reasons, his study cannot be interpreted as providing a fully developed ordinary-memory interpretation for flashbulb memories. As I discuss in a later section, however, Larsen's work has important implications for the special-mechanism hypothesis when viewed from a different perspective.

Although I have discussed the difficulty of estimating the performance expected from ordinary memory mechanisms in the context of the Larsen study, the point is a general one. At current levels of understanding of ordinary memory mechanisms, we are usually not in a position to make trustworthy estimates of how these mechanisms would perform under the critical conditions specified in the various forms of the special-mechanism hypothesis. As a consequence, one of the major elements of any well-developed argument for or against a special mechanism cannot be adequately specified. Although researchers have occasionally made strong assumptions about the effects of variables on ordinary memory mechanisms, and used these assumptions as a basis for estimating the performance of the ordinary mechanisms under the critical conditions, the assumptions have been of questionable validity.

### The Neisser and Harsch study

Consider next the study by Neisser and Harsch (this volume). These researchers present a variety of fascinating results concerning inaccurate high-confidence recollections, and also offer some interesting conjectures concerning how the inaccuracies might have come about. Further, Neisser and Harsch quite rightly emphasize the importance of asking why people are often so confident of their erroneous recollections.

Nevertheless, much of the attention that the Neisser and Harsch study will undoubtedly attract will have to do with its implications for the special-mechanism hypothesis. When I first learned of the results, my immediate reaction was that the high levels of inaccuracy obtained in the study clearly disconfirmed the special-mechanism hypothesis. Upon reflection, however, I realized that this reaction was off the mark – high levels of inaccuracy do not in and of themselves refute the special-mechanism hypothesis. A fully fleshed-out argument against this hypothesis requires a comparison of any observed level of performance with the performance expected from ordinary memory mechanisms. If the observed performance conforms to what we expect from ordinary mechanisms, then there is no need to appeal to a special mechanism. On the other hand, if we would expect ordinary memory mechanisms to yield performance even worse than that observed, the data would constitute support for the special-mechanism hypothesis. Unless we have an estimate of performance expected from ordinary memory mechanisms, we have no standard against which to compare the observed performance.

It may seem absurd even to entertain the possibility that ordinary memory mechanisms are incapable of supporting the level of performance observed in the Neisser and Harsch study. However, not all of the subjects in the study were completely inaccurate. Three years after the *Challenger* explosion, many subjects correctly recalled some information about the circumstances in which they learned of the explosion, and a few subjects recalled quite a lot. Hence, it cannot be taken for granted that ordinary memory mechanisms are adequate to explain the results, especially given Larsen's finding that recall of the context in which one learned a piece of news is often very poor even at short retention intervals.

*Implications of the studies for the special-mechanism hypothesis*

I have suggested that neither the Larsen study nor the Neisser and Harsch study definitively refutes the hypothesis of a special flashbulb memory mechanism. Does this mean that the hypothesis is alive and well, that it emerges unscathed? Absolutely not. Even though the Neisser and Harsch study, and the Larsen study, and other recent studies (e.g., Christianson, 1989; McCloskey, Wible, & Cohen, 1988) do not provide a definitive refutation, these studies nevertheless have strong implications for the special-mechanism hypothesis, in that they undercut the motivation for entertaining the hypothesis.

The original motivation for proposing the special-mechanism hypothesis – and the motivation for continuing to entertain this hypothesis in the absence of clear support – is a largely intuitive argument that goes something like the following:

1. People have surprisingly good memory for the circumstances in which they learned about shocking events like the assassination of John F. Kennedy or the explosion of the Space Shuttle *Challenger*.
2. Intuitively, it seems that ordinary memory mechanisms would yield very poor memory for these circumstances of learning.
3. Thus, there seems to be a major gap between the memories we would expect from ordinary memory mechanisms, and the memories that are actually generated under flashbulb conditions.
4. In fact, this gap seems sufficiently large to motivate postulation of a special flashbulb memory mechanism, or at least to entertain a special-mechanism hypothesis.

The Neisser and Harsch study, the Larsen study, and other recent studies undermine this argument in two ways. First, the results reported by Neisser and Harsch suggest that memory for circumstances of learning about shocking events is not as good as was initially assumed. The original assumption was based on the observation that people can frequently offer, with considerable confidence, reports of the circumstances in which they learned of events such as the Kennedy assassination or the *Challenger* explosion. However, Neisser and Harsch's data, and other recent results, suggest that it is not safe to infer good memory from confident reports.

Furthermore, Larsen, Neisser, and others have called into question the intuition that ordinary memory mechanisms would yield very poor memory for circumstances of learning about flashbulb events. Larsen suggests that the context of learning about such an event may be rehearsed more than other learning contexts; Neisser (1982) has previously suggested that learning about a shocking public event represents a significant personal experience and therefore may be well retained by ordinary memory mechanisms; and other researchers have made similar suggestions.

As I have emphasized, these suggestions cannot be taken as fully fleshed-out, strongly motivated arguments about how ordinary memory mechanisms would perform under flashbulb conditions. Further, various sorts of data have been presented as evidence against many of the suggestions (although in my view the data are quite weak). At present, then, the suggestions are probably best viewed simply as responses in kind to the original intuitive argument that ordinary mechanisms would perform very poorly under flashbulb conditions. As such, their force is that the original intuitive argument is not persuasive; a firmer basis for the assumption of poor performance by ordinary memory mechanisms is needed.

The results of Neisser and Harsch, Larsen, and others also suggest that proponents of the special-mechanism hypothesis face an uphill battle as they attempt to place the hypothesis on a more solid foundation. Given that flashbulb memories may not be all that good, and the performance expected from ordinary memory mechanisms may not be all that bad, motivation for postulating a special flashbulb memory mechanism may not be easy to come by.

## An agenda for flashbulb memory research

Perhaps the time has not yet come to close the book on the special-mechanism hypothesis. However, the discussions at the Emory conference, and some of the recent flashbulb memory literature, suggest that attention may be shifting away from this hypothesis, and toward the goal of interpreting flashbulb memories in terms of ordinary memory mechanisms. The pursuit of this goal raises a wealth of difficult and unresolved questions concerning the workings of ordinary memory mechanisms. For example, which of the variables that may affect the operation of ordinary memory mechanisms are important in the genesis of accurate or inaccurate flashbulb memories? What is the role, if any, of emotion, rehearsal, distinctiveness, surprise, and personal significance? And how do these variables have their effects? Thus far, discussion of these questions has been characterized by drawing strong conclusions from weak data, and by a relative absence of specific theoretical proposals concerning underlying cognitive representations and processes. If we can be more empirically and theoretically rigorous in the future, we may succeed not only in explaining the inherently interesting flashbulb memory phenomena, but also in advancing our understanding of memory in general. And that, after all, is what we are trying to do.

## NOTE

1 Any well-articulated argument for or against a special-mechanism hypothesis must also of course specify the critical conditions *C*, because different assumptions about these conditions define different versions of the special-mechanism hypothesis, and data bearing on one version of the hypothesis (e.g., a version holding that the special mechanism is triggered by high levels of surprise and consequentiality) may not be relevant to other versions (e.g., a version holding that the special mechanism is triggered by strong emotional reactions). The potential for variation in assumptions about critical conditions for triggering the presumed special mechanism has been a source of some confusion in flashbulb memory research.

## REFERENCES

Brown, R., & Kulik, J. (1977). Flashbulb memories. *Cognition, 5,* 73–99.

Christianson, S-Å. (1989). Flashbulb memories: Special, but not so special. *Memory & Cognition, 17,* 435–443.

McCloskey, M., Wible, C. G., & Cohen, N. J. (1988). Is there a special flashbulb-memory mechanism? *Journal of Experimental Psychology: General, 117,* 171–181.

Neisser, U. (1982). Snapshots or benchmarks? In U. Neisser (Ed.), *Memory observed: Remembering in natural contexts* (pp. 43–48). San Francisco: W. H. Freeman.

# 12

# Remembering personal circumstances: A functional analysis

DAVID B. PILLEMER

In the classic paper on "flashbulb" memories, Brown and Kulik (1977) identified an aspect of autobiographical memory that had received scant attention from cognitive psychologists – memory for one's own personal circumstances (such as location, ongoing activities, and feelings) when receiving an important and shocking piece of news (such as first learning that President Kennedy had been shot), as opposed to memory for the newsworthy event itself. A second contribution of Brown and Kulik's original papers, and Neisser's (1982b) subsequent commentary, was a focus on memory function. What is the psychological value or adaptive significance of remembering personal details at such times?

In this chapter I examine memories of personal circumstances from a functional perspective. First, I argue that memories of personal circumstances are essential components of a fully functioning autobiographical memory system. Second, I critically examine the emphasis on memory accuracy in recent studies of flashbulb memories, and I conclude that the research agenda should be expanded to include memory functions that have heretofore fallen outside the realm of cognitive psychology. Third, I identify and describe three broad categories of memory function, none of which depends on absolute veridicality in recall:

1.  *Communicative* functions: The act of recounting a detailed personal memory to others communicates meaning that transcends the surface content of the particular recollection, and this specialized form of communication appears to be rule governed.
2.  *Psychodynamic* functions: Remembering personal circumstances in vivid detail can have a profound emotional and psychological impact on the rememberer, and on others with whom the memories are shared. Detailed recollection of specific episodes is frequently identified by clinicians as an essential component of psychotherapeutic process.
3.  *Directive* functions: Memories of personal circumstances provide prescriptions for present and future behavior. In some instances, the directive is obtained through conscious, purposeful analysis of memory content; in other instances, memory influences feelings and behaviors outside of conscious awareness.

The analysis of memory function will be based on research, theory, and illustrations from several diverse areas of study, including communications, psychotherapy, and textual analysis as well as cognitive psychology.

## Personal circumstances and autobiographical memory

Brown and Kulik (1977) defined flashbulb memories as "memories for the circumstances in which one first learned of a very surprising and consequential (or emotionally arousing) event," and identified hearing the news that President Kennedy had been shot as the "prototype case" (p. 73). Following Brown and Kulik, researchers examining the flashbulb concept have focused almost exclusively on learning about shocking public tragedies or near-tragedies: the attempted assassination of President Reagan (Pillemer, 1984), the space shuttle disaster (Bohannon, 1988; McCloskey, Wible, & Cohen, 1988; Neisser & Harsch, this volume; Warren & Swartwood, this volume), and the assassination of Swedish prime minister Olof Palme (Christianson, 1989). Another research strategy has been to compare memories of shocking events to memories of anticipated but still newsworthy events, such as President Nixon's resignation and the 1969 moon landing (Winograd & Killinger, 1983).

Newsworthy events are an attractive data source for large-scale memory studies, because many people have experienced the same target event at a known time. But the almost exclusive focus on public events is also limiting. The evolutionary model proposed by Brown and Kulik (1977) was based on directly experienced events: "Probably the same 'Now Print!' mechanism accounts both for the enduring significant memories in which one has played the role of protagonist and those in which one has only been a member of an interested audience of millions" (pp. 98–99). Memories of a personal shock (Brown & Kulik, 1977) or the first menstrual period (Pillemer, Koff, Rhinehart, & Rierdan, 1987) are structurally similar to conventional flashbulb memories. I will broaden the research agenda to include events happening directly to the rememberer as well as public events.

Where do memories of personal circumstances fit in broader conceptualizations of autobiographical memory? Brewer (1986, 1988) made a distinction between personal memory and autobiographical facts. *Autobiographical facts* represent knowledge about a particular episode in which the person has participated, but without an imagistic representation of the specific event. In contrast, a *personal memory* approximates a "'reliving' of the individual's phenomenal experience during the earlier episode" (1988, p. 22). According to Brewer, a personal memory is accompanied by visual imagery and a belief that the event represented in memory was personally experienced by the self. People can have access to autobiographical facts without having access to the corresponding personal memory. For example,

Brewer *knew* that he took a plane home from a conference on memory at Emory University, but he had no personal memory of the trip (1988, p. 22).

Remembering personal circumstances is more than a curious side effect of receiving shocking news: It is probably the *defining* characteristic of personal memory. When do we feel that we actually experienced an event first-hand, whether it is a national disaster, a personal tragedy, or a routine plane trip? How can we convince other people that we were participants? By mentally reliving the original circumstances and recounting them to others. Without such an awareness, there are no personal memories, only learned autobiographical facts. Tulving (1989) described an amnesic patient, K. C., who apparently is without personal memory in Brewer's sense of the term. K. C. "cannot remember himself experiencing situations and participating in life's events" (Tulving, 1989, p. 362), but he does have access to autobiographical facts. For example, when asked to report the saddest moment in his life, K. C. responded with a specific episode: the death of his brother. Yet although K. C. appears to *know* that he experienced his brother's death, he is totally unaware of his personal activities and feelings during this, and all other, life experiences.

Whenever autobiographical facts are accompanied by a personal memory, it is possible to distinguish between memory for the target event itself, peripheral details connected with the target event, and one's own personal circumstances at the time (Pillemer, 1990). In the case of the death of a family member, one could potentially remember the simple fact that the death had occurred, factual details of this occurrence, and personal details about how the tragedy was experienced by the rememberer. As in the case of a national disaster, the third type of information (the flashbulb memory of the event) is what distinguishes personal memory from general knowledge.

Because the term flashbulb memory is associated with the specific model proposed by Brown and Kulik (1977), the more general and inclusive term *memory of personal circumstances* may be preferable (Pillemer, 1990). Personal circumstances can be vividly remembered in the absence of intense surprise or perceived consequentiality (Pillemer, 1984; Rubin & Kozin, 1984; Winograd & Killinger, 1983). For example, a subject in a list learning experiment may remember personal details about his or her participation one month after the test session for a variety of reasons: (1) Someone suddenly entered the testing room with the news of the space shuttle disaster, (2) a stream of obscenities appeared in the middle of a word list, (3) the subject was romantically interested in the experimenter and a relationship blossomed in the weeks that followed, (4) the subject was an advanced graduate student in experimental psychology, and was designing a similar study for a dissertation, and (5) immediately after the test session, the experimenter explained that the real goal was to remember as many personal details as possible. It makes little sense from either a theoretical or a research perspective to isolate prematurely the memory associated with the first reason for remembering in an exclusive category of flashbulb memories (Brewer, 1986; McCloskey et al., 1988; Pillemer, 1990; Rubin & Kozin, 1984).

In short, personal details are an essential component of all memories that are actively experienced as a part of one's life history. When attempting to remember the event of, say, eating dinner on your last birthday, you search for information about where you were, what you ate, who was there, and what you saw or heard or felt. It is not necessary to recollect all of this information, but remembering some fragment of personal experience is probably necessary to feel and believe with conviction that "I was there."

## Memory functions, memory accuracy, and underlying mechanisms

Following Bruce (1985, 1989), I use the term function to refer to the usefulness or adaptive significance of memory. One obvious function of memory in general is the veridical reconstruction of earlier events. Evaluating this function with accuracy tests is a prominent aspect of almost all experimental memory research. One can trace the emphasis on "objective" rather than "subjective" aspects of remembering to historical tradition and to research preferences of cognitive psychologists (Tulving, 1983, pp. 128–129).

In the last decade, scientific interest in functions of autobiographical memory other than veridical recall has increased (Baddeley, 1988; Bruce, 1985, 1989; Bruner, 1987; Edwards & Middleton, 1986; Neisser, 1982a, 1988a; Neisser & Winograd, 1988; Nelson, 1989; Robinson & Swanson, 1990; Rubin, 1986). Yet despite the shift away from an exclusive focus on veridicality in studies of autobiographical memory, accuracy continues to be a central concern in critical commentaries on flashbulb memories. For some researchers, accuracy is a yardstick for testing hypotheses about underlying memory mechanisms. Cohen, McCloskey, & Wible (1990) stated that the aim of research in cognitive psychology is to characterize the "mental machinery" underlying human cognition: "From this perspective, the aim of flashbulb-memory research is not simply to provide descriptions of the memories or the circumstances in which they occur but rather to elucidate the underlying memory mechanisms" (1990, p. 97). These authors held that "'research hypotheses' are of interest only to the extent that they are tied to specific contentions about underlying mechanisms" (p. 98). If flashbulb memories are not only subjectively vivid, but also unusually accurate, then the idea of a special memory mechanism is tenable. On the other hand, if the memories are not exceptionally accurate, special-mechanism hypotheses can be discarded or at least set aside (Cohen et al., 1990; Harsch & Neisser, 1989; McCloskey et al, 1988; Neisser, 1982b; Neisser & Harsch, this volume).

The aim of cognitive research identified by Cohen et al. (1990) – to uncover underlying mechanisms – is not as "uncontroversial" (p. 97) as these authors suggest. Methods for examining flashbulb memories appear to be inadequate for conducting strong tests of hypotheses about neuro-biological structures. Brown and Kulik (1977) acknowledged this deficiency: "we could not very well provide any direct evidence as to [the 'Now Print!' theory's] truth value with a paper-and-pencil study" (p. 76). Nevertheless, if remembering personal circumstances is an essential component of all memories that are actively tied to one's life history, then such remembering is worthy of study in its own right, apart from abstract hypotheses about specialized memory structures. In addition, with respect to the question of whether specialized memory systems exist, analyzing memory function actually appears to be a better long-term research strategy than testing memory accuracy. If flashbulb memories were in fact shown to be perfectly accurate under certain circumstances, this would by itself say little about the existence of a functionally separate memory mechanism. Another possibility would be that we are simply observing the optimal performance of a single underlying mechanism (Pillemer, 1990). Visual identification of letters is perfect under certain conditions (close proximity, adequate light), but a special, functionally distinct ocular system is not required to explain the extremely high level of visual accuracy.

Functional analysis provides a different basis for making inferences about multiple memory systems. According to Sherry and Schacter (1987), "it is only justifiable to speak of multiple memory systems when the systems are characterized by different rules of operation" (p. 440). New memory systems evolve in response to environmental demands that are incompatible with the properties of existing systems: "we would be hesitant to postulate a new memory system to accommodate a particular experimental finding or pattern of findings unless a good case could be made that the proposed system performs a function that cannot be performed by another memory system" (Sherry & Schacter, 1987, p. 449). With respect to flashbulb memories, is remembering one's own personal circumstances functionally incompatible with other types of memory? Questions such as this are best addressed by first conducting detailed functional analyses: "it should be possible to specify more clearly the range of functions that a system can serve and, hence, set the stage for meaningful analyses of functional incompatibilities" (Sherry & Schacter, 1987, p. 450).

# Why are personal circumstances remembered and recounted?

*Initial proposals: Brown and Kulik (1977) and Neisser (1982b)*

According to Brown and Kulik (1977), whenever a surprising and consequential event occurs, an imagistic record of personal circumstances is automatically encoded. If the event is overtly or covertly rehearsed, a narrative account is also constructed that can be purposefully accessed and shared with others. Flashbulb memories would have had survival value for our early ancestors because, unlike presidential assassinations, surprising and consequential events were often experienced *directly*. By recording information about concomitant circumstances, including where the event occurred, what activities were ongoing, what emotions were expressed, and what ensued, similar situations could be anticipated and quickly identified, and appropriate actions could be taken. Brown and Kulik (1977) saw "no obvious utility" (p. 74) in flashbulb memories of contemporary newsworthy events; in fact, the lack of an obvious function for flashbulb memories, rather than their apparent vividness or accuracy, suggested to Brown and Kulik that there was a "mystery" (p. 98) to be solved. They concluded that flashbulb memories accompanying news of shocking events happening elsewhere, to other people, are formed because the ancient encoding mechanism operates automatically and relatively indiscriminately.

Neisser (1982b) forcefully questioned Brown and Kulik's (1977) evolutionary model. He argued that the existence of flashbulb memories is not explained by automatic encoding. Rather, the memories are constructed in an active effort to link one's own personal life history with the flow of world events: "We are aware of this link at the time and aware that others are forging similar links. We discuss 'how we heard the news' with our friends and listen eagerly to how *they* heard. We rehearse the occasion often in our minds and our conversations, seeking some meaning in it" (Neisser, 1982b, p. 48). Neisser's account anticipated recent functional analyses of autobiographical memory: Memory is seen as a vehicle for constructing a coherent and meaningful self-concept and for promoting social interaction (e.g., Baddeley, 1988; Fivush, 1988; Neisser, 1988a; Nelson, 1988; Robinson & Swanson, 1990).

Although Neisser (1982b) offered his account as an alternative to Brown and Kulik's (1977) evolutionary model, the two types of functions need not be mutually exclusive: "memory systems that evolve initially as solutions to one environmental problem may come to serve many other functions" (Sherry & Schacter, 1987, p. 449). Rather than attempt to settle on a single preferred functional explanation, I will broaden the discussion to include a wide range of social and personal activities that may be influenced or enhanced by remembering, and recounting, personal circumstances.

### Communicative functions

Recounting memories of personal circumstances is undoubtedly guided by communicative conventions. The *act* of sharing personal details with others communicates meaning over and above the particular informational content of the memories, and thereby helps the speaker achieve important interpersonal goals. Effective communication requires that memories be shared in accordance with a system of rules, a *grammar* of memorial expression, that has yet to be formally described.

*Rules of memory sharing.* Spoken conversation is a good starting point for functional analyses of memory sharing. Conversations are clearly rule-governed (Myllyniemi, 1986; Schank, 1977): "The typical regularities of conversation occur because the participants know the rules of discussing, and follow them" (Myllyniemi, 1986, p. 148). Providing explicit descriptions of personal memories is not the usual mode of discourse, and under certain circumstances this activity clearly violates Grice's (1975) conversational maxims of relevance, clarity, and brevity. For example, "when people tell narratives, they occupy a larger portion of social time and space than in most other conversational turns" (Labov, 1982, p. 227). What circumstances allow for such violations of protocol?

Deciphering rules of memory sharing is more complicated in naturally occurring conversation than in laboratory settings. The "communicative frame" (Edwards & Middleton, 1986) of the laboratory is structured by the experimenter so that accurate reporting is the explicit goal, but other settings elicit different and more subtle communicative agendas. For example, Tenney (1989) analyzed phone conversations in which new parents announced the arrival of their baby. The patterns of discourse supported a "communication model" over a "memory model": "salient events are not simply retrieved as they occur to the reporter, but rather are selected with respect to criteria that foster social interaction" (p. 231). New parents responded to their own needs and the needs of the listener by presenting events out of chronological order, withholding negative details until the listener began to reminisce about similar problems, suppressing embarrassing information and elaborating on entertaining topics. Tenney concluded that "the art of conversation requires more than a good memory," and that "it is this creative aspect of conversational reporting that poses the biggest challenge to our understanding" (p. 232).

Because memory sharing is influenced by characteristics of the particular communicative frame, it is misleading to draw inferences about the contents of autobiographical memory based on observed recall in one specific context. Situational influences must be taken into account (Jacoby, 1988). For example, sharing detailed personal episodes is undoubtedly influenced, as is politeness (Brown, 1990), by the relationship between speaker and listener. If during an encounter with a casual acquaintance the speaker repeatedly described personal memories, the listener would attempt to decipher the meaning of this unusual conversational style: a hidden agenda, perhaps, or a subtle indication of psychopathology. On the other hand, recounting personal details is acceptable and even desirable in other settings, such as the psychotherapy office or when talking to one's intimates.

Data reported by Barsalou (1988) illustrate the complexities of attempting to infer underlying memory organization from conversational reports. An experimenter stopped people on a college campus and asked them to "describe events that occurred during your summer in the order in which they come to mind" (p. 199). Narratives produced during the 5-minute response period were tape-recorded. The researchers were surprised to find that respondents "spent only 21% of their time recalling specific events" (p. 201). Subjects in a follow-up study found it difficult to obey explicit instructions to report specific events only. Barsalou's data suggested that when adults recall their past experiences, they "provide information about what usually happens" (Fivush, 1988, p. 278), and that "individual episodes have no privileged status in memory" (Neisser, 1988b, p. 362).

When Barsalou's (1988) interview procedure is evaluated from the point of view of the respondent, it is questionable whether the 21% incidence of specific episodes provides direct evidence about the absolute contents of autobiographical memory or about memory sharing in other contexts. It is unusual to share personal details of past experiences with a stranger, and even more unusual to do so after being stopped unexpectedly and asked to talk uninterruptedly into a tape recorder. Speakers might censor embarrassing episodes and exclude trivial or uninteresting events. In order to integrate and provide meaning to a list of singular episodes, the speaker must also supply a general organizational framework, as demonstrated by the prominence of Barsalou's "extended-event time lines" (p. 222). Even when the request to provide specific events only is clearly understood, it may nevertheless be difficult to override usual conversational protocol without considerable effort.

The incidence of episodic reporting is in fact demonstrably variable across different retrieval contexts. When college students were asked to provide written descriptions of four separate memories of their first year in college, 74% of the memories were specific (Pillemer, Rhinehart, & White, 1986, Study 1). In contrast, when similar students were asked to describe their first year in college by talking into a tape recorder for 20 minutes, the incidence of specific episodes was only 14% (Pillemer, Krensky, Kleinman, Goldsmith, & White, 1991). In Barsalou's (1988) study, variations in procedure could have had similarly dramatic effects. Personal episodes, including embarrassing or trivial events, may flow more freely if the interviewer were a peer rather than a researcher, the same rather than a different gender, or a close acquaintance rather than a stranger. Or, if the interviewer were to spontaneously share his or her own personal memories of college, this could encourage episodic reporting by the respondent.

Memory incidences obtained in different studies indicate how particular contexts and cultural conventions constrain or enhance episodic remembering. Barsalou (1988) acknowledged that people may employ narrative styles that "do not reflect underlying memory organization but instead reflect various cultural and linguistic conventions" (p. 217). Although no single study can provide a clear window into autobiographical memory, studies that elicit memories under a variety of retrieval conditions, taken together, can pinpoint situations in which reporting of personal circumstances is high or low, acceptable or unacceptable, free-flowing or forced.

In addition to situational constraints, people undoubtedly vary in their ability or willingness to share specific episodes. For example, suicide attempters have difficulty retrieving specific positive memories in an experimental setting (Williams & Broadbent, 1986). Person–situation interactions must be represented in models of personal memory sharing.

*Meanings of memory sharing.* The act of sharing personal memories communicates an implicit message about the speaker's abilities, intentions, or feelings. Recounting detailed memories of personal circumstances can make a communication appear more *truthful, accurate,* or *believable.* As a result, the communication is more *persuasive.* Persuasion is an "ultimate function of all story-telling memory mechanisms" (Bruce, 1989, p. 50), and recounting specific instances is a very effective way to get a point across: "Except perhaps in academic circles, a remembered episode is almost impossible to beat in an argument – it carries more persuasive weight than a wealth of scientific studies and can only be countered by the common rejoinder: 'But that reminds me of another occasion . . .'" (Larsen & Plunkett, 1987, p. 18). Even in academic psychology, detailed case studies and clinical anecdotes can have a sustained impact (Light & Pillemer, 1984, chapter 4).

Bell and Loftus (1989) examined the influence of detailed testimony on juror decision making. They found that "even seemingly insignificant and irrelevant information, such as the store items a customer dropped prior to a crime, can influence mock juror judgments" (p. 677). Bell and Loftus labeled this phenomenon "trivial persuasion," which may occur "through a process in which people form inferences about the communicator" (p. 679). Jurors may believe that individuals who recount trivial details have exceptional memories.

Descriptions of personal circumstances that are usually contained in flashbulb memories, such as the informant's own activities and feelings when the target event occurred, could have a similarly persuasive effect. For example, Secretary of State George Shultz's testimony before the Senate and House committees concerning covert military assistance to Iran frequently contained personal details:

> So I picked up the phone Sunday morning, and I called the President. I said, "Mr. President, I have something I should bring over here and tell you about right now." So he said, "Fine, come over." . . . I went up to the family quarters, and Al Keel, who was then Acting National Security Advisor, went with me at my request. And I told the President the items on this agenda, including such things as doing something about the Dawa prisoners, which made me sick to my stomach that anybody would talk about that as something we would consider doing. And the President was astonished, and I have never seen him so mad. He is a very genial, pleasant man and doesn't – very easy going. But his jaws set and his eyes flashed, and both of us, I think, felt the same way about it, and I think in that meeting I finally felt that the President deeply understands that something is radically wrong here." (Select Committees on the Iran-Contra Investigation, 1988, p. 5)

The verbatim quotes, vivid descriptions of emotional reactions, and visual imagery are not necessarily indicative of an accurate memory (Neisser, 1981), but they could well add to the believability of Shultz's testimony. Shultz was not only "there" when the event occurred, but the vividness of his recall suggests a reliving at the time of retelling.

In addition to enhancing the persuasiveness of a communication, sharing detailed memories of personal circumstances signals *emotionality*, *intimacy*, and *immediacy*. Personal memories can draw in the listener and evoke empathic responses more readily than can general, scripted accounts. Beals's (1991) study of communication patterns over a computer network identified a consistent pattern of responsiveness to specific event memories. Harvard has a computer network for graduates and faculty members of teacher training programs. The network is a vehicle through which novice teachers discuss problems, seek advice, and offer support. The network is more than a source of information: It also fosters "conversations" and "philosophical discussions" (Merseth, 1990).

Many of the messages sent by teachers over the computer network are general, but occasionally they describe specific classroom episodes, replete with details about location, activities, and feelings. Beals (1991) found that specific event narratives were more likely than general statements to evoke responses from other members of the network. One possible explanation is that specific episodes more vividly transmit the feelings and emotional needs of the speaker: "The writers of general descriptions avoid detail, and thus keep their emotional distance. Providing specific details and evaluations of events peels back one's personal armor, so to speak, exposing what really matters to the teacher. This vulnerability demonstrated by the storyteller invokes the response (and support) of peers more frequently than do the safer, more distant descriptions" (Beals, 1991, p. 35).

If recounting memories of personal circumstances is an indication of the speaker's openness and emotionality, then it may trigger a similar mode of communication in others. A personal event narrative may be interpreted as an overture to the listener to join the speaker emotionally, to transcend usual conversational conventions and "go deeper." Responding to a specific anecdote with a personal memory of one's own is a show of *empathy*: The listener also has experienced a similar situation first-hand. If the recipient accepts the overture, the conversational maxims of brevity, relevance, and so forth are temporarily put aside in favor of a more intimate interchange. If the recipient maintains a detached posture and continues to converse in general terms, the overture to move the communication to a more personal level is rebuffed. If recounting specific rather than general memories often triggers a move to a qualitatively different, more intimate level of discourse, then joint remembering should be marked by periods in which personal event narratives are shared, embedded in periods of more general responding.

What characteristics of personal memories suggest that the original event was emotionally charged and that the speaker is reexperiencing the emotion at retelling? The vividness of images contained in the narrative provides one clue. A possible marker of memory vividness is particularly interesting from a communications perspective: *verb tense*, or more precisely, a temporary shift from the past to the present tense at critical junctures in the narrative. The historical present conveys "the sense of more vivid narrative" (Labov, 1972, p. 47). Novelist John Updike (1990) extolled the virtues of the present tense compared to the past tense: "Instead of writing 'she said and he said' it's 'he says and she says,' and not 'he jumped' at some past moment, but 'he jumps,' right now in front of you. Action takes on a wholly different, flickering quality; thought and feeling and event are brought much closer together" (p. 1). Beals (1991) found that the small number of computer network messages that were written in the historical present tense elicited a high number of responses from others.

A dramatic shift from past to present tense may indicate that the narrator is no longer simply *retelling* an event – he or she is *reliving* some salient aspect of it. Spence (1988) observed that a discontinuity in verb tense is one indication that narrators are "shifting their attention from the outside world to their inner experiences" (p. 317). When testifying about covert arms transactions with Iran, George Shultz made an uncharacteristic shift from past to present while describing the personal trauma of having his loyalty questioned:

So I was in a battle to try to get what I saw as the facts to the President and get – and see that he understood them. Now, this was a very traumatic period for me because everybody was saying I'm disloyal to the President, I'm not speaking up for the policy, and I'm battling away here, and I could see people were calling for me to resign if I can't be loyal to the President, even including some of my friends and people who had held high office and should know that maybe there's more involved than they're seeing. (Select Committees on the Iran-Contra Investigation, 1988, p. 40)

The shift to the present tense suggests that Shultz still felt the hurt and anger of that earlier time.

Harvey (1986) analyzed the use of the present tense in oral descriptions of momentous personal experiences. Following Labov and Waletzky (1967), Harvey collected "danger of death" narratives – stories of how the speaker narrowly escaped death. She hypothesized that "if the narrator were reliving the experience in retelling it, this would be indicated in the narration by a switch from the past tense to the present tense at the crucial point of the story – the point where the narrator believed that he or she was about to die" (p. 154). The narrative analysis supported her hypothesis: There was "consistent use of the historical present tense at the crucial point in these stories and at no other time" (p. 157). For example, a man recounted his experience as a naval officer when a small boat in which he was sitting plunged from a troop carrier toward the water: "Then I remember falling . . . and there's all kinds of debris around . . . and the debris was closing in . . . and there was . . . water around and I'm under water . . . there is ripping, crashing . . . say something hit me on the head as I'm . . . lurching about falling and then . . . there's sort of things closing in on me, debris and then the debris is jo/it's wet so it's water and debris and foam bubbles and I'm under water" (pp. 158–159).

In summary, the implicit meanings of personal memory sharing are determined in part by how the memories are described to others. Characteristics of personal event narratives that reveal the speaker's emotions, elicit emotional responses from others, and contribute to the persuasiveness of the communication probably include (but are by no means limited to) changes in verb tense, verbatim quotations, and other unusually detailed descriptions of visual or auditory imagery, feelings, and personal circumstances.

*Psychodynamic functions*

Why is the recounting of vivid personal details interpreted by other people as an indication of heightened emotionality in the speaker? People may infer from their own experiences that detailed images of personal circumstances are especially likely to accompany memories of highly emotional events. In addition, they have had their own current emotions elevated by remembering and retelling past episodes. When listening to someone else describe vivid memory images, the listener tacitly assumes that both the original event and the mental reliving of the event have a strong affective component. The connection between detailed recollection and emotion does not require that the remembered details be accurate; emotional expression is linked to the rememberer's *perceptions* of past realities.

Memories of the specific circumstances of an earlier trauma can have a continuing psychological impact on the rememberer. Salient details are replayed in an almost automatic, involuntary fashion: "Following a sudden consequential automobile accident, one of us finds his covert rehearsal of the circumstances as uncontrollable as the tongue that seeks an aching tooth" (Brown & Kulik, 1977, p. 86). Similarly, the assassination of President Kennedy evoked in many people "the tendency to recapitulate the disastrous event repeatedly, in an effort to assimilate it and master the disorganizing distress it has caused" (Wolfenstein & Kliman, 1966, p. xvi).

The connection between vivid personal memories, emotion, and psychological functioning is a prominent component of contemporary theories of psychotherapy. Remembering detailed personal circumstances triggers emotional expression, which provides an opportunity to master the emotion and thereby lessen its nonconscious influence. Wachtel and Wachtel (1986) emphasized the psychotherapeutic importance of asking "questions that convert general statements into descriptions of specific behaviors" (p. 79). Similarly, Williams and Dritschel (1988) observed that "difficulty in being specific may also impede the processes by which change is brought about in psychotherapy," because "the type of affect which is associated with generic memory is unhelpful for therapeutic process" (p. 232). For example, "greater benefit is obtained in cognitive therapy if depressed patients are able to go beyond general statements such as 'I've always been a failure' or 'I used to be so happy' to describe the details of particular instances when they felt they had failed or felt fulfilled" (p. 232).

Detailed memories of early episodes can influence later psychological functioning. These "critical identity images" (Kantor, 1980) or "nuclear scenes" (Carlson, 1981) may persist as "potent, unresolved problems in later life" (Carlson, 1981, p. 504). A major task of psychotherapy involves bringing the concrete, flashbulb-like image into awareness, and also recognizing and responding to the feelings it has aroused: "The therapist, while permitting and encouraging the expression of feelings, also explores and enlarges on other structural details – visual, behavioral, conceptual – how old are you in this scene? in what room of the house does the scene take place? who else is there? what is mother wearing? how do you feel about what your brother is doing?" (Kantor, 1980, p. 158). Kantor's technique involves retelling the earlier episode in the present tense; in accordance with the analysis of verb tense in memory narratives presented earlier, use of the present tense may facilitate direct emotional expression. Even psychological disturbances that are often treated behaviorally, such as phobias, frequently are traceable to a memory of a specific traumatic incident (McNally, 1989).

Emotional expression accompanying the process of remembering specific episodes also has been identified in nonclinical settings. Davis (1988) observed intense emotional distress in a research subject who had been asked to recall anger experiences from her life. Following the outward expression of her emotions and personal discussion with the researcher, "both subjective and physiological measures revealed a substantial reduction in tension" (p. 19). The observations suggested that the unanticipated emotional release was beneficial or "cathartic." Greenstein (1966) observed a similar reaction among male college students who were interviewed in the days following the Kennedy assassination. Students were encouraged to "describe in detail the circumstances under which they learned of the shooting, and their immediate and subsequent thoughts and actions" (p. 194). Students appeared to benefit emotionally from the opportunity to rehash their personal circumstances: "It was clear that the students *wanted* to talk. The interviews had a cathartic, confessional quality" (p. 194).

The connection between trauma and vivid memories, and the potential healing effects of recounting personal circumstances, is demonstrated in public reactions to tragedy. Following the San Francisco earthquake of 1989, the media focused on personal experiences of individuals as well as on more global effects of the disaster. *The Boston Globe* (Grossfeld, 1989) published interviews with a bartender who had to escape flying glass ("Then the glasses started flying and the kegs in back started knocking around. I ran for cover"), and with an 11-year-old boy who was doing his math homework when the earthquake hit ("I'm scared in the house, any house"). Psychologists warned that victims might experience "intrusive images," and stressed the therapeutic benefits of talking about what happened (Robb, 1989). Memory sharing appeared to facilitate both individual and collective "working through."

Exaggerated images of emotion and catharsis accompanying vivid recollection are common in literature and the arts. In *Ironweed*, William Kennedy (1983) described a father's tearful visit to the grave of his infant son, who died when accidentally dropped by the father 22 years earlier:

"I remember everything," Francis told Gerald in the grave. "It's the first time I tried to think of those things since you died. I had four beers after work that day. It wasn't because I was drunk that I dropped you. Four beers, and I didn't finish the fourth. Left it next to the pigs'-feet jar on Brady's bar so's I could walk home with Cap Lawlor. Billy was nine then. He knew you were gone before Peggy knew. She hadn't come home from choir practice yet. Your mother said two words, 'Sweet Jesus,' and then we both crouched down to snatch you up. But we both stopped in that crouch because of the looks of you. Billy come in then and saw you. 'Why is Gerald crooked?' he says . . . I remember the linoleum you fell on was yellow with red squares. You suppose now that I can remember this stuff out in the open, I can finally start to forget it? (pp. 18–19)

The immediate psychological impact of mentally reliving traumatic episodes need not always be positive or liberating. For example, stage hypnosis can have deleterious psychological consequences if age regression unintentionally uncovers memories of early traumas (Kleinhauz, Dreyfuss, Beran, Goldberg, & Azikri, 1979). In one extreme case "the regression in age and the re-awakening of traumatic childhood experiences probably broke down tenuously established defense mechanisms which had enabled the patient to function adequately" (p. 223), and therapy was necessary to undo the damage.

Whether the emotional impact of recalling detailed personal episodes will be positive or negative is probably determined by complex interactions between memory content, the person's psychological makeup, and the recall context. Although the remembered events may be reconstructions or even fabrications, the *psychological* effects of remembering are real, and should be represented in cognitive as well as clinical models.

### Directive functions

Remembering specific episodes influences not only feelings, but also behaviors and attitudes. Memories of personal circumstances provide directives or prescriptions for current and future activities. The directive can be identified purposefully and consciously, or the memory can influence behavior outside of conscious awareness. I will consider conscious influences first, and then turn to nonconscious influences in the following section.

Prediction is a primary function of memory, and semantic knowledge or scripts are frequently identified as the primary predictive agents (e.g., Abelson, 1981; Fivush, 1988; Nelson, 1988). More generally, Tulving (1983) observed that "knowledge of the world, by and large, is more useful to people than are personal memories" (1983, p. 52). Expectations represented in scripts help individuals negotiate the customary routines of life, whereas the store of memories that comprise the individual's personal history has "its own value independent of the general memory function of prediction and preparation for future events" (Nelson, 1988, p. 267).

Because scripts contain information about what "usually happens," they are invaluable for predicting what is likely to happen. Nevertheless, vivid memories of specific, one-moment-in-time events are often equally capable of fulfilling a predictive or directive function (Barsalou, 1988; Schank, 1980; Tulving, 1983). Schank (1980) asked, "Why should scripts be the only kind of past experience that aid processing by making predictions and filling in causal chain inferences? . . . A person who has experienced something only once might well expect his or her second time around to conform to the initial experience" (pp. 42–43). Similarly, Tulving (1983) observed not only that attending many dinners at old Oxford colleges produces a script that includes guidelines for proper behavior, but also that "if you have only been to one such dinner, you may still be able to answer many of the same questions on the basis of your recollection of the particular event" (p. 64). More generally, "questions that are assumed to be directed at the semantic system could be answered in terms of the information retrieved from the episodic system" (Tulving, 1983, p. 64).

When is the predictive value of specific episodes paramount? Analysis of detailed personal memories should be especially useful when scripts are violated and predictions fail: "when we have failed to predict accurately what will happen next is when we are most in need of a specific memory to help us through the rough spots" (Schank, 1980, p. 41). Specific memories also are valuable in novel situations, where scripts are sketchy or missing. For example, memories of the first year in college are overrepresented in September, the point of transition and novelty (Pillemer et al., 1986; Pillemer, Goldsmith, Panter, & White, 1988). Mackavey, Malley, and Stewart's (1991) analysis of consequential experiences described in eminent psychologists' autobiographies also indicated that episodic memories were more likely than nonepisodic memories to involve transitional life events. People often report detailed personal memories of first-time happenings, especially if the events were unanticipated. College women who reported feeling less knowledgeable at menarche provided more personal details about the first menstrual episode (Pillemer et al., 1987). Specific memories contain information about what happened in the novel environment, and this information can guide subsequent behavior.

A directive function is identifiable even in "classic" flashbulb memory circumstances, where the central event is public rather than personal. When John F. Kennedy was assassinated, "some college students spoke of not knowing how to react, of watching those around them to get clues" (Wolfenstein & Kliman, 1966, p. 224). Most of these young observers had not previously experienced a presidential assassination and so relevant prior episodes did not exist in memory. In contrast, college professors in Pillemer's (1984) study of the assassination attempt on President Reagan were less naive. A substantial number of respondents reported first thinking of their own personal circumstances when hearing about prior assassinations or attempts. These recollections appeared to establish standards for current behavior: "They had experienced this *before*, a president had been shot, work had momentarily stopped, emotions were high, and yet the world went on pretty much as usual, without mass chaos" (Pillemer, 1984, p. 79).

Memories of specific episodes can exert an active influence on current behavior, but this does not establish a causal link between the original experience and later adaptations. The *memory* rather than the original event is the active agent and enduring influence. For example, Pillemer, Law, and Reichman (1990) elicited memories of influential college experiences from Wellesley alumnae. Specific events, replete with vivid details of personal circumstances, were frequently identified as influential. For example, a graduate offered this memory:

I remember sitting in a _____ class on the day that a midterm on _____ was handed back. I was a freshman and felt that I was in over my head. The professor gave a stern lecture on the value of good writing before she handed back the papers. As she reproached us, my terror grew because her remarks seemed to be personally directed at *me*. I was from a small town, did not have the same background as anyone in my class, and had immediately felt my inadequacies when class began in September. Suddenly she turned and looked directly at me – I thought I would die of humiliation. Then she said, "But _____ has answered the question well and has an unusual lyrical and personal style that enhanced her answer." I couldn't believe that she was talking about my paper, but she was. I can still envision that dimly lit little room in the bottom of _____ and smell its peculiar musty odor. I can still picture her stern but kind face and feel the relief and pride that I felt at that moment.

The memory is in many ways similar to flashbulb memories of assassinations except that the "news" is about the person's *own* well-being. She rated the impact of this singular episode on her life as extremely strong, and stated that the experience had influenced her decision to get a PhD and pursue an academic career.

The directive aspects of the memory – that you are exceptionally talented academically and that the study of poetry will make you proud rather than ashamed – do not hinge on the precise accuracy of remembered details. In his comments following my presentation at the Emory conference, David Rubin observed that the memory itself undoubtedly became more important in the woman's life than anything that "really happened that day" in the classroom. The clarity of the recollection, the vividness of minute personal details, the strong emotions, and the speaker's confidence that the event "really happened" probably contributed to its persistence and perceived influence: "the vividness or extensiveness of phenomenal experience may increase the level of subjective confidence in a recollection, and that may have an impact on the decisions we make about current or pending situations" (Robinson & Swanson, 1990, p. 328).

Groups of people also extract lessons from their shared memories of specific instances. The memory serves as a communal touchstone and guide. Members of the Detroit Pistons, reigning champions of the National Basketball Association, attributed their current success in part to a specific basketball game or, more precisely, a fleeting *moment* in a game played several years earlier: "How were they to know that this moment of immeasurable regret and sorrow would turn out to be so beneficial? Three years later, the Detroit Pistons will admit without hesitation that what happened to them on the night of May 26, 1987, helped mold them into what they are today" (Ryan, 1990, p. 81). In the crucial earlier game, the Pistons were leading the Boston Celtics by a point with only seconds to go. All the Pistons had to do was inbound the ball and let the time expire, but Boston star player Larry Bird dramatically and unexpectedly intercepted the pass and threw it to a teammate who scored the winning basket. The Piston coaches and players carry the memory of that moment with them to this day, and as several current quotes attest, the recollection continues to have a strong directive influence: "How often do we think about it? . . . Try last night, just prior to going out on the floor." "[That game] cemented our mental toughness . . . It taught us to persevere mentally." "Ever since [that game] in Boston . . . we've learned that you never give up. If we're down 10 points with two minutes to go, we always believe we've got a chance to win the game." "It's become a positive thing for us . . . We now react to that situation with a certain set we should have used that night." (Ryan, 1990, pp. 81, 88). In this particular instance, we know that the event really happened – it was shown on television and observed by millions. But the memory now has a life of its own, and for the Detroit players the vivid and emotionally charged image is far more persuasive and instructive than any number of general discussions about the virtues of "never giving up."

The corporate world is another arena in which specific episodes influence that attitudes and behaviors of groups of people. Employees are exposed not only to the explicit, formal structure and reward system of a company, but also to an implicit "corporate culture." Remembered and retold episodes are an important source of information about what "really counts" in the organization: "Employees also take note of all critical incidents that stem from management action – such as the time that so-and-so was reprimanded for doing a good job when not asked to do it beforehand or the time that another worker was fired for publicly disagreeing with the company's position. Incidents such as these become an enduring part of the company folklore, indicating what the corporation really wants . . . They are the unwritten rules of the game" (Kilmann, 1985, p. 64).

### Nonconscious processing of specific memories

The directive functions discussed in the preceding section are conscious and deliberate: A memory of a specific past event is retrieved and inspected, and the "lessons" are applied to a present or future situation. In this section I identify directive memory functions that occur outside of focal attention. Research on the relationship between cognition and behavior has been limited by the frequent failure to distinguish between processes operating at different levels of consciousness (Brewin, 1989), although recent research in cognitive psychology has identified several types of nonconscious mental activity (Kihlstrom, 1987). Purposeful evaluation of prior episodes is apparently not the only way that specific memories can influence behavior – it may not even be the most common channel of influence.

*Nonverbal memory images.* Brown and Kulik's (1977) model of flashbulb memory formation can be characterized as a two-stage process

(Pillemer, 1990). The basic memory, formed at the time of the original experience, "is not a narrative and not even in verbal form, but represented in other, perhaps imaginal, ways" (Brown & Kulik, 1977, p. 85). The basic memory is "not directly accessible" (Brown & Kulik, 1977, p. 87). Narrative representations are actively constructed from the primary sensory image through overt and covert rehearsal. Although Brown and Kulik (and all other researchers who have examined flashbulb memories) focused their empirical analysis on subjects' narrative memories, the more primitive memory images would appear to play a role in the authors' evolutionary account. For our early ancestors, critical events would include such things as "the appearance in one's territory of a new dangerous carnivore or the sight of a serious injury to a dominant male of the same species" (p. 97). One way to prevent a future disaster would be to create a narrative representation or "story" of the tragic event, and to verbally alert others to the event's occurrence. But participants in the original episode could also benefit from the automatic activation of the memory image when confronting a similar situation: "Walking in the tall grass, near an unfamiliar waterhole, with few companions, at dusk, these characteristics must trigger an emotional reaction and recollection of the earlier tragedy. To depend solely on purposeful, deliberate reconstruction of prior similar episodes is risky – an attack may occur before relevant information is accessed" (Pillemer, 1984, p. 78).

Recent theoretical analyses of autobiographical memory are consistent with Brown and Kulik's (1977) memory model. White and Pillemer (1979; Pillemer & White, 1989) posited the existence of two functionally distinct memory systems. A basic system, "present from birth and operational throughout life, is addressable by situational and affective cues. Past experiences are evoked by feelings, locations, or people. The memories are expressed through images, behaviors, or emotions" (Pillemer & White, 1989, p. 326). A second, "socially accessible" system "emerges during the preschool years. Memories are addressable through intentional retrieval efforts, apart from the original learning conditions ... Event representations entering the higher-order system are actively thought about or mentally processed and thus are encoded in narrative form" (p. 326). Similar dualities are part of recent clinical formulations. Brewin (1989) offered a distinction between "situationally accessible knowledge" and "verbally accessible knowledge" (p. 382). According to Terr (1988), traumatic events experienced before about age 3 are encoded visually and imagistically, but narrative as well as visual memories can be formed thereafter.

*A model of preconscious personal memory processes.* How might the automatic retrieval of a specific memory image influence attitudes and behaviors outside of conscious awareness? I will first present a speculative theoretical model, and then discuss its main components.

The hypothesized sequence, baldly put, is as follows: Encountering a novel or problematic situation frequently triggers a preconscious memory of a specific past episode that is structurally similar to the present predicament. The preconscious memory evokes an emotional response, and action consistent with the felt emotion is taken:

Triggering Situation --> Preconscious Memory --> Emotional Response --> Action

The use of the term "preconscious" (or "subconscious"; see Kilhstrom's [1987] taxonomy of nonconscious processes) rather than "unconscious" is deliberate, because the memories are potentially available to consciousness. As will be discussed shortly, bringing these preconscious memories into focal awareness is an essential component of psychotherapeutic attempts to modify the depicted sequence of events.

This proposal has a different emphasis than existing models in which mood influences memory (e.g., Bower, 1981). The usual sequence is as follows:

Triggering Situation --> Emotional Mood --> Mood Consistent Memories

In the present model, the order is reversed: The preconscious memory either evokes the corresponding affective response or the emotional reaction is an integral component of the memory image itself.

*Triggering situations.* Under what circumstances would the automatic activation of specific memory images be adaptive? Schank (1980) proposed that lasting episodic memories are created when script-based processing fails: "When we detect a failure of an action to conform to our expectations, we remember that failure. In a sense, we are attempting to jot it down for next time, so that we won't fail that way again" (p. 44). In this way, "entire episodic memories can be stored at critical script junctures" (p. 43). At the point of a future processing failure, the individual is *reminded* of structurally similar past episodes, which may contain clues about how to proceed. Memories should "come to mind at just the point where that memory would be most useful for processing. This tends to be necessary when things have not gone exactly as planned" (p. 41).

Processing will stall not only when established scripts are violated, but also when new situations are encountered. In the absence of scripts, the "best that memory can do" under novel circumstances is to activate specific episodes representing different surface topics, but with similar structural characteristics.

*Preconscious event memories.* Schank's (1980) analysis of remindings focused on conscious mental processes, but the activation of memory images also can occur outside of conscious awareness. According to Brewin (1989), *preconscious* stimuli "may also be accessible to consciousness if we are alerted to their presence. These stimuli have not been deliberately ignored, but are part of the enormous number of sensations, images, and so forth, which are automatically filtered out of the material potentially available to our limited consciousness" (p. 380). Singer (1970) employed Neisser's (1967) concept of *preattentive* processes to account for the "continuous processing of material from memory": "fleeting images and bits and pieces of uncoded material are held temporarily in iconic storage . . . Only if focal attention is brought to bear on the material . . . are we likely to get reportable content" (Singer, 1970, p. 143). The internal stimuli include "short-term memories, the elaborations upon events perceived and events drawn from long-term memory storage, and associations and combinations of old memories with recently perceived events or with images just aroused" (Singer, 1975, p. 77). Spence (1988) described "passive remembering – the general experience of having things come to mind without their being requested" (p. 311). When passive memory first appears, "it may speak in a whisper, and we may not notice its presence" (p. 314). Mandler (1989) made a distinction between conscious and unconscious reminding: "sometimes events come to mind that are simply accepted as fitting the stream of our productions, at other times they are specially noticed" (p. 103).

The ongoing stream of internally generated stimuli is potentially accessible to focal attention, although it will often fail to achieve conscious recognition. External and internal sources of stimulation compete, in a sense, for limited conscious processing resources. Singer (1970, 1975) observed that under many circumstances conscious attention will be occupied by demands imposed by external rather than internal stimuli. Similarly, Pillemer and White (1989) proposed that purposeful mental activities can inhibit conscious expression of internal memory images: "The social memory system is engaged when the situation calls for an intentional, purposeful memory search . . . When the higher-order system is inactive, as during free association, sleep, or undirected rumination, stored images, feelings, and behaviors may be reinstated automatically by affective or contextual cues" (p. 326).

Preconscious material can take many forms, but specific memory images, once identified, often have a strong *visual* component. Brewer (1988) observed that personal memories are almost always accompanied by visual imagery, and clinical researchers have described primary, visual, "core" memories that form the basis of secondary, narrative accounts. Terr (1988) concluded that "traumatic events create lasting visual images" (p. 103) and that visual rather than verbal memory is the primary instigator of behavioral reenactments of the trauma. Kantor's (1980) critical identity images also are primarily visual and spatial: "One can think of them as pictorialized representations of events, as thoughts in visual form, or as pictorialized thought schemas" (p. 148). The therapist responds to an interpersonal impasse (or to borrow Schank's information processing term, a processing failure) among family members by eliciting concrete "memory pictures," and then by pinning down "enough of the concrete 'elements' to 'fix the picture' in awareness" (Kantor, 1980, p. 157). Once the influential but preconscious image is brought into conscious awareness, therapy can advance.

*Memory-emotion-action sequence.* The traditional experimental paradigm for studying the relationship between mood and memory involves manipulating the mood state and observing effects on memory (Bower, 1981). In the present model, specific memories elicit emotions rather than the reverse, and the elicited emotions can influence behaviors without the initiating memory reaching conscious awareness. Memories can influence emotional states as well as be influenced by them (e.g., Brewin, 1989; Oatley, 1988; Singer, 1970). According to Singer (1970), "just as affects are evoked by the pattern of processing external stimuli, so too can they be evoked by the processing of material from long-term memory" (p. 140). Standard mood induction procedures provide a concrete example: Hypnotized subjects put themselves into a happy or sad mood by remembering a happy or sad scene (Bower, 1981, p. 130). Although attempts to change moods in this fashion are purposeful, feelings can be evoked or altered without conscious awareness of the specific emotional trigger (Zajonc, 1980). This view is prominent in contemporary theories of psychotherapy: "Clearly, powerful emotional and behavioral effects can be observed without the necessity for representing relevant past experiences at a conscious level" (Brewin, 1989, p. 382).

How might a preconscious memory exert a powerful influence on emotion and subsequent action but nevertheless fail to achieve conscious awareness? Specific memory images are activated *automatically* by the underlying structural characteristics of a problematic or unscripted situation, and this preconscious processing often goes unnoticed. Singer (1978) observed that "most people simply do not recall a great deal of such [private mental] processing because they have moved on rapidly to new externally generated materials or to new thoughts" (p. 204). Focal attention is occupied by the mobilization of thought and activity in response to the felt emotions, and action is prompted by feelings rather than by a cognitive evaluation of the memory image. The person who feels afraid when confronting an unanticipated situation will find his or her thoughts and behaviors directed toward immediate anxiety reduction, rather than toward a purposeful analysis of transient memory images.

Psychotherapeutic work points to the unattended-to memory image as a critical first link in the emotion–action sequence. One therapeutic strategy involves "the therapist attempting to specify the exact content of the nonconscious memory in order to help the patient discriminate precisely which situational features elicit inappropriate fear, sadness, or other emotions" (Brewin, 1989, p. 387). Similarly, Kantor's (1980) technique, described previously, involves bringing a critical memory image into conscious awareness, and tying the analysis of emotion to the now-concrete image.

Memory awareness is enhanced in psychotherapy, where the patient is encouraged to "stay with" the anxiety or other strong emotion, to resist the urge to reduce it immediately by shifting thoughts and actions, and instead to reflect on and verbalize concomitant feelings and images. Memory images also are potentially retrievable in nontherapeutic contexts. A recent personal experience provides an illustration. When my wife proposed buying a tricycle for my 3-year-old daughter, my immediate reaction was concern. My thoughts and energies were focused on anxiety reduction: postponing the purchase, blocking off our driveway from the street, and so on. Sustained reflection produced a vivid memory image of my own early bike-riding experience. I rode in the street without permission, and my father forcefully told me to stop. In my eagerness to comply, I fell off the bike. My childhood feelings of anxiety and embarrassment remain a prominent part of the memory. According to the memory model presented here, activation of the childhood memory, initially at a preconscious level, triggered the inappropriately strong emotional reaction. The memory image vividly portrayed what could "go wrong," and it appeared to "explain" the high level of present discomfort and the thoughts and behaviors aimed at anxiety reduction.

In the present model, memory images are identified as emotional triggers, but it is also possible that the memories themselves are simply triggered by the feelings evoked by the situation. Nevertheless, two factors suggest that specific nonconscious memories can produce conscious emotional reactions. First, the emotions evoked by some situations are experienced as alien, or at least as too strong for present circumstances. Emotional incongruity would be expected if feelings are determined by preconscious memory images of remote events rather than by "objective" characteristics of the current situation: "Any new context similar in structure to the original identity image can invoke an emotional response and a behavioral response similar to what was experience earlier" (Kantor, 1980, p. 149). Irrational fears may arise when "the person's conscious recollection of events did not correspond to the representation of them that was automatically created by the system mediating nonconscious causal perception" (Brewin, 1989, p. 382). When relationships between present and past are unclear and when the memory image is fleeting, emotions can be inexplicable and unwanted.

A second reason why specific memories appear to trigger emotions rather than simply to follow them is the psychotherapeutic importance, discussed earlier, of eliciting concrete, detailed, flashbulb-like images. According to Brewin (1989, p. 385), "therapists can modify access to nonconscious situational memories that contain information about past experience." If nonconscious memories are mere by-products of emotional expression, it is unclear why therapeutic progress should be tied to the identification and detailed analysis of preconscious memories.

Brown and Kulik's (1977) model of flashbulb memory formation resembles current psychodynamic models in several respects. The primary systemic distinction may not be between flashbulb memories and ordinary memories, but rather between nuclear imagistic traces and narrative event descriptions that are constructed after the fact. Brown and Kulik's assertion that the nonverbal memory image (as opposed to the narrative construction) is "fixed for a very long time, and conceivably permanently . . . once created, always there, and in need of no further strengthening" (p. 85), although jolting to cognitive psychologists, is consistent with some current psychotherapeutic conceptions. Brewin (1989) commented that "original situational memories are unlikely to be changed" (p. 387). Terr (1988) asserted that "traumatic events create lasting visual images" or "'burned-in' visual impressions" (p. 103), although words can later be affixed to the picture. Kantor (1980) stressed the therapeutic importance of changing the meaning of the image rather than the image itself: "these memory imprints are indelible, they do not erase – a therapy that tries to alter them will be uneconomical" (p. 163). Just as a narrative flashbulb account is created by rehearsal (Brown & Kulik, 1977, p. 86), so too are memory narratives actively constructed and reconstructed as part of the process of psychotherapy.

For present purposes, the major point is that detailed memories of personal circumstances may serve psychological functions of which we are unaware. Somewhat paradoxically, as the memory images are brought into awareness and narrated, they may lose some of their influence, because automatic emotional responses are moderated by conscious control and deeper understanding.

## Conclusions

Functional analysis of memories of personal circumstances has suggested several directions for a reorientation of memory research. First, functional analysis extends the domain of relevant empirical studies well beyond traditional boundaries of research on memory – into sociolinguistics, psychotherapy, autobiography, textual analysis, and communications. Second, the issue of memory accuracy should not dominate research simply by fiat. For each memory function, one can ask: "Is veridicality important in this particular instance?" Memories can serve communicative, directive, and psychodynamic functions even though some of the remembered details are imprecise or inaccurate. The person's subjective belief that the event "really happened" appears to be more important than "objective" accuracy in these areas of application.

From a functional perspective, overarching questions about memory can and should be reformulated in more specific fashion. For example, whereas current questions about development include "When does autobiographical memory originate?" and "How does autobiographical memory develop?" identifying developmental trajectories of particular autobiographical memory functions may prove more tractable: How do children learn to produce personal memory narratives in conversation? How and when do they learn to decode the meanings implicit in the act of sharing personal memories? Do discussions with parents about the causes and consequences of specific past events enhance children's ability to glean useful directives from their own memories of specific episodes? Does verbal expression of memories of personal circumstances following extreme shock or trauma serve as an emotional release for young children as well as for adults? Certain functions – communicative, directive – may show rapid development in early childhood, whereas other functions – psychodynamic, preconscious – may remain relatively stable throughout the lifespan, but these are questions for research. The functional approach not only provides a way to think about research findings, it is itself a general research strategy, one that can imbue the study of memory with practical meaning.

## NOTE

Preparation of this chapter was supported by a grant from the Spencer Foundation. Ulric Neisser, Jane Traupmann Pillemer, Avril Thorne, Sheldon White, and Eugene Winograd provided valuable comments on an earlier draft.

## REFERENCES

Abelson, R. P. (1981). Psychological status of the script concept. *American Psychologist, 36*, 715–729.

Baddeley, A. (1988). But what the hell is it for? In M. M. Gruneberg, P. E. Morris, & R. N. Sykes (Eds.), *Practical aspects of memory: Current research and issues: Vol. 1. Memory in everyday life* (pp. 3–18). Chichester: John Wiley & Sons.

Barsalou, L. W. (1988). The content and organization of autobiographical memories. In U. Neisser & E. Winograd (Eds.), *Remembering reconsidered: Ecological and traditional approaches to the study of memory* (pp. 193–243). New York: Cambridge University Press.

Beals, D. E. (1991). Stories from the classroom: Rate of response to personal event narratives told by beginning teachers. *The Quarterly Newsletter of the Laboratory of Comparative Human Cognition, 13*, 31–38.

Bell, B. E., & Loftus, E. F. (1989) Trivial persuasion in the courtroom: The power of (a few) minor details. *Journal of Personality and Social Psychology, 56*, 669–679.

Bohannon, J. N. III. (1988). Flashbulb memories for the Space Shuttle disaster: A tale of two theories. *Cognition, 29*, 179–196.

Bower, G. H. (1981). Mood and memory. *American Psychologist, 36*, 129–148.

rewer, W. F. (1986). What is autobiographical memory? In D. C. Rubin (Ed.), *Autobiographical memory* (pp. 25–49). New York: Cambridge University Press.

rewer, W. F. (1988). Memory for randomly sampled autobiographical events. In U. Neisser & E. Winograd (Eds.), *Remembering reconsidered: Ecological and traditional approaches to the study of memory* (pp. 21–90). New York: Cambridge University Press.

Brewin, C. R. (1989). Cognitive change processes in psychotherapy. *Psychological Review, 96*, 379–394.

Brown, R. (1990). Politeness theory: Exemplar and exemplary. In I. Rock (Ed.), *The legacy of Solomon Asch: Essays in cognition and social psychology* (pp. 23–38). Hillsdale, NJ: Erlbaum.

Brown, R., & Kulik, J. (1977). Flashbulb memories. *Cognition, 5*, 73–99.

Bruce, D. (1985). The how and why of ecological memory. *Journal of Experimental Psychology: General, 114*, 78–90.

Bruce, D. (1989). Functional explanations of memory. In L. W. Poon, D. C. Rubin, & B. A. Wilson (Eds.), *Everyday cognition in adulthood and late life* (pp. 44–58). New York: Cambridge University Press.

Bruner, J. S. (1987). Life as narrative. *Social Research, 54*, 11–32.

Carlson, R. (1981). Studies in script theory: I. Adult analogs of a childhood nuclear scene. *Journal of Personality and Social Psychology, 40*, 501–510.

Christianson, S-Å. (1989). Flashbulb memories: Special, but not so special. *Memory & Cognition, 17*, 435–443.

Cohen, N. J., McCloskey, M., & Wible, C. G. (1990). Flashbulb memories and underlying cognitive mechanisms: Reply to Pillemer. *Journal of Experimental Psychology: General, 119*, 97–100.

Davis, P. J. (1988). Physiological and subjective effects of catharsis: A case report. *Cognition and Emotion, 2*, 19–28.

Edwards, D., & Middleton, D. (1986). Joint remembering: Constructing an account of shared experience through conversational discourse. *Discourse Processes, 9*, 423–459.

Fivush, R. (1988). The functions of event memory: Some comments on Nelson and Barsalou. In U. Neisser & E. Winograd (Eds.), *Remembering reconsidered: Ecological and traditional approaches to the study of memory* (pp. 277–282). New York: Cambridge University Press.

Greenstein, F. I. (1966). Young men and the death of a young president. In M. Wolfenstein & G. Kliman (Eds.), *Children and the death of a president* (pp. 193–216). Garden City, NY: Anchor Books.

Grice, H. P. (1975). Logic and conversation. In P. Cole & J. L. Morgan (Eds.), *Syntax and semantics: Vol. 3. Speech acts* (pp. 41–58). New York: Academic Press.

Grossfeld, S. (1989, October 22). Not everyone is running down from life on the fault line. *The Boston Globe*, pp. 1, 27.

Harsch, N., & Neisser, U. (1989, November). *Substantial and irreversible errors in flashbulb memories of the Challenger explosion.* Poster presented at the Psychonomic Society Meeting, Atlanta, GA.

Harvey, A. D. (1986). Evidence of a tense shift in personal experience narratives. *Empirical Studies of the Arts, 4*, 151–162.

Jacoby, L. L. (1988). Memory observed and memory unobserved. In U. Neisser & E. Winograd (Eds.), *Remembering reconsidered: Ecological and traditional approaches to the study of memory* (pp. 145–177). New York: Cambridge University Press.

Kantor, D. (1980). Critical identity image: A concept linking individual, couple, and family development. In J. K. Pearce & L. J. Friedman (Eds.), *Family therapy:*

*Combining psychodynamic and family systems approaches* (pp. 137–167). New York: Grune & Stratton.

Kennedy, W. (1983). *Ironweed*. New York: The Viking Press.

Kihlstrom, J. F. (1987). The cognitive unconscious. *Science, 237,* 1445–1452.

Kilmann, R. H. (1985). Corporate culture. *Psychology Today, 19,* 62–68.

Klein.auz, M., Dreyfuss, D. A., Beran, B., Goldberg, T., & Azikri, D. (1979). Some after-affects of stage hypnosis: A case study of psychopathological manifestations. *The International Journal of Clinical and Experimental Hypnosis, 27,* 219–226.

Labov, W. (1972). *Language in the inner city*. Philadelphia: University of Pennsylvania Press.

Labov, W. (1982). Speech actions and reactions in personal narrative. In D. Tannen (Ed.), *Analyzing discourse: Text and talk* (pp. 219–247). Washington, DC: Georgetown University Press.

Labov, W., & Waletzky, J. (1967). Narrative analysis: Oral versions of personal experience. In J. Helm (Ed.), *Essays on the verbal and visual arts* (pp. 12–44). Seattle: University of Washington Press.

Larsen, S. F., & Plunkett, K. (1987). Remembering experienced and reported events. *Applied Cognitive Psychology, 1,* 15–26.

Light, R. J., & Pillemer, D. B. (1984). *Summing up: The science of reviewing research*. Cambridge, MA: Harvard University Press.

McCloskey, M., Wible, C. G., & Cohen, N. J. (1988). Is there a special flashbulb-memory mechanism? *Journal of Experimental Psychology: General, 117,* 171–181.

Mackavey, W. R., Malley, J. E., & Stewart, A. J. (1991). Remembering autobiographically consequential experiences: Content analysis of psychologists' accounts of their lives. *Psychology and Aging, 6,* 50–59.

McNally, R. J. (1989). On "stress-induced recovery of fears and phobias." *Psychological Review, 96,* 180–181.

Mandler, G. (1989). Memory: Conscious and unconscious. In P. R. Solomon, G. R. Goethals, C. M. Kelley, & B. R. Stephens (Eds.), *Memory: Interdisciplinary approaches* (pp. 84–106). New York: Springer-Verlag.

Merseth, K. K. (1990, April). *The power of multiple contexts: Beginning teachers, electronic networks and induction support*. Paper presented at the Annual Meetings of the American Educational Research Association, Boston, MA.

Myllyniemi, R. (1986). Conversation as a system of social interaction. *Language & Communication, 6,* 147–169.

Neisser, U. (1967). *Cognitive psychology*. New York: Appleton-Century-Crofts.

Neisser, U. (1981). John Dean's memory: A case study. *Cognition, 9,* 1–22.

Neisser, U. (1982a). Memory: What are the important questions? In U. Neisser (Ed.), *Memory observed* (pp. 3–19). San Francisco: Freeman.

Neisser, U. (1982b). Snapshots or benchmarks? In U. Neisser (Ed.), *Memory observed* (pp. ∙3–48). San Francisco: Freeman.

Neisser, U. (1988a). Time present and time past. In M. M. Gruneberg, P. E. Morris, & R. N. Sykes (Eds.), *Practical aspects of memory: Current research and issues: Vol. 2 Clinical and educational implications* (pp. 545–560). Chichester: John Wiley & Sons.

Neisser, U. (1988b). What is ordinary memory the memory of? In U. Neisser & E. Winograd (Eds.), *Remembering reconsidered: Ecological and traditional approaches to the study of memory* (pp. 356–373). New York: Cambridge University Press.

Neisser, U., & Winograd, E. (Eds.) (1988). *Remembering reconsidered: Ecological and traditional approaches to the study of memory*. New York: Cambridge University Press.

Nelson K. (1988). The ontogeny of memory for real events. In U. Neisser & E. Winograd (Eds.), *Remembering reconsidered: Ecological and traditional approaches to the study of memory* (pp. 244–276). New York: Cambridge University Press.

Nelson K. (1989). Remembering: A functional developmental perspective. In P. R. Solomon, G. R. Goethals, C. M. Kelley, & B. R. Stephens (Eds.), *Memory: Interdisciplinary approaches* (pp. 127–150). New York: Springer-Verlag.

Oatley, K. (1988). Gaps in consciousness: Emotions and memory in psychoanalysis. *Cognition and Emotion*, 2, 3–18.

Pillemer, D. B. (1984). Flashbulb memories of the assassination attempt on President Reagan. *Cognition*, 16, 63–80.

Pillemer, D. B. (1990). Clarifying the flashbulb memory concept: Comment on McCloskey, Wible, and Cohen (1988). *Journal of Experimental Psychology: General*, 119, 92–96.

Pillemer, D. B., Goldsmith, L. R., Panter, A. T., & White, S. H. (1988). Very long-term memories of the first year in college. *Journal of Experimental Psychology: Learning, Memory, and Cognition*, 14, 709–715.

Pillemer, D. B., Koff, E., Rhinehart, E. D., & Rierdan, J. (1987). Flashbulb memories of menarche and adult menstrual distress. *Journal of Adolescence*, 10, 187–199.

Pillemer, D. B., Krensky, L., Kleinman, S. N., Goldsmith, L. R., & White, S. H. (1991). Chapters in narratives: Evidence from oral histories of the first year in college. *Journal of Narrative and Life History*, 1, 3–14.

Pillemer, D. B., Law, A. B., & Reichman, J. S. (1990). [Memories of educational episodes]. Unpublished raw data.

Pillemer, D. B., Rhinehart, E. D., & White, S. H. (1986). Memories of life transitions: The first year in college. *Human Learning*, 5, 109–123.

Pillemer, D. B., White, S. H. (1989). Childhood events recalled by children and adults. In H. W. Reese (Ed.), *Advances in child development and behavior: Vol. 21* (pp. 297–340). Orlando, FL: Academic Press.

Robb, C. (1989, October 19). For survivors of earthquakes, the shocks linger on. *Boston Globe*, pp. 93, 98.

Robinson, J. A., & Swanson, K. L. (1990). Autobiographical memory: The next phase. *Applied Cognitive Psychology*, 4, 321–335.

Rubin, D. C. (Ed.). (1986). *Autobiographical memory*. New York: Cambridge University Press.

Rubin, D. C., & Kozin, M. (1984). Vivid memories. *Cognition*, 16, 81–95.

Ryan, B. (1990, June 8). Detroit's character was built in Boston. *The Boston Globe*, pp. 81, 88.

Schank, R. C. (1977). Rules and topics in conversation. *Cognitive Science*, 1, 421–441.

Schank, R. C. (1980). Failure-driven memory. *Cognition and Brain Theory*, 4, 41–60.

Select Committees on the Iran-Contra Investigation. (1988). *Testimony of George P. Shultz and Edwin Meese, III, July 23, 24, 28, and 29, 1987*. Washington, DC: U.S. Government Printing Office.

Sherry, D. F., & Schacter, D. L. (1987). The evolution of multiple memory systems. *Psychological Review*, 94, 439–454.

Singer, J. L. (1970). Drives, affects, and daydreams: The adaptive role of spontaneous imagery of stimulus-independent mentation. In J. S. Antrobus (Ed.), *Cognition and affect* (pp. 131–158). Boston: Little, Brown and Company.

Singer, J. L. (1975). *The inner world of daydreaming*. New York: Harper & Row.

Singer, J. L. (1978). Experimental studies of daydreaming and the stream of thought. In K. S. Pope & J. L. Singer (Eds.), *The stream of consciousness* (pp. 187–223). New York: Plenum.

Spence, D. P. (1988). Passive remembering. In U. Neisser & E. Winograd (Eds.), *Remembering reconsidered: Ecological and traditional approaches to the study of memory* (pp. 311–325). New York: Cambridge University Press.

Tenney. Y. J. (1989). Predicting conversational reports of a personal event. *Cogniti Science*, *13*, 213–233.

Terr, L. (1988). What happens to early memories of trauma? A study of twent children under age five at the time of documented traumatic events. *Journal of th American Academy of Child and Adolescent Psychiatry*, *27*, 96–104.

Tulving, E. (1983). *Elements of episodic memory*. Oxford: Clarendon Press.

Tulving, E. (1989). Remembering and knowing the past. *American Scientist*, *77*, 361–367.

Updike, J. (1990, August 5). Why Rabbit had to go. *The New York Times Book Review* pp. 1, 24–25.

Wachtel, E. F., & Wachtel, P. L. (1986). *Family dynamics in individual psychotherapy: A guide to clinical strategies*. New York: The Guilford Press.

White, S. H., & Pillemer, D. B. (1979). Childhood amnesia and the development of a socially accessible memory system. In. J. F. Kihlstrom & F. J. Evans (Eds.), *Functional disorders of memory* (pp. 29–73). Hillsdale, NJ: Erlbaum.

Williams, J. M. G., & Broadbent, K. (1986). Autobiographical memory in suicide attempters. *Journal of Abnormal psychology*, *95*, 144–149.

Williams, J. M. G., & Dritschel, B. H. (1988). Emotional disturbance and the specificity of autobiographical memory. *Cognition and Emotion*. *2*, 221–234.

Winograd, E., & Killinger, W. A., Jr. (1983). Relating age at encoding in early childhood to adult recall: Development of flashbulb memories. *Journal of Experimental Psychology: General*, *112*, 413–422.

Wolfenstein, M., & Kliman, G. (Eds.). (1966). *Children and the death of a president*. Garden City, NY: Anchor Books.

Zajonc, R. B. (1980). Feeling and thinking: Preferences need no inferences. *American Psychologist*, *35*, 151–175.

# 13

# Constraints on memory

DAVID C. RUBIN

Commenting on this conference is a hard task. Every clever slant I could think of, and many I could not, were covered by comments in the continuing open discussion. I reflected on what others might do in this situation, and chose Allen Newell as a model. What he did to organize his discussion, on at least one occasion like this, was to spend half of his space on an issue not directly related to the papers of the conference. He had something worth saying that is as appropriate to this conference as it was to his, so I will just use his talk again. After all, he first gave his discussion in 1972 and we have heard here how confused memories can get over time. Newell began as follows.

I am a man who is half and half. Half of me is half distressed and half confused. Half of me is quite content and clear on where we are going.

My confused and distressed half has been roused by my assignment to comment on the papers of this symposium. It is curious that it should be so. We have just listened to a sample of the best work . . .

Psychology, in its current style of operation, deals with phenomena. . . . The number is so large it scares me. . . . [Our phenomenon is "flashbulb" memory.]

Psychology also attempts to conceptualize what it is doing, as a guide to investigating these phenomena. How do we do that? Mostly, so it seems to me, by the construction of oppositions – usually binary ones. We worry about nature versus nurture, about central versus peripheral, about serial versus parallel, and so on. . . . [Our opposition is are flashbulb memories qualitatively different from other memories: an opposition McCloskey and Brewer analyze in detail in chapters 11 and 14.]

As I examine the fate of our opposition, looking at those already in existence as a guide to how they fare and shape the course of science, it seems to me that clarity is never achieved. Matters simply become muddier and muddier as we go down through time. Thus, far from providing the rungs of a ladder by which psychology gradually climbs to clarity, this form of conceptual structure leads rather to an ever increasing pile of issues, which we weary of or become diverted from, but never really settle. (Newell, 1973, pp. 283–289)

Newell offers three possible paradigms that might help science cumulate more efficiently: build a complete processing model, analyze a complex task, and use one program for many tasks. As this conference was convened to discuss the complex task of the formation and recall of flashbulb memories, the second paradigm is the most applicable. Newell described it in the following way.

Focus a series of experimental and theoretical studies around a single complex task the aim being to demonstrate that one has a sufficient theory of a genuine slab of human behavior. All of the studies would be designed to fit together and add up to a total picture in detail. (Newell, 1973, p. 303)

The key words are "in detail." Illustrations of the beginnings of this strategy included studies of mental arithmetic and chess.

We are better off now than in 1972. Instead of being half content and half confused, I am closer to 80% content and 20% confused, and had Newell been the discussant at this conference, I hope that he would be too. Some closure has come. This conference supports Newell's suggestion of analyzing a complex task or phenomenon as a good way for cognitive psychology to proceed, especially when a phenomenon provides regularities or extends the range of our database in a way that challenges and extends existing theory (Rubin, 1989). It also convinces me that Newell was correct in worrying about the damage done by our tendency to develop dichotomies to explain complex human behavior. As Newell argued, more complex, but well-defined, theories are more likely to increase our understanding. Over the last 18 years the field has begun to follow his advice. In Newell's view, we need to view flashbulb memories as "a genuine slab of human behavior" rather than just as a small isolated phenomenon or as half of a dichotomy with normal memory as the other half, and we need to develop "a sufficient theory" of those memories known as flashbulb memories. This is something this volume begins to do. Even its framings of the dichotomy question look to a general and sufficient theory of memory (McCloskey, chapter 11; Brewer, chapter 14). With this caution in mind let us return to flashbulb memories.

## The blind people and the flashbulb

We came to the study of flashbulb memories with different biases and interests. These shaped what we expected, what we looked for, what data we collected, and what theoretical ax we ground. Our papers are a projective test of our theories and measures. They are a reasonable survey of approaches to cognitive psychology as it is practiced today. We have viewed flashbulb memories in about as many ways as the blind men viewed the elephant.

Let us start at the beginning. Flashbulb memories are a phenomenon that Brown and Kulik named in 1977, though they had been studied much earlier in psychology (Colgrove, 1899). Roger Brown is very good at naming and describing such fertile phenomena; the tip-of-the-tongue phenomenon is another well-known terms of his (Brown & McNeill, 1966). In a fashion not nlike Newell's, he views describing and trying to understand phenomena as n important contribution to psychology (Brown, 1989). Brown and Kulik tudied what they saw as the phenomenon's distinctive feature, the detailed ecall of personal circumstances that were of no real importance to the entral event. Thus, in large part, what defined the phenomenon was the ifelike recall of what a historian would consider irrelevant details. At this conference, Larsen (chapter 3) and others extended this view.

To provide a concrete example of how varied the perspectives are, I will consider my work first. Kozin and I (Rubin & Kozin, 1984) probably grabbed the elephant's tail. To us, vividness was the defining feature that made flashbulb memories special. We asked undergraduates for their three most vivid memories because we thought that Brown and Kulik were correct for their database but needed a broader database to check their theorizing: a standard move I had made before in extending other areas of my PhD adviser's work (Rubin, 1975, 1988). As a measure of the diversity of opinion (or the influence Kozin and I had on the field) note that no one here shared our view that vividness was the defining feature of flashbulb memories and many participants did not even measure it.

At the conference there were two invited outside views. They were expected to be different from the others, and so there is no problem here. Gold (chapter 7) viewed flashbulb memories from the point of view of the physiological mechanisms underlying the behaviors that the rest of us are studying. Loftus and Kaufman (chapter 10) viewed flashbulb memories from their relevance, irrelevance, and annoyance to the study of eyewitness testimony, a topic in which, from a practical standpoint, accuracy and distortion are everything. The rest of the participants, to whom the elephant was our central topic of study, however, showed as much variance.

Larsen (chapter 3) defined "flashbulb-like" memories using confidence. The memories that he was confident he would later recall were explored. Larsen studied central versus peripheral events because of a prior interest in a similar issue (Larsen, 1988) and confidence fell out of his measures and theoretical ideas. Christianson (chapter 9) as well as Reisberg and Heuer (chapter 8) were brave enough to examine flashbulb memories from the perspective of the role of emotions in memory in general.

Others including Warren and Swartwood (chapter 5) looked at consistency, and Gold told us clearly this was not the same part of the elephant as accuracy. Consistency was used partly because accuracy could not be and partly because it is interesting in its own right. People's memories are their memories whether or not they accurately reflect an actual event. The stability of those memories is a valid and theoretically informative question independent of the issue of accuracy.

Pillemer (chapter 12) examined the functions of telling flashbulb memories: the emotional impact of their telling for catharsis, their role in establishing trust, and the increase in communication that specific details can give Examining function is a useful approach to add, and as Bruce (1989) has noted, one we should consider more often. Consistent with this functional approach, Pillemer (chapter 6) as well as Warren and Swartwood added developmental data and considerations.

Neisser and Harsch (chapter 2) grabbed the elephant at two places at once. Their contrast between accuracy and confidence has concerned others, including Brewer (1986), and is part of Neisser's long-standing attempt to argue against the reappearance hypothesis: the hypothesis that fixed stored memories reappear to consciousness (Neisser, 1967).

It is hard to fit the work of Bohannon and Symons (chapter 4) and their colleagues into the blindman metaphor. They appear to be so interested in the phenomenon and have spent so much time with it (Bohannon, 1988; Bohannon & Schmidt, 1989; Schmidt & Bohannon, 1988) that they have made most of the possible approaches.

The study of flashbulb memories is rich in part because of this diversity. We could not do without any of them. But we must be careful that the diversity does not lead to Newell's (1973) conclusion that "Clarity is never achieved. Matters simply become muddier and muddier as we go down through time" (p. 289). The way Newell might suggest we avoid this is to keep the problem of flashbulb memories as "a genuine slab of human behavior" in need of a detailed theory, and not let it become a dichotomy or a phenomenon that is isolated from related behavior.

## Putting it all together

Can we integrate these views and the data they produce?

I have very few ideas, so I keep using the same one again, with a little modification. Here Steen Larsen, Ira Hyman, Jr., and others helped with the modification of ideas about multiple constraints that have been developing at Duke (Hyman & Rubin, 1990; Rubin 1988; Rubin, Stolzfus, & Wall, 1991; Rubin & Wallace, 1989; Wallace & Rubin, 1988, 1991).

Flashbulb memories are constrained by many factors. The original stimulus is not always the most important of these. The following are a number of constraints drawn from this conference and the earlier literature.

As Neisser (1982) pointed out in his criticism of Brown and Kulik, the canonical categories of flashbulb memories are part of narrative structure. Flashbulb memory must be in good narrative form in order to make a good story to tell and to recall. Fivush and Slackman (1986) and Pillemer (chapter 6) note that if you have the mind of a 3-year-old, you do not create a mature narrative structure, and free recall suffers.

As Pillemer, Fivush, and others have commented, our culture helps organize and specify what we should recall. Thus when we tell someone about the

*Challenger* explosion, we try to present new information and that information
is more likely to be about our experiences than what was on the evening
news. Besides, Pillemer notes that concrete details are needed to serve the
other functions of memory, such as the functions of insuring response and
establishing trust. The two constraints of having good narrative form and
fitting into cultural norms for communication combine to make flashbulb
memories good stories full of personal details.

Our life narratives, independent of the particular event being recalled, are
a constraining factor. This life story defines the self in terms of a sequence of
consistent memories (Barclay, 1986; Brewer, 1986; Greenwald, 1980; Robinson, 1986). This consistent life story imposes constraints on the contents of
flashbulb memories and was probably central in Pillemer's example of a
student's comments on her essay leading to a career choice.

There are also the standard constraints of memory itself. Memories without vivid images are less likely to be recalled. Moreover, the imagery of
details leads to a sense of the memory being real (Brewer, 1986; Johnson &
Raye, 1981) and functions to increase communication as noted by Pillemer
(chapter 6). Emotionality of the events in flashbulb memories helps recall, as
noted by Christianson (chapter 9), or at least seems to slow forgetting, as
noted by Reisberg and Heuer (chapter 8).

Brown and Kulik postulate rehearsal as a mechanism to insure access to
flashbulb memories. Rehearsal, especially spaced, helps people remember.
Rehearsal in the first few hours and then very spaced, as Neisser and Harsch
(chapter 2) have noted, may increase the likelihood of recall, though it might
not help its consistency or accuracy. Rehearsal at 2 weeks and 2 months will
help people remember 2 years later, as Warren and Swartwood (chapter 5)
found. There are also the details of the event itself, but these have to be
considered in terms of how well they fit the other constraints. From the data
and Gold's comments (chapter 7), it may take a week or so for all of this to
settle down.

From the combination of these factors we would expect flashbulb memories to be in good narrative form, containing information that is new and
potentially interesting to the listener, consistent with the teller's view of the
self, and to contain concrete, imageable details as well as emotional impact
and reactions. Distortions from the original event should be in the direction
of these constraints. When emotional arousal increases rehearsal, often in the
form of information seeking, it should lead to a greater amount of recall, but
not necessarily to greater accuracy or consistency. This list of factors is far
from exhaustive and further still from Newell's call for a complete detailed
theory, but I am only a discussant and flashbulb memories are not chess.
Nonetheless, it is hard to imagine a detailed theory that would not include
the interplay of at least these factors.

## Suggestions for the ambulance chaser

What is the minimum set of experimental conditions that could begin to answer the questions considered at the conference? Although the previous sections were greatly influenced by those who attended the conference, the answer to this question is entirely theirs. My only role is as a collector, distorter, and reporter of ideas. Portions of this section came not only from the participants listed in this book, but also from those who participated but did not deliver papers, including Darryl Bruce, Henry Ellis, Joe Fitzgerald, Robyn Fivush, Ira Hyman, Jr., Makiko Naka, and Colwyn Trevarthyn, among others.

All data can be useful in some way, but we now have issues that cannot be settled without more controlled study. Research should continue even if all conditions of an ideal experiment cannot be met, but formulating an ideal experiment and therefore making it open to consideration and debate is a useful undertaking, especially when the phenomenon under study leaves little time for planning once an incident occurs.

The minimum ideal experiment needs recalls to be taken both at a short retention interval and a long retention interval, from a single person, after an emotionally arousing event. An accurate description of the event and the subject's first exposure to it would be useful to distinguish accuracy from consistency. The long retention interval should be one month or longer to be well beyond the 1-week interval that the data presented here indicate may be a turning point for flashbulb memories. For different subjects, the short retention interval should be either: (a) as soon as possible, but definitely within 24 hours, (b) about three days, or at (c) about 1 week. These intervals were chosen because, for the data presented at the conference by different experimenters, there is much better agreement between the memories at 1 week and 1 year than between memories at 1 day and 1 year. Some probing of these times is therefore needed within one experiment to see if the differences observed are artifacts of different experimental procedures or subject populations. If the difference in consistency between 1 day and 1 week and later recalls is real we need the three short intervals to begin to understand the time course of this effect. Different subjects were suggested for each short time, to prevent the repeated recall from fixing the recall. A within-group procedure, however, with recalls taken at many intervals would be a good addition to track the changes, although this procedure should lead to more stability than a design with one only long and one short retention interval (Cofer, 1943).

For some subjects, a complete log of every time they gained new information about the event, or talked about it, is needed for at least the first day or two after the event. This is because some of Neisser and Harsch's (chapter 2) subjects who appear to be wildly constructing memories could be reportng accurately about two or more different times in which they heard about he *Challenger* exploding, although they were always asked for the *first* time. This is Brewer's (1988) "wrong time slice" response (p. 53). We need to know whether the differences between short and long retention periods are he result of a major reconstruction or just a lapse in memory for the first time in favor of a more vivid second, third, or fourth time.

Several factors have been postulated as playing an important role in flashbulb memories, and measures of these should be taken close to encoding (i.e., at the short retention interval) and at the time of later recall (i.e., at the long retention interval) to begin to distinguish effects present at encoding and retrieval, as opposed to encoding and retrieval effects (Watkins, 1990). The factors include at least general emotional arousal, specific emotional arousal for aspects of the event that might be recalled, and measures of rehearsal. Both "thought about" and "told about" measures might be taken or combined as rehearsal (e.g., Rubin, Groth, & Goldsmith, 1984). The number of times the event was talked about, in contrast to being thought about, includes the number of times that new information could have been added, possibly distorting the final recall.

In all of this there is a need to compare flashbulb memories to "control" memories. The concept of control is difficult because theoretical constructs that differ across experiments determine which aspects of flashbulb memories need to be controlled. There is also the practical problem of getting "control" events to be recalled at all at the long retention interval. In any case, the "control" memories cannot be replaced by a vague idea of what people would recall or by the assumption of perfect recall (Schmidt & Bohannon, 1988).

Another vexing problem for the especially ambitious ambulance chaser is the distinction between central and peripheral events. Brown and Kulik stressed that the observation in need of explanation is not why people remember the nationally important event, but why they remember trivial details of their lives that occurred at the time. The problem is how to define what is central and what is peripheral. The issue in the conference that hinged most on this is whether emotionality focuses attention on the central, emotion-provoking aspects of the event or not.

By clever experimentation and thoughtful theory we have made progress, but in doing so we have set ourselves a difficult task. I wish us all good luck.

## REFERENCES

Barclay, C. R. (1986). Schematization of autobiographical memory. In D. C. Rubin (Ed.), *Autobiographical memory* (pp. 82–99). New York: Cambridge University Press.

272    D. C. RUBIN

Bohannon, J. N. (1988). Flashbulb memories of the space shuttle disaster: A tale of two theories. *Cognition, 29*, 179–196.

Bohannon, J. N., & Schmidt, S. R. (1989). Flashbulb memories for the space shuttle disaster: Three lags and three theories. Unpublished manuscript.

Brewer, W. F. (1986). What is autobiographical memory? In U. Neisser & E. Winograd (Eds.), *Remembering reconsidered: Ecological and traditional approaches to the study of memory* (pp. 21–90). New York: Cambridge University Press.

Brewer, W. F. (1988). Memory of randomly sampled autobiographical events. In D. C. Rubin (Ed.), *Autobiographical memory* (pp. 25–49). New York: Cambridge University Press.

Brown, R. (1989). Roger Brown. In G. Lindzey (Ed.), *A history of psychology in autobiography. Vol. VIII* (pp. 37–60). Stanford: Stanford University Press.

Brown, R., & Kulik, J. (1977). Flashbulb memories. *Cognition, 5*, 73–99.

Brown, R., & McNeill, D. (1966). The "tip of the tongue" phenomenon. *Journal of Verbal Learning and Verbal Behavior, 5*, 325–337.

Bruce, D. (1989). Functional explanations of memory. In L. W. Poon, D. C. Rubin, & B. A. Wilson (Eds.), *Everyday cognition in adult and later life* (pp. 44–58). New York: Cambridge University Press.

Cofer, C. N. (1943). An analysis of errors made in learning prose material. *Journal of Experimental Psychology, 32*, 399–410.

Colgrove, F. (1899). Individual memories. *American Psychologist, 10*, 228–255.

Fivush, R., & Slackman, E. A. (1986). The acquisition and development of scripts. In K. Nelson (Ed.), *Event knowledge: Structure and function in development* (pp. 71–96) Hillsdale, NJ: Erlbaum.

Greenwald, A. G. (1980). The totalitarian ego: Fabrication and revision of personal history. *American Psychologist, 35*, 605–618.

Hyman, I. E., Jr., & Rubin, D. C. (1990). Memorabeatlia: A naturalistic study of long-term memory. *Memory and Cognition, 18*, 205–214.

Johnson, M. K., & Raye, C. L. (1981). Reality monitoring. *Psychological Review, 88*, 67–85.

Larsen, S. F. (1988). Remembering without experiencing: Memory for reported events. In U. Neisser & E. Winograd (Eds.), *Remembering reconsidered: Ecological and traditional approaches to the study of memory* (pp. 326–355). New York: Cambridge University Press.

Neisser, U. (1967). *Cognitive psychology*. New York: Appleton-Century-Crofts.

Neisser, U. (1982). Snapshots or benchmarks? In U. Neisser (Ed.), *Memory observed* (pp. 43–48). San Francisco: Freeman.

Newell, A. (1973). You can't play 20 questions with nature and win: Projective comments on the papers of this symposium. In W. G. Chase (Ed.), *Visual information processing* (pp. 283–308). New York: Academic Press.

Robinson, J. A. (1986). Temporal reference systems and autobiographical memory. In D. C. Rubin (Ed.), *Autobiographical memory* (pp. 159–188). New York: Cambridge University Press.

Rubin, D. C. (1975). Within word structure in the tip-of-the-tongue phenomenon. *Journal of Verbal Learning and Verbal Behavior, 14*, 392–397.

Rubin, D. C. (1988). Learning poetic language. In F. Kessel (Ed.), *The development of language and language researchers: Essays in honor of Roger Brown* (pp. 339–351). Hillsdale, NJ: Erlbaum.

Rubin, D. C. (1989). Issues of regularity and control: Confessions of a regularity freak. In L. W. Poon, D. C. Rubin, & B. A. Wilson (Eds.), *Everyday cognition in adult and later life* (pp. 84–103). New York: Cambridge University Press.

ubin, D. C., Groth, L., & Goldsmith, D. (1984). Olfactory cuing of autobiographical memory. *American Journal of Psychology, 97,* 493–507.

ubin, D. C., & Kozin, M. (1984). Vivid memories. *Cognition, 16,* 81–95.

ubin, D. C., Stolzfus, E. R., & Wall, K. L. (1991). The abstraction of form in
semantic categories. *Memory and Cognition, 19,* 1–7.

ubin, D. C., & Wallace, W. T. (1989). Rhyme and reason: Analyses of dual cues.
*Journal of Experimental Psychology: Learning, Memory, and Cognition, 15,* 698–709.

chmidt, S. R., & Bohannon, J. N. (1988). In defense of the flashbulb-memory
hypothesis: A comment on McCloskey, Wible, and Cohen. *Journal of Experimental
Psychology: General, 117,* 332–335.

Wallace, W. T., & Rubin, D. C. (1988). "The Wreck of the Old 97": A real event
remembered in song. In U. Neisser & E. Winograd (Eds.), *Remembering reconsidered: Ecological and traditional approaches to the study of memory* (pp. 283–310). New
York: Cambridge University Press.

Wallace, W. T., & Rubin, D. C. (1991). Characteristics and constraints in ballads
and their effects on memory. *Discourse Processes, 14,* 181–202.

Watkins, M. J. (1990). Mediationism and the obfuscation of memory. *American
Psychologist, 45,* 328–335.

## 14

# The theoretical and empirical status of the flashbulb memory hypothesis

WILLIAM F. BREWER

The purpose of this chapter is to analyze the concept of "flashbulb" memory and contrast it with other forms of human memory. The construct of flashbulb memory was introduced in a seminal paper by Brown and Kulik (1977) to account for memories of events such as the assassination of John F. Kennedy. Brown and Kulik described flashbulb memories as memories for the circumstances of hearing about a highly surprising and consequential event. These memories were said to be like a photograph, to show very little forgetting, and to be produced by a special purpose biological mechanism. Most recent work on this topic derives from the Brown and Kulik paper, and this chapter will begin with a conceptual analysis of that paper. The analysis will examine, in turn, each of the major theoretical and empirical claims of the original Brown and Kulik paper.

## Brown and Kulik – theory

### Circumstances (news reception context)

The core phenomenon described by Brown and Kulik (1977) is that certain events give rise to memories that show little forgetting. These flashbulb memories include both the central event *and* the circumstances in which one learned of the event.

### Mental imagery

It appears to me that Brown and Kulik believe that the recollection of flashbulb memories involves the occurrence of visual images. Brown and Kulik do not state this explicitly, but it is the only interpretation I can give to their statement that flashbulb memories have a "primary, 'live' quality that is almost perceptual" (p. 74).

274

### Memory for details

Brown and Kulik make a number of statements that suggest that they believe that flashbulb memories contain an exceptional degree of detail. For example, they state that flashbulb memories are "very like a photograph that indiscriminately preserves the scene" (p. 74).

### Initiating conditions

Brown and Kulik hypothesized that the events that lead to flashbulb memories are highly surprising and highly consequential. This dual criterion is presumably designed to include events such as the assassination of major political figures, but to eliminate events such as having your shoelace break off in your hand as you tie your shoe (high surprise; low consequentiality), or gradually learning that the ozone layer is becoming depleted (low surprise; high consequentiality).

### Representation

Brown and Kulik suggested that flashbulb memories have two parallel forms of representation: The flashbulb event itself is represented in a nonverbal, "imaginal" form (p. 86). With rehearsal, the initial nonverbal representation leads to a second representation in the form of a "verbal narrative" (p. 86).

### Veridicality

There is no explicit discussion in Brown and Kulik of the accuracy of flashbulb memories. However, they did make such statements such: "[a flashbulb memory] is very like a photograph that indiscriminately preserves the scene" (p. 74). Statements such as this certainly do invite the inference that flashbulb memories are veridical records of the flashbulb event and its circumstances, and most subsequent researchers (e.g., Christianson, 1989; McCloskey, Wible, & Cohen, 1988; Neisser, 1982; ) have interpreted Brown and Kulik's paper as asserting that flashbulb memories are veridical.

If Brown and Kulik had chosen to elaborate this aspect of their proposal, it is possible they would have adopted a two-factor theory. The flashbulb metaphor and the proposed biological "Now Print!" mechanism certainly suggest a veridical memory trace. However, in a discussion of flashbulb recalls, they note that these verbal narratives might be produced through a "constructive process." Therefore they might have proposed a two-factor theory, in which the original nonverbal flashbulb representation is veridical, whereas the narrative description of this event is reconstructed in ways that may not be veridical. The scientific value of such a two-factor theory would be considerably strengthened if it were combined with proposals about how to investigate the two forms of representation independently.

### Forgetting

Brown and Kulik took a strong position on the issue of the forgetting of flashbulb memories. In several places they referred to such memories as "permanent," and in their most qualified discussion of the issue they stated that a flashbulb memory is "fixed for a very long time, and conceivably permanently" (p. 85).

### Retention theories

Brown and Kulik's discussions of the mechanisms that lead to extraordinary retention for flashbulb memories are hard to follow. They proposed that rehearsals play an important role in flashbulb memory. They suggested that the rehearsal might be covert (i.e., just thinking about the event) or overt (i.e., telling someone about the event). Finally, they hypothesized that consequentiality leads to rehearsal, and rehearsal allows easier access to more elaborated flashbulb memories. At first glance it is not obvious why they need a rehearsal mechanism, given that they also postulate a special biological mechanism that produces permanent traces for flashbulb memories. Perhaps the best interpretation of their position is that there is a permanent nonverbal flashbulb memory representation, but that rehearsal operates to produce very high retention of the verbal narrative describing that nonverbal memory. This interpretation gives a fairly good account of the text except that Brown and Kulik also have a discussion of the possible role of a nonverbal rehearsal mechanism that presumably operates on the original nonverbal representation. This mechanism would once again lead to the paradox of postulating a rehearsal mechanism to strengthen an already permanent memory trace.

### Core theoretical claims

Brown and Kulik's basic theoretical proposal is that when a consequential event occurs that exceeds a particular threshold for surprise it causes a biological "Now Print!" mechanism to operate and to record permanently all immediately previous and contemporaneous brain events" (p. 87). They hypothesized that the initial imaginal representation is rehearsed, leading to the formation of a structured narrative representation.

### Type of memory

In essence, the Brown and Kulik paper can be taken as a claim to have discovered a new form of memory. They characterize the new form of memory and give it a new name. They assert that it is produced under unique circumstances (of surprise and consequentiality) and has unique properties (little or no forgetting). Finally, they propose that it is produced by a special purpose biological mechanism.

## Brown and Kulik – data and evaluation

The next section of this chapter describes Brown and Kulik's empirical findings and then evaluates each aspect of their theory in light of their data.

### Experiment

Brown and Kulik gathered data on flashbulb memories from 80 subjects. They gave these subjects a series of nine events (e.g., the assassination of John F. Kennedy) and asked them if "you recall the circumstances in which you first heard [about the event]" (1977, p. 78). For those events receiving an affirmative answer, subjects were asked to recall the episode, rate it on a scale of consequentiality, and indicate their estimate of the number of times they had rehearsed the event (type of rehearsal left unspecified).

### Circumstances (news reception context)

Brown and Kulik state that flashbulb memories include both the initiating event and the circumstances in which one learned about the event. From the data presented one can calculate that 99% of the subjects recalled the circumstances in which they heard about the assassination of John F. Kennedy and 56% of the subjects recalled the circumstances in which they heard about the assassination of Robert F. Kennedy (these two were the strongest of the nine historical events investigated). It does seem impressive that these subjects were able to recall the circumstances of hearing of events that occurred 8 and 13 years earlier. This is one of the strongest pieces of evidence for Brown and Kulik's characterization of flashbulb memories as a distinct form of memory.

### Mental imagery

Brown and Kulik gathered no data on their subjects' reports of imagery during the recall process and so they provide no evidence in their study to support the view that flashbulb memories involve the occurrence of mental imagery.

### Memory for details

In support of the hypothesis that flashbulb memories contain unusual amounts of detail Brown and Kulik note that in attempting to classify the information in subjects' recall protocols there was often "completely idiosyncratic content" that could not be classified (e.g., "We all had on our little blue uniforms" p. 80). They give no further details about this category of information, but in the conclusion of the paper they argue that the fact that "many accounts included utterly idiosyncratic and, in a sense, accidental content" (p. 95) was strong evidence for the "Now Print!" memory mechanism. Obviously, Brown and Kulik do not provide enough information to allow an evaluation of their empirical claim. However, even if they had provided more information about the recall protocols it is not clear that it would have been interpretable without equivalent data from nonflashbulb events.

### Initiating conditions

Brown and Kulik provide no direct evidence to support the position that a high level of surprise is required to produce a flashbulb memory. Most of the events they asked about would probably have been fairly surprising, but without a measure of surprise and a control group of nonsurprising events, this aspect of their theory remains untested. Brown and Kulik did obtain data to test their hypothesis that a high level of consequentiality is required to produce flashbulb memories. Examination of the data shows that for the events that led to flashbulb memories, in 5 of the 9 cases the mean score on consequentiality was less than 2.0 on a scale where 5.0 indicated "very high" consequentiality. Thus, the data on rated consequentiality is inconsistent with their hypothesis.

### Recall content (canonical categories)

Brown and Kulik carried out a qualitative analysis of the content of the flashbulb memories. They found a number of recurring categories in these recalls: place, ongoing event, own affect, informant, affect in others, and aftermath. They assert (p. 95) that the occurrence of these "canonical" forms in flashbulb memory recalls is direct evidence for their basic "Now Print!" theory.

This issue requires some conceptual analysis. First, one needs to be very careful to distinguish: (a) the event, (b) the representation of the event, and

(c) the narrative recall of the representation. Let us first focus on the *event*. It seems to me that any event experienced by a human being must contain at least the following categories: a place, a time, an experiencing person, the person's actions, the person's thoughts, and the person's affect. For more complex events (e.g., events involving additional individuals) other categories will be added to this minimal list.

All of these event categories have the potential to be *represented in memory*. My earlier work on memory for randomly selected events (Brewer, 1988) suggests that most of these categories are represented in memory for ordinary, everyday events. The one exception is time. Although autobiographical memories of this type are memories of a unique moment in time (e.g., 10:05 a.m. on September 21, 1990) the time information is not explicitly encoded in the memory representation in the way that location is (e.g., at my desk in my office at the Beckman Institute). Instead, time information is typically derived by inference from the other categories of information ("The sun was just setting so it must have been about 7:00 p.m." or "I was in class so it had to be either a Monday or Wednesday").

Finally, one must consider the *narrative form of the recall* of an event. Individuals carrying out a recall obey a variety of conventions about what to include in a narrative (Brewer, 1980). They do not include information that they think will be obvious to the listener/reader. Thus, in recalling recent personally experienced events, individuals typically do not explicitly mention their own age and gender although they will typically give that type of information about other individuals mentioned in the narrative who are not known to the listener/reader. Another important aspect of the narrative structure is the order in which information is presented. Brown and Kulik do not present any data on the ordering of canonical recall categories for their flashbulb memories even though this is an aspect of the recalls that could be influenced by repeated telling or repeated rehearsals.

With these issues in mind, we can examine Brown and Kulik's assertion about the canonical categories in flashbulb recalls. First, we need to consider the ecology of the environment (cf. Brewer, 1988, pp. 77–78; Neisser, 1986) associated with flashbulb memory events. Brown and Kulik focused on flashbulb memories for traumatic public events. For most individuals, events of this type will not be personally experienced; instead, the individual will first hear of the event from the news media or from another person. Larsen (this volume) has referred to this special type of event as the "reception context." Thus, for the events studied by Brown and Kulik the canonical situation consisted of the individual going about his or her normal daily activities (school, work, home), having those events interrupted by someone bringing the news of the traumatic public event, and then experiencing a strong emotional reaction to this event. Overall, this analysis of the ecology of the environment associated with Brown and Kulik's flashbulb events suggests that the canonical recall categories (place, ongoing event, own affect, informant, affect in others, and aftermath) are simply reflections in the recalls of the canonical *event structure* of an individual learning about a traumatic public event. This analysis shifts the locus of the observed regularity from the structure of recall to the structure of reception situations for traumatic public events. Nevertheless one might still want to argue that the regularity obtained in recall remains a unique, though indirect, index for flashbulb events. There are, however, severe problems with this attempt to retain the use of canonical recalls as a criterion for flashbulb memory.

First, consider the case of nonflashbulb memory for an ordinary reception event such as someone coming in to an individual's office and reporting that it had begun to snow. The results of my study of memory for randomly chosen events (Brewer, 1988) strongly suggest that subjects' successful recalls for these everyday events would contain much the same information as Brown and Kulik's canonical recalls (except possibly for reduced mention of affect).

Second, consider the case of flashbulb memories for events other than news reception events. Rubin and Kozin (1984) carried out a study examining flashbulb memories that used free recall rather than the cued recall technique of Brown and Kulik. It appears that the vast majority of flashbulb memories obtained with this open-ended procedure were not news reception situations. Instead, they tended to be of such events as being in an accident or appearing in front of an audience. Rubin and Kozin note (p. 87) that they were unable to use all of Brown and Kulik's canonical scoring categories because for most of the events there was no informant – a finding consistent with the view that many flashbulb recalls do not have the canonical structure described by Brown and Kulik.

Overall then, this analysis suggests that Brown and Kulik's canonical recall categories can occur for nonflashbulb memories and that most flashbulb memories do not give rise to the full set of canonical categories. Thus, the occurrence of the canonical recall categories cannot be taken to provide evidence for a unique "Now Print!" theory of memory as argued by Brown and Kulik.

### Representation

Brown and Kulik provide no data relevant to their hypothesis that flashbulb memories are represented in both a nonverbal, imaginal form and in a verbal, narrative form.

### Experimental definition

The experimental definition of flashbulb memory used by Brown and Kulik consisted of two criteria: (a) that the subjects answer "yes" to the question

"Do you recall the circumstances in which you first heard that . . .?" and (b) that the subjects recall some information from at least one of the six canonical categories. This choice of criteria seems dramatically unconstrained by their theory. It includes no information about the type of event so it could easily apply to such ordinary events as "Do you recall the circumstances in which you heard today's weather?" It includes no criteria associated with the "almost perceptual clarity" of the memories. The requirement that the recalls include merely one canonical category seems extremely weak given their claims about the permanence of the memory trace and the biological "Now Print!" mechanism.

### Veridicality

The flashbulb memory recalls analyzed by Brown and Kulik were gathered from 1 to 13 years after the original event and so with this set of data there was no way to examine the accuracy of the subjects' reports. In a later discussion of this issue Brown (1986) agreed that the term "flashbulb" memory did suggest that the memories were veridical even though there was no evidence in the earlier study to support this view.

### Forgetting

Brown and Kulik found that after 13 years only 1% of their subjects appeared to show forgetting for the circumstances in which they heard about the assassination of John F. Kennedy and after 8 years only 44% appeared to show forgetting for the circumstances associated with hearing about the assassination of Robert F. Kennedy. These are certainly the most interesting data in Brown and Kulik's study. However, they can only be suggestive. First, we do not know if the circumstances that the subjects' report are accurate. If the circumstances reported by the subjects are not the actual ones that occurred years earlier, then they do not provide evidence for exceptional recall. If flashbulb reports do contain significantly different amounts of (nonveridical) circumstances compared to other forms of memory, this would be an interesting phenomenon, but not one necessarily related to the issue of retention. The second and more fundamental problem with Brown and Kulik's retention data is that there are no comparable data from a set of nonflashbulb memories to provide differential support for the claim that flashbulb memories show little or no forgetting.

### Retention theories

Brown and Kulik predicted that events with higher consequentiality would show more frequent rehearsals and their data showed a high positive correlation between rated consequentiality and reported number of rehearsals. They also predicted that more frequent rehearsal would lead to longer and more elaborate narratives and they found high correlations supporting this prediction. These data are consistent with a rehearsal explanation of the high retention of flashbulb events. However, the puzzle here is why Brown and Kulik need such a mechanism. If flashbulb events lead to a more or less permanent nonverbal memory trace it would seem that the subjects should be able to use the nonverbal trace to generate a narrative description whenever they are asked for recall, and there would be little need to postulate a rehearsal mechanism to account for low rates of forgetting.

### Type of memory

Brown and Kulik do not provide an explicit contrast between their description of flashbulb memory (i.e., unique memory for circumstances, no forgetting, biological mechanism) and other forms of memory such as rote memory or semantic memory. However, the present analysis of their paper would not support a claim that flashbulb memories are a unique type of memory. Their data do not provide evidence for a unique role of surprise and consequentiality in producing flashbulb memories. In addition, it appears that the occurrence of the canonical recall categories is due to the structure of the reception event episode and is not the indicator of a special type of memory. Brown and Kulik do offer suggestive evidence that people recall the circumstances of flashbulb events for long periods of time, but without appropriate control items it is not clear if this is specific to flashbulb memories. Finally, they provide no evidence for a specific biological memory mechanism.

### Overall evaluation

The Brown and Kulik (1977) paper is innovative and opened up a new field of research. Yet, it seems clear that a careful analysis of this paper shows that the theory is inconsistent, that the data presented in the paper are not appropriate for testing the theory, and that for the few instances where there is relevant data it sometimes goes against the theory (see McCloskey, Wible, & Cohen, 1988, for a similar conclusion).

## Importance of the Brown and Kulik study

Given the severe problems found with many aspects of Brown and Kulik's (1977) study an obvious question arises – why has this paper been so influential?

## An original topic of investigation

One clear reason for the impact of this paper is that it dealt with a phenomenon that had rarely been studied, and that tapped the shared intuitions of almost every reader. They caught the attention of the scientific community to such a degree that 13 years later this chapter is part of a volume that is entirely devoted to the topic of flashbulb memory!

## Personal memory

At the time that Brown and Kulik wrote their paper, the major focus of memory research was on topics of rote memory and semantic memory. They were asserting that flashbulb memory was a different form of memory. I agree that they were studying a different form of memory, but have argued (Brewer, 1986, pp. 35–36) that flashbulb memories are best treated as a subclass of a broader class of memory that I called "personal memory." I described personal memory as "a recollection of a particular episode from an individual's past. It frequently appears to be a 'reliving' of the individual's phenomenal experience during that earlier moment. The content almost always includes reports of visual imagery, with less frequent occurrences of other forms of imagery. Other aspects of the earlier mental experience, such as occurrent thoughts and felt affect, are also found in the reports . . . Finally, personal memories are typically accompanied by a belief that they are a veridical record of the originally experienced episode" (Brewer, 1986, pp. 34–35). Brown and Kulik's description of flashbulb memory is essentially identical to this description of personal memory, except that they restrict the subject matter to surprising and consequential events, whereas the class of personal memories is not restricted in that way, but can include memories of any event, mundane or extraordinary. Therefore, it seems to me, that another major reason for the importance of the Brown and Kulik paper is that it was one of the first papers on the topic of personal memory to appear at a time when modern empirical work on this topic was just beginning with the studies of Crovitz and Schiffman (1974) and Robinson (1976).

## A copy theory

The Brown and Kulik theory is an example of a "copy theory" of memory (i.e., a theory that assumes that the memory representation is a mental copy of some aspect of the world). This is a clear and simple type of memory theory and has always been attractive to memory researchers. Brown and Kulik provide a very compelling account of this form of theory with the name "flashbulb memory" and descriptions such as "[at the moment of hearing about the Kennedy assassination] much of the world stopped still to have its picture taken" (p. 80). Copy theories have been particularly attractive for theorists in the area of personal memory. I have noted (Brewer, 1986, p. 41) that this affinity for copy theories in the area of personal memory may be partly due to the strong belief that the *theorists* have in the veridicality of their own personal memories.

Thus, it seems to me that there were good reasons for researchers to be excited by the Brown and Kulik paper even though there were serious problems with both its theory and its data.

## Current status of the flashbulb memory hypothesis

In the next section I will go through each aspect of Brown and Kulik's theory of flashbulb memory and evaluate the theory in light of recent work on this topic.

### Circumstances (news reception context)

A large number of studies of flashbulb memory have been published since Brown and Kulik's initial paper. These studies clearly show that for flashbulb events (e.g., traumatic public events) most subjects report being able to recall the circumstances of hearing about the event many months or years later (Bohannon, 1988; Christianson, 1989; McCloskey, Wible, & Cohen, 1988; Neisser & Harsch, this volume; Pillemer, 1984; Winograd & Killinger, 1983; Yarmey & Bull, 1978).

*Conclusion.* There can now be little doubt that people report being able to recall the circumstances of receiving news about dramatic events. Much of the recent work on flashbulb memory to be reviewed in this section can be thought of as attempts to provide an interpretation of these findings.

### Mental imagery

Rubin and Kozin (1984) found that high degrees of visual imagery were associated with the occurrence of flashbulb memories. On a scale of visual imagery 58% of their flashbulb memories were given ratings of 6 or 7 on a scale where 7 was defined as "vivid as normal vision," and not a single flashbulb memory was rated as "no image at all." Pillemer (1984) found that 73% of his college faculty sample reported visual images associated with their flashbulb memories of the assassination attempt on Ronald Reagan. Neisser and Harsch (this volume) found that 3 years after the *Challenger* explosion their undergraduate subjects gave a mean rating of 5.35 on a scale of visual imagery (maximum imagery = 7) for their flashbulb memories of hearing about the explosion.

*Conclusions.* The evidence seems to show that most and perhaps all flashbulb memories are associated with strong visual imagery.

### Vividness versus mental imagery

It seems to me that there has been some confusion in the flashbulb literature about the terms "vividness" and "imagery." The original Brown and Kulik paper did not use either term, but I have interpreted their description of flashbulbs as "very like a photograph" and having a "quality that is almost perceptual" (p. 74) to be a description of visual imagery. Their avoidance of the term mental imagery is perhaps understandable in light of the fact that Brown (1958, pp. 82–93) has taken a rather harsh view on the possible role of imagery in a number of mental processes.

However, it is not so clear what is meant in many of the later papers. *The Random House Dictionary* (1968) gives a number of meanings for "vivid," such as "strong" and "lively." It seems to me that these meanings can be applied to human memory without necessarily implying anything about mental imagery. However, the dictionary *also* gives a definition of vivid that explicitly refers to mental imagery ("forming distinct and striking mental images").

Some researchers investigating flashbulb memory overtly use the term "visual imagery" in their discussions of flashbulb memory (Pillemer, 1984). Other researchers (McCloskey, Wible, & Cohen, 1988; Winograd & Killinger, 1983) use "vividness" with no further elaboration. Rubin and Kozin (1984) use the term "vividness" in the theoretical parts of their paper in ways that are perhaps more consistent with the first set of definitions from the *Random House Dictionary*, but the instructions for the subjects asked them to rate their memory on a vividness scale where "1 means no image at all and 7 means as vivid as normal vision" (p. 86). Reisberg, Heuer, McLean, and O'Shaughnessy (1988) report a study examining the vividness of flashbulb memories where vividness was defined as how "complete and detailed" the memory was. These researchers also included an independent scale of mental imagery in their Experiment 1 and found very high correlations between rated vividness and rated imagery (D. Reisberg personal communication, November 27, 1990).

*Conclusions.* The ambiguity of the term "vividness" in English has a number of implications for work in this area. If researchers mean mental imagery by the term, then they should stop being coy and include this in their theoretical treatment and then they should gather appropriate mental imagery data from their subjects. If researchers mean something other than mental imagery by the term "vividness," then they need to explain what they do mean and gather appropriate data from subjects to test their position.

*Memory for details*

There has been little explicit attempt to investigate the claim that flashbulb memories contain an unusual amount of idiosyncratic details. Rubin and Kozin (1984) reported that 71% of their subjects' recalls contained "extraneous details" (p. 87). Christianson (1989) reports data on two questions of "specific detailed information" (e.g., information about the clothing worn at the time) and finds that these items show moderate rates of retention. It is not clear how to interpret these findings. Many of the recalls from my study of ordinary personal memories (Brewer, 1988) contained "idiosyncratic" and "extraneous details." For example, one subject's recall of walking home from the grocery store included the following information: "Bag was heavy – old lady & white shaggy on leash just passed me. Girl across street who looks like C. Birds bickering on tree limb."

*Conclusions.* The claim that flashbulb memories contain unusual amounts of detail cannot be evaluated without: (a) more explicit descriptions of what counts as idiosyncratic detail, and (b) comparisons with appropriate nonflashbulb events.

*Initiating conditions*

Neisser (1982) argued against the hypothesis that surprisingness is essential for the development of flashbulb memories and stated that one can have flashbulb memories for expected, nonsurprising events (e.g., the resignation of Richard Nixon). Winograd and Killinger (1983) provided data showing that two nonsurprising events (the first moon landing; Nixon's resignation) lead to significant numbers of flashbulb memories. Rubin and Kozin (1984) found that many of the flashbulb memories that they obtained were rated low on a scale of surprisingness. Reisberg, Heuer, McLean, and O'Shaughnessy (1988) found no significant correlation between surprise and vividness. However, Christianson (1989) studied several possible initiating conditions and found that only rated surprise was significantly related to higher recall of the circumstances of a flashbulb event.

Pillemer (1984) and Bohannon (1988) reported data on the intensity of emotion and amount of recall. In both cases the effects of emotional intensity on recall were somewhat inconsistent, but generally positive. Reisberg, Heuer, McLean, and O'Shaughnessy (1988) found a strong relation between the intensity of emotion and the rated vividness of flashbulb memories in three separate experiments. Christianson (1989) found no significant relation between intensity of emotion and recall consistency. Neisser and Harsch (this volume) found no significant relationship between intensity of emotion and recall accuracy.

Neisser (1982) proposed that the crucial initiating condition for flashbulb memories is that the timeline for public history is momentarily brought into alignment with an individual's personal timeline. Rubin and Kozin (1984) used a free recall technique to obtain flashbulb memories ([recall the] "3 clearest memories from your past"). With this procedure only 3% of the obtained flashbulb memories were above the midpoint on a scale of "national importance." These data raise severe problems for a theory of flashbulb memories based on a public event timeline.

Rubin and Kozin's (1984) data on freely recalled flashbulb memories also do not support Brown and Kulik's hypothesis that consequentiality is crucial for the occurrence of flashbulb memories. Many of the flashbulb memories in Rubin and Kozin's sample were rated low on a scale of consequentiality. However, Reisberg, Heuer, McLean, and O'Shaughnessy (1988) found a strong relation between rated vividness of flashbulb memories and a rating for personal consequentiality. In Rubin and Kozin's (1984) data on unconstrained recall of flashbulb memories the characteristic of the events that showed the highest rated value was a scale of "personal importance."

*Conclusions.* Clearly, the research in this area does not provide a consistent characterization of the psychological properties of the type of events that lead to flashbulb memories. There are a number of possible explanations for this state of affairs. It may be that one or more of the psychological states postulated to be crucial are in fact crucial, but that the particular techniques used to measure these states have been faulty. Another possibility is that the researchers in the area of flashbulb memory have not focused on the relevant variables. For example, in my work on ordinary personal memories, the uniqueness (distinctiveness) of events was the major determiner of successful memory, yet measures of this dimension have rarely been used in the study of flashbulb memories. However, my guess is that there is some set of personally experienced emotional states associated with that flashbulb memory phenomenon and that future work will be able to resolve this issue.

### Recall content (canonical categories)

Neisser (1982) argued that Brown and Kulik's canonical recall categories are due to narrative conventions. Although there may be some role for narrative conventions in the occurrence of the canonical recall categories, it seems to me, as discussed earlier, that it is the structure of the subjects' environment that is most directly responsible for Brown and Kulik's canonical recall categories.

Christianson (1989) suggested that the canonical recall categories are "reconstructed from recollections of the gist of the event" (p. 441). In particular, he suggested that subjects recalled some core information (e.g., "I heard the news in the morning") and then filled in the details of the canonical categories with script information (e.g., "I must have been in my bed reading the newspaper as I do every Saturday morning"). This is a very strong reconstructive hypothesis and makes clear predictions. Essentially, all of the information in the recalls gathered by Christianson should be script information and none should be unique and specific to the particular day of the Palme assassination. Christianson does not provide a qualitative analysis of his recall data to support this strong reconstructive hypothesis. However, there are a few examples of recalls given in his paper, and they suggest that a qualitative analysis of the full data set would not support the extreme reconstructive approach. For example, one subject stated, "My daughter called and woke me up in the morning – she had heard on the radio that Olof Palme was murdered" (p. 438). It appears to me that most of the information in this recall was unique information about the events of the day of the assassination and not reconstructed from this woman's script for her usual morning activities. If many of the recalls were of this form then the data would not support a reconstructive script theory of the canonical recall categories. Instead, they would support the position that the categories were reflections of the particular event situation on the day of the Palme assassination.

*Conclusions.* Overall, the data on the occurrence of the canonical recall categories seem to me best interpreted as reflecting the events that occur in a news reception situation. It also seems likely that some additional structure (e.g., category order) is imposed on the information in the narrative recalls, but there is no evidence for this in the current studies.

### Representation

There has been little discussion of the issue of the form of representation of flashbulb memories. The discussion given earlier in this chapter distinguishing the characteristics of the events, the representation of the events, and the narrative description of the events is probably the most detailed account of this topic since the original proposals of Brown and Kulik (1977).

### Experimental definition

There has been little progress in developing theory-based criteria for defining the category of flashbulb memories. Some researchers (e.g., Winograd & Killinger, 1983) have followed Brown and Kulik's criteria of a "yes" answer to the circumstances question plus the recall of one or more canonical categories. Other researchers have used an even weaker criterion, requiring only a positive answer to a question about memory for the circumstances of hearing about the event (Pillemer, 1984; Yarmey & Bull, 1978). Some researchers have assumed that if subjects give answers to a number of questions about the circumstances of their hearing about an event, then the memory is a flashbulb memory (Christianson, 1989; McCloskey, Wible, & Cohen, 1988). It would appear that all of these definitions dramatically underspecify the phenomenon being studied. Almost all of them would also include memories for the circumstances of ordinary reception events. In practice all of these studies involve the recall of traumatic public events over long time intervals and thus have implicit criteria (i.e., type of events, little forgetting) for flashbulb memories that are usually not made explicit in the criteria. Rubin and Kozin (1984) adopted an interesting approach. They provided subjects with an abstract definition of flashbulb memories (e.g., "when your brain 'takes a picture' of an event"), gave examples of the type of memories they were interested in (e.g., hearing about Pearl Harbor, seeing an accident), and asked their subjects to give their three clearest examples of this type of memory. This approach, unlike most of the others, makes some use of theory in defining the memories.

*Conclusions.* Overall, this analysis of recent work suggests the need for the development of experimental definitions of flashbulb memory that provide a full and explicit test of the particular researcher's theory of flashbulb memory.

## Veridicality

Neisser (1982) described a long-time personal flashbulb memory for the bombing of Pearl Harbor, which he had later (when he became a reconstructive memory theorist?) decided was inaccurate. However, Thompson and Cowan (1986) have provided evidence about the public announcement of that event that suggests that Neisser's memory was much more accurate than he thought it was. Pillemer (1984) reported data that showed that flashbulb memory recalls over a 6-month interval were "quite consistent" (p. 75). McCloskey, Wible, and Cohen (1988) found about 8% of errors between two flashbulb memory recalls separated by about 9 months and note that none of these errors were "grossly incongruent" (p. 175). Larsen (this volume) reports that his memory for the reception context of two of the traumatic public events in his diary study were quite inaccurate. However, the force of this finding is somewhat reduced because these two items did not reach his experimental criterion for flashbulb status and apparently his recall of the contexts of his five clearest flashbulbs ("High Context Confidence" memories) was, in fact, fairly accurate.

Neisser and Harsch (this volume) provide the clearest data that have been gathered on the topic of the veridicality of flashbulb memories. They collected data on memory of hearing about the *Challenger* explosion 24 hours after the event and obtained recalls 2.5 and 3 years later. They found that the subjects showed high confidence (mean of 4.17 on a scale with 5.0 as maximum confidence). Yet 25% of their subjects' recalls were totally inaccurate and only 7% showed essentially perfect recalls, with the remainder showing intermediate degrees of accuracy. The Neisser and Harsch data seem to me to show definitively that a proportion of "classic" flashbulb memories reporting the circumstances involved in hearing about an emotional event are simply in error.

However, I want to make an argument that the *type* of error may not be as dramatic as suggested by Neisser and Harsch. In my study of memory for randomly sampled events (Brewer, 1988) I classified errors into: wrong events, wrong time slice, and overt errors. Recalls were classified as *wrong events* when the subject simply recalled some totally different event from the one originally recorded. Recalls were classified as *wrong time slice* when the subject appeared to be recalling the correct event, but the particular moment recalled was slightly (seconds to minutes) offset in time from the originally recorded event. Recalls were classified as *overt errors* when it appeared that the subject was trying to recall the originally recorded event, but there were overt contradictions between the two records. In my data the vast majority of errors (97% for event recalls) were of the first two types and I argued that these were better thought of as retrieval errors, not as reconstructive errors.

It is interesting to examine the Neisser and Harsch findings in light of this data on errors in ordinary personal memories. Neisser and Harsch give one protocol as evidence of how completely wrong a subject's flashbulb memory could be. This subject appears to have heard something about the explosion while in a class and then went to her room after class and watched TV accounts of the accident with her roommate. In her recall 2.5 years later she reports that she first heard about the event while she was in her dorm room with her roommate and later called her parents. It seems to me quite plausible that she did, in fact, watch TV with her roommate and call her parents, but that, 2.5 years later, when she tried to recall where she first heard the news, she retrieved the later event of watching the news in her dorm. By this account what she forgot was merely where she *first* heard the news, a form of source amnesia (Larsen, this volume; Schacter, Harbluk, & McLachlan, 1984). Neisser and Harsch report that their analysis of the recalls showed that 12 of 42 subjects shifted the source of their initial information from some other informant to a TV source. This suggests that the retrieval account given above for the one reported protocol might be a relatively general effect. However, note that a retrieval analysis cannot account for all of the data. In the recall carried out 2.5 years after the event the subject states that she first heard about the *Challenger* explosion on TV in ner room ("it came on a news flash," Neisser and Harsch, this volume). This would appear to be a true reconstructive error driven by the need to provide a plausible account of how she first came to hear about the event. Overall, it appears to me that many of the errors reported by the subjects in Neisser and Harsch's study are retrieval errors, although some proportion are also clearly reconstructive errors.

The thrust of my discussion of Neisser and Harsch's data has been to show that their data on accuracy of flashbulb memories may be much more consistent with my data on memory for ordinary events than it might appear on a first reading. However, given the Neisser and Harsch data, I think it is possible that future work using appropriate controls might find that flashbulb memories *do* show a somewhat higher rate of reconstructive recall errors than do ordinary personal memories. This possibility should not be that surprising. One of the basic characteristics of flashbulb memories is that they are retained for long periods of time and it may be that the memory processes involved in producing the slow forgetting lead to errors in recall (though I know of no clear evidence for this hypothesis). There is, of course, a certain irony in this proposal that flashbulb memories may be *less* accurate than other forms of memory, given that many researchers in this area have favored copy theories for flashbulb memories and have therefore implied that flashbulb memories are likely to be *more* accurate than other forms of memory.

*Conclusions.* It seems to me that with the Neisser and Harsch data we now know that some proportion of flashbulb memories are not veridical. However, at this point, we do not know if flashbulb memories differ from other personal memories in this respect.

### Memory confidence

McCloskey, Wible, and Cohen (1988) report that three of their subjects who produced inconsistent responses (from their first recall to their second) gave high confidence scores to these recalls. However, examination of the data for all of the inconsistent responses suggests that they are, in fact, somewhat lower than those for the consistent responses. Larsen's (this volume) data for his five flashbulb memories (HCC) suggests that there was a fairly strong relation between his confidence in his memory and his recall accuracy.

However, Neisser and Harsch (this volume) report some rather different data. In essence, they find that there is little or no relation between ratings of memory confidence and memory accuracy. Neisser and Harsch find nonsignificant correlations between several different measures of memory confidence and accuracy of recall. They also report that for the subjects who gave the maximum ratings on confidence (5 on a 5-point scale), the distribution of accuracy scores ranged across the entire scale. Clearly, these data suggest a severe breakdown of the relation between the subjects' beliefs about the accuracy of their memories and their actual accuracy. An initial question raised by this finding is its generality – what is the relation of confidence and accuracy for nonflashbulb memories? I, for one, find it hard to believe that my beliefs about the accuracy of my memories for the events in my life are a total delusion. There are also data to support this opinion. In my study of memory for ordinary events (Brewer, 1988, Experiment 2) there is a variety of evidence showing a strong relation between memory confidence and memory accuracy. The events with the highest accuracy score ("correct with detail") received a mean confidence score ("Overall Memory") of 6.0, whereas those events for which the subjects could recall nothing ("omit") received a mean confidence score of 1.3. The confidence ratings were on a 1–7 scale in which 7 was defined as "certain that remember the event." Clearly, the subjects' confidence in the accuracy of their memories for the randomly sampled events that had occurred on the average 1 month earlier was highly related to the experimenter's independent scoring of their written recalls.

There seem to me to be two possible explanations for the inconsistency between the data on ordinary memories and Neisser and Harsch's data on flashbulb memories. The first explanation makes use of my argument that the low accuracy scores in the Neisser and Harsch study are predominantly due to the subjects' retrieving the wrong event. If this retrieval error hypothesis is correct then the subjects' confidence scores might well correlate highly with the accuracy of the event they are describing – it is just not the event that Neisser and Harsch are scoring it against. There is evidence to support this line of argument from my data on ordinary event memory (Brewer, 1988, Experiment 2). The clearest example of retrieval errors in that study were events classified as "wrong time slice"(the recall of the wrong moment of an overall correct event). The subjects' mean rated confidence ("Overall Memory") for these "errors" was 4.9, which is roughly the same as the mean rated confidence (4.5) for the general class of accurate recalls ("corrects"). This suggests that, both in my study of ordinary personal memories, and in Neisser and Harsch's study of flashbulb memories, the subjects sometimes recall an event other than the one the experimenter has asked for and give it a high confidence rating (not realizing that they have made a retrieval error). If most of the errors in the Neisser and Harsch study are retrieval errors, then this line of argument suggests there is no essential difference in the relationship of confidence and accuracy for flashbulb memories and for ordinary memories.

If we assume that the retrieval error analysis does not account for all of the Neisser and Harsch data, then we still need an explanation of the dissociation of memory confidence and memory accuracy for flashbulb memories. Neisser and Harsch suggest that the dissociation may occur because the subjects have strong emotions and strong visual images associated with the flashbulb event and these give rise to erroneous confidence ratings. There is evidence to support part of their argument in my data on ordinary personal memories. In that study (Brewer, 1988) there was a very strong relation between memory confidence and visual imagery. For the items with the highest confidence scores ("Overall memory") subjects rated every item either a 6 or a 7 on a 7-point visual imagery scale. There is a second form of evidence that supports Neisser and Harsch's proposal. John Pani and I carried out an experiment that follows up on my earlier research on inferences in memory for locations (Brewer & Treyens, 1981). In this new study (Brewer & Pani, unpublished ms.) we show that erroneous schema-driven recalls exhibit roughly the same strength of imagery as correct recalls. Thus, I think it is possible to postulate that some memory process or processes lead to the long-term retention of flashbulb memories and during this time period they are reconstructed while retaining strong images and strong beliefs about their accuracy. This would, of course, lead to a dissociation between accuracy and confidence for flashbulb memories.

*Conclusions.* In order to resolve these issues we need additional research directed at understanding the relationship of confidence to imagery, strength of emotion, and memory accuracy (cf. Brewer, 1988, pp. 83–85).

### Forgetting

Yarmey and Bull (1978) studied the recall of the reception circumstances for the Kennedy assassination. They found recall rates as high as 97.5% in some age groups 12 years after the event. Rubin and Kozin's (1984) sample of flashbulb memories obtained with an unconstrained sampling procedure showed a median rated age of 6 years before the time of recall. McCloskey, Wible, & Cohen's (1988) study found that essentially 100% of their subjects showed flashbulb memories for the *Challenger* explosion 9 months after the event; however, they also found that the specific information in the recalls became somewhat more general over that period. They found that between 48% and 55% of their subjects reported flashbulb memories for the assassination attempt on Ronald Reagan 5 years after the incident.

Bohannon (1988) attempted to show the special nature of the forgetting function for flashbulb memories by comparing recall of the circumstances of hearing about the *Challenger* explosion with recall of semantic information about the event (e.g., how many men were on the shuttle?). However, comparing the retention of personal memories with retention of facts confounds type of memory and thus would not appear to be the appropriate control condition. What is needed here is a comparison of the forgetting of the circumstances surrounding the hearing about some *nonflashbulb event* (e.g., "your keys are on the coffee table" or "today's weather will be mostly sunny with a chance of light showers") with the forgetting of the circumstances associated with a flashbulb event.

Christianson (1989) studied the flashbulb memories of Swedish subjects for the assassination of Olof Palme. In a phone interview he asked specific questions about seven different aspects of the reception event (informant, time, place, activity, other persons, clothes, first thought). Six weeks after the assassination the subjects' mean recall for information in these categories was 91%. When tested a year later mean consistent recall was 80% by a lenient scoring criterion and 53% by a strict scoring criterion.

In addition, Christianson gathered information on a nonflashbulb event in order to have a baseline for the forgetting of the flashbulb events. In the initial interview he asked the subjects to describe their most vivid memory from a day roughly a week earlier and 89% were able to do so. When tested 1 year later the subjects gave only 22% consistent responses by the lenient criterion and a mere 11% correct responses by the strict criterion, thus suggesting that forgetting of ordinary autobiographical events is much more rapid than that of flashbulb memories. The control information in this study consisted of autobiographical events and so it is more appropriate than semantic facts as control items (e.g., Bohannon, 1988). However, there are several difficulties with this control condition. First, the subjects are not given a content cue for these events that corresponds to being told that they are to recall the circumstances associated with the assassination of Olof Palme in the flashbulb case. Second, the subjects were simply asked to recall an autobiographical event and not asked to give the circumstances associated with the event, so on several accounts the data are still not quite the appropriate control. However, note that there is evidence (Larsen, this volume) that the circumstances for an ordinary event will be forgotten more rapidly than the event itself; if this is so, then Christianson's control condition might *underestimate* the differences between flashbulb memories and ordinary autobiographical memories.

There is another aspect of this study that highlights the need for additional theoretical and empirical work on the issue of selecting appropriate nonflashbulb control events. Christianson states that when contacted for the second interview 100% of his subjects remembered the phone call that they had received 1 year earlier. Thus, it would appear that for some aspects of this particular nonflashbulb event, the subjects' memories were actually better than for the circumstances of the flashbulb event itself! Yet, Neisser and Harsch (this volume) report that only 25% of their subjects recalled filling out a questionnaire about the *Challenger* explosion 2.5 years earlier. Obviously, much more research on forgetting of ordinary events is needed before it will be possible to make unambiguous statements about the relative rate of forgetting of flashbulb memories.

Larsen (this volume) has carried out a study on his own memory for news events that includes an appropriate set of control events. Larsen recorded one news event and one personally experienced event each day for 6 months and then carried out a variety of memory tests for these events. For the news events he recorded information about both the content of the event itself and the circumstances involved in the reception of the news event. Overall, he found that memory for personal events was better than for news events and that memory for news context was poorer than that for the news events. The finding that memory of the reception context of ordinary news events is poor is consistent with an ecological analysis of this situation (cf., Brewer, 1988, pp. 77–78), in which many different forms of content are received in roughly the same context (e.g., repeatedly listening to the news on the TV in your living room). However, the same form of ecological analysis for flashbulb events might give a very different result if the news content is dramatic enough to disrupt the reception context (e.g., running out of the room to tell someone the news). In this case a distinctiveness argument would predict strong recall of the reception context for flashbulb events.

Out of his large sample of news events Larsen selected five events as having flashbulb quality (maximum scores on two memory confidence scales). He found that for this small subset of events the relation between memory for the news content versus memory for the news context was the reverse of that for ordinary news events. For the flashbulb events memory for the circumstances of hearing of the event was better recalled than the content of the event. There is a certain degree of circularity in the selection of these items (they were classified as flashbulb memories because Larsen gave them high *confidence* ratings for source and context) and they are based on one (hard working!) subject; nevertheless, the results are certainly intriguing.

*Conclusion.* The evidence suggests that the recall of the reception context for flashbulb events shows strong memory. However, confidence in this conclusion should remain low until there are more studies that provide a clear comparison between memory of the reception context for flashbulb events and memory of the reception context for ordinary events.

### Retention theories

*Hypothetical data.* In order to evaluate theories of the retention of flashbulb memories we need to make some assumptions about the eventual outcome of empirical studies of the forgetting of flashbulb memories. Clearly, if flashbulb reception contexts do not show superior retention compared to appropriate control events, there is no need for special theories to account for the memory of flashbulb events. In addition, to give a clear account of retrieval theories I think it is necessary to incorporate the analysis given earlier of the structure of the news reception event. Therefore, for this discussion, I will assume that future studies of flashbulb memory will show less forgetting (compared to appropriate control events) for (a) the local circumstances and ongoing events, (b) the informant, and (c) the content of the informant's message.

*Strong initial representation.* Many memory theorists have assumed that certain events have characteristics that lead to strong initial representations and therefore show high retention. This theory has a long history (James, 1890, Vol. 1, pp. 670–673) and was applied to the area of flashbulb memory by Brown and Kulik (1977). Neisser and Harsch (this volume) use their discovery of a high percentage of nonveridical flashbulb memories to attack this position. However, I think a version of the strong trace theory survives. First, I have argued above that many of the errors in the Neisser and Harsch data may be due to inaccurate retrievals of other very strong memory representations. Second, I do not accept the assumption that the hypothesis of a strong initial representation must be a strict copy theory. Although particular theories such as the "Now Print!" mechanism proposed by Brown and Kulik do seem to be copy theories, I see no reason why a theory that postulates a strong initial representation could not include the possibility of constructive processes working on this trace and thus, allowing reconstructive errors (cf. Brewer & Pani's, 1983, pp. 32–33, discussion of copy images vs. reconstructed images). Therefore, I think that theories that postulate a strong initial representation are still viable hypotheses in this area and can account for the data outlined above. However, this approach does seem to suffer because the theory is so close to the phenomenon it is trying to explain. Some way is needed to make an independent assessment of the assumed strength of the representation.

A version of the strong initial representation hypothesis that is more specific is the proposal that flashbulb memory situations lead to the strong focus of attention and that it is the effect of the increased attention that leads to better retention (cf. Reisberg & Heuer, this volume). This hypothesis is open to fairly direct test because there are a variety of techniques (e.g., eye movement records) that should make it possible to measure attention independently of recall.

*Image theories.* Rubin and Kozin (1984) briefly suggest that the superior recall of flashbulb memories could be related to the images associated with flashbulb recall. Although it is known that imageable words and sentences show higher recall than nonimageable words and sentences (Paivio, 1971), it is not clear that this approach can provide an account of the particularly high recall shown for flashbulb events. My data (1988) on memory for ordinary personal memories shows that they give rise to strong images, and so it is not obvious that one can use imagery to give a unique account of the retention of flashbulb memories compared to other personal memories.

*Rich interconnections.* Rubin and Kozin (1984) suggest that the low rate of forgetting for flashbulb memories might be due to the numerous links that they have to other memories. This hypothesis might be plausible for certain personal milestone events discussed by Rubin and Kozin, such as a flashbulb memory for walking across the stage to receive one's high school diploma. However, it does not seem to fit many other types of isolated events that led to flashbulb memories in their subjects (e.g., witnessing an automobile accident involving strangers).

*Distinctiveness.* In my study of ordinary personal memories (Brewer, 1988) the most consistent and most powerful variables for predicting memory were the subjects' original ratings of a sampled episode in terms of its frequency of occurrence or the frequency of its location (with low frequency leading to better memory). This relationship held for both the characteristics of the episodes themselves and for the characteristics of the episodes used as retrieval cues in recall. Thus, a subject's memory for his or her only visit to a shoe store in the local shopping center would typically be much better than the memory for sitting at a desk working the seventh weekly set of homework problems for introductory calculus. Regression techniques showed that, for this sample of ordinary events, the frequency effect was independent of the emotionality of the events. Thus, a subject would typically show better memory for the unique shoe store episode than he or she would for an episode that included one more emotional argument as part of a long, stormy, interpersonal relationship. In my 1988 chapter I interpreted this data on the powerful role of frequency in recall and recognition of personal memories as supporting the position that distinctive memory representations lead to higher recall.

A number of researchers have argued that distinctiveness could account for some or all of the apparent high rates of recall of flashbulb memories (e.g., Rubin & Kozin, 1984). However, the distinctiveness hypothesis must be elaborated in terms of the earlier analysis of the news reception situation. It seems to me that most theorists would concede that the *content* of most flashbulb memories is distinctive information. Therefore we need to consider the issue of the distinctiveness of the circumstances of hearing of a flashbulb event. Larsen (this volume) has found that the reception contexts for ordinary news reception episodes are poorly recalled and suggested that this may be due to a lack of distinctiveness. Several researchers (McCloskey, Wible, & Cohen, 1988; Winograd & Killinger, 1983) in the area of flashbulb memory have argued that the reception context for flashbulb memory situations may become overtly distinctive, for example, an ordinary school day is disrupted by an informant bursting into the classroom with the news.

This hypothesis also has the advantage that discussing it allows me to add *my Challenger* reception event to those of the other researchers already in the literature. I have a private carrel in the university library that I use to hide away from the world when I need to work intensively on some project. On the day of the *Challenger* explosion I was working in my carrel when a maintenance worker came over, knocked on the window, and gestured for me to open the door. I stepped out and he told me the news of the *Challenger* explosion. This is clearly consistent with the hypothesis that reception events frequently make the flashbulb event distinctive because this is the only time in the 6 years that I have had the library carrel that someone has interrupted me while I was working.

However, Winograd and Killinger (1983) point out that their memory protocols for people hearing about the bombing of Pearl Harbor do not show as much event disruption. Thus, in addition to the disruption hypothesis one may need to postulate another less overt form of distinctiveness. In my 1988 chapter I suggested the possibility that "the addition of affect to a memory representation increases its distinctiveness and thus its accessibility in memory" (p. 79).

Schmidt and Bohannon (1988) make several criticisms of the distinctiveness hypothesis. They argue that it is not consistent with laboratory findings showing that distinctive events sometimes suppress memory for surrounding material. This criticism does not seem to carry for the forms of the distinctiveness hypothesis outlined above, because each of these hypotheses provides a way for the reception event itself to become distinctive. Schmidt and Bohannon also argue that the addition of the construct of "distinctiveness" adds nothing to the explanation of the high rates of recall of flashbulb events. Although I agree that there are some problems here, it seems to me that the use of event and location frequency to predict later memory (Brewer, 1988) shows that the distinctiveness hypothesis does have independent explanatory force.

The last class of retention theories to be examined are theories that explain the recall of flashbulb events in terms of rehearsal. There are a range of possible rehearsal theories. They can be analyzed into theories that postulate overt or covert rehearsal and, within these two types, those that postulate rehearsal of content or context or some combination of content and context.

*Overt rehearsal of content.* A simple form of overt rehearsal theory might postulate that the content of flashbulb memories (e.g., knowing that the *Challenger* exploded) is particularly salient and that salient events are rehearsed more than other information. Rubin and Kozin (1984) suggest this as one possible explanation for the long-term retention of "vivid" memories.

However, this simple form of rehearsal theory does not predict the data (i.e., it doesn't predict strong retention for the *circumstances* or *informant*). In addition, the hypothesis of content rehearsal also has only limited empirical support. Rubin and Kozin (1984) found that a number of the vivid memories in their sample were reported not to have been overtly rehearsed ("how many times have you discussed this event"); however many of Rubin and Kozin's flashbulb memories involved sexual events and personally embarrassing events that might well have been thought about repeatedly (covert rehearsal) and yet not discussed with others. Larsen (this volume) found that his estimate of the number of his own overt and covert rehearsals of ordinary news events was significantly related to memory for the content of the events, but not to their context.

*Overt rehearsal of context, informant, and content.* If rehearsal theories are to succeed they have to account for the hypothesized memory superiority of context, informant, and content information. Brown and Kulik (1977) proposed that subjects might rehearse the reception event of flashbulb memories and Neisser (1982) outlined a similar proposal in which he suggested that recall of the circumstances of hearing of an event in flashbulb memories is high because individuals rehearse "how we heard the news" (p. 48). Larsen (this volume) adopts this approach and proposes that for flashbulb memories there is a "reversal of rehearsal" in which subjects chose to tell others about the circumstances of their learning about a flashbulb event whereas they do not do this for ordinary news events. If these hypotheses about the rehearsal of the reception event were supplemented with a proposal that subjects also rehearse the content of flashbulb events, they would give an account of the hypothesized flashbulb retention findings.

However, the data have not tended to support this hypothesis. Winograd and Killinger (1983) found that subjects' self-reports of "how often they had talked about [the reception event]" showed only a low correlation (.23) with the number of categories recalled for flashbulb memories. Pillemer's (1984) study of flashbulb memories for the attempted assassination of Ronald Reagan showed that only 24% of his subjects reported any overt rehearsals. Larsen (this volume) found that his estimate of the number of his own overt and covert rehearsals was significantly related to memory for personal events and the content of ordinary news events but *not* for the circumstances associated with the reception of ordinary news events. Larsen's own rehearsal data do not look as if they support his theory that rehearsals are crucial for maintaining flashbulb memories because his five flashbulb (MCC) memories show rehearsal rates lower than many of his relatively ordinary events. Neisser and Harsch (this volume) gathered data the day after the *Challenger* explosion about how much time their subjects had spent talking about the event on the day of the explosion. They found no significant relation between this measure of rehearsal and the quality of the subject's recalls. However, this measure of rehearsal is not comparable to those used in other studies. It is an index of rehearsal of the content and, in addition, most theories of rehearsal would predict that rehearsals distributed over the years before the test would play the major role in sustaining retention. Therefore Neisser and Harsch's measure does not appear to be an adequate index of the long-term rehearsal of context. On the other hand, all of the other studies use the subjects' retrospective accounts of the amount they had rehearsed. It is not clear if the subjects' recall of their rehearsals is valid data and it is possible that the subjects' confidence in their memories influences their estimates about number of rehearsals. Overall, the evidence does not lend much support to the overt rehearsal theories; however, it has proved difficult to carry out an appropriate test of this theory and so the negative evidence should not be weighted too heavily.

*Overt rehearsal that involves context and informant information.* Another solution to the problem of having rehearsal affect all three aspects of a flashbulb event is to hypothesize that subjects carry out overt rehearsals of the content of the event and that this then strengthens the informant and context information. In light of my analysis of the characteristics of personal memories (Brewer, 1986) this hypothesis seems quite plausible for *personally experienced events.* Thus, if an individual has observed an automobile accident and tells another person about the accident (content), it seems quite likely that the individual telling about the accident will relive his or her own experience of seeing the event while telling about the accident.

However, for the case of the *news reception context* the situation is not so clear. When someone is talking about the content of a flashbulb event, do they frequently reexperience the circumstances of how they heard about the event? Note the interesting implications of the two alternative answers to this question. If people do spontaneously reexperience the circumstances of how they heard about an event, then this hypothesis will predict the hypothesized retention data. However, if people do not reexperience the circumstances of reception when retelling an event, then this hypothesis would predict that memory for the circumstances of a news reception event would be *worse* than memory for the circumstances of a personally experienced event – a prediction that is somewhat in opposition to the original Brown and Kulik flashbulb memory hypothesis.

*Covert rehearsal.* A number of researchers in this area have mentioned the possibility that subjects carry out "covert rehearsals" (Brown & Kulik, 1977, p. 87; Larsen, this volume; McCloskey, Wible, & Cohen, 1988, p. 180; Pillemer, 1984, p. 77; Winograd & Killinger, 1983, p. 418). However, there has been little additional description of these "covert rehearsals." I assume that the "covert rehearsals" correspond to thinking about (recollecting) some event from the past. More specifically, it involves having a personal memory (Brewer, 1986). It seems to me that there are at least three possible phenomena here – voluntary covert rehearsals, remindings, and unbidden recalls.

In the same way that an individual can choose to talk to someone about an event they can chose to think about the event. Thus, there is clearly the possibility of voluntary covert rehearsals. A second form of covert rehearsal is a reminding (Schank, 1982). If subjects are consciously aware of a connection between a current stimulus and some past event, the situation is usually referred to as a reminding. On other occasions thoughts about a past event seem to intrude into the ongoing train of thought (cf. Salaman's, 1982, "involuntary memories"). Although it seems to me that there is a clear experiential difference between these two types of recalls, it may, of course, be that the same mechanisms operate in both cases (cf. Norman, 1982, p. 34). For lack of a better word I will use "covert rehearsal" as the general term to cover all three of these memory situations.

*Covert rehearsal of content.* A simple theory that postulates that subjects covertly rehearse the content of flashbulb memories suffers from the problem that it does not predict the data. It will not lead to superior recall of the reception event.

*Covert rehearsal of context, informant, and content.* One can hypothesize that subjects covertly rehearse the news reception events of flashbulb episodes; this would predict the data. Currently, there is little evidence to support this hypothesis, and yet it seems important for rehearsal theorists to provide such data because the covert rehearsal hypothesis certainly could give the appearance of being a retreat to an ad hoc position in the face of the failure to find the predicted overt rehearsals.

*Event content leading to covert rehearsal of context and informant information.* One could hypothesize that when subjects are exposed to the content of a flashbulb event they are reminded of the original news reception episode involving that content. Pillemer (1984) reported data that lends some support to this hypothesis. He found that when his subjects heard the news of the attempted assassination of Ronald Reagan many were reminded of earlier assassinations and that between 23% and 29% were reminded of the reception event for the earlier episode.

Overall, this examination of rehearsal theories suggests that there are a number of rehearsal theories that could account for the data, but few of the rehearsal theories have been given a clear, strong test and, to the degree that they have been tested, the data have not been particularly supportive.

*Retention theories – conclusions.* It is clear that many of the theories outlined in this section can account for the retention of the reception event of a flashbulb episode over long periods of time, but there is no overwhelming evidence for any particular one of these theories. Currently, I think the most promising hypotheses are: (a) a strong initial representation associated with some forms of strong emotions, (b) exposure to event content leading to remindings of the reception event, and (c) distinctiveness arising from disruptions of ongoing episodes and the emotional coloring of the event.

### Flashbulb reception context versus semantic memory reception context

Most discussions of flashbulb memory assume that there is a qualitative difference in the recall of the reception context for flashbulb memories and for semantic memories. Most theorists in this area assume that you can recall the context of hearing about the *Challenger* explosion, but not the context of hearing that matter can be converted into energy. I also believe that there is a fundamental difference here (cf. Brewer, 1986; Brewer & Pani, 1983). However, it seems to me that it would be better for all of us if this assumption was backed up with empirical work showing that, in fact, memory for the reception context of semantic memories does differ from the memory of the reception context of other forms of memory.

### Types of memory

One of the most interesting aspects of the Brown and Kulik paper is the assumption that flashbulb memories are a unique and qualitatively different form of memory. There is now fairly general agreement that this claim has not been supported (Brewer, 1986, pp. 35–36; Christianson, 1989, p. 442; Larsen, this volume; McCloskey, Wible, & Cohen, 1988, p. 171; Pillemer, 1990, p. 95; Rubin & Kozin, 1984, p. 94). When Brown and Kulik first began the investigation of flashbulb memory very little empirical work had been done on autobiographical memory and so it seems likely that when they compared the form of memory they were interested in with the textbook descriptions (e.g., semantic memory, rote memory), they assumed that flashbulb memory was a unique form of memory. I have argued several times in this chapter that the description of flashbulb memories is essentially identical to that of ordinary personal memory.

### Conclusions

Are flashbulb memories special? Research over the last decade has clearly established that: (a) People report being able to recall the reception context for flashbulb events, (b) the recall of the reception context occurs over long periods of time, (c) much of the recall content in flashbulb memory protocols can be classified into a set of canonical recall categories, (d) people are confident about the accuracy of their memories, and (e) they report strong visual images during the recollection process. The question is: Do these findings support Brown and Kulik's hypotheses about the special nature of flashbulb memories? In this chapter I have argued that the observed canonical recall categories are merely the reflection of the fact that the subjects have been recalling a particular type of news reception event. I have also argued that the description of flashbulb memories (e.g., imagery, confidence, recollection of specific events) shows that flashbulb memories are a form of personal memory. This analysis suggests that the type of memory involved in flashbulb memories is special in the sense that it is different from other forms of memory such as semantic memory and rote memory; however, it is not special in the sense that it is merely a subclass of personal memory.

Several recent studies have suggested that some flashbulb memories are in error and Neisser and Harsch's (this volume) important study argues that most are erroneous. In this chapter I have proposed that many of the errors found in these studies are not reconstructive errors, but retrieval errors, in which the subjects have recollected the wrong event and thus the "erroneous" recalls may be accurate descriptions of some other experienced event. However, there is clear evidence for reconstruction in some flashbulb memory recalls and I suggested that flashbulb memories might eventually turn out to show more reconstructive errors than ordinary personal memories.

It is not yet clear if the data on memory for reception context information in flashbulb memory is unusual. Much of the work in this area has not used appropriate control events so it cannot speak to this issue. There has also been considerable confusion about what would constitute an appropriate control item. However, the recent work of Larsen (this volume) makes clear that one appropriate control is the recall of the context information for ordinary reception events.

If one assumes that flashbulb memory events do show an unusually high rate of recall then is it necessary to postulate a special form of memory mechanism? It does not seem to me that we need to invoke a special mechanism until we have thoroughly explored more ordinary mechanisms. Currently, I think there are at least three viable explanations for a finding of exceptional retention of reception context information in flashbulb memories: (a) Strong emotion (surprise? personal involvement?) may lead to a strong memory representation (e.g., a moderated form of Brown and Kulik's hypothesis), (b) the flashbulb memory situation may lead to covert rehearsal of the reception event, and (c) the reception events for flashbulb memory events may be unusually distinctive. There is no reason to think that there has to be a single mechanism to account for the data, and so that all of these processes could be jointly contributing to the retention findings. Overall, it would appear that flashbulb memories are not a special type of memory, but they may show an unusual degree of retention over time due to known memory mechanisms.

## NOTE

I would like to thank Steen Larsen and Dan Reisberg for influential discussions on the topic of this chapter. I would also like to thank Brian Ross for his very helpful comments on an earlier draft of this chapter. Finally, I would like to thank Gene Winograd and Dick Neisser for inviting me down to the Flashbulb Memory Conference and for exposing me to the provocative flashbulb memory debate.

## REFERENCES

Bohannon, J. N. III. (1988). Flashbulb memories for the Space Shuttle disaster: A tale of two theories. *Cognition, 29,* 179–196.

Brewer, W. F. (1980). Literary theory, rhetoric, and stylistics: Implications for psychology. In R. J. Spiro, B. C. Bruce, & W. F. Brewer (Eds.), *Theoretical issues in reading comprehension* (pp. 221–239). Hillsdale, NJ: Erlbaum.

Brewer, W. F. (1986). What is autobiographical memory? In D. C. Rubin (Ed.), *Autobiographical memory* (pp. 25–49). New York: Cambridge University Press.

Brewer, W. F. (1988). Memory for randomly sampled autobiographical events. In U. Neisser & E. Winograd (Eds.), *Remembering reconsidered: Ecological and traditional approaches to the study of memory* (pp. 21–90). New York: Cambridge University Press.

Brewer, W. F., & Pani, J. R. (1983). The structure of human memory. In G. H. Bower (Ed.), *The psychology of learning and motivation: Advances in research and theory* (pp. 1–38). New York: Academic Press.

Brewer, W. F., & Pani, J. R. (unpublished ms.). Evidence for reconstructive imagery in memory for rooms.

Brewer, W. F., & Treyens, J. C. (1981). Role of schemata in memory for places. *Cognitive Psychology, 13,* 207–230.

Brown, R. (1958). *Words and things.* Glencoe, IL: Free Press.

Brown, R. (1986). *Social psychology* (2nd ed.). New York: Free Press.

Brown, R., & Kulik, J. (1977). Flashbulb memories. *Cognition, 5,* 73–99.

Christianson, S.-Å. (1989). Flashbulb memories: Special, but not so special. *Memory & Cognition, 17,* 435–443.

Crovitz, H. F., & Schiffman, H. (1974). Frequency of episodic memories as a function of their age. *Bulletin of the Psychonomic Society, 4,* 517–518.

James, W. (1890). *The principles of psychology* (Vol. 1). New York: Henry Holt.

McCloskey, M., Wible, C. G., & Cohen, N. J. (1988). Is there a special flashbulb-memory mechanism? *Journal of Experimental Psychology: General, 117,* 171–181.

Neisser, U. (1982). Snapshots or benchmarks? In U. Neisser (Ed.), *Memory observed: Remembering in natural contexts* (pp. 43–48). San Francisco: W. H. Freeman.

Neisser, U. (1986). Remembering Pearl Harbor: Reply to Thompson and Cowan. *Cognition, 23,* 285–286.

Norman, D. A. (1982). *Learning and memory*. San Francisco: W. H. Freeman.

Paivio, A. (1971). *Imagery and verbal processes*. New York: Holt, Rinehart and Winston.

Pillemer, D. B. (1984). Flashbulb memories of the assassination attempt on President Reagan. *Cognition, 16*, 63–80.

Pillemer, D. B. (1990). Clarifying the flashbulb memory concept: Comment on McCloskey, Wible, and Cohen (1988). *Journal of Experimental Psychology: General, 119*, 92–96.

*Random House dictionary of the English language. College edition.* (1968). New York: Random House.

Reisberg, D., Heuer, F., McLean, J., & O'Shaughnessy, M. (1988). The quantity, not the quality of affect predicts memory vividness. *Bulletin of the Psychonomic Society, 26*, 100–103.

Robinson, J. A. (1976). Sampling autobiographical memory. *Cognitive Psychology, 8*, 578–595.

Rubin, D. C., & Kozin, M. (1984). Vivid memories. *Cognition, 16*, 81–95.

Salaman, E. (1982). A collection of moments. In U. Neisser (Ed.), *Memory observed: Remembering in natural contexts* (pp. 49–63). San Francisco: W. H. Freeman.

Schacter, D. L., Harbluk, J. L., & McLachlan, D. R. (1984). Retrieval without recollection: An experimental analysis of source amnesia. *Journal of Verbal Learning and Verbal Behavior, 23*, 593–611.

Schank, R. C. (1982). *Dynamic memory: A theory of reminding and learning in computers and people*. Cambridge: Cambridge University Press.

Schmidt, S. R., & Bohannon, J. N. III. (1988). In defense of the flashbulb-memory hypothesis: A comment on McCloskey, Wible, and Cohen (1988). *Journal of Experimental Psychology: General, 117*, 332–335.

Thompson, C. P., & Cowan, T. (1986). Flashbulb memories: A nicer interpretation of a Neisser recollection. *Cognition, 22*, 199–200.

Winograd, E., & Killinger, W. A., Jr. (1983). Relating age at encoding in early childhood to adult recall: Development of flashbulb memories. *Journal of Experimental Psychology: General, 112*, 413–422.

Yarmey, A. D., & Bull, M. P. III. (1978). Where were you when President Kennedy was assassinated? *Bulletin of the Psychonomic Society, 11*, 133–135.

# Author index

# Subject index

313